# The D Programming Language

# The D Programming Language

Andrei Alexandrescu

✦Addison-Wesley

Upper Saddle River, NJ • Boston • Indianapolis • San Francisco
New York • Toronto • Montreal • London • Munich • Paris • Madrid
Capetown • Sydney • Tokyo • Singapore • Mexico City

Many of the designations used by manufacturers and sellers to distinguish their products are claimed as trademarks. Where those designations appear in this book, and the publisher was aware of a trademark claim, the designations have been printed with initial capital letters or in all capitals.

The authors and publisher have taken care in the preparation of this book, but make no expressed or implied warranty of any kind and assume no responsibility for errors or omissions. No liability is assumed for incidental or consequential damages in connection with or arising out of the use of the information or programs contained herein.

The publisher offers excellent discounts on this book when ordered in quantity for bulk purchases or special sales, which may include electronic versions and/or custom covers and content particular to your business, training goals, marketing focus, and branding interests. For more information, please contact:

U.S. Corporate and Government Sales
(800) 382-3419
corpsales@pearsontechgroup.com

For sales outside the United States please contact:

International Sales
international@pearson.com

Visit us on the Web: informit.com/aw

*Library of Congress Cataloging-in-Publication Data*
Alexandrescu, Andrei.
    The D Programming Language / Andrei Alexandrescu.
        p.   cm.
    Includes bibliographical references and index.
    ISBN 978-0-321-63536-5 (pbk. : alk. paper)   1.   D (Computer program language)   I. Title.
    QA76.73.D138A44 2010
    005.13'3—dc22
                                                                            2010009924

Pearson Education, Inc.
Rights and Contracts Department
501 Boylston Street, Suite 900
Boston, MA  02116
Fax: (617) 671-3447

ISBN 13: 978-0-321-63536-5
ISBN 10:      0-321-63536-1
Text printed in the United States  on recycled paper at Courier in Stoughton, Massachusetts.
2nd Printing, June 2010

# Contents

# Foreword

by Walter Bright

There's a line in a science fiction novel I read long ago that says a scientist would fearlessly peer into the gates of hell if he thought it would further knowledge in his field. In one sentence, it captures the essence of what it means to be a scientist. This joy in discovery, this need to know, is readily apparent in the videos and writings of physicist Richard Feynman, and his enthusiasm is infectious and enthralling.

Although I am not a scientist, I understand their motivation. Mine is that of an engineer—the joy of creation, of building something out of nothing. One of my favorite books is a chronicle of the step-by-step process the Wright brothers went through to solve the problems of flight one by one, *The Wright Brothers as Engineers* by Wald, and how they poured all that knowledge into creating a flying machine.

My early interests were summed up in the opening pages of *Rocket Manual for Amateurs* by Brinley with the phrase "thrilled and fascinated by things that burn and explode," later matured into wanting to build things that went faster and higher.

But building powerful machines is an expensive proposition. And then I discovered computers. The marvelous and seductive thing about computers is the ease with which things can be built. You don't need a billion-dollar fab plant, a machine shop, or even a screwdriver. With just an inexpensive computer, you can create worlds.

So I started creating imaginary worlds on the computer. The first was the game Empire, Wargame of the Century. The computers of the day were too underpowered to run it properly, so I became interested in how to optimize the performance of programs. This led to studying the compilers that generated the code and naturally to the hubris of "I can write a better compiler than that." Enamored with C, I gravitated toward implementing a C compiler. That wasn't too hard, taking a couple of years part-time. Then I discovered Bjarne Stroustrup's C++ language, and I thought that I could add those extensions to the C compiler in a couple of months (!).

Over a decade later, I was still working on it. In the process of implementing it, I became very familiar with every detail of the language. Supporting a large user base meant a lot of experience in how other people perceived the language, what worked, and what didn't. I'm not able to use something without thinking of ways to improve the design. In 1999, I decided to put this into practice. It started out as the Mars programming language, but my colleagues called it D first as a joke, but the name caught on and the D programming language was born.

D is ten years old as of this writing and has produced its second major incarnation, sometimes called D2. In that time D has expanded from one man toiling over a keyboard to a worldwide community of developers working on all facets of the language and supporting an ecosystem of libraries and tools.

The language itself (which is the focus of this book) has grown from modest beginnings to a very powerful language adept at solving programming problems from many angles. To the best of my knowledge, D offers an unprecedentedly adroit integration of several powerful programming paradigms: imperative, object-oriented, functional, and meta.

At first blush, it would appear that such a language could not be simple. And indeed, D is not a simple language. But I'd argue that is the wrong way to view a language. A more useful view is, what do programming solutions in that language look like? Are D programs complicated and obtuse, or simple and elegant?

A colleague of mine who has extensive experience in a corporate environment observed that an IDE (Integrated Development Environment) was an essential tool for programming because with one click a hundred lines of boilerplate code could be generated. An IDE is not as essential a tool for D, because instead of relying on wizard-based boilerplate generation, D obviates the boilerplate itself by using introspection and generational capabilities. The programmer doesn't have to see that boilerplate. The inherent complexity of the program is taken care of by the language, rather than an IDE.

For example, suppose one wanted to do OOP (object-oriented programming) using a simpler language that has no particular support for the paradigm. It can be done, but it's just awful and rarely worthwhile. But when a more complex language supports OOP directly, then writing OOP programs becomes simple and elegant. The language is more complicated, but the user code is simpler. This is worthwhile progress.

The ability to write user code for a wide variety of tasks in a simple and elegant manner pretty much requires a language that supports multiple programming paradigms. Properly written code should just look beautiful on the page, and beautiful code oddly enough tends to be correct code. I'm not sure why that relationship holds, but it tends to be true. It's the same way an airplane that looks good tends to fly well, too. Therefore, language features that enable algorithms to be expressed in a beautiful way are probably good things.

Simplicity and elegance in writing code, however, are not the only metrics that characterize a good programming language. These days, programs are rapidly increasing in size with no conceivable end in sight. With such size, it becomes less and less practical to rely on convention and programming expertise to ensure the code is correct, and more and more worthwhile to rely on machine-checkable guarantees. To that end, D sports a variety of strategies that the programmer can employ to make such guarantees. These include contracts, memory safety, various function attributes, immutability, hijack protection, scope guards, purity, unit tests, and thread data isolation.

No, we haven't overlooked performance! Despite many predictions that performance is no longer relevant, despite computers running a thousand times faster than when I wrote my first compiler, there never seems to be any shortage of demand for faster programs. D is a systems programming language. What does that mean? In one sense, it means that one can write an operating system in D, as well as device drivers and application code. In a more technical sense, it means that D programs have access to all the capabilities of the machine. This means you can use pointers, do pointer aliasing and pointer arithmetic, bypass the type system, and even write code directly in assembly language. There is nothing completely sealed off from a D programmer's access. For example, the implementation of D's garbage collector is entirely written in D.

But wait! How can that be? How can a language offer both soundness guarantees and arbitrary pointer manipulation? The answer is that the kinds of guarantees are based on the language constructs used. For example, function attributes and type constructors can be used to state guarantees enforcible at compile time. Contracts and invariants specify guarantees to be enforced at runtime.

Most of D's features have appeared in other languages in one form or another. Any particular one doesn't make the case for a language. But the combination is more than the sum of the parts, and D's combination makes for a satisfying language that has elegant and straightforward means to solve an unusually wide variety of programming problems.

Andrei Alexandrescu is famous for his unconventional programming ideas becoming the new mainstream (see his seminal book *Modern C++ Design*). Andrei joined the D programming language design team in 2006. He's brought with him a sound theoretical grounding in programming, coupled with an endless stream of innovative solutions to programming design problems. Much of the shape of D2 is due to his contributions, and in many ways this book has co-evolved with D. One thing you'll happily discover in his writing about D is the *why* of the design choices, rather than just a dry recitation of facts. Knowing why a language is the way it is makes it much easier and faster to understand and get up to speed.

Andrei goes on to illustrate the whys by using D to solve many fundamental programming problems. Thus he shows not only how D works, but why it works, and how to use it.

I hope you'll have as much fun programming in D as I've had working to bring it to life. A palpable excitement about the language seeps out of the pages of Andrei's book. I think you'll find it exciting!

Walter Bright
January 2010

# Foreword

by Scott Meyers

By any measure, C++ has been a tremendous success, but even its most ardent proponents won't deny that it's a complicated beast. This complexity influenced the design of C++'s most widely used successors, Java and C#. Both strove to avoid C++'s complexity—to provide most of its functionality in an easier-to-use package.

Complexity reduction took two basic forms. One was elimination of "complicated" language features. C++'s need for manual memory management, for example, was obviated by garbage collection. Templates were deemed to fail the cost/benefit test, so the initial versions of these languages chose to exclude anything akin to C++'s support for generics.

The other form of complexity reduction involved replacing "complicated" C++ features with similar, but less demanding, constructs. C++'s multiple inheritance morphed into single inheritance augmented with interfaces. Current versions of Java and C# support templatesque generics, but they're simpler than C++'s templates.

These successor languages aspired to far more than simply doing what C++ did with reduced complexity. Both defined virtual machines, added support for runtime reflection, and provided extensive libraries that allow many programmers to shift their focus from creating new code to gluing existing components together. The result can be thought of as C-based "productivity languages." If you want to quickly create software that more or less corresponds to combinations of existing components—and much software falls into this category—Java and C# are better choices than C++.

But C++ isn't a productivity language; it's a *systems* programming language. It was designed to rival C in its ability to communicate with hardware (e.g., in drivers and embedded systems), to work with C-based libraries and data structures without adaptation (e.g., in legacy systems), to squeeze the last drop of performance out of the hardware it runs on. It's not really an irony that the performance-critical components of the virtual machines beneath Java and C# are written in C++. The high-performance implementation of virtual machines is a job for a *systems* language, not a productivity language.

D aims to be C++'s successor in the realm of systems programming. Like Java and C#, D aims to avoid the complexity of C++, and to this end it uses some of the same techniques. Garbage collection is in, manual memory management is out.[1] Single inheritance and interfaces are in, multiple inheritance is out. But then D starts down a path of its own.

It begins by identifying functional holes in C++ and filling them. Current C++ offers no Unicode support, and its nascent successor version (C++0x) provides only a limited amount. D handles Unicode from the get-go. Neither current C++ nor C++0x offers support for modules, Contract Programming, unit testing, or "safe" subsets (where memory errors are impossible). D offers all these things, and it does so without sacrificing the ability to generate high-quality native code.

Where C++ is both powerful and complicated, D aims to be at least as powerful but less complicated. Template metaprogrammers in C++ have demonstrated that compile-time computation is an important technology, but they've had to jump through hoops of syntactic fire to practice it. D offers similar capabilities, but without the lexical pain. If you know how to write a function in current C++, you know nothing about how to write the corresponding C++ function that's evaluated during compilation. If you know how to write a function in D, however, you know exactly how to write its compile-time variant, because the code is the same.

One of the most interesting places where D parts ways with its C++-derived siblings is in its approach to thread-based concurrency. Recognizing that improperly synchronized access to shared data (data races) is a pit that's both easy to fall into and hard to climb out of, D turns convention on its head: by default, data isn't shared across threads. As D's designers point out, given the deep cache hierarchies of modern hardware, memory often isn't truly shared across cores or processors anyway, so why default to offering developers an abstraction that's not only an illusion, it's an illusion known to facilitate the introduction of difficult-to-debug errors?

All these things and more make D a noteworthy point in the C heritage design space, and that is reason enough to read this book. The fact that the author is Andrei Alexandrescu makes the case even stronger. As codesigner of D and an implementer of substantial portions of its library, Andrei knows D like almost no one else. Naturally, he can describe the D programming language, but he can also explain *why* D is the way it is. Features present in the language are there for a reason, and would-be features that are missing are absent for a reason, too. Andrei is in a unique position to illuminate such reasoning.

This illumination comes through in a uniquely engaging style. In the midst of what might seem to be a needless digression (but is actually a waystation en route to a destination he needs you to reach), Andrei offers reassurance: "I know you are asking yourself what this has to do with compile-time evaluation. It does. Please bear with me." Regarding the unintuitive nature of linker diagnostics, Andrei observes, "If you forget about `--main`, don't worry; the linker will fluently and baroquely remind you of that

---

1. Actually, it's optional. As befits a systems programming language, if you really want to perform manual memory management, D will let you.

in its native language, encrypted Klingon." Even references to other publications get the Alexandrescu touch. You're not simply referred to Wadler's "Proofs are programs," you're referred to "Wadler's fascinating monograph 'Proofs are programs.'" Friedl's "Mastering regular expressions" isn't just recommended, it's "warmly recommended."

A book about a programming language is filled with sample code, of course, and the code samples also demonstrate that Andrei is anything but a pedestrian author. Here's his prototype for a search function:

```
bool find(int[] haystack, int needle);
```

This is a book by a skilled author describing an interesting programming language. I'm sure you'll find the read rewarding.

Scott Meyers
January 2010

# Preface

Programming language design seeks power in simplicity and, when successful, begets beauty.

Choosing the trade-offs among contradictory requirements is a difficult task that requires good taste from the language designer as much as mastery of theoretical principles and of practical implementation matters. Programming language design is software-engineering-complete.

D is a language that attempts to consistently do the right thing within the constraints it chose: system-level access to computing resources, high performance, and syntactic similarity with C-derived languages. In trying to do the right thing, D sometimes stays with tradition and does what other languages do, and other times it breaks tradition with a fresh, innovative solution. On occasion that meant revisiting the very constraints that D ostensibly embraced. For example, large program fragments or indeed entire programs can be written in a well-defined memory-safe subset of D, which entails giving away a small amount of system-level access for a large gain in program debuggability.

You may be interested in D if the following values are important to you:

- *Performance.* D is a systems programming language. It has a memory model that, although highly structured, is compatible with C's and can call into and be called from C functions without any intervening translation.
- *Expressiveness.* D is not a small, minimalistic language, but it does have a high power-to-weight ratio. You can define eloquent, self-explanatory designs in D that model intricate realities accurately.
- *"Torque."* Any backyard hot-rodder would tell you that power isn't everything; its availability is. Some languages are most powerful for small programs, whereas other languages justify their syntactic overhead only past a certain size. D helps you get work done in short scripts and large programs alike, and it isn't unusual for a large program to grow organically from a simple single-file script.
- *Concurrency.* D's approach to concurrency is a definite departure from the languages it resembles, mirroring the departure of modern hardware designs from the architectures of yesteryear. D breaks away from the curse of implicit memory sharing (though it allows statically checked explicit sharing) and fosters mostly independent threads that communicate with one another via messages.

- *Generic code.* Generic code that manipulates other code has been pioneered by the powerful Lisp macros and continued by C++ templates, Java generics, and similar features in various other languages. D offers extremely powerful generic and generational mechanisms.
- *Eclecticism.* D recognizes that different programming paradigms are advantageous for different design challenges and fosters a highly integrated federation of styles instead of One True Approach.
- *"These are my principles. If you don't like them, I've got others."* D tries to observe solid principles of language design. At times, these run into considerations of implementation difficulty, usability difficulties, and above all human nature that doesn't always find blind consistency sensible and intuitive. In such cases, all languages must make judgment calls that are ultimately subjective and are about balance, flexibility, and good taste more than anything else. In my opinion, at least, D compares very favorably with other languages that inevitably have had to make similar decisions.

## Intended Audience

This book assumes you're a programmer, meaning that you know how to accomplish typical programming tasks in a language of your choice. Knowledge of any language in particular is not assumed or particularly recommended. If you know one of the Algol-derived languages (C, C++, Java, or C#), you will enjoy a slight advantage because the syntax will feel familiar from the get-go and the risk of finding false friends (similar syntax with different semantics) is minimal. (In particular, if you paste a piece of C code into a D file, it either compiles with the same semantics or doesn't compile at all.)

A book introducing a language would be boring and incomplete without providing insight into the motivation behind various features, and without explaining the most productive ways to use those features to accomplish concrete tasks. This book discusses the rationale behind all non-obvious features and often explains why apparently better design alternatives weren't chosen. Certain design choices may disproportionately aggravate the implementation effort, interact poorly with other features that have stronger reasons to stay put, have hidden liabilities that are invisible in short and simple examples, or simply aren't powerful enough to pull their own weight. Above all, language designers are as fallible as any other human, so it's very possible that good design choices exist that simply haven't been seen.

## Organization of the Book

The first chapter is a brisk walk through the major parts of the language. At that point, not all details are thoroughly explored, but you can get a good feel for the language and build expertise to write small programs in it. Chapters 2 and 3 are the obligatory reference chapters for expressions and statements, respectively. I tried to combine the required uniform thoroughness with providing highlights of the "deltas," differences from traditional languages. With luck, you'll find these chapters easy to read sequentially and also handy to return to for reference. The tables at the end of these chapters are "cheat sheets"—quick refreshers expressed in terse, intuitive terms.

Chapter 4 describes built-in arrays, associative arrays, and strings. Arrays can be thought of as pointers with a safety switch and are instrumental in D's approach to memory safety and in your enjoyment of the language. Strings are arrays of UTF-encoded Unicode characters. Unicode support throughout the language and the standard library makes string handling correct and effective.

After reading the first four chapters, you can use the abstractions provided by the language to write short script-style programs. Subsequent chapters introduce abstraction building blocks. Chapter 5 describes functions in an integrated manner that includes compile-time parameterized functions (template functions) and functions evaluated during compilation. Such concepts would normally be confined to an advanced chapter, but D makes them simple enough to justify early introduction.

Chapter 6 discusses object-oriented design with classes. Again, compile-time parameterized classes are presented in an integrated, organic manner. Chapter 7 introduces additional types, notably `struct`, which is instrumental in building high-efficiency abstractions, often in concert with classes.

The following four chapters describe features that are relatively separate and specialized. Chapter 8 deals with type qualifiers. Qualifiers provide strong guarantees that are very handy in single-threaded and multithreaded applications alike. Chapter 9 covers the exception model. Chapter 10 introduces D's powerful facilities for Contract Programming and is intentionally separate from Chapter 9 in an attempt to dispel the common misconception that error handling and Contract Programming are practically the same topic; they aren't, and Chapter 10 explains why.

Chapter 11 gives information and advice for building large programs out of components and also gives a brief tour through D's standard library. Chapter 12 covers operator overloading, without which a host of abstractions such as complex numbers would be severely affected. Finally, Chapter 13 discusses D's original approach to concurrency.

## A Brief History

Cheesy as it sounds, D is a work of love. Walter Bright, a C and C++ compiler writer, decided one day in the 1990s that he didn't want to continue his career maintaining his compilers, so he set out to define a language as he thought "it should be done." Many of us dream at some point or another of defining the Right Language; luckily, Walter already had a significant portion of the infrastructure handy—a back-end code generator, a linker, and most of all extensive experience with building language processors. The latter skill offered Walter an interesting perspective. Through some mysterious law of nature, poor language feature design reflects itself, in a Dorian Gray-esque manner, in convoluted compiler implementation. In designing his new language, Walter attempted systematically to eliminate such disfluencies.

The then-nascent language was similar to C++ in spirit so the community called it simply D, in spite of Walter's initial attempt to dub it Mars. Let's call that language D1 for reasons that will become apparent soon. Walter worked on D1 for years and through sheer passion and perseverance amassed a growing crowd of followers. By 2006 D1 had grown into a strong language that could technically compete head to head with much more established languages such as C++ and Java. However, by that time it had become clear that D1 would not become mainstream because it did not have enough compelling features to make up for the backing that other languages had. At that time Walter decided to make a daring gambit: he decided that D1 would be the mythical throwaway first version, put D1 in maintenance mode, and embarked on a revamped design for the second iteration of the language that had the discretion to break backward compatibility. Current D1 users continued to benefit from bug fixes, but D1 would not add new features; D2 would become the flagship language definition, which I'll henceforth call D.

The gambit paid off. The first design iteration provided insights into things to do and things to avoid. Also, there was no rush to advertise the new language—newcomers could work with the stable, actively maintained D1. Since compatibility and deadline pressures were not major issues, there was time to analyze design alternatives carefully and to make the right decisions through and through. To further help the design effort, Walter also enlisted the help of collaborators such as Bartosz Milewski and me. Important features pertaining to D's approach to immutability, generic programming, concurrency, functional programming, safety, and much more were decided in long, animated meetings among the three of us at a coffee shop in Kirkland, WA.

In time, D firmly outgrew its "better C++" moniker and became a powerful multipurpose language that could gainfully steal work from system-level, enterprise, and scripting languages alike. There was one problem left—all of this growth and innovation has happened in obscurity; little has been documented about the way D approaches programming.

The book you're now reading attempts to fill that void. I hope you will enjoy reading it as much as I enjoyed writing it.

## Acknowledgments

D has a long list of contributors that I can't hope to produce in its entirety. Of these, the participants in the Usenet newsgroup `digitalmars.D` stand out. The newsgroup has acted as a sounding board for the designs we brought up for scrutiny and also generated many ideas and improvements.

Walter has benefited from community help with defining the reference implementation `dmd`, and two contributors stand out: Sean Kelly and Don Clugston. Sean has rewritten and improved the core runtime library (including the garbage collector) and has also authored most of D's concurrency library implementation. He's very good at what he does, which sadly means that bugs in your concurrent code are more likely to be yours than his. Don is an expert in math in general and floating point numerics issues in particular. He has enormously helped D's numeric primitives to be some of the best around and has pushed D's generational abilities to their limit. As soon as the source code for the reference compiler was made available, Don couldn't resist adding to it, becoming the second-largest dmd contributor. Both Sean and Don initiated and carried through proposals that improved D's definition. Last but not least, they are awesome hackers all around and very enjoyable to interact with in person and online. I don't know where the language would be without them.

For this book, I'd like to warmly thank my reviewers for the generosity with which they carried out a difficult and thankless job. Without them this book would not be what it now is (so if you don't like it, take solace—just imagine how much worse it could have been). So allow me to extend my thanks to Alejandro Aragón, Bill Baxter, Kevin Bealer, Travis Boucher, Mike Casinghino, Àlvaro Castro Castilla, Richard Chang, Don Clugston, Stephan Dilly, Karim Filali, Michel Fortin, David B. Held, Michiel Helvensteijn, Bernard Helyer, Jason House, Sam Hu, Thomas Hume, Graham St. Jack, Robert Jacques, Christian Kamm, Daniel Keep, Mark Kegel, Sean Kelly, Max Khesin, Simen Kjaeraas, Cody Koeninger, Denis Koroskin, Lars Kyllingstad, Igor Lesik, Eugene Letuchy, Pelle Månsson, Miura Masahiro, Tim Matthews, Scott Meyers, Bartosz Milewski, Fawzi Mohamed, Ellery Newcomer, Eric Niebler, Mike Parker, Derek Parnell, Jeremie Pelletier, Pablo Ripolles, Brad Roberts, Michael Rynn, Foy Savas, Christof Schardt, Steve Schveighoffer, Benjamin Shropshire, David Simcha, Tomasz Stachowiak, Robert Stewart, Knut Erik Teigen, Cristian Vlăsceanu, and Leor Zolman.

Andrei Alexandrescu
Sunday, May 2, 2010

# "D"iving In

You know what's coming first, so without further ado:

```
import std.stdio;
void main() {
    writeln("Hello, world!");
}
```

Depending on what other languages you know, you might have a feeling of déjà vu, a mild appreciation for simplicity, or perhaps a slight disappointment that D didn't go the scripting languages' route of allowing top-level statements. (Top-level statements invite global variables, which quickly turn into a liability as the program grows; D does offer ways of executing code outside main, just in a more structured manner.) If you're a stickler for precision, you'll be relieved to hear that void main is equivalent to an int main that returns "success" (code zero) to the operating system if it successfully finishes execution.

But let's not get ahead of ourselves. The purpose of the traditional "Hello, world!" program is not to discuss a language's capabilities, but instead to get you started on writing and running programs using that language. If you don't have some IDE offering transparent builds, the command line is an easy route. After you have typed the code above in a file called, say, hello.d, fire a shell and type the following commands:

```
$ dmd hello.d
$ ./hello
Hello, world!
$ _
```

where $ stands in for your command prompt (it could be `C:\Path\To\Dir>` on Windows or `/path/to/dir%` on Unix systems, such as OSX, Linux, and Cygwin). You can even get the program to compile and run automatically if you apply a bit of your system-fu skills. On Windows, you may want to associate the shell command "Run" with the program `rdmd.exe`, which is part of the installation. Unix-like systems support the "shebang notation" for launching scripts, syntax that D understands; adding the line

```
#!/usr/bin/rdmd
```

to the very beginning of your `hello.d` program makes it directly executable. After you make that change, you can simply type at the command prompt:

```
$ chmod u+x hello.d
$ ./hello.d
Hello, world!
$ _
```

(You need to do the `chmod` thing only once.)

On all operating systems, the `rdmd` program is smart enough to cache the generated executable, such that compilation is actually done only after you've changed the program, not every time you run it. This, combined with the fact that the compiler proper is very fast, fosters a rapid edit-run cycle that helps short scripts and large programs alike.

The program itself starts with the directive

```
import std.stdio;
```

which instructs the compiler to look for a module called `std.stdio` and make its symbols available for use. `import` is akin to the `#include` preprocessor directive found in C and C++ but is closer in semantics to Python's `import`: there is no textual inclusion taking place—just a symbol table acquisition. Repeated `import`s of the same file are of no import.

Per the venerable tradition established by C, a D program consists of a collection of declarations spread across multiple files. The declarations can introduce, among other things, types, functions, and data. Our first program defines the `main` function to take no arguments and return "nothingness"—`void`, that is. When invoked, `main` calls the `writeln` function (which, of course, was cunningly defined by the `std.stdio` module), passing it a constant string. The `ln` suffix indicates that `writeln` appends a newline to the printed text.

The following sections provide a quick drive through Deeville. Little illustrative programs introduce basic language concepts. At this point the emphasis is on conveying a feel for the language, rather than giving pedantic definitions. Later chapters will treat each part of the language in greater detail.

## 1.1 Numbers and Expressions

Are you ever curious how tall foreigners are? Let's write a simple program that displays a range of usual heights in feet + inches and in centimeters.

```
/*
  Compute heights in centimeters for a range of heights
  expressed in feet and inches
*/
import std.stdio;

void main() {
    // Values unlikely to change soon
    immutable inchesPerFoot = 12;
    immutable cmPerInch = 2.54;

    // Loop'n write
    foreach (feet; 5 .. 7) {
        foreach (inches; 0 .. inchesPerFoot) {
            writeln(feet, "'", inches, "'\t",
                (feet * inchesPerFoot + inches) * cmPerInch);
        }
    }
}
```

When executed, this program will print a nice two-column list:

```
5'0''    152.4
5'1''    154.94
5'2''    157.48
...
6'10''   208.28
6'11''   210.82
```

The construct `foreach (feet; 5 .. 7) { ... }` is an iteration statement that defines an integer variable `feet` and binds it in turn to 5 and then 6, but not 7 (the interval is open to the right).

Just like Java, C++, and C#, D supports `/*multiline comments*/` and `//single-line comments` (plus documentation comments, which we'll get to later). One more interesting detail is the way our little program introduces its data. First, there are two constants:

```
immutable inchesPerFoot = 12;
immutable cmPerInch = 2.54;
```

Constants that will never, ever change are introduced with the keyword `immutable`. Constants, as well as variables, don't need to have a manifest type; the actual type can be inferred from the value with which the symbol is initialized. In this case, the literal 12 tells the compiler that `inchesPerFoot` is an integer (denoted in D with the familiar `int`); similarly, the literal 2.54 causes `cmPerInch` to be a floating-point constant (of type `double`). Going forth, we notice that the definitions of `feet` and `inches` avail themselves of the same magic, because they look like variables all right, yet have no explicit type adornments. That doesn't make the program any less safe than one that states:

```
immutable int inchesPerFoot = 12;
immutable double cmPerInch = 2.54;
...
foreach (int feet; 5 .. 7) {
    ...
}
```

and so on, only less redundant. The compiler allows omitting type declarations only when types can be unambiguously inferred from context. But now that types have come up, let's pause for a minute and see what numeric types are available.

In order of increasing size, the signed integral types include `byte`, `short`, `int`, and `long`, having sizes of exactly 8, 16, 32, and 64 bits, respectively. Each of these types has an unsigned counterpart of the same size, named following a simple rule: `ubyte`, `ushort`, `uint`, and `ulong`. (There is no "unsigned" modifier as in C.) Floating-point types consist of `float` (32-bit IEEE 754 single-precision number), `double` (64-bit IEEE 754), and `real` (which is as large as the machine's floating-point registers can go, but no less than 64 bits; for example, on Intel machines `real` is a so-called IEEE 754 double-extended 79-bit format).

Getting back to the sane realm of integral numbers, literals such as 42 can be assigned to any numeric type, but note that the compiler checks whether the target type is actually large enough to accommodate that value. So the declaration

```
immutable byte inchesPerFoot = 12;
```

is as good as the one omitting `byte` because 12 fits as comfortably in 8 bits as in 32. By default, if the target type is to be deduced from the number (as in the sample program), integral constants have type `int` and floating-point constants have type `double`.

Using these types, you can build a lot of expressions in D using arithmetic operators and functions. The operators and their precedence are much like the ones you'd find in D's sibling languages: `+`, `-`, `*`, `/`, and `%` for basic arithmetic, `==`, `!=`, `<`, `>`, `<=`, `>=` for comparisons, `fun(argument1, argument2)` for function calls, and so on.

Getting back to our centimeters-to-inches program, there are two noteworthy details about the call to `writeln`. One is that `writeln` takes five arguments (as opposed to one in the program that opened the hailing frequencies). Much like the I/O facilities found in Pascal (writeln), C (printf), or C++ (cout), D's writeln function accepts a variable number of arguments (it is a "variadic function"). In D, however, users can define their own variadic functions (unlike in Pascal) that are always typesafe (unlike in C) without needing to gratuitously hijack operators (unlike in C++). The other detail is that our call to writeln awkwardly mixes formatting information with the data being formatted. Separating data from presentation is often desirable, so let's use the formatted write function writefln instead:

```
writefln("%s'%s''\t%s", feet, inches,
    (feet * inchesPerFoot + inches) * cmPerInch);
```

The newly arranged call produces exactly the same output, with the difference that writefln's first argument describes the format entirely. % introduces a format specifier similar to C's printf, for example, %i for integers, %f for floating-point numbers, and %s for strings.

If you've used printf, you'd feel right at home were it not for an odd detail: we're printing ints and doubles here—how come they are both described with the %s specifier, which traditionally describes only strings? The answer is simple. D's variadic argument facility gives writefln access to the actual argument types passed, a setup that has two nice consequences: (1) the meaning of %s could be expanded to "whatever the argument's default string representation is," and (2) if you don't match the format specifier with the actual argument types, you get a clean-cut error instead of the weird behavior specific to misformatted printf calls (to say nothing about the security exploits made possible by printf calls with untrusted format strings).

## 1.2 Statements

In D, just as in its sibling languages, any expression followed by a semicolon is a statement (for example, the "Hello, world!" program's call to writeln has a ; right after it). The effect of the statement is to simply evaluate the expression.

D is a member of the "curly-braces block-scoped" family, meaning that you can group several statements into one by surrounding them with { and }—something that's necessary, for example, when you want to do several things inside a foreach loop. In the case of exactly one statement, you can omit the curly braces entirely. In fact, our entire height conversion double loop could be rewritten as follows:

```
foreach (feet; 5 .. 7)
  foreach (inches; 0 .. inchesPerFoot)
    writefln("%s'%s''\t%s", feet, inches,
      (feet * inchesPerFoot + inches) * cmPerInch);
```

Omitting braces for single statements has the advantage of shorter code and the disadvantage of making edits more fiddly (during code maintenance, you'll need to add or remove braces as you mess with statements). People tend to be pretty divided when it comes to rules for indentation and for placing curly braces. In fact, so long as you're consistent, these things are not as important as they might seem, and as a proof, the style used in this book (full bracing even for single statements, opening braces on the introducing line, and closing braces on their own lines) is, for typographical reasons, quite different from the author's style in everyday code. If he could do this without turning into a werewolf, so could anyone.

The Python language made popular a different style of expressing block structure by means of indentation—"form follows structure" at its best. Whitespace that matters is an odd proposition for programmers of some other languages, but Python programmers swear by it. D normally ignores whitespace but is especially designed to be easily parsed (e.g., parsing does not need to understand the meaning of symbols), which suggests that a nice pet project could implement a simple preprocessor allowing usage of Python indentation style with D without suffering any inconvenience in the process of compiling, running, and debugging programs.

The code samples above also introduced the `if` statement. The general form should be very familiar:

> **if** (‹*expression*›) ‹*statement*$_1$› **else** ‹*statement*$_2$›

A nice theoretical result known as the *theorem of structure* [10] proves that we can implement any algorithm using compound statements, `if` tests, and loops à la `for` and `foreach`. Of course, any realistic language would offer more than just that, and D is no exception, but for now let's declare ourselves content as far as statements go and move on.

## 1.3   Function Basics

Let's go beyond the required definition of the `main` function and see how to define other functions in D. Function definitions follow the model found in other Algol-like languages: first comes the return type, then the function's name, and finally the formal parameters[1] as a parenthesized comma-separated list. For example, to define a function called `pow` that takes a `double` and an `int` and returns a `double`, you'd write

```
double pow(double base, int exponent) {
    ...
}
```

Each function parameter (`base` and `exponent` in the example above) has, in addition to its type, an optional *storage class* that decides the way arguments are passed to

---

[1]. This book consistently uses *parameter* to refer to the value accepted and used inside the function and *argument* when talking about the value passed from the outside to the function during invocation.

the function when invoked. By default, arguments are passed into pow by value. If storage class ref is prepended to a parameter's type, the parameter is bound directly to the incoming argument such that changing the parameter is directly and immediately reflected in the value received from the outside. For example:

```
import std.stdio;

void fun(ref uint x, double y) {
    x = 42;
    y = 3.14;
}
void main() {
    uint a = 1;
    double b = 2;
    fun(a, b);
    writeln(a, " ", b);
}
```

This program prints 42 2 because x is a ref uint, meaning that assigning to x really means assigning to a. On the other hand, assigning to y has no effect on b because y is a private copy at fun's disposal.

The last adornments we'll discuss in this brief introduction are in and out. Simply put, in is a promise on the part of the function that it wants only to look at, not touch, the parameter. Using out with a function parameter works similarly to ref, with the amendment that the parameter is forcibly initialized to its default value upon the function's entry. (Each type T defines an initial value, denoted as T.init. User-defined types can define their own init.)

There is a lot more to say about functions. You can pass functions to other functions, nest them into one another, allow a function to save its local environment (full-fledged syntactic closures), create and comfortably manipulate unnamed functions (lambdas), and some additional juicy little bits. We will get to each of these in good order.

## 1.4   Arrays and Associative Arrays

Arrays and associative arrays (the latter colloquially referred to as hashtables or hashes) are arguably the most used compound data structures in the history of computing, enviously followed by Lisp's lists. A lot of useful programs need no more than some sort of array and associative array, so it's about time to see how D implements them.

### 1.4.1   Building a Vocabulary

For example, let's write a simple program following this specification:

> Read a text consisting of words separated by whitespace, and associate a unique
> number with each distinct word. Output lines of the form ID word.

This little script can be quite useful if you want to do some text processing; once
you have built a vocabulary, you only need to manipulate numbers (cheaper), not full-
fledged words. A possible approach to building such a vocabulary is to accumulate already seen words in a sort of a dictionary that maps words to integers. When adding a
new mapping we only need to make sure the integer is unique (a solid option is to just
use the current length of the dictionary, resulting in the IDs 0, 1, 2, . . . ). Let's see how we
can do that in D.

```d
import std.stdio, std.string;

void main() {
   uint[string] dictionary;
   foreach (line; stdin.byLine()) {
      // Break sentence into words
      // Add each word in the sentence to the vocabulary
      foreach (word; splitter(strip(line))) {
         if (word in dictionary) continue; // Nothing to do
         auto newID = dictionary.length;
         dictionary[word] = newID;
         writeln(newID, '\t', word);
      }
   }
}
```

In D, the type of an associative array (a hashtable) that maps values of type K to values of type V is denoted as V[K]. So the variable dictionary of type uint[string] maps
strings to unsigned integers—just what we needed to store word-to-ID mappings. The
expression word in dictionary is nonzero if the key word could be found in associative
array dictionary. Finally, insertion in the dictionary is done with dictionary[word] =
newID.

Although not made explicit in the script above, the type string is really an array of
characters. Generally, dynamically sized arrays of T are denoted as T[] and are allocated
in a number of ways, such as

```d
int[] a = new int[20]; // 20 zero-initialized integers
int[] b = [ 1, 2, 3 ]; // An array containing 1, 2, and 3
```

Unlike C arrays, D arrays know their own length, accessible as arr.length for any
array arr. Assigning to arr.length reallocates the array. Array accesses are bounds
checked; code that enjoys risking buffer overruns can scare the pointer out of the array

(by using `arr.ptr`) and then use unchecked pointer arithmetic. Also, a compiler option disables bounds checking if you really need everything that silicon wafer could give. This places the path of least resistance on the right side of safety: code is safe by default and can be made a tad faster with more work.

Here's how to iterate over an array using a new form of the already familiar `foreach` statement:

```
int[] arr = new int[20];
foreach (elem; arr) {
    /* ... use elem ... */
}
```

The loop above binds `elem` to each element of `arr` in turn. Assigning to `elem` does not assign back to elements in `arr`. To change the array, just use the `ref` keyword:

```
// Zero all elements of arr
foreach (ref elem; arr) {
    elem = 0;
}
```

And now that we know how `foreach` works with arrays, let's look into one more useful thing. If you also need the index of the array element while you're iterating, `foreach` can do that for you:

```
int[] months = new int[12];
foreach (i, ref e; months) {
    e = i + 1;
}
```

The code above creates an array containing 1, 2, ..., 12. The loop is equivalent to the slightly more verbose code below, which uses `foreach` to iterate over a range of numbers:

```
foreach (i; 0 .. months.length) {
    months[i] = i + 1;
}
```

D also offers statically sized arrays denoted as, for example, `int[5]`. Outside a few specialized applications, dynamically sized arrays are to be preferred because more often than not you don't know the size of the array in advance.

Arrays have shallow copy semantics, meaning that copying one array variable to another does not copy the entire array; it just spawns a new view to the same underlying storage. If you do want to obtain a copy, just use the `dup` property of the array:

```
int[] a = new int[100];
```

```
int[] b = a;
// ++x increments value x
++b[10];      // b[10] is now 1, as is a[10]
b = a.dup;    // Copy a entirely into b
++b[10];      // b[10] is now 2, a[10] stays 1
```

### 1.4.2   Array Slicing. Type-Generic Functions. Unit Tests

Array slicing is a powerful feature that allows referring to a portion of an array without actually copying array data. To exemplify, let's write a function binarySearch implementing the eponymous algorithm: given a sorted array and a value, binarySearch
quickly returns a Boolean value that tells whether the value is in the array. D's standard
library offers a function that does this in a more general way and returns something
more informative than just a Boolean, but that needs to wait for more language features.
Let us, however, bump our ambitions up just a notch, by setting to write a binarySearch
that works not only with arrays of integers, but with arrays of any type as long as values
of that type can be compared with <. It turns out that that's not much of a stretch. Here's
what a generic binarySearch looks like:

```
import std.array;

bool binarySearch(T)(T[] input, T value) {
   while (!input.empty) {
      auto i = input.length / 2;
      auto mid = input[i];
      if (mid > value) input = input[0 .. i];
      else if (mid < value) input = input[i + 1 .. $];
      else return true;
   }
   return false;
}

unittest {
   assert(binarySearch([ 1, 3, 6, 7, 9, 15 ], 6));
   assert(!binarySearch([ 1, 3, 6, 7, 9, 15 ], 5));
}
```

The (T) notation in binarySearch's signature introduces a *type parameter* T. The
type parameter can then be used in the regular parameter list of the function. When
called, binarySearch will deduce T from the actual arguments received. If you want to
explicitly specify T (for example, for double-checking purposes), you may write

```
assert(binarySearch!(int)([ 1, 3, 6, 7, 9, 15 ], 6));
```

which reveals that a generic function can be invoked with two pairs of parenthesized arguments. First come the compile-time arguments enclosed in !(...), and then come the runtime arguments enclosed in (...). Mixing the two realms together has been considered, but experimentation has shown that such uniformity creates more trouble than it eliminates.

If you are familiar with similar facilities in Java, C#, or C++, you certainly noticed that D made a definite departure from these languages' use of angle brackets < and > to specify compile-time arguments. This was a deliberate decision aimed at avoiding the crippling costs revealed by experience with C++, such as increased parsing difficulties, a hecatomb of special rules and arbitrary tiebreakers, and obscure syntax to effect user-directed disambiguation.[2] The difficulty stems from the fact that < and > are at their heart comparison operators,[3] which makes it very ambiguous to use them as delimiters when expressions are allowed *inside* those delimiters. Such would-be delimiters are very difficult to pair. Java and C# have an easier time exactly because they do not allow expressions inside < and >, but that limits their future extensibility for the sake of a doubtful benefit. D does allow expressions as compile-time arguments and chose to simplify the life of both human and compiler by extending the traditional unary operator ! to binary uses and using the classic parentheses (which (I'm sure) you always pair properly).

Another detail of interest in binarySearch's implementation is the use of auto to leverage type deduction: i and mid have their types deduced from their initialization expressions.

In keeping with good programming practices, binarySearch is accompanied by a unit test. Unit tests are introduced as blocks prefixed with the unittest keyword (a file can contain as many unittests as needed, and you know what it's like—too many are almost enough). To run unit tests before main is entered, pass the -unittest flag to the compiler. Although unittest looks like a small feature, it helps you observe good programming style by making it so easy to insert small tests that it's embarrassing not to. Also, if you're a top-level thinker who prefers to see the unittest first and the implementation second, feel free to move unittest before binarySearch; in D, the semantics of a module-level symbol never depends on its relative ordering with others.

The slice expression input[a .. b] returns a slice of input from index a up to, and excluding, index b. If a == b, an empty slice is produced, and if a > b, an exception is thrown. A slice does not trigger a dynamic memory allocation; it's just an alias for a part of the array. Inside an index expression or a slice expression, $ stands in for the length of the array being accessed; for example, input[0 .. $] is exactly the same thing as input.

---

2. If one of your C++ fellow coders has Superman-level confidence, ask him or her what the syntax object.template fun<arg>() does and you'll see Kryptonite at work.

3. To add insult to injury, << and >> are operators, too.

Again, although it might seem that `binarySearch` does a lot of array shuffling, no array is ever allocated; all of `input`'s slices share space with the original `input`. The implementation is in no way less efficient than a traditional one maintaining indices but is arguably easier to understand because it manipulates less state. Speaking of state, let's write a recursive implementation of `binarySearch` that doesn't reassign `index` at all:

```
import std.array;

bool binarySearch(T)(T[] input, T value) {
   if (input.empty) return false;
   auto i = input.length / 2;
   auto mid = input[i];
   if (mid > value) return binarySearch(input[0 .. i]);
   if (mid < value) return binarySearch(input[i + 1 .. $]);
   return true;
}
```

The recursive implementation is arguably simpler and terser than its iterative counterpart. It's also every bit as efficient because the recursive calls can easily be optimized away by a popular compiler technique known as *tail call elimination:* in brief, if a function's `return` simply calls itself with different arguments, the compiler modifies the argument and issues a jump to the beginning of the function.

### 1.4.3   Counting Frequencies. Lambda Functions

Let's set out to write another useful program: counting distinct words in a text. Want to know what words were used most frequently in *Hamlet*? You're in the right place.

The following program uses an associative array mapping strings to `uints` and has a structure similar to the vocabulary-building example. Adding a simple printing loop completes a useful frequency-counting program:

```
import std.stdio, std.string;

void main() {
  // Compute counts
  uint[string] freqs;
  foreach (line; stdin.byLine()) {
    foreach (word; split(strip(line))) {
      ++freqs[word.idup];
    }
  }
  // Print counts
  foreach (key, value; freqs) {
```

```
    writefln("%6u\t%s", value, key);
  }
}
```

All right, now after downloading `hamlet.txt` off the Net (you can find a permanent link at `http://erdani.com/tdpl/hamlet.txt`), running our little program against the Bard's chef d'oeuvre prints

```
    1   outface
    1   come?
    1   blanket,
    1   operant
    1   reckon
    2   liest
    1   Unhand
    1   dear,
    1   parley.
    1   share.
    ...
```

which sadly reveals that output doesn't come quite ordered, and that whichever words come first are not quite the most frequent. This isn't surprising; in order to implement their primitives as fast as possible, associative arrays are allowed to store them internally in any order.

In order to sort output with the most frequent words first, you can just pipe the program's output to `sort -nr` (sort numerically and reversed), but that's in a way cheating. To integrate sorting into the program, let's replace the last loop with the following code:

```
// Print counts
string[] words = freqs.keys;
sort!((a, b) { return freqs[a] > freqs[b]; })(words);
foreach (word; words) {
   writefln("%6u\t%s", freqs[word], word);
}
```

The property `.keys` yields only the keys of the `freqs` associative array as an array of strings. The array is newly allocated, which is necessary because we need to shuffle the strings. We now get to the code

```
sort!((a, b) { return freqs[a] > freqs[b]; })(words);
```

which features the pattern we've already seen:

```
sort!(‹compile-time arguments›)(‹runtime arguments›);
```

Peeling one layer of parentheses off ! ( . . . ), we reach this notation, which looks like an incomplete function that forgot to mention parameter types, result type, and the name of the function itself:

```
(a, b) { return freqs[a] > freqs[b]; }
```

This is a *lambda function*—a short anonymous function that is usually meant to be passed to other functions. Lambda functions are so useful in so many places, D did its best to eliminate unnecessary syntactic baggage from defining a lambda: parameter types as well as the return type are deduced. This makes a lot of sense because the body of the lambda function is by definition right there for the writer, the reader, and the compiler to see, so there is no room for misunderstandings and no breakage of modularity principles.

There is one rather subtle detail to mention about the lambda function defined in this example. The lambda function accesses the freqs variable that is local to main; that is, it is not a global or a static. This is more like Lisp than C and makes for very powerful lambdas. Although traditionally such power comes at a runtime cost (by requiring indirect function calls), D guarantees no indirect calls (and consequently full opportunities for inlining).

The modified program outputs

```
929    the
680    and
625    of
608    to
523    I
453    a
444    my
382    in
361    you
358    Ham.
...
```

which is as expected, with commonly used words being the most frequent, with the exception of "Ham." That's not to indicate a strong culinary preference of the dramatis personae, it's just the prefix of all of Hamlet's lines. So apparently he has some point to make 358 times throughout, more than anyone else. If you browse down the list, you'll see that the next speaker is the king with only 116 lines—fewer than a third of Hamlet's. And at 58 lines, Ophelia is downright taciturn.

## 1.5   Basic Data Structures

Now that we've gotten into *Hamlet*, let's analyze the text a bit further. For example, for all dramatis personae, we'd like to collect some information, such as how many words they say in total, and how rich their vocabulary is. To do that, we need to associate several data items with one persona.[4] To group such information in one place, we can define a data structure as follows:

```d
struct PersonaData {
    uint totalWordsSpoken;
    uint[string] wordCount;
}
```

In D you get `structs` and then you get `classes`. They share many amenities but have different charters: `structs` are value types, whereas `classes` are meant for dynamic polymorphism and are accessed solely by reference. That way confusion, slicing-related bugs, and comments à la `// No! Do NOT inherit!` do not exist. When you design a type, you decide up front whether it'll be a monomorphic value or a polymorphic reference. C++ famously allows defining ambiguous-gender types, but their use is rare, error-prone, and objectionable enough to warrant simply avoiding them by design.

In our case, we just need to collect some data and we have no polymorphic ambitions, so using `struct` is a good choice. Let's now define an associative array mapping persona names to `PersonaData` values:

```d
PersonaData[string] info;
```

All we have to do is fill `info` appropriately from `hamlet.txt`. This needs some work because a character's paragraph may extend for several lines, so we need to do some simple processing to coalesce physical lines into paragraphs. To figure out how to do that, let's take a look at a short fragment from `hamlet.txt`, dumped verbatim below (with leading spaces made visible for clarity):

```
␣␣Pol. Marry, I will teach you! Think yourself a baby
␣␣␣␣That you have ta'en these tenders for true pay,
␣␣␣␣Which are not sterling. Tender yourself more dearly,
␣␣␣␣Or (not to crack the wind of the poor phrase,
␣␣␣␣Running it thus) you'll tender me a fool.
␣␣Oph. My lord, he hath importun'd me with love
␣␣␣␣In honourable fashion.
␣␣Pol. Ay, fashion you may call it. Go to, go to!
```

Whether or not Polonius's enthusiasm about `goto` was a factor in his demise is, even to this day, a matter of speculation. Regardless of that, let's note how each character's line is preceded by exactly two spaces, followed by the (possibly contracted) character's name, followed by a period and a space, finally followed by the actual content of the line. If a logical line extends to multiple physical lines, the continuations are always

---

4. Apologies for the slightly pretentious *persona*. The problem with the worldlier *character* is that it creates confusion with the likes of `char`.

preceded by exactly four spaces. We could do such simple pattern matching by using a regular expression engine (found in the `std.regex` module), but we want to learn arrays so let's match things "by hand." We enlist the help of only the Boolean function `a.startsWith(b)`, defined by `std.algorithm`, which tells whether `a` starts with `b`.

The `main` driver reads input lines, concatenates them in logical paragraphs (ignoring everything that doesn't fit our pattern), passes complete paragraphs to an accumulator function, and at the end prints the desired information.

```
import std.algorithm, std.conv, std.ctype, std.regex,
    std.range, std.stdio, std.string;

struct PersonaData {
    uint totalWordsSpoken;
    uint[string] wordCount;
}

void main() {
    // Accumulates information about dramatis personae
    PersonaData[string] info;
    // Fill info
    string currentParagraph;
    foreach (line; stdin.byLine()) {
        if (line.startsWith("     ")
                && line.length > 4
                && isalpha(line[4])) {
            // Persona is continuing a line
            currentParagraph ~= line[3 .. $];
        } else if (line.startsWith("   ")
                && line.length > 2
                && isalpha(line[2])) {
            // Persona just started speaking
            addParagraph(currentParagraph, info);
            currentParagraph = to!string(line[2 .. $]);
        }
    }
    // Done, now print collected information
    printResults(info);
}
```

After we've equipped ourselves with information on how arrays work, the code should be self-explanatory, save for the presence of `to!string(line[2 .. $])`. Why is it needed, and what if we forgot about it?

The `foreach` loop that reads from `stdin` deposits successive lines of text in the variable `line`. Because it would be wasteful to allocate a brand-new buffer for each line read, `byLine` reuses the contents of `line` every pass through the loop. The type of `line` itself is `char[]`—an array of characters.

As long as you just inspect each line as it comes and then forget about it, everything works smoothly. But code that wants to squirrel away the contents of a line better makes a copy of it. Obviously `currentParagraph` is meant to indeed save text, so duplication is needed; hence the presence of `to!string`, which converts any expression into a `string`. The `string` type itself is impossible to overwrite, and `to` takes care of whatever duplication is necessary to observe that guarantee.

Now, if we forgot `to!string` and subsequently the code still compiled, the results would have been nonsensical and the bug rather hard to find. Having a part of a program modify data held in a different part of the program is very unpleasant to track down because it's a non-local effect (just how many `to` calls could one forget in a large program?). Fortunately, that's not the case because the types of `line` and `currentParagraph` reflect their respective capabilities: `line` has type `char[]`, that is, an array of characters that could be overwritten at any time; whereas `currentParagraph` has type `string`, which is an array of characters that cannot be individually modified. (For the curious: the full name of `string` is `immutable(char)[]`, which means precisely "contiguous region of immutable characters." We'll get to talk more about strings in Chapter 4.) The two cannot refer to the same memory content because `line` would break the promise of `currentParagraph`. So the compiler refuses to compile the erroneous code and demands a copy, which you provide in the form of the conversion `to!string`, and everybody's happy.

On the other hand, when you copy `string` values around, there's no more need to duplicate the underlying data—they can all refer to the same memory because it's known neither will overwrite it, which makes `string` copying at the same time safe and efficient. Better yet, `strings` can be shared across threads without problems because, again, there's never contention. Immutability is really cool indeed. If, on the other hand, you need to modify individual characters intensively, you may want to operate on `char[]`, at least temporarily.

`PersonaData` as defined above is very simple, but in general `structs` can define not only data, but also other entities such as `private` sections, member functions, `unittests`, operators, constructors, and destructor. By default, each data member of a structure is initialized with its default initializer (zero for integral numbers, Not a Number (NaN) for floating-point numbers,[5] and `null` for arrays and other indirect-access types). Let's now implement `addParagraph`, which slices and dices a line of text and puts it into the associative array.

---

5. NaN is a good default initializer for floats, but unfortunately, no equivalent initializer exists for integral numbers.

The line as served by main has the form "Ham. To be, or not to be- that is the question." We need to find the first ". " to distinguish the persona's name from the actual line. To do so, we use the find function. haystack.find(needle) returns the right-hand portion of haystack starting with the first occurrence of needle. (If no occurrence is found, find returns an empty string.) While we're at it, we should also do a little cleanup while collecting the vocabulary. First, we must convert the sentence to lowercase such that capitalized and non-capitalized words count as the same vocabulary element. That's easily taken care of with a call to tolower. Second, we must eliminate a strong source of noise: punctuation that makes, for example, "him." and "him" count as distinct words. To clean up the vocabulary, all we need to do is pass an additional parameter to split mentioning a regular expression that eliminates all chaff: regex("[ \t,.;:?]+"). With that argument, the split function will consider any sequence of the characters mentioned in between [ and ] as part of word separators. That being said, we're ready to do a lot of good stuff in just a little code:

```
void addParagraph(string line, ref PersonaData[string] info) {
   // Figure out persona and sentence
   line = strip(line);
   auto sentence = std.algorithm.find(line, ". ");
   if (sentence.empty) {
      return;
   }
   auto persona = line[0 .. $ - sentence.length];
   sentence = tolower(strip(sentence[2 .. $]));
   // Get the words spoken
   auto words = split(sentence, regex("[ \t,.;:?]+"));
   // Insert or update information
   if (!(persona in info)) {
      // First time this persona speaketh
      info[persona] = PersonaData();
   }
   info[persona].totalWordsSpoken += words.length;
   foreach (word; words) ++info[persona].wordCount[word];
}
```

The bulk of addParagraph consists of updating the associative array. In case the person hasn't been heard from yet, the code inserts an empty, default-constructed PersonaData object in the associative array. Since the default-constructed uint is zero and the default-constructed associative array is empty, the newly inserted slot is ready to start absorbing meaningful information.

Finally, let's implement printResults to print a quick summary for each persona:

```
void printResults(PersonaData[string] info) {
```

```
foreach (persona, data; info) {
   writefln("%20s %6u %6u", persona, data.totalWordsSpoken,
      data.wordCount.length);
}
}
```

Ready for a test drive? Save and run!

|            |       |      |
|-----------:|------:|-----:|
| Queen      | 1104  | 500  |
| Ros        | 738   | 338  |
| For        | 55    | 45   |
| Fort       | 74    | 61   |
| Gentlemen  | 4     | 3    |
| Other      | 105   | 75   |
| Guil       | 349   | 176  |
| Mar        | 423   | 231  |
| Capt       | 92    | 66   |
| Lord       | 70    | 49   |
| Both       | 44    | 24   |
| Oph        | 998   | 401  |
| Ghost      | 683   | 350  |
| All        | 20    | 17   |
| Player     | 16    | 14   |
| Laer       | 1507  | 606  |
| Pol        | 2626  | 870  |
| Priest     | 92    | 66   |
| Hor        | 2129  | 763  |
| King       | 4153  | 1251 |
| Cor., Volt | 11    | 11   |
| Both [Mar  | 8     | 8    |
| Osr        | 379   | 179  |
| Mess       | 110   | 79   |
| Sailor     | 42    | 36   |
| Servant    | 11    | 10   |
| Ambassador | 41    | 34   |
| Fran       | 64    | 47   |
| Clown      | 665   | 298  |
| Gent       | 101   | 77   |
| Ham        | 11901 | 2822 |
| Ber        | 220   | 135  |
| Volt       | 150   | 112  |
| Rey        | 80    | 37   |

Now that's some fun stuff. Unsurprisingly, our friend "Ham" gets the lion's share by a large margin. Voltemand's ("Volt") role is rather interesting: he doesn't have many words to say, but in these few words he does his best to display a solid vocabulary, not to mention the Sailor, who hardly repeats a word. Also compare the well-rounded Queen with Ophelia: the Queen has about 10% more words to say than Ophelia, but her vocabulary is no less than 25% larger.

The output has some noise in it (such as `"Both [Mar"`), easy for a diligent programmer to fix and hardly affecting the important statistics. Nevertheless, fixing the last little glitches would be an instructive (and recommended) exercise.

## 1.6   Interfaces and Classes

Object-oriented features are important for large projects; therefore, introducing them by means of small examples is at high risk of looking goofy. Add to that a pressing desire to stay away from overused examples featuring shapes, animals, or employees, and we're faced with quite a pickle. Oh, and there's one more thing—small examples usually gloss over the issue of polymorphic object creation, which is important. Talk about writer's block! Fortunately, the real world provides a useful example in the form of a problem that's relatively small, yet has no satisfactory procedural solution. The code we'll discuss below is the rewrite of a small useful awk script that had grown well beyond the implicit limits set by its design. We will work together toward an object-oriented solution that is at the same time small, complete, and elegant.

Consider writing a small statistics program called `stats` with a simple interface: `stats` takes the statistical functions to compute as command-line parameters, gathers the numbers to operate on via standard input as a whitespace-separated list, and prints the statistical results one per line. Here is a sample session:

```
$ echo 3 5 1.3 4 10 4.5 1 5 | stats Min Max Average
1
10
4.225
$ _
```

A quick-and-dirty script can perform such tasks with no problem, yet the "dirty" tends to overshadow the "quick" as the number of statistical functions grows. So let's put together a better solution. For now, we start with the simplest statistical functions: minimum, maximum, and average. After we figure out an extensible design, the door is open to implementing more complex statistical functions.

A simple way to approach things is to just loop through the input and compute all needed statistics. This is not a scalable design because each time we need to add a new statistical function, we'd have to do surgery on existing code. The modifications will be nontrivial if we want to perform only the computations asked for in the command line. Ideally, we'd confine each statistical function to one contiguous piece of code. That way, we can add new functionality to the program by simply appending new code—the Open-Closed principle [39] at its best.

Such an approach entails figuring out what all, or at least most, statistical functions have in common, with the goal of manipulating them all from one place and in a uniform manner. Let's start by remarking that Min and Max take their input one number at a time and have the result handy as soon as the input is finished. The final result is only one number. In addition, Average must do a post-processing step (divide the accumulated sum by the number of inputs). Moreover, each algorithm maintains its own state. When different computations obey a uniform interface and need to keep state, it makes sense to make them objects and define a formal interface to manipulate any and all of them.

```
interface Stat {
   void accumulate(double x);
   void postprocess();
   double result();
}
```

An interface defines a required behavior as a set of functions. Of course, anyone claiming to implement the interface must define all functions as specified by their declarations. Speaking of implementation, let's see how we can define Min to obey Stat's iron fist:

```
class Min : Stat {
   private double min = double.max;
   void accumulate(double x) {
      if (x < min) {
         min = x;
      }
   }
   void postprocess() {} // Nothing to do
   double result() {
      return min;
   }
}
```

Min is a *class*—a user-defined type that brings lots of object orientation goodies into D. Min manifestly implements Stat through the syntax class Min : Stat and indeed defines Stat's three functions exactly with the same arguments and return types (otherwise the compiler would not have allowed Min to get away with it). Min keeps only one private member variable min, which is the smallest value seen so far, and updates it inside accumulate. The initial value of Min is the *largest* possible number, such that the first input number will replace it.

Before defining more statistical functions, let's write a driver for our stats program that reads the command-line parameters, creates the appropriate objects to do computations (such as Min when Min is passed in the command line), and uses the objects through the interface Stat.

```d
import std.contracts, std.stdio;

void main(string[] args) {
    Stat[] stats;
    foreach (arg; args[1 .. $]) {
        auto newStat = cast(Stat) Object.factory("stats." ~ arg);
        enforce(newStat, "Invalid statistics function: " ~ arg);
        stats ~= newStat;
    }
    for (double x; readf(" %s ", &x) == 1; ) {
        foreach (s; stats) {
            s.accumulate(x);
        }
    }
    foreach (s; stats) {
        s.postprocess();
        writeln(s.result());
    }
}
```

This program does quite a lot but is only one mouthful. First off, main has a signature different from what we've seen so far—it takes an array of strings. The D runtime support initializes the array from the command-line parameters. The first loop initializes the stats array from args. Given that in D (as in other languages) the first argument is the name of the program itself, we skip that first argument by taking the slice args[1 .. $]. We now hit the statement

```d
auto newStat = cast(Stat) Object.factory("stats." ~ arg);
```

which is quite long, but, to quote a sitcom cliché, "I can explain." First, ~, when used as a binary operator, concatenates strings, so if the command-line argument was Max, the concatenation results in the string "stats.Max", which is passed to the function Object.factory. Object is the root of all class objects, and it defines the static method factory that takes a string, looks up a little database built during compilation, magically creates an object of the type named by the passed-in string, and returns it. If the class is not present, Object.factory returns null. For that call to succeed, all you need is to have a class called `Max` defined somewhere in the same file. Creating an object given the name of its type is an important facility with many useful applications—so important, in fact, that some dynamic languages make it a central feature; languages with a more static approach to typing need to rely on runtime support (such as D or Java) or leave it to the programmer to devise a manual registration and discovery mechanism.

Why `stats.Max` and not just `Max`? D is serious about modularity so it does not have a global namespace in which anyone can put anything. Each symbol lives in a named module, and by default the name of the module is the base name of the source file. So given that our file is called `stats.d`, D reckons that every name defined in that file belongs to module `stats`.

There is one more hitch left. The static type of the just-obtained `Min` object is actually not `Min`. That sounds dumb, but it's justified by the fact that you could create *any* object by invoking `Object.factory("whatever")`, so the return type should be some common denominator of all possible object types—`Object`, that is. To get the appropriate handle on the newly created object, we must make it into a `Stat` object, an operation known as *casting*. In D, the expression `cast(T) expr` casts expression `expr` into type `T`. Casts involving class and interface types are always checked, so our code is foolproof.

Looking back, we notice that we've done a lot of solid work in `main`'s first five lines. That was the hardest part, because the rest of the code writes itself. The second loop reads one number at a time (`readf` takes care of that) and calls `accumulate` for all statistical objects. The `readf` function returns the number of items read successfully according to the specified format. In our case, the format is `" %s "`, which means one item surrounded by any amount of whitespace. (The item's type is decided by the type of the element being read, in this case `x` of type `double`.) Finally, the program prints all results.

### 1.6.1 More Statistics. Inheritance

Implementing `Max` is as trivial as implementing `Min`; aside from a slight change in `accumulate`, everything is exactly the same. Whenever a new task looks a lot like an old one, "interesting" and not "boring" is what should come to mind. A repetitive task is an opportunity for reuse, and rightly languages that can better exploit various flavors of similarity should rate higher on a certain quality scale. What we need to figure out is the particular kind of similarity that `Min` and `Max` (and we hope other statistical functions) enjoy. As we think it through, it looks like they both belong to the kind of statistical functions that build their result incrementally and need only one number to characterize the result. Let's call this category of statistical functions, *incremental functions*.

```d
class IncrementalStat : Stat {
   protected double _result;
   abstract void accumulate(double x);
   void postprocess() {}
   double result() {
```

```
        return _result;
    }
}
```

An abstract class can be seen as a partial commitment: it implements a number of methods, but not all, and as such cannot work stand-alone. The way to materialize an abstract class is to inherit it and complete its implementation. IncrementalStat takes care of Stat's boilerplate code but leaves accumulate to be implemented by the derived class. Here's what the new Min looks like:

```
class Min : IncrementalStat {
    this() {
        _result = double.max;
    }
    void accumulate(double x) {
        if (x < _result) {
            _result = x;
        }
    }
}
```

Class Min defined a constructor, too, in the form of a special function called this(), needed to initialize the result appropriately. Even with the constructor in place, the resulting code marks good savings from the initial state of affairs, particularly if we take into account the fact that many other statistical functions follow a similar pattern (e.g., sum, variance, average, standard deviation). Let's look at implementing average, because it's a great occasion to introduce a couple of more concepts:

```
class Average : IncrementalStat {
    private uint items = 0;
    this() {
        _result = 0;
    }
    void accumulate(double x) {
        _result += x;
        ++items;
    }
    override void postprocess() {
        if (items) {
            _result /= items;
        }
    }
}
```

First off, `Average` introduces one more member variable, `items`, which is initialized with zero through the syntax `= 0` (just to showcase initialization syntax, but redundant in this case because integral types are zero-initialized anyway, as discussed on page 17). Second, `Average` defines a constructor that sets `result` to zero; this is because, unlike minimum or maximum, the average of zero numbers is defined to be zero. Although it might seem that initializing `result` with NaN just to overwrite it later with zero is needless busywork, optimizing away the so-called dead assignment is low-hanging fruit for any optimizer. Finally, `Average` overrides `postprocess` even though `IncrementalStat` already defined it. In D, by default, you can override (inherit and redefine) member functions of all classes, but you must specify `override` so as to avoid various accidents (e.g., failing to override because of some typo or a change in the base type, or overriding something by mistake). If you prepend `final` to a member function, that prohibits derived classes from overriding the function, effectively stopping the dynamic method lookup mechanism.

## 1.7 Values versus References

Let's run a simple experiment:

```
import std.stdio;

struct MyStruct {
    int data;
}
class MyClass {
    int data;
}

void main() {
    // Play with a MyStruct object
    MyStruct s1;
    MyStruct s2 = s1;
    ++s2.data;
    writeln(s1.data); // Prints 0
    // Play with a MyClass object
    MyClass c1 = new MyClass;
    MyClass c2 = c1;
    ++c2.data;
    writeln(c1.data); // Prints 1
}
```

It seems like playing with a `MyStruct` object is quite a different game from playing with a `MyClass` object. In both cases we create a variable that we copy into another variable, after which we modify the copy (recall that `++` is a unary operator that increments its argument). The experiment seems to reveal that after a copy, `c1` and `c2` refer to the same underlying storage, while on the contrary, `s1` and `s2` have independent lives.

The behavior of `MyStruct` obeys *value semantics:* each variable refers to exactly one value, and assigning one variable to another really means copying the state of the variable over the state of the other variable. The source of the copy is unchanged, and the two variables continue to evolve independently. The behavior of `MyClass` obeys *reference semantics:* values are created explicitly (in our case by invoking `new MyClass`), and assigning a class variable to another simply means that the two variables refer to the same value.

Value semantics are easy to deal with, simple to reason about, and allow efficient implementation for small sizes. On the other hand, nontrivial programs are difficult to implement without some means to refer to a value without copying it. Value semantics alone preclude, for example, forming self-referential types (lists or trees), or mutually referential structures such as a child window knowing about its parent window. Any serious language implements some sort of reference semantics; it could be argued that it all depends on where the default is. C has value semantics exclusively and allows forming references explicitly, by means of pointers. In addition to pointers, C++ also defines reference types. Interestingly, pure functional languages are free to use reference or value semantics as they see fit, because user code cannot tell the difference. This is because pure functional languages don't allow mutation, so you can't tell if they snuck a copy of a value or just a reference to it—it's frozen anyway, so you couldn't verify whether the value is shared by changing it. On the contrary, pure object-oriented languages are traditionally mutation-intensive and employ reference semantics exclusively, some to the extent of allowing a disconcerting amount of flexibility such as changing system-wide constants dynamically. Finally, some languages take a hybrid approach, embracing both value and reference types, with various levels of commitment.

D makes a systematic approach to the hybrid method. To define reference types you use `class`. To define value types or hybrid types you use `struct`. As Chapters 6 and 7 (respectively) describe in detail, each of these type constructors is endowed with amenities specific to this fundamental design choice. For example, `struct`s do not have support for dynamic inheritance and polymorphism (the kind we've shown in the `stats` program above), as such behaviors are not compatible with value semantics. Dynamic polymorphism of objects needs reference semantics, and any attempt to mess with that can only lead to terrible accidents. (For example, a common danger to watch for in C++ is slicing, i.e., suddenly stripping the polymorphic abilities of an object when inadvertently using it as a value. In D, slicing could never occur.)

A closing thought is that `struct`s are arguably a more flexible design choice. By defining a `struct`, you can tap into any semantics that you want, be it eager-copy value, lazy copying à la copy-on-write or reference counting, or anything in between. You can even define reference semantics by using `class` objects or pointers inside your `struct` object. On the other hand, some of these stunts may require quite advanced technical savvy; in contrast, using `classes` offers simplicity and uniformity across the board.

## 1.8 Summary

Because of the introductory nature of this chapter, some concepts and examples glossed over a few details and assumed passing familiarity with some others. Also, an experienced programmer could easily find ways to complete and improve the examples.

With luck, this chapter included something for everyone. If you are the kind of practical, no-nonsense coder, you might have looked at the cleanliness of arrays and associative arrays with an appreciative eye. These two concepts alone make a world of difference in simplifying code day in and day out, for projects small and large. If you enjoy object orientation, no doubt interfaces and classes seemed dearly familiar to you and suggest good upward scalability of the language to large projects. If you need to use D for short scripts as well, this chapter has shown that short scripts that manipulate files are easy to write and get running.

As always, the whole story is a fair amount longer. However, it's useful to get back to the basics and make sure that simple things remain simple.

# Basic Types. Expressions

If you've ever programmed in C, C++, Java, or C#, you'll feel right at home understanding D's basic types and expressions—fortunately with quite a few home improvements. Manipulating values of basic types is the bread and butter of many programming tasks, and a language's offering interacting with your personal preferences can go a long way toward making your life either pleasant or miserable. There is no perfect approach; many desiderata are conflicting, which brings the subjective factor into play. In turn, that makes it impossible for a language to find a solution that pleases everyone. Too strict a system puts the burden in the wrong place as the programmer must fight the compiler into accepting the simplest idioms; make it too lax, and all of a sudden you're on the wrong side of verifiability, efficiency, or both.

D's basic type system works little wonders inside the boundaries dictated by its membership in the family of statically typed, compiled languages. Type inference, value range propagation, various operator overloading decisions, and a carefully designed web of automatic conversions work together to make D's type system a thorough, discreet assistant that starts nagging and asking for attention mostly when it has a real reason.

The fundamental types can be classified in the following categories:

- *The type without a value:* void, which fills in for cases where a type is formally required but no meaningful value is ever produced
- *Boolean type:* bool, with two possible values, true and false
- *Integral types:* byte, short, int, and long, and their unsigned counterparts ubyte, ushort, uint, and ulong
- *Real floating-point types:* float, double, and real

29

- *Character types:* char, wchar, and dchar, which are numeric but are understood by the language to be encodings of Unicode strings

Table 2.1 briefly describes the garden variety of basic types, with their sizes and default initializers. In D, all variables are initialized if you just define them without initializing. The default value is accessible as ‹*type*›.init; for example, int.init is zero.

**Table 2.1:** D basic types

| Name | Description | Default initializer (‹*type*›.init) |
|------|-------------|-------------------------------------|
| void | no value | n/a |
| bool | Boolean value | false |
| byte | signed 8 bits | 0 |
| ubyte | unsigned 8 bits | 0 |
| short | signed 16 bits | 0 |
| ushort | unsigned 16 bits | 0 |
| int | signed 32 bits | 0 |
| uint | unsigned 32 bits | 0 |
| long | signed 64 bits | 0 |
| ulong | unsigned 64 bits | 0 |
| float | 32-bit floating-point | float.nan |
| double | 64-bit floating-point | double.nan |
| real | largest in hardware | real.nan |
| char | unsigned 8-bit UTF-8 | 0xFF |
| wchar | unsigned 16-bit UTF-16 | 0xFFFF |
| dchar | unsigned 32-bit UTF-32 | 0x0000FFFF |

## 2.1  Symbols

A symbol is a case-sensitive string of characters starting with a letter or an underscore followed by any number of letters, underscores, or digits. The only exception to this rule is that symbols starting with two underscores are reserved by the D implementation. Symbols starting with only one underscore are allowed and actually are a popular convention for denoting member variables.

An interesting detail about D symbols is that they are international: in the definition above, "letter" means not only the Roman alphabet letters A through Z and a through z, but also universal characters as defined by the C99 standard [33, Annex D].

For example, abc, α5, _, Γ_1, _AbC, Ab9C, and _9x are valid symbols, but 9abc, __, and __abc are not.

If a symbol is prefixed by a dot `.likeThis`, then the symbol is looked up at module scope, not at the current lexically nested scope. The prefix dot operator has the same precedence as a regular symbol.

### 2.1.1 Special Symbols

Certain symbols, shown in Table 2.2, are language-reserved keywords. User code cannot define them in any circumstance.

**Table 2.2:** D keywords

| | | | |
|---|---|---|---|
| abstract | double | long | super |
| alias | . | . | switch |
| align | else | macro | synchronized |
| asm | enum | mixin | . |
| assert | export | module | template |
| auto | extern | . | this |
| . | . | new | throw |
| body | false | null | true |
| bool | final | . | try |
| break | finally | out | typeid |
| byte | float | override | typeof |
| . | for | . | . |
| case | foreach | package | ubyte |
| cast | function | pragma | uint |
| catch | . | private | ulong |
| char | goto | protected | union |
| class | . | public | unittest |
| const | if | . | ushort |
| continue | import | real | . |
| . | in | ref | version |
| dchar | inout | return | void |
| debug | int | . | . |
| default | interface | scope | wchar |
| delegate | invariant | short | while |
| deprecated | is | static | with |
| do | . | struct | |

A few symbols are recognized as primitive expressions. The special symbol `this` denotes the current object inside a method's definition; `super` restricts both static and dynamic lookup to the base subobject of the current object, as Chapter 6 discusses. The

$ symbol is valid only inside an index expression or a slice expression and evaluates to the length of the array being indexed.  The `null` symbol denotes a null object, array, or pointer.

The `typeid(T)` primary expression returns information about the type `T` (consult your implementation's documentation for more information).

## 2.2   Literals

### 2.2.1   Boolean Literals

The `bool` literals are `true` and `false`.

### 2.2.2   Integral Literals

D features decimal, octal, hexadecimal, and binary integral literals. A decimal constant is a sequence of digits optionally suffixed by `L`, `U`, `u`, `LU`, `Lu`, `UL`, or `uL`. The type of decimal literals is deduced as follows:

- *No suffix:* the type is the first of `int` and `long` that can accommodate the value.
- *U/u only:* the type is the first of `uint` and `ulong` that can accommodate the value.
- *L only:* the type is `long`.
- *Both U/u and L:* the type is `ulong`.

For example:

```
auto
   a = 42,           // a has type int
   b = 42u,          // b has type uint
   c = 42UL,         // c has type ulong
   d = 4000000000,   // long; wouldn't fit in an int
   e = 4000000000u,  // uint; it does fit in a uint
   f = 5000000000u;  // ulong; wouldn't fit in a uint
```

You can freely insert underscores in a number (just not in the first position lest you'd actually create an identifier). Underscores are helpful in writing large numbers clearly:

```
auto targetSalary = 15_000_000;
```

To write a hexadecimal integral literal, use the prefix `0x` or `0X` followed by a sequence of the letters 0–9, a–f, A–F, or _. A leading 0 followed by a possibly empty sequence of 0–7 or _ forms an octal literal. Finally, you can create binary literals with `0b` or `0B` followed by a string of 0s, 1s, and again underscores. All of these literals can be suffixed similarly to the decimal constants, and the rules governing their types are identical to those for decimal literals.

Figure 2.1, worth the proverbial 1024 words, defines the syntax of integral literals concisely and rigorously. The rules of walking the automaton are: (1) each edge consumes the input corresponding to its label; (2) the automaton tries to consume as much input as possible.[1] Stopping in a final (i.e., doubly circled) state means that a number was successfully parsed.

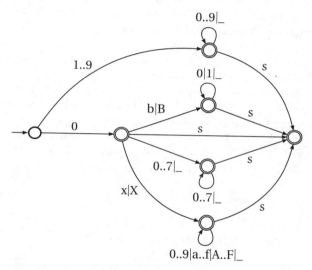

**Figure 2.1:** Understanding D integral literals. The automaton tries to take successive steps (consuming the input corresponding to the edge taken) until it must stop. Stopping in a terminal (doubly circled) state means that a number was successfully parsed. *s* stands for the suffix, which can be U|u|L|UL|uL|Lu|LU.

### 2.2.3 Floating-Point Literals

Floating-point literals can be decimal or hexadecimal. Decimal floating-point literals are easy to define in terms of the just-defined integral literals: a decimal floating-point literal consists of a decimal literal that may also contain one dot (.) in any position, optionally followed by an exponent and/or a suffix. The exponent is one of e, E, e+, E+, e-, or E- followed by an unsigned decimal literal. The suffix can be f, F, or L. Obviously, at least one of ., e/E, or f/F must be present, lest the floating-point number quite literally

---

1. For the theoretically inclined, the automata in Figure 2.1 and Figure 2.2 are "deterministic finite automata" (DFAs).

miss the point and become an integral literal. The f/F suffix, when present, forces the type of the literal to float, and L forces it to real. Otherwise, the literals type is double.

It would appear that hexadecimal floating-point constants are an oddity, but they turn out to be very useful in writing constants *precisely*. Internally, floating-point values are stored in base 2, so a real number expressed in base 10 involves a base conversion, which is approximate because 10 is not a power of 2. In contrast, hexadecimal notation allows you to write down floating-point numbers exactly as they will be represented. A full treatise on how floating-point numbers are stored is beyond the scope of this book, but all D implementations are guaranteed to use the IEEE 754 format, for which plentiful good references are just a Web search away (e.g., look for "IEEE 754 floating-point format").

A hexadecimal floating-point constant consists of the prefix 0x or 0X followed by a string of hexadecimal digits containing a dot in any position. Then comes the mandatory exponent, which is introduced by one of p, P, p+, P+, p-, or P- followed by *decimal* (not hexadecimal!) digits. Only the so-called mantissa—the fractional portion before the exponent—is expressed in hexadecimal; the exponent itself is a decimal integer. The exponent of a hexadecimal floating-point constant represents the exponent of 2 in the final number (not 10 as in the decimal case). Finally, the optional suffix f, F, or L completes the constant.[2] Let's look at some relevant examples:

```
auto
   a = 1.0,       // a has type double
   b = .345E2f,   // b = 34.5 has type float
   c = 10f,       // c has type float due to suffix
   d = 10.,       // d has type double
   e = 0x1.fffffffffffffp1023, // e is the largest double
   f = 0XFp1F;    // f = 30.0 has type float
```

Figure 2.2 on the facing page concisely describes D's floating-point literals. The rules for walking the automaton are the same as for the integral constants automaton: transition is made on reading characters in the literal and the longest path is attempted. The automaton representation clarifies a few points that would be tedious to describe informally: For example, 0x.p1 and even 0xp1 are legal, albeit odd, ways of expressing zero, but constructs such as 0e1, .e1, and 0x0.0 are disallowed.

## 2.2.4   Character Literals

A character literal is one character enclosed in single quotation marks, as in 'a'. The actual quote character must be escaped by a backslash, as in '\''. In fact, like other languages, D defines a number of escape sequences, and Table 2.3 on page 36 shows them

---

2. Yes, the syntax is odd, but D copied C99s syntax rather than devising yet another notation with its own inevitable set of quirks.

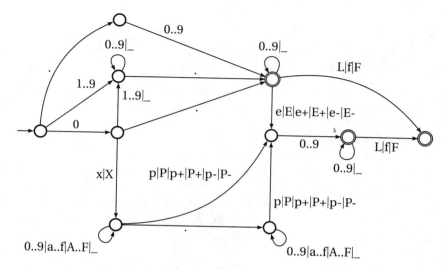

**Figure 2.2:** Understanding floating-point literals.

all. In addition to the standard fare of control characters, D defines ways to form Unicode characters by using one of the notations `'\u03C9'` (\u followed by exactly four hex digits), `'\U0000211C'` (\U followed by exactly eight hex digits), or `'\&copy;'` (a named entity starting with \& and ending with ;). The first one is Unicode for ω, the second is a nicely calligraphed $\mathscr{R}$, and the last one is the dreaded copyright symbol ©. Search the Net for "Unicode table" in case you're in need of a complete list.

### 2.2.5 String Literals

Now that we know how to represent characters, literal strings are a breeze. D is great at manipulating strings, and that is partly because of its powerful ways of representing string literals. Just like other string-bashing languages, D differentiates between *quoted* strings (inside which the escape sequences in Table 2.3 on the following page apply) and *What You See Is What You Get (WYSIWYG)* strings (which the compiler just parses blindly, without attempting to decipher escape sequences). The WYSIWYG style is very useful for representing strings that would require a flurry of escapes, two notorious examples being regular expressions and Windows path names.

Quoted strings are sequences of characters enclosed in double quotation marks, `"like this"`. All escape sequences in Table 2.3 on the next page are meaningful inside a quoted string. Strings of all kinds are automatically concatenated when juxtaposed:

```
auto crlf = "\r\n";
auto a = "This is a string with \"quotes\" in it, and also
a newline, actually two" "\n";
```

The line break after `also` in the code above is intentional: a string literal can embed a newline (an actual newline in the source code, not a backslash followed by an n), which will be stored as such.

**Table 2.3:** D escape sequences

| Sequence | Type | Description |
| --- | --- | --- |
| \' | char | Single quote (when ambiguous) |
| \" | char | Double quote (when ambiguous) |
| \\ | char | Backslash |
| \a | char | Bell (ASCII 7) |
| \b | char | Backspace (ASCII 10) |
| \f | char | Form feed (ASCII 14) |
| \n | char | Line feed (ASCII 12) |
| \r | char | Carriage return (ASCII 15) |
| \t | char | Tab (ASCII 9) |
| \v | char | Vertical tab (ASCII 11) |
| \‹*one to three octal digits*› | char | UTF-8 character in octal (must be $\leq 377_8$) |
| \x‹*two hex digits*› | char | UTF-8 character in hexadecimal |
| \u‹*four hex digits*› | wchar | UTF-16 character in hexadecimal |
| \U‹*eight hex digits*› | dchar | UTF-32 character in hexadecimal |
| \&‹*named character entity*›; | dchar | Symbolic Unicode character |

### 2.2.5.1   WYSIWYG, Hex, and `imported` String Literals

WYSIWYG strings either start with `r"` and end with a `"` (`r"like this"`), or start and end with a backquote (`‘like that’`). Any character (aside from the respective terminating characters) can occur within a WYSIWYG string and is stored at face value. This implies that you cannot represent, say, the double quote character itself within a double-quoted WYSIWYG string. That's not a big problem because you can concatenate literal strings obtained with various syntaxes. For example:

```
auto a = r"String with a \ and a " ‘"’ " inside.";
```

For practical purposes, you can consider that a double quote inside an `r"string"` is encoded by the sequence ⟨`"‘"’`⟩, and that a backquote inside a `‘string’` is encoded as ⟨`‘"‘"‘`⟩. Happy quote counting.

D defines a third kind of literal string: a hex string, which is a string of hex digits and (ignored) whitespace, delimited by `x"` and `"`. Hex strings are useful for defining raw data; the compiler makes no attempt whatsoever to interpret the contents as Unicode characters or anything else but hexadecimal digits. Spaces inside a hex string are ignored.

```
auto
  a = x"0A",            // Same as "\x0A"
  b = x"00 F BCD 32";   // Same as "\x00\xFB\xCD\x32"
```

In case your hacker mind immediately started thinking about embedding binary resources into D programs, you'll be happy to hear about a very powerful means to define a string: from a file!

```
auto x = import("resource.bin");
```

During compilation, `x` will be initialized with the actual *contents* of the file `resource.bin`. (This is not the same as C's `#include` facility because the above includes the file as data, not code.) For safety reasons, only relative paths are accepted and the search paths are controlled via a compiler switch. The reference implementation `dmd` uses the `-J` flag to control string include paths.

The string resulting from an `import` is not checked for UTF-8 correctness. This is intentional in order to allow importing binary resources.

### 2.2.5.2   Type of a Literal String

What's the type of a literal string? Let's run a simple experiment:

```
import std.stdio;
void main() {
    writeln(typeid(typeof("Hello, world!")));
}
```

The built-in operator `typeof` fetches the type of an expression, and `typeid` makes that type into a printable string. Our little program prints

```
immutable(char)[]
```

revealing that literal strings are *arrays of immutable characters*. In fact, the type `string` that we used in our code examples is a shortcut notation for the longer type `immutable(char)[]`. Let's look in detail at these three aspects of string literal types: immutability, length, and base character type.

**Immutability**    Literal strings live in "read-only" memory. That doesn't necessarily mean they are stored on actual non-erasable memory chips or in memory protected by the operating system, but it does mean that the language makes a pledge against overwriting of the string's memory. The `immutable` keyword embodies that pledge by disallowing, during compilation, any operation that would modify the contents of an `immutable` piece of data:

```
auto a = "Nobody can change me";
a[0] = 'X'; // Error! Cannot modify an immutable string!
```

The `immutable` keyword is a *type qualifier* (Chapter 8 discusses qualifiers) that operates on whatever type comes to its right, obeying parentheses. If you say `immutable(char)[] str`, then the characters in `str` are not individually mutable, but `str` can be made to refer to a different string:

```
immutable(char)[] str = "One";
str[0] = 'X';               // Error! Can't assign immutable(char)!
str = "Two";                // Fine, rebind str
```

On the other hand, if the parentheses are not present, `immutable` will qualify the entire array:

```
immutable char[] a = "One";
a[0] = 'X';              // Error!
a = "Two";               // Error!
```

Immutability has many virtues. To wit, `immutable` provides enough guarantees to allow indiscriminate data sharing across module and thread boundaries (Chapter 13). Since the characters of a string are not changeable, there is never contention, and sharing is safe and efficient.

**Length**    The length of the literal string (which is 13 for `"Hello, world!"`) is obviously known during compilation. It might seem natural, then, to give the most precise type to each string; for example, `"Hello, world!"` could be typed as `char[13]`, that is, an array of exactly 13 characters. However, experience with the Pascal language has shown that static sizes are highly inconvenient. Therefore, in D the type of literals does not include length information. However, if you really want a fixed-size string you can create one by specifying it explicitly:

```
immutable(char)[13] a = "Hello, world!";
char[13] b = "Hello, world!";
```

Fixed-size array types `T[N]` are implicitly convertible to dynamically sized array types `T[]` for all types `T`. Information is not lost in the process because dynamically sized arrays remember their length:

```
import std.stdio;
```

```
void main() {
    immutable(char)[3] a = "Hi!";
    immutable(char)[] b = a;
    writeln(a.length, " ", b.length); // Prints "3 3"
}
```

**Base Character Type**   Last but not least, string literals can have either char, wchar, or dchar as their base character type. You don't need to use the long-winded type names: string, wstring, and dstring are handy aliases for immutable(char)[], immutable(wchar)[], and immutable(dchar)[], respectively. If the literal string contains at least a 4-byte character dchar, it is of type dstring; otherwise, if the literal contains at least a 2-byte character wchar, it is of type wstring; otherwise the string is of familiar type string. If a different type of string from the one inferred is expected, a literal will silently comply, as in this example:

```
wstring x = "Hello, wide world!";        // UTF-16-encoded
dstring y = "Hello, even wider world!"; // UTF-32-encoded
```

In case you want to override string type inference, you can suffix a string literal with either c, w, or d, which, similarly to the homonym character literal suffixes, force the type of the string literal to string, wstring, and dstring, respectively.

### 2.2.6   Array and Associative Array Literals

Strings are a particular kind of arrays featuring their own literal syntax; now, how do we express array literals of other types, for example, int or double? An array literal is represented as a comma-separated sequence of values enclosed in square brackets:

```
auto somePrimes = [ 2u, 3, 5, 7, 11, 13 ];
auto someDoubles = [ 1.5, 3, 4.5 ];
```

The size of the array is computed from the length of the comma-separated list. Unlike string literals, array literals are not immutable, so you can change them after initialization:

```
auto constants = [ 2.71, 3.14, 6.023e22 ];
constants[0] = 2.21953167;  // The "moving sofa" constant
auto salutations = [ "hi", "hello", "yo" ];
salutations[2] = "Ave Caesar";
```

Notice how you can reassign a slot in salutations, but you cannot alter the content of the string stored in the slot. This is to be expected because membership in an array does not change what you can do with a string.

The element type of the array is determined by agreement among all elements of the array, which is computed by means of the conditional operator ? : (anticipating § 2.3.16). For a literal `lit` of more than one element, the compiler applies the expression `true ? lit[0] : lit[1]` and stores the type of that expression as a type L. Then for each $i^{th}$ element `lit[2]` up to the last element in `lit`, the compiler computes the type of `true ? L.init : lit[i]` and stores that type back in L. The final L is the element type of the array.

This sounds a whole lot more complicated than it really is, which is simply that the element type of the array is established by a Polish democracy consensus—a type is found to which all elements agree to implicitly convert. For example, the type of [ 1, 2, 2.2 ] is `double`, and the type of [ 1, 2, 3u ] is `uint` because taking ? : between an `int` and a `uint` yields a `uint`.

Associative array literals are defined with the following syntax:

```
auto famousNamedConstants =
  [ "pi" : 3.14, "e" : 2.71, "moving sofa" : 2.22 ];
```

Each slot in an associative array literal has the form `key : value`. The key type of the associative array literal is computed by conceptually putting all keys in one array and computing the type of that array as discussed above. The value type is computed in a similar fashion. Once the key type K and the value type V are computed, the literal is typed as `V[K]`. The type of `famousNamedConstants` is, for example, `double[string]`.

### 2.2.7  Function Literals

In some languages, each function has a name chosen at the point of its definition; subsequent calls of that function use its name. Other languages offer the possibility to define anonymous functions (also known as *lambda functions*) right at the point of their use. Such a feature is useful in powerful idioms using higher-order functions, that is, functions that take as parameters and/or return other functions. D's function literals offer the ability to define an anonymous function *in situ* wherever a function name is expected.

This chapter's sole preoccupation is to show how function literals are defined, at the expense of showcasing some interesting use cases. For illustrations of the powerful uses of this mighty feature, please accept a rain check, to be redeemed in Chapter 5. Here's the basic syntax of a function literal:

```
auto f = function double(int x) { return x / 10.; };
auto a = f(5);
assert(a == 0.5);
```

Function literal definitions follow the same syntax as regular function definitions, the only difference being that the keyword `function` precedes the definition and that the name is missing. The code above doesn't even use much anonymity because the anonymous function is immediately bound to the symbol f. The type of f is "pointer to function taking an int and returning a double." That type itself is spelled as double function(int) (notice that the keyword function got swapped after the return type), so an equivalent definition of f would be

```
double function(int) f = function double(int x) { return x / 10.; };
```

The seemingly odd swap of function and double actually makes everybody's life considerably easier because it allows distinguishing a function literal from its type. To easily remember things: in a literal function comes first, whereas in the type of a function, function replaces the name of the function.

To simplify definition of a function literal, you can omit the return type and the compiler will deduce it for you because it has the body available straightaway:

```
auto f = function(int x) { return x / 10.; };
```

Our function literal above uses only its own parameter x, so its meaning can be figured by looking inside the body of the function literal alone, and not the environment in which it is used. But what if the function literal needs to use data present at the point of call yet not passed as a parameter? In that case you must replace function with delegate:

```
int c = 2;
auto f = delegate double(int x) { return c * x / 10.; };
auto a = f(5);
assert(a == 1);
c = 3;
auto b = f(5);
assert(b == 1.5);
```

The type of f is now double delegate(int). All type deductions for function apply unchanged to delegate. This raises a legitimate question: Given that delegates can do anything functions do (after all, a delegate *can* but is not *obligated* to use variables within its environment), why bother with functions in the first place? Can't we just use delegates throughout? The answer is simple: efficiency. Clearly delegate has access to more information, so by some immutable law of nature, it must pay for that access. In practice, the size of function is that of a pointer, while delegate is twice as big (one pointer for the function, the other for the environment).

## 2.3  Operators

The following subsections describe in detail all of D's operators, in decreasing order of precedence. This order corresponds to the natural order in which you'd group together and compute small subexpressions in increasingly larger chunks.

Operators are tightly linked to two orthogonal notions: lvalues versus rvalues and numeric conversion rules. The following two subsections introduce the needed definitions.

### 2.3.1  Lvalues and Rvalues

Many operators work only when their left-hand side satisfies certain conditions. For example, there isn't a need for a sophisticated justification to deem the assignment 5 = 10 invalid. For an assignment to succeed, the left-hand side operator must be an *lvalue*. It's about time we defined lvalues precisely (together with *rvalues*, their complement). Historically, the terms originated indeed from the position of values in an assignment expression such as a = b: a stands on the **l**eft-hand side so it's an **l**value, and b stands on the **r**ight-hand side, hence it's an **r**value.

Defined by sheer enumeration, lvalues are composed of

- All variables, including function parameters, even if they cannot be effectively modified (e.g., are qualified with immutable)
- Elements of arrays and associative arrays
- struct and class fields (which we'll discuss later)
- Function returns of ref type (which we'll discuss even later).

Any lvalue can act as an rvalue. Rvalues also comprise everything not explicitly mentioned above, such as literals, enumerated values (introduced with enum; see § 7.3 on page 272) and the result of expressions such as x + 5. Notice that being an lvalue is a necessary, but not sufficient, condition to allow assignment: several other semantic checks must be satisfied, such as access rights (Chapter 6) and mutability rights (Chapter 8).

### 2.3.2  Implicit Numeric Conversions

We've touched on the topic of implicit conversions already, so it's time for a thorough treatment. As far as numeric conversions go, there really are only a few simple rules to remember:

1. If a numeric expression compiles in the C language and *also* compiles in D, its type will be the same in both languages (note that not all C expressions must be accepted by D).
2. No integral value converts implicitly to a narrower one.

3. No floating-point value converts implicitly to an integral value.
4. Any numeric value (integral or floating-point) converts implicitly to any floating-point value.

Rule 1 makes things just a tad more complicated than they would otherwise be, but D overlaps enough with C and C++ to inspire people to simply copy and paste entire functions into D programs. Now it's all right if D occasionally refuses to compile certain constructs for safety or portability reasons; but if it compiled that 2000-line encryption package and ran it with different results, life would definitely not be good for the hapless victim. However, rule 2 tightens the screws more than C and C++. So when porting code, the occasional diagnostic will point you to rough portions of code and prompt you to insert the appropriate checks and explicit casts.

Figure 2.3 on the next page illustrates the conversion rules for all numeric types. In a conversion, the shortest path is taken; when two paths have equal length, the result of the conversion is the same. Regardless of the number of steps, the conversion is considered a one-step process, and there are no priorities or orderings among conversions—either a type converts to another or not.

### 2.3.2.1  Value Range Propagation

By the rules described above, a banal number such as 42 would be considered unequivocally of type `int`. Now consider the following equally banal initialization:

```
ubyte x = 42;
```

Following the inexorable laws of typechecking, 42 is first recognized as an `int`. That `int` is subsequently assigned to `x`, a process that incurs a coercion. Allowing such an unqualified coercion is dangerous (there are many `int`s that can't actually fit in a `ubyte`). On the other hand, requiring a cast for code that is so obviously correct would be thoroughly unpleasant.

D breaks this conundrum in an intelligent way inspired by a compiler optimization known as *value range propagation:* each value in an expression is associated with a range consisting of the minimum and maximum possible values. These bounds are tracked during compilation. When some value is assigned to a narrower type, the compiler allows the assignment if and only if the value's range fits within the target type. For a constant such as 42, obviously the minimum and maximum possible values are 42 and 42, so the assignment goes through.

Of course, that trivial case could have been figured much more easily, but value range propagation checks correctness in much more interesting situations. Consider a function that extracts the least significant and the most significant bytes from an `int`:

```
void fun(int val) {
  ubyte lsByte = val & 0xFF;
```

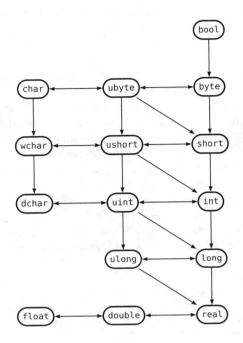

**Figure 2.3:** Implicit integral conversions.  A type is automatically convertible to another type if and only if there is a directed path in the graph from the source type to the destination type. The shortest path is taken, and conversion is considered one-step regardless of the actual path length. Conversions in the opposite directions are possible if value range propagation (§ 2.3.2.1 on the previous page) verifies validity.

```
    ubyte hsByte = val >>> 24;

    ...
}
```

The code is correct regardless of the input value val. The first expression masks the value eliminating all high-order bits, and the second shifts the expression such that the most significant byte of val migrates to the least significant byte, and everything else is zeroed.

Indeed, the compiler types fun correctly because in the first case it computes the range of val & 0xFF between 0 and 255 regardless of val, and in the second case it computes the range of val >>> 24, again from 0 through 255. If you tried operations yielding values that don't necessarily fit in a `ubyte` (such as `val & 0x1FF` or `val >>> 23`), the compiler would not have accepted the code.

Value range propagation "understands" all arithmetic and logic operations; for example, a `uint` divided by 100,000 will always fit within a `ushort` and also works correctly in complex expressions, such as a masking followed by a division. For example:

```
void fun(int val) {
   ubyte x = (val & 0xF0F0) / 300;
   ...
}
```

In the example above, the `&` operator sets the bounds to 0 through `0xF0F0`, which is 61,680 in decimal. Then the division sets the bounds to 0 through 205. Any number within that range fits in a `ubyte`.

Using value range propagation to differentiate between correct and incorrect narrowing conversions is an imperfect, conservative mechanism. For one thing, tracking of value ranges is carried only myopically, inside an expression but not across consecutive expressions. For example:

```
void fun(int x) {
   if (x >= 0 && x < 42) {
      ubyte y = x; // Error!
                   // Cannot coerce int to ubyte!
      ...
   }
}
```

Clearly the initialization is correct, but the compiler does not recognize it. It could, but that would complicate the implementation and slow down the compilation process. It was decided to go with the less sensitive per-expression value range propagation. Experience with the feature as implemented reveals that this conservative estimate tends to remove most undue coercion errors in a program. For the remaining false positives, you may want to use the `cast` expression (§ 2.3.6.7 on page 53).

### 2.3.3 Typing of Numeric Operators

Many of the coming sections introduce operators applicable to numeric types. The type of the value yielded by operators on numbers is computed by using a few rules. They aren't the best rules that could be devised but are simple enough, uniform, and systematic.

The type yielded by unary operators is the same as the operand, except for the negation operator `!`, to be defined in § 2.3.6.6 on page 53, which always yields `bool`. For binary operators, the type of the result is computed as follows:

- If at least one participant in the operator application has a floating-point type, then the result type is that of the largest floating-point type involved.
- Otherwise, if at least one participant has type `ulong`, the other is implicitly converted to `ulong` prior to the application and the result has type `ulong`.
- Otherwise, if at least one participant has type `long`, the other is implicitly converted to `long` prior to the application and the result has type `long`.
- Otherwise, if at least one participant has type `uint`, the other is implicitly converted to `uint` prior to the application and the result has type `uint`.
- Otherwise, implicitly convert both operands to `int` and apply the operator. The result has type `int`.

All implicit conversions take the shortest path depicted in Figure 2.3 on page 44. This is an important detail; consider, for example, the following:

```
ushort x = 60_000;
assert(x / 10 == 6000);
```

In the division operation, `10` has type `int` and according to the rules above x is implicitly converted to `int` prior to the operation. Figure 2.3 shows several possible paths, among which are the direct conversion ushort → int and the slightly longer (one hop) ushort → short → int. The second is undesirable because converting `60000` to `short` yields `-5536`, which is further promoted to an `int` and causes the `assert` to fail. Choosing the shortest path in the conversion graph ensures better value preservation.

### 2.3.4    Primary Expressions

Primary expressions are atoms of evaluation. We've already met with symbols (§ 2.1 on page 30), the Boolean literals `true` and `false` (§ 2.2.1 on page 32), integral literals (§ 2.2.2 on page 32), floating-point literals (§ 2.2.3 on page 33), character literals (§ 2.2.4 on page 34), string literals (§ 2.2.5 on page 35), array literals (§ 2.2.6 on page 39), and function literals (§ 2.2.7 on page 40); they are all primary expressions, as is the literal `null`. The following subsections describe the other primary subexpressions: `assert` expressions, `mixin` expressions, `is` expressions, and parenthesized expressions.

#### 2.3.4.1    The `assert` Expression

Several expressions and statements, including `assert` itself, use the notion of *nonzero* values. These values can be of (a) numeric or character type, in which case nonzero has the obvious meaning; (b) Boolean type (nonzero means `true`); or (c) array, reference, and pointer types (nonzero means non-`null`).

The expression `assert(expr)` evaluates `expr`. If `expr` is nonzero, there is no effect. Otherwise, the `assert` expression throws an exception of type `AssertError`. The form `assert(expr, message)` makes `message` (which must be convertible to a string type) part of the error message contained within the `AssertError` object. (`message` is not evaluated if `expr` is nonzero.) In all cases, `assert`'s own type is `void`.

When you want to build a program for ultimate efficiency, the D compiler offers a switch (`-release` for the reference implementation `dmd`) to ignore all `assert` expressions in a module (not evaluate `expr` at all). As such, `assert` should be seen as a debugging tool and not a means for testing conditions that might legitimately fail. For the same reason it's incorrect to put expressions with side effects inside `assert` expressions if the program behavior depends on those side effects. For more details about release builds, refer to Chapter 11.

The case `assert(false)`, `assert(0)`, or in general `assert` against a statically known zero value is handled in a particular manner. That assertion is always enabled (regardless of build flags) and issues the `HLT` machine code instruction that abruptly stops execution of the process. Such an interrupt may prompt the operating system to generate a core dump or to start the debugger on the offending line.

Foreshadowing the logical OR expression (§ 2.3.15 on page 59), a simple idiom for always evaluating an expression and asserting on its result is `(expr) || assert(false)`.

Chapter 10 discusses in depth `assert` and other mechanisms for ensuring program correctness.

### 2.3.4.2 The `mixin` Expression

If expressions were various kinds of screwdrivers, `mixin` would be a power screwdriver with exchangeable heads, adjustable clutch, a brain surgery adapter, built-in wireless camera, and speech recognition. It's *that* powerful.

In short, the `mixin` expression allows you to make a string into executable code. The expression's syntax is `mixin(expr)`, where `expr` must be a compile-time-known string. The restriction rules out dynamic scripting abilities such as reading a string from the terminal and interpreting it; no, D is not an interpreted language, and neither does it make the compiler part of the standard runtime support. The good news is that D does run a full-fledged interpreter *during compilation*, which means that you can build strings in ways as sophisticated as needed.

The ability to manipulate strings and transform them into code during compilation enables the creation of the so-called domain-specific embedded languages, fondly called DSELs by their fans. A typical DSEL implemented in D would accept DSEL statements as a string literal, process it during compilation, create the corresponding D code in string form, and use `mixin` to transform the string into D. As fancy as they sound, DSELs are very down-to-earth and practical. Good examples of useful DSELs are SQL commands, regular expressions, and grammar specifications (à la `yacc`). In fact, if you've ever used `printf`, you did DSELs. The format specifier used by `printf` is really a small language that specializes in describing textual data layouts.

D allows you to create any DSEL without using any additional tools (parsers, binders, code generators, ...); to wit, the standard library function `bitfields` (in module std.bitmanip) accepts bit field definitions and generates optimal D code for reading and writing them, even though the language itself does not support bit fields.

### 2.3.4.3  is Expressions

The is expressions answer queries about types ("Does a type called Widget exist?" or "Does Widget inherit Gadget?") and are an important part of D's powerful compile-time introspection. Evaluation of all is expressions occurs during compilation and returns an answer to a query as a bool constant. There are multiple forms of is expressions, as shown below.

1. The forms is(Type) and is(Type Symbol) check whether a type exists. The type may be illegal or, most often, just not exist. For example:

```
bool
    a = is(int[]),    // True, int[] is a valid type
    b = is(int[5]),   // True, int[5] is also valid
    c = is(int[-3]),  // False, array size is invalid
    d = is(Blah);     // False (if Blah wasn't defined)
```

In all cases, Type must be syntactically valid even if it is semantically invalid; for example, is([]x[]) is a compile-time error, not a false constant. In other words, you can make queries only about things that syntactically look like types.

If Symbol is present, it becomes an alias of Type in the true case. This can be useful if Type is long and complicated. The as-yet-unseen static if statement distinguishes the true case from the false one. Chapter 3 discusses static if in full detail, but the basic plot is simple—static if evaluates a compile-time expression and compiles the controlled statement only if the expression is true.

```
static if (is(Widget[100][100] ManyWidgets)) {
   ManyWidgets lotsOfWidgets;
   ...
}
```

2. The forms is(Type1 == Type2) and is(Type1 Symbol == Type2) yield true if Type1 is identical to Type2. (They might have different names through the use of alias.)

```
alias uint UInt;
assert(is(uint == UInt));
```

If Symbol is present, it becomes an alias of Type1 in the true case.

3. The forms is(Type1 : Type2) and is(Type1 Symbol : Type2) yield true if Type1 is identical to, or implicitly convertible to, Type2. For example:

```
bool
  a = is(int[5] : int[]),   // True, int[5] convertible to int[]
  b = is(int[5] == int[]),  // False; they are distinct types
  c = is(uint : long),      // True
  d = is(ulong : long);     // True
```

Again, if `Symbol` is present and the `is` expression evaluates to `true`, `Symbol` becomes an alias of `Type1`.

4. The forms `is(Type == Kind)` and `is(Type Symbol == Kind)` check the kind of `Type`. A kind is one of the following keywords: `struct`, `union`, `class`, `interface`, `enum`, `function`, `delegate`, and `super`. The expression is `true` if `Type` is of the respective kind. If present, `Symbol` is defined depending on the kind, as shown in Table 2.4.

**Table 2.4:** Bindings for `Symbol` in the form `is(Type Symbol == Kind)`

| Kind | Symbol is an alias for... |
|------|---------------------------|
| struct | Type |
| union | Type |
| class | Type |
| interface | Type |
| super | Base class (see Chapter 6) |
| enum | The base type of the enum (see Chapter 7) |
| function | Function type |
| delegate | Function type of the delegate |
| return | Type returned by function, delegate, or function pointer |

#### 2.3.4.4 Parenthesized Expressions

Parentheses override usual precedence order: for any expression ‹*expr*›, (‹*expr*›) is a primary expression.

### 2.3.5 Postfix Expressions

#### 2.3.5.1 Member Access

The member access operator `a.b` accesses the member named `b` within the object or type `a`. If `a` is a complicated value or type, it may be parenthesized. `b` can also be a new expression (see Chapter 6).

### 2.3.5.2    Increment and Decrement

All numeric and pointer types support the postincrement operator (`lval++`) and the postdecrement operator (`lval--`) with semantics similar to the homonym operators found in C and C++: evaluating postincrement or postdecrement increments `lval` but yields a copy of it before the modification. `lval` must be an lvalue. (For the related preincrement and predecrement operators see § 2.3.6.3 on page 53.)

### 2.3.5.3    Function Call

The familiar function call operator `fun()` invokes function `fun`. The syntax `fun(`‹*comma-separated list*›`)` also passes `fun` an argument list. All arguments are evaluated left to right before `fun` gets invoked. The function type must be in agreement with the number and types of the values in the argument list. If the function was defined with the `@property` attribute, specifying the function name alone is equivalent to invoking that function without any arguments. Usually `fun` is the name of a defined function, but it may also be a function literal (§ 2.2.7 on page 40) or an expression yielding a pointer to a function or delegate. Chapter 5 describes functions in detail.

### 2.3.5.4    Indexing

The expression `arr[i]` accesses the $i^{th}$ (zero-based) element of array or associative array `arr`. If the array is non-associative, `i` must be of an integral type. Otherwise, `i` must be implicitly convertible to `arr`'s key type. If the indexing expression is on the left-hand side of an assignment operation (e.g., `arr[i] = e`) and `a` is an associative array, the expression inserts an element in the array if it wasn't present. In all other cases, if `i` does not refer to an existing element of `arr`, the expression throws a `RangeError` object. The expression `arr[i]` also works if `arr` has pointer type and `i` has integral type. Pointer indexing is unchecked. Certain build modes (release unsafe builds; see § 4.1.2 on page 95) may disable bounds checking for non-associative arrays altogether.

### 2.3.5.5    Array Slices

If `arr` is a linear (non-associative) array, the expression `arr[i .. j]` returns an array referring to a window inside `arr` starting at index `i` and ending at (without including) index `j`. The bounds `i` and `j` must be convertible to integral types. The expression `arr[]` takes a slice of `arr` as large as `arr` itself. No actual data is copied, so modifying the array returned by the slice operator modifies `arr`'s contents. For example:

```
int[] a = new int[5]; // Create an array of five integers
int[] b = a[3 .. 5];  // b refers to the last two elements of a
b[0] = 1;
b[1] = 3;
```

```
assert(a == [ 0, 0, 0, 1, 3 ]); // a was modified
```

If i > j or j > a.length, the operator throws a RangeError object. Otherwise, if i == j, an empty array is returned. The expression arr[i .. j] also works if arr has pointer type and returns an array reflecting the memory region from arr + i up to (and excluding) arr + j. If i > j, a RangeError object is thrown, but otherwise range slicing from pointers is unchecked. Again, release unsafe builds (§ 4.1.2 on page 95) may disable all bounds checking for slices.

### 2.3.5.6 Nested Class Creation

An expression of the form a.new T, where a is of class type, creates an object of type T whose definition is nested inside a's definition. If it is confusing, it is because classes, nested classes, and even new expressions haven't been defined yet. The definition of the new expression is right around the corner (§ 2.3.6.1), but for the definition of classes and nested classes please wait until Chapter 6 (specifically § 6.11 on page 222). Until then, this paragraph is a placeholder inserted for completeness purposes.

## 2.3.6 Unary Expressions

### 2.3.6.1 The new Expression

A new expression has one of the following forms:

```
new (‹addr›)opt ‹Type›
new (‹addr›)opt ‹Type›(‹arglist›opt)
new (‹addr›)opt ‹Type›[‹arglist›]
new (‹addr›)opt ‹AnonymousClass›
```

Let's ignore the optional (‹addr›) for the moment. The first two forms new T and new T(‹arglist›opt) dynamically allocate an object of type T. The latter form optionally passes some arguments to T's constructor. (The forms new T and new T() are entirely equivalent and create a default-initialized object.) We haven't yet looked at types with constructors, so let's defer that discussion to the treatment of classes in Chapter 6 (specifically § 6.3 on page 181) and of other user-defined types in Chapter 7 (see § 7.1.3 on page 243). Let's also defer anonymous class allocation (last line above) to Chapter 6, § 6.11.3 on page 226.

Here, let's focus on allocating the already familiar arrays. The expression new T[n] allocates a contiguous chunk of memory large enough to accommodate n objects back to back, fill those slots with T.init, and return a handle to them in the form of a T[] value. For example:

```
auto arr = new int[4];
assert(arr.length == 4);
```

```
assert(arr == [ 0, 0, 0, 0 ]); // Default-initialized
```

The same result can be achieved with a slightly different syntax:

```
auto arr = new int[](4);
```

This time, the expression is interpreted as new T(4), where T is int[]. Again, the net result is an array of four elements handled by arr, which has type int[].

The second form is actually more generous than the first. If you want to allocate an array of arrays, you can specify multiple arguments in the parentheses. They count as dimension initializers, in row order. For example, here's how you allocate an array of four arrays, each having eight elements:

```
auto matrix = new int[][](4, 8);
assert(matrix.length == 4);
assert(matrix[0].length == 8);
```

The first line in the snippet above supplants the more verbose

```
auto matrix = new int[][](4);
foreach (ref row; matrix) {
    row = new int[](8);
}
```

All allocations discussed so far grab memory off the garbage-collected heap. Memory that becomes unused and inaccessible to the program is automatically recycled. The runtime support of the reference implementation offers a number of specialized primitives for manipulating garbage-collected memory in module core.gc, including changing the size of an already allocated block or manually freeing memory. Manual memory management is risky, so you should avoid it unless absolutely necessary.

The optional address addr passed right after the new keyword introduces a construct known as *placement new*. The semantics of new(addr) T in that case is different: instead of allocating memory for a new object, just create an object in place at the given address addr. This is a low-level feature that does not occur in normal code; for example, you could use it if you want to allocate memory off C's heap with malloc and then use it to store D values.

### 2.3.6.2 Address and Dereference

Since pointers are a future topic, we'll just mention the dual operators address-of and dereference in passing. The expression &lval fetches the address of lval (as its name suggests, lval must be an lvalue) and returns a pointer of type T*, for lval of type T.

The converse operator *p dereferences a pointer in a way that cancels out & and makes *&lval the same as lval. A detailed discussion of pointers is intentionally deferred to Chapter 7 because you should be able to write a great deal of good D code without relying on pointers—a low-level and dangerous feature *par excellence.*

### 2.3.6.3 Preincrement and Predecrement

The expressions ++lval and --lval respectively increment and decrement lval and also offer as a result the freshly changed value of lval. lval must have numeric or pointer type.

### 2.3.6.4 Bitwise Complement

The expression ~a toggles (reverses) every bit in a and has the same type as a itself. a must have integral type.

### 2.3.6.5 Unary Plus and Unary Minus

The expression +val does nothing noteworthy—it's present for completeness only. The expression -val computes 0 - val and applies to numeric types.

One surprising behavior of unary minus is that, when applied to an unsigned value, it still yields an unsigned value (according to the rules in § 2.3.3 on page 45). For example, -55u is 4_294_967_241, which is uint.max - 55 + 1.

The fact that unsigned types are not really natural numbers is a fact of life. In D and many other languages, two's complement arithmetic with its simple overflow rules is an inescapable reality that cannot be abstracted away. One way to think of -val for any integral value val is to consider it a short form of ~val + 1; in other words, flip every bit in val and then add 1 to the result. This manipulation does not raise particular questions about the signedness of val.

### 2.3.6.6 Negation

The expression !val has type bool and yields false if val is nonzero (see the definition of *nonzero* 46) and true otherwise.

### 2.3.6.7 Cast Expressions

The cast operator is like the mighty and well-intended lamp genie hurrying to save the day. Much like a cartoonish lamp genie, the cast is mischievous, hard of hearing, and prone to taking advantage of poorly worded wishes by fulfilling them all too mechanically—often with disastrous consequences.

That being said, casts can occasionally be useful when the static type system isn't smart enough to keep pace with your exploits. The cast syntax is cast(Type) a. There are several kinds of casts, ranked below in decreasing order of safety:

- Reference casts allow you to convert among references to class and interface objects. These casts are always checked dynamically.
- Numeric casts coerce data from any numeric type to any other numeric type.
- Array casts allow you to convert across different array types, as long as the total size of the source array is divisible by the element size of the target array.
- Pointer casts take a pointer to one type and transform it into a pointer to another type.
- Pointer-numeric casts deposit a pointer into an integral type large enough to hold it, and vice versa.

Be extremely careful with all unchecked casts, particularly the last three, which may violate the integrity of the type system.

### 2.3.7 The Power Expression

The power expression has the form base ^^ exp and raises base to the power of exp. Both base and exp must be of numeric type. The offered functionality is the same as that of the library function pow(base, exp) found in C's and D's standard libraries (consult your documentation for the std.math module). However, certain numeric applications do benefit from the syntactic simplification.

Raising zero to power zero is one, and raising zero to any nonzero power is zero.

### 2.3.8 Multiplicative Expressions

The multiplicative expressions are multiplication (a * b), division (a / b), and remainder (a % b). They operate on numeric types only.

If b is zero in the integral operation a / b or a % b, a hardware exception is thrown. If the division would yield a fractional number, it is always truncated toward zero (for example, 7 / 3 yields 2 and -7 / 3 yields -2). The expression a % b is defined such that a == (a / b) * b + a % b, so 7 % 3 yields 1 and -7 / 3 yields -1.

D also defines modulus for floating-point numbers. The definition is more involved. When at least one of a and b is a floating-point value in a % b, the result is the largest (in absolute value) floating-point number r satisfying the following conditions:

- a and r do not have opposite signs.
- r is smaller than b in absolute value, abs(r) < abs(b).
- There exists an integer q such that r == a - q * b.

If such a number cannot be found, a % b yields the Not A Number (NaN) special value.

### 2.3.9 Additive Expressions

The additive expressions are addition a + b, subtraction a - b, and concatenation a ~ b.

Addition and subtraction operate on numeric types only. The type of the result is determined as described in § 2.3.3 on page 45.

Concatenation requires that at least one of a and b be an array type holding elements of some type T. The other value must be either an array of T or a value implicitly convertible to type T. The result is a new array composed of the juxtaposition of a and b.

### 2.3.10 Shift Expressions

There are three shift operators in D, all taking two integral values: a << b, a >> b, and a >>> b. In all cases, b must be of an unsigned type; if all you have is a signed value, you must cast it to an unsigned type (likely after ensuring that b >= 0; shifting by a negative amount yields an unspecified value). a << b shifts a to the left (i.e., in the direction of a's most significant bit) by b bits, and a >> b shifts a to the right by b bits. If a is negative, shifting preserves its sign.

a >>> b is an unsigned shift regardless the signedness of a. This means that a zero will be shifted into a's most significant bit, guaranteed. To exemplify the sometimes surprising effects of shifts over signed numbers:

```
int a = -1;              // That's 0xFFFF_FFFF
int b = a << 1;
assert(b == -2);         // 0xFFFF_FFFE
int c = a >> 1;
assert(c == -1);         // 0xFFFF_FFFF
int d = a >>> 1;
assert(d == +2147483647); // 0x7FFF_FFFF
```

Shifting by more than the number of bits in a's type is disallowed during compilation if b is a statically known value, and it leaves an implementation-dependent value in a if b is a runtime value:

```
int  a = 50;
uint b = 35;
a << 33;              // Compile-time error
auto c = a << b;      // Implementation-defined result
auto d = a >> b;      // Implementation-defined result
```

In all cases, the type of the result is determined according to the rules in § 2.3.3 on page 45.

A historically popular use of shifting was as an inexpensive integral multiplication by 2 (a << 1) or division by 2 (a >> 1)—or, in general, multiplication and division by various powers of 2. This technique has gone the way of the videotape. Just write a * k or

a / k; as long as k is a compile-time-known quantity, your trusty compiler will generate
the optimal code for you with shift and all, without you having to worry about getting
the sign subtleties right. Shift happens.

### 2.3.11   in Expressions

If key is a value of type K and map is an associative array of type V[K], then key in
map yields a value of type V* (pointer to V). If the associative array contains the pair
⟨key, val⟩, then the pointer points to val. Otherwise, the pointer yielded is null.

For the converse negative test, you may of course write !(key in map) but also the
terser form key !in map, which has the same precedence as key in map.

Why all the pointer aggravation instead of just having a in b yield a bool? It's for
efficiency. Oftentimes, you want to look up an index in an associative array and use the
mapped element if present. A possibility would be

```
double[string] table;
...
if ("hello" in table) {
    ++table["hello"];
} else {
    table["hello"] = 0;
}
```

The problem with the code above is that it performs two lookups on the successful
path. Using the returned pointer, the code can be written more efficiently like this:

```
double[string] table;
...
auto p = "hello" in table;
if (p) {
    ++*p;
} else {
    table["hello"] = 1;
}
```

### 2.3.12   Comparison Operators

#### 2.3.12.1   Comparing for Equality

a == b, of type bool, has the following semantics: First, if the two operands don't have
the same type, an implicit conversion brings them to the same type. Then the operands
are compared for equality as follows:

- For integral types and pointers, equality is defined as an exact bitwise comparison of the bit pattern of the values.
- For floating-point types, -0 is considered equal to +0, and NaN is considered unequal to NaN.[3] In all other cases equality is defined as bit pattern equality.
- For objects of class type, equality is defined with the help of the opEquals operator (see § 6.8.3 on page 205).
- For arrays, equality means element-for-element equality.
- For objects of struct type, equality is by default defined as field-for-field equality. User-defined types may override this behavior (see Chapter 12).

The form a != b tests for non-equality.

The expression a is b compares for *alias equality* and returns true if a and b refer to the same actual object.

- If a and b are arrays or class references, the result is true if and only if a and b are two names for the same actual object;
- Otherwise, a is b is the same as a == b.

We haven't looked into classes yet, but an example with arrays should be helpful:

```d
import std.stdio;

void main() {
   auto a = "some thing";
   auto b = a; // a and b refer to the same array
   a is b && writeln("Yep, they're the same thing really");
   auto c = "some (other) thing";
   a is c || writefln("Indeed... not the same");
}
```

The code above prints both messages because a and b are bound to the same actual array, whereas c is bound to a different one. In general, it's possible that the content of two arrays is equal (so a == c is true), but they point to different regions of memory so they fail the a is c test. Of course, if a is c is true, definitely a == c is true as well, unless you bought your RAM chips at a very, very deep discount.

The inequality operator a !is b is shorthand for !(a is b).

---

3. IEEE 754 floating-point numbers have two distinct bit patterns for zero, denoted as -0 and +0. They cause minor aggravations such as the special case herein but also speed up many calculations. You'd seldom use the -0.0 literal in D, but it may be produced surreptitiously as the result of a calculation that asymptotically approaches zero with negative values.

### 2.3.12.2   Comparing for Ordering

D defines the expressions a < b, a <= b, a > b, and a >= b, of type bool, with the usual meanings: less than, less than or equal, greater than, greater than or equal. When numbers are compared, one of them must be implicitly convertible to the other's type. For floating-point operands, -0 and 0 are considered equal so -0 < 0 yields false, whereas 0 <= -0 yields true. All ordering comparison operators return false whenever at least one of their operands is a NaN (as paradoxical as this might seem).

As always, NaNs tend to mess things up whenever legit floating-point numbers are trying to have a good time. All comparisons that receive at least one NaN engenders a floating-point exception. That is not an actual exception in the usual programming language terminology, but a hardware-level state that can be checked explicitly. D offers an interface with the floating-point hardware via the std.c.fenv module.

### 2.3.12.3   Non-associativity

One important characteristic of all of D's comparison operators is that they are *not associative*. Any chaining of comparison operations, such as a <= b < c, is illegal.

One simple way to define comparison operators is to have them yield bool. Boolean values can be compared themselves, which would create the unfortunate state of affairs that a <= b < c does not have the meaning expected by the little mathematician inside all of us struggling to get out. Instead, the expression would be parsed as (a <= b) < c, or "Compare the Boolean resulting from a <= b with c." For example, 3 <= 4 < 2 would yield true! Such semantics is almost never what you'd want.

A possible solution would be to allow a <= b < c and impart to it the intuitive mathematical meaning, which is a <= b && b < c, with the perk that b gets evaluated only once. Languages such as Python and Perl 6 have embraced this semantics, allowing arbitrary chains of comparisons such as a < b == c > d < e. D, on the other hand, has a different heritage. Allowing C expressions but with subtly different semantics (albeit arguably in the right direction) would add more confusion than convenience, so D chose to simply disallow the construct.

### 2.3.13   Bitwise OR, XOR, AND

Expressions a | b, a ^ b, and a & b evaluate the OR, XOR, and AND bitwise operations, respectively. Both sides are evaluated (no short-circuit) even when the result would be entirely determined by one side alone.

Both a and b must have integral types. The type of the result is determined according to § 2.3.3 on page 45.

### 2.3.14   Logical AND

In light of the above, it should come as no surprise that the semantics of the expression
a && b depends on the type of b.

- If the type of b is not void, then the expression has type bool. If a is nonzero, the
  expression evaluates b and yields true if and only if b is nonzero. Otherwise, the
  expression evaluates to false.
- If b has type void, the expression has type void as well. If a is nonzero, b is evaluated. Otherwise, b is not evaluated.

Using && with a void expression on the right-hand side is useful as shorthand for an
if statement:

```
string line;
...
line == "#\n" && writeln("Got a # successfully");
```

### 2.3.15   Logical OR

The semantics of the expression a || b depends on the type of b.

- If the type of b is not void, then the expression has type bool.  If a is nonzero,
  the expression evaluates to true. Otherwise, the expression evaluates b and yields
  true if and only if b is nonzero.
- If b has type void, the expression has type void as well.  If a is nonzero, b is not
  evaluated. Otherwise, b is evaluated.

The second instance is useful for handling contingency cases:

```
string line;
...
line.length > 0 || line = "\n";
```

### 2.3.16   The Conditional Operator

The conditional operator is an if-then-else expression with the syntax a ? b : c, with
which you might be familiar already. If a is nonzero, the conditional expression evaluates and yields b; otherwise, the expression evaluates and yields c. The compiler makes
heroic efforts to find the "tightest" common type of b and c, which becomes the type
of the conditional expression.  That type (let's call it T) is computed by using a simple
algorithm (shown below with examples):

1. If a and b have the same type, T is that type;
2. else if a and b are integrals, first promote anything smaller than 32-bit to int, then choose T as the larger type, with a preference for unsigned type if tied in size;
3. else if one is an integral and the other is a floating-point type, T is the floating-point type;
4. else if both have floating-point types, T is the larger of the two;
5. else if the types have a common supertype (e.g., base class), T is that supertype (we will return to this topic in Chapter 6);
6. else try implicitly converting a to b's type and b to a's type; if exactly one of these succeeds, T is the type of the successful conversion target;
7. else the expression is in error.

Moreover, if b and c have the same type and are both lvalues, the result is an lvalue as well, allowing you to write

```
int x = 5, y = 5;
bool which = true;
(which ? x : y) += 5;
assert(x == 10);
```

Many generic programming idioms use the conditional operator to assess the common type of two values.

### 2.3.17  Assignment Operators

Assignment operators take the form a = b or a $\omega$= b, where $\omega$ stands for one of the following: ^^, *, /, %, +, -, ~, <<, >>, >>>, |, ^, &, and "obligatory use of Greek letters in a programming book." The previous sections have already introduced the stand-alone versions of these operators.

The semantics of a $\omega$= b is identical to that of a = a $\omega$ b, with the notable difference that a is evaluated only once (imagine a and b as arbitrarily complex expressions, as in array[i * 5 + j] *= sqrt(x)).

Regardless of the precedence of $\omega$, the precedence of $\omega$= is the same as that of = itself, just below the conditional operator (discussed just above) and a notch tighter than the comma operator's precedence (discussed just below). Also, regardless of $\omega$'s associativity, all $\omega$= operators (and also =) collectively associate right to left; for example, a /= b = c -= d is the same as a /= (b = (c -= d)).

### 2.3.18  The Comma Operator

Expressions separated by commas are evaluated in sequence. The result of the entire expression is the result of the rightmost expression. Example:

```
int a = 5;
int b = 10;
int c = (a = b, b = 7, 8);
```

After the snippet above is executed, the values of a, b, and c are 10, 7, and 8, respectively.

## 2.4  Summary and Quick Reference

This about concludes D's rich ways to build expressions. Table 2.5 summarizes all of D's operators and is the place to which you may want to return whenever you're in need of a quick reference.

**Table 2.5:** Expressions in decreasing order of precedence

| Expression | Description |
|---|---|
| ‹*symbol*› | Symbol (§ 2.1 on page 30) |
| . ‹*symbol*› | Symbol accessed at module scope (bypassing all other scopes) (§ 2.1 on page 30) |
| this | The current object inside a method (§ 2.1.1 on page 31) |
| super | Guide symbol lookup and dynamic method lookup through the base subobject (§ 2.1.1 on page 31) |
| $ | Current array size (valid inside an index or slice expression) (§ 2.1.1 on page 31) |
| null | The null reference, array, or pointer (§ 2.1.1 on page 31) |
| typeid(T) | Get the TypeInfo object associated with T (§ 2.1.1 on page 31) |
| true | Boolean true (§ 2.2.1 on page 32) |
| false | Boolean false (§ 2.2.1 on page 32) |
| ‹*num*› | Numeric literal (§ 2.2.2 on page 32, § 2.2.3 on page 33) |
| ‹*char*› | Character literal (§ 2.2.4 on page 34) |
| ‹*string*› | String literal (§ 2.2.5 on page 35) |
| ‹*array*› | Array literal (§ 2.2.6 on page 39) |
| ‹*function*› | Function literal (§ 2.2.7 on page 40) |
| assert(a) | In debug mode, if a is not nonzero, halt program; in release mode, do nothing (§ 2.3.4.1 on page 46) |
| assert(a, b) | Same as above; make b part of the error information (§ 2.3.4.1 on page 46) |
| mixin(a) | Mixin expression (§ 2.3.4.2 on page 47) |
| ‹*IsExpr*› | is expression (§ 2.3.4.3 on page 48) |

**Table 2.5:** Expressions in decreasing order of precedence *(continued)*

| Expression | Description |
|---|---|
| ( a ) | Parenthesized expression (§ 2.3.4.4 on page 49) |
| a.b | Member access (§ 2.3.5.1 on page 49) |
| a++ | Postincrement (§ 2.3.5.2 on page 50) |
| a-- | Postdecrement (§ 2.3.5.2 on page 50) |
| a(‹*csl*$_{opt}$›) | Function call operator (‹*csl*$_{opt}$› = optional comma-separated list of arguments) (§ 2.3.5.3 on page 50) |
| a[‹*csl*›] | Indexing operator (‹*csl*› = comma-separated list of arguments) (§ 2.3.5.4 on page 50) |
| a[] | Slicing an entire collection (§ 2.3.5.5 on page 50) |
| a[b .. c] | Slicing (§ 2.3.5.5 on page 50) |
| a.‹*new-expr*› | Creation of an instance of a nested class (see § 2.3.5.6 on page 51) |
| & a | Address (§ 2.3.6.2 on page 52) |
| ++a | Increment (§ 2.3.6.3 on page 53) |
| --a | Decrement (§ 2.3.6.3 on page 53) |
| *a | Dereference (§ 2.3.6.2 on page 52) |
| -a | Unary minus (§ 2.3.6.5 on page 53) |
| +a | Unary plus (§ 2.3.6.5 on page 53) |
| !a | Negation (§ 2.3.6.6 on page 53) |
| ~a | Bitwise complement (§ 2.3.6.4 on page 53) |
| (T).a | Static member access |
| cast(T) a | Cast expression to type |
| ‹*new-expr*› | Object creation (see § 2.3.6.1 on page 51) |
| a ^^ b | Exponentiation (§ 2.3.7 on page 54) |
| a * b | Multiplication (§ 2.3.8 on page 54) |
| a / b | Division (§ 2.3.8 on page 54) |
| a % b | Modulus (§ 2.3.8 on page 54) |
| a + b | Addition (§ 2.3.9 on page 55) |
| a - b | Subtraction (§ 2.3.9 on page 55) |
| a ~ b | Concatenation (§ 2.3.9 on page 55) |
| a << b | Left shift (§ 2.3.10 on page 55) |
| a >> b | Right shift (§ 2.3.10 on page 55) |
| a >>> b | Unsigned right shift (most significant bit of the result is zero regardless of a's type and value) (§ 2.3.10 on page 55) |
| a in b | Membership test for associative arrays (§ 2.3.11 on page 56) |
| a == b | Equality test; all operators in this group are not associative; for example, a == b == c is not legal (§ 2.3.12.1 on page 56) |

**Table 2.5:** Expressions in decreasing order of precedence *(continued)*

| Expression | Description |
|---|---|
| a != b | Non-equality test (§ 2.3.12.1 on page 56) |
| a is b | Identity test (true if and only if a and b refer to the same object) (§ 2.3.12.1 on page 56) |
| a !is b | Same as !(a is b) |
| a < b | Less than (§ 2.3.12.2 on page 58) |
| a <= b | Less than or equal (§ 2.3.12.2 on page 58) |
| a > b | Greater than (§ 2.3.12.2 on page 58) |
| a >= b | Greater than or equal (§ 2.3.12.2 on page 58) |
| a \| b | Bitwise OR (§ 2.3.13 on page 58) |
| a ^ b | Bitwise XOR (§ 2.3.13 on page 58) |
| a & b | Bitwise AND (§ 2.3.13 on page 58) |
| a && b | Logical AND (b can have type void) (§ 2.3.14 on page 59) |
| a \|\| b | Logical OR (b can have type void) (§ 2.3.15 on page 59) |
| a ? b : c | Conditional operator; if a is nonzero then b, else c (§ 2.3.16 on page 59) |
| a = b | Assignment; all assignment operators in this group bind right to left; for example, a *= b += c is the same as a *= (b += c) (§ 2.3.17 on page 60) |
| a += b | In-place add; all compute-and-assign operators a $\omega$= b in this group evaluate in sequence (1) a (which must be an lvalue), (2) b, and (3) $a_l = a_l \, \omega \, b$, where $a_l$ is the lvalue resulting from a's evaluation |
| a -= b | In-place subtract |
| a *= b | In-place multiply |
| a /= b | In-place divide |
| a %= b | In-place modulo |
| a &= b | In-place bitwise AND |
| a \|= b | In-place bitwise OR |
| a ^= b | In-place bitwise XOR |
| a ~= b | In-place concatenation (append b to a) |
| a <<= b | In-place left shift |
| a >>= b | In-place right shift |
| a >>>= b | In-place unsigned right shift |
| a , b | Sequencing; expressions are evaluated left to right, and the result is the rightmost expression (§ 2.3.18 on page 60) |

# Statements

This chapter contains the obligatory definitions for all statements that D defines. D builds on the C family's look and feel—there's `if`, `while`, `for`, and others. However, there are a few new, interesting statements and tweaks on the existing statements. In case you are likely to get bored by the inevitable litany describing each statement in detail, here are some "deltas"—interesting bits original to D.

If you want to conditionally compile code, `static if` (§ 3.4 on page 68) may be of interest. Its usefulness goes well beyond simple flag-directed customizations; if you use generic code in any capacity, `static if` is an enormous boon. The `switch` statement (§ 3.5 on page 71) looks and acts much like its C counterpart but works with strings, too, and allows you to match entire ranges at once. For correctly handling small closed sets of values, `final switch` (§ 3.6 on page 72) may be of interest; it works with enumerated types and forces you to handle each and every one of the possible values. The `foreach` statement (§ 3.7.4 to 3.7.5 on pages 74–75) is very handy for straight iterations, whereas the classic `for` is more general but a bit more verbose. The `mixin` statement (§ 3.12 on page 82) expands predefined boilerplate code. The `scope` statement (§ 3.13 on page 84) greatly simplifies writing correct transactional code with correct error recovery by replacing convoluted `try/catch/finally` statements that you'd otherwise have to write.

## 3.1 The Expression Statement

As mentioned before (§ 1.2 on page 5), an expression becomes a statement if you append a semicolon to it:

```
a = b + c;
transmogrify(a + b);
```

However, not just any expression can become a statement. If the resulting statement
has no effect, as in

```
1 + 1 == 2; // A profound truth
```

then the compiler issues an error.

## 3.2   The Compound Statement

The compound statement is a (possibly empty) sequence of statements enclosed in
curly braces. The statements are executed in sequence. The braces introduce a lexical
scope: symbols defined inside a compound statement are not visible outside of it.

A symbol defined inside a scope hides a homonym symbol hanging outside all
scopes:

```
uint widgetCount;
...
void main() {
   writeln(widgetCount); // Writes the global symbol
   auto widgetCount = getWidgetCount();
   writeln(widgetCount); // Writes the local symbol
}
```

The first call to `writeln` prints the global `widgetCount` symbol and the second accesses the locally defined `widgetCount`. Should there be a need for accessing the global symbol after it has been masked, prefixing it with a dot—as in
`writeln(.widgetCount)`—will do, as first mentioned on page 31. However, it is illegal
to define a symbol that would mask a symbol in an enclosing compound statement:

```
void main() {
   auto widgetCount = getWidgetCount();
   // Let's now open a nested block
   {
      auto widgetCount = getWidgetCount(); // Error!
   }
}
```

As long as masking does not occur, it's legal to reuse the same symbol in different
compound statements:

```
void main() {
   {
      auto i = 0;
      ...
```

```
    }
    {
        auto i = "eye"; // Fine
        ...
    }
    double i = 3.14;    // Fine too
}
```

The rationale of this setup is simple. Allowing global symbol masking is necessary for writing good modular code that's assembled out of separately compiled parts; you don't want the addition of a global variable to suddenly render various innocent bystanders uncompilable. On the other hand, enclosing-scope masking is useless as a modularity device (as there's never a case of a compound statement spanning multiple modules in D) and most often indicates either an oversight aspiring to become a bug, or a cancerous function that's grown out of control.

## 3.3 The if Statement

Various examples have already used D's if statement, which is pretty much what you'd expect:

```
if (‹expression›) ‹statement₁›
```

or

```
if (‹expression›) ‹statement₁› else ‹statement₂›
```

One detail about the statements controlled by if is worth noting. Unlike other languages, D does not have an "empty statement" construct; in particular, a colon present by itself is *not* a statement and will be flagged as an error. This design automatically steers programmers away from bugs like

```
if (a == b);
    writeln("a and b are equal");
```

code that looks obviously silly when it's short and when you've been primed for it, but not so much so when the expression is longer, the entire construct is buried in swaths of code, and it's two o'clock in the morning. If you do want to control an empty statement with an if, you may want to use the closest approximation of an empty statement—a compound statement with no statements inside:

```
if (a == b) {}
```

which is useful as you refactor code and occasionally comment in and out various portions of code.

The `else` clause always binds to the closest `if`, so the following code is correctly indented:

```
if (a == b)
    if (b == c)
        writeln("All are equal");
    else
        writeln("a is different from b. Or is that so?");
```

The second `writeln` kicks in when a == b and b != c because the `else` binds to the innermost (second) `if`. If you instead want to bind the `else` to the first `if`, "buffer" the second `if` with a pair of braces:

```
if (a == b) {
    if (b == c)
        writeln("All are equal");
    else
        writeln("a is different from b");
}
```

Cascading multiple `if-else` statements is achieved in the time-honored C style:

```
auto opt = getOption();
if (opt == "help") {
    ...
} else if (opt == "quiet") {
    ...
} else if (opt == "verbose") {
    ...
} else {
    stderr.writefln("Unknown option '%s'", opt);
}
```

## 3.4   The `static if` Statement

Now that we've gotten warmed up a bit with some simple statements (thanks for suppressing that yawn), let's take a look at something just a bit more unusual.

If you want to "comment out" (or not) some statements depending on a compile-time Boolean condition, then the `static if` statement[1] comes in handy. For example:

```
enum size_t
```

---

1. Insert the obligatory "yet another use of the `static` keyword."

```
    g_maxDataSize = 100_000_000,
    g_maxMemory = 1_000_000_000;
...
double transmogrify(double x) {
    static if (g_maxMemory / 4 > g_maxDataSize) {
        alias double Numeric;
    } else {
        alias float Numeric;
    }
    Numeric[] y;
    ... // Complicated computation
    return y[0];
}
```

The static if statement is a compile-time selector, much like C's #if construct. When encountering a static if, the compiler evaluates the controlling expression. If the expression is nonzero, the corresponding code is compiled; otherwise, the code corresponding to the else clause (if any) gets compiled. In the example above, static if is used to switch between a memory-saving operation mode (by using the smaller float) and an accurate mode (by using the more precise double). Uses of considerably more power and expressiveness are possible inside generic code.

The expression tested by static if is any if-testable expression that can be evaluated during compilation. Allowed expressions include a large subset of the language, including arithmetic on all numeric types, array manipulation, is expressions that operate on types (§ 2.3.4.3 on page 48), and even function calls, an absolutely remarkable feature called compile-time function evaluation. Chapter 5 discusses compile-time evaluation in depth.

**Peeling Braces**   There's a glaring oddity about the transmogrify example. See, the numeric type is introduced inside a pair of { and } braces. As such, it should be visible only locally inside that scope (and consequently invisible to the enclosing function), thus foiling our entire plan quite thoroughly. Such behavior would also render the promising static if statement practically useless. For that reason, static if uses braces for *grouping*, but not for *scoping*. As far as scope and visibility are concerned, static if peels the outermost braces away, if any (they are not required when you have only one controlled statement; our example above uses them only out of stylistic obsession). If you do want braces, just add another pair:

```
import std.stdio;

void main() {
    static if (real.sizeof > double.sizeof) {{
```

```
    auto maximorum = real.max;
    writefln("Really big numbers - up to %s!", maximorum);
  }}
  ... /* Maximorum is invisible here */ ...
}
```

**The Statement That Wasn't**    What is the name of this chapter? "Statements." What is the name of this section? "The `static if` Statement." You're right to be a little surprised hearing that `static if` is not only a statement but also a *declaration*. The non-statement-ness of `static if` shows not only in the peeling braces behavior, but also in the fact that `static if` can occur anywhere a declaration may occur, and that includes module, `struct`, and `class` levels, which are inaccessible to statements; for example, we could define `numeric` globally by simply pulling the pertinent code outside `transmogrify` as follows:

```
enum size_t
   g_maxDataSize = 100_000_000,
   g_maxMemory = 1_000_000_000;
...

// The declaration of Numeric will be seen at module scope
static if (g_maxMemory / 4 > g_maxDataSize) {
   alias double Numeric;
} else {
   alias float Numeric;
}

double transmogrify(double x) {
   Numeric[] y;
   ... // Complicated computation
   return y[0];
}
```

**Two ifs, One else**    `static if` does not come with a corresponding `static else`. Instead, it just reuses the regular `else`. Logically, `else` binds to the nearest `if`, be it `static` or regular:

```
if (a)
   static if (b) writeln("a and b are nonzero");
   else writeln("b is zero");
```

## 3.5   The switch Statement

It's best to illustrate switch with a quick example:

```d
import std.stdio;

void classify(char c) {
    write("You passed ");
    switch (c) {
        case '#':
            writeln("a hash sign.");
            break;
        case '0': .. case '9':
            writeln("a digit.");
            break;
        case 'A': .. case 'Z': case 'a': .. case 'z':
            writeln("an ASCII character.");
            break;
        case '.', ',', ':', ';', '!', '?':
            writeln("a punctuation mark.");
            break;
        default:
            writeln("quite a character!");
            break;
    }
}
```

The general form of the switch statement is

```
switch (‹expression›) ‹statement›
```

‹*expression*› can have numeric, enumerated, or string type. ‹*statement*› may contain labels defined as follows:

1. case ‹*e*›:
   Jump here if ‹*expression*› == ‹*e*›. To use the comma operator (§ 2.3.18 on page 60) in e, you need to wrap the entire expression in parentheses.
2. case ‹$e_1$›, ‹$e_2$›, ..., ‹$e_n$›:
   Each ‹$e_k$› is an expression. The construct is equivalent to case ‹$item_1$›: case ‹$item_2$›:, ..., case ‹$item_n$›:.
3. case ‹$e_1$›: .. case ‹$e_2$›:
   Jump here if ‹*expression*› >= ‹$e_1$› and ‹*expression*› <= ‹$e_2$›.
4. default:
   Jump here if no other jump was taken.

In all of these tests, ‹*expression*› is evaluated only once. The expression in each case label is any legal expression comparable for equality with ‹*expression*›, and also for inequality if the .. syntax is used. Usually the case expressions are compile-time constants, but D allows variables, too, and guarantees lexical-order evaluation up to the first match. After evaluation, a jump is taken to the corresponding case or default label and execution proceeds from there. Just as in C and C++, execution inside the switch does not automatically stop when the next case label is reached; you must insert a break if you want that to happen. This arguably suboptimal behavior was decided in order to not surprise programmers coming from other languages.

For labels evaluated during compilation, it is enforced that no overlap exists. For example, this code is illegal:

```
switch (s) {
    case 'a' .. case 'z': ... break;
    // Trying a special case for 'w'
    case 'w': ... // Error! Case labels cannot overlap!
}
```

If no jump is taken at all, a runtime exception is thrown. This is to prevent the common programming error of overlooking a subset of values. If there is no such danger, insert a default: break; in the controlled statement, thus nicely documenting your assumption. Check the next section for a static enforcement of the same condition.

## 3.6   The `final switch` Statement

It is often the case that switch is used in conjunction with enumerated types and is meant to handle all of their possible values. If, during maintenance, the number of cases is changing, all of the dependent switch statements suddenly fall out of sync and must be manually searched for and modified.

Now clearly the scalable solution is to replace tag-based switching with virtual function dispatch; that way there's no more need to handle all different cases in one place, but instead the processing is distributed across different interface implementations. However, it is a reality of life that defining interfaces and classes incurs a high initial effort, which switch-based solutions may avoid. For such situations, the final switch statement comes in handy by statically forcing the case labels to cover all possible values of an enumerated type:

```
enum DeviceStatus { ready, busy, fail }
...
void process(DeviceStatus status) {
    final switch (status) {
    case DeviceStatus.ready:
        ...
```

```
    case DeviceStatus.busy:
        ...
    case DeviceStatus.fail:
        ...
    }
}
```

Say that code maintenance adds another possible device status:

```
enum DeviceStatus { ready, busy, fail, initializing /* added */ }
```

After that change, attempting to recompile `process` is met with refusal on the following grounds:

```
Error: final switch statement must handle all values
```

The `final switch` statement requires that all labels of the `enum` be explicitly handled. Ranged `case` labels of the form `case ‹e₁›: .. case ‹e₂›:` or the `default` label are disallowed.

## 3.7  Looping Statements

### 3.7.1  The `while` Statement

Yes, you are absolutely right:

```
while (‹expression›) ‹statement›
```

Execution starts by evaluating ‹*expression*›. If it is nonzero, ‹*statement*› is executed and the cycle resumes with another evaluation of ‹*expression*›. Otherwise, the `while` statement is done and execution flows past it.

### 3.7.2  The `do-while` Statement

If a loop with at least one execution is needed, the `do-while` statement comes in handy:

```
do ‹statement› while (‹expression›);
```

Notice the required semicolon at the end of the construct. Again, ‹*statement*› must be non-empty. The `do-while` statement is equivalent to a `while` statement that forces one initial execution of ‹*statement*›.

### 3.7.3   The `for` Statement

The `for` statement has the syntax

```
for (‹decl-expr› ‹expr₁›; ‹expr₂›) ‹statement›
```

Any and all of ‹*decl-expr*›, ‹*expr*$_1$›, and ‹*expr*$_2$› can be missing; if ‹*expr*$_1$› is missing, it is considered to be `true`. The ‹*decl-expr*› construct either introduces a value declaration (such as `auto i = 0;` or `float w;`) or is an expression followed by `;` (such as `i = 10;`). The semantics is similar to that of the homonym construct in other languages: ‹*decl-expr*› is evaluated first, then ‹*expr*$_1$› is evaluated; as long as it is true, ‹*statement*› is executed, then ‹*expr*$_2$›, after which the cycle resumes by evaluating ‹*expr*$_1$› again.

### 3.7.4   The `foreach` Statement

The most convenient, safe, and often fast means to iterate is the `foreach` statement, which comes in several flavors. The simplest form of `foreach` is

```
foreach (‹symbol›; ‹expression₁› .. ‹expression₂›) ‹statement›
```

The two expressions must be of numeric or pointer types.  Simply put, ‹*symbol*› spans the interval from (and including) ‹*expression*$_1$› to (and excluding) ‹*expression*$_2$›. This informal explanation achieves conciseness at the expense of leaving out quite a few details; for example, is ‹*expression*$_2$› evaluated only once or multiple times throughout? Or what happens if ‹*expression*$_1$› >= ‹*expression*$_2$›?  Such details can be easily figured out by looking at the semantically equivalent code below.  The technique of expressing high-level constructs in terms of equivalent constructs in a simpler (sub)language is called *lowering* and will be put to good use throughout this chapter.

```
{
    auto __n = ‹expression₂›;
    auto ‹symbol› = true ? ‹expression₁› : ‹expression₂›;
    for (; ‹symbol› < __n; ++‹symbol›) ‹statement›
}
```

where `__n` is a symbol generated by the compiler, guaranteed to never clash with other symbols ("fresh" symbol in compiler writer lingo).

(What do the top braces do? They ensure that ‹*symbol*› doesn't leak past the `foreach` statement, and also that the entire construct is a single statement.)

It's now clear that both ‹*expression*$_1$› and ‹*expression*$_2$› are evaluated only once, and ‹*symbol*›'s type is computed according to the rules of the ternary operator (§ 2.3.16 on page 59)—that's why the `?:` is there, as it has no runtime role. The careful type conciliation made by `?:` ensures that some potential confusion between numbers of different sizes and precisions, as well as conflicts between signed and unsigned types, are properly prevented or at least exposed.

It is also worth mentioning that the compiler doesn't enforce a specific type for `__n`; consequently, you can make this form of `foreach` work with a user-defined type too, as long as that type defines operators for less-than comparison and increment (we'll learn how to do that in Chapter 12). Better yet, if the type does not define less-than comparison but does define comparison for equality, the compiler automatically replaces `<` with `!=` in the lowering. In that case, the range cannot be checked for validity so you must make sure that the upper limit can be reached by starting from the lower limit and applying `++` repeatedly. Otherwise, the iteration may go astray.[2]

You can specify an actual type with ‹*symbol*›. That type is often redundant, but it is useful when you want to ensure that the iterated type fits a certain expectation, solve a signed/unsigned ambiguity, or insert an implicit conversion:

```
import std.math, std.stdio;

void main() {
    foreach (float elem; 1.0 .. 100.0) {
        writeln(log(elem)); // Logarithms in single precision
    }
    foreach (double elem; 1.0 .. 100.0) {
        writeln(log(elem)); // Double precision
    }
    foreach (elem; 1.0 .. 100.0) {
        writeln(log(elem)); // Same
    }
}
```

### 3.7.5 foreach on Arrays

Moving on to a different form of `foreach`, here's a form that works with arrays and slices:

`foreach (‹symbol›; ‹expression›) ‹statement›`

‹*expression*› must be of array (linear or associative), slice, or user-defined type. Chapter 12 will deal with the latter case, so for now let's focus on arrays and slices. After ‹*expression*› is evaluated once, a reference to it is stored in a private temporary. (The actual array is not copied.) Then ‹*symbol*› is bound in turn to each element of the array and ‹*statement*› is executed. Just as with the range `foreach`, you can specify a type in front of ‹*symbol*›.

---

2. C++'s STL consistently uses `!=` to test for iteration's end, on the grounds that (in)equality is more general as it applies to a larger category of types. D's approach is no less general but speculatively uses `<` when available, to the goal of increased safety of iteration at no overall cost in abstraction or efficiency.

The `foreach` statement assumes there will be no changes in the array length during iteration; if you plan otherwise, you may want to use a plain `for` loop and the appropriate amount of care.

**Updating during Iteration**    Assigning to ‹*symbol*› inside ‹*statement*› is not reflected in the array. If you do want to change the element being iterated, define ‹*symbol*› as a reference type by prefixing it with `ref` or `ref` ‹*type*›. For example:

```
void scale(float[] array, float s) {
   foreach (ref e; array) {
      e *= s; // Updates array in place
   }
}
```

You could specify a full type with `ref`, such as `ref float e` in the code above. However, this time the type match must be *exact*; conversions don't work with `ref`!

```
float[] arr = [ 1.0, 2.5, 4.0 ];
foreach (ref float elem; arr) {
   elem *= 2; // Fine
}
foreach (ref double elem; arr) { // Error!
   elem /= 2;
}
```

The reason is simple: to ensure proper assignment, `ref` counts on and exact match of representation; although you can create a `double` from a `float` at any time, you can't use a `double` assignment to update a `float` for multiple reasons, the simplest one being that they don't even have the same size.

**Where Was I?**    Sometimes, having access to the iteration index is useful. You can bind a symbol to it with the form

**foreach** (‹*symbol*$_1$›, ‹*symbol*$_2$›; ‹*expression*›) ‹*statement*›

So you can write

```
void print(int[] array) {
   foreach (i, e; array) {
      writefln("array[%s] = %s;", i, e);
   }
}
```

This function prints the contents of an array as actual D code: `print([5, 2, 8])` produces

```
array[0] = 5;
array[1] = 2;
array[2] = 8;
```

Accessing the iteration index becomes much more interesting with associative arrays:

```
void print(double[string] map) {
    foreach (i, e; map) {
        writefln("array['%s'] = %s;", i, e);
    }
}
```

Now calling print(["Moon": 1.283, "Sun": 499.307, "Proxima Centauri": 133814298.759]) prints

```
array['Proxima Centauri'] = 1.33814e+08;
array['Sun'] = 499.307;
array['Moon'] = 1.283;
```

Notice how the order of elements is not the same as the order specified in the literal. In fact, if you experiment with the same code on a different implementation or version of the same implementation, you may experience a different ordering. This is because associative arrays use several occult techniques to make storage and retrieval of elements efficient, at the expense of guaranteed ordering.

The type of the index and that of the element are deduced. Alternatively, you can impose them by specifying types for one or both of ‹*symbol*$_1$› and ‹*symbol*$_2$›. However, ‹*symbol*$_1$› can never be a ref type.

**Shenanigans**   Arbitrarily changing the underlying array during iteration has the following possible effects:

- *Array mutates in place:* Iteration will "see" mutation to not-yet-visited slots of the array.
- *Array changes in size:* Iteration will iterate up to the length that the array had upon loop entry. It's possible that the size change moves the new array to a different region of memory, in which case subsequent mutation of the array is invisible to the iteration, and also subsequent mutations effected by the iteration itself are not visible to the array. Not recommended because the rules that trigger moving the array are implementation-dependent.
- *Array is deallocated or shrunk in place using low-level allocation control functions:* You wanted ultimate control and efficiency and you took the time to read about low-level allocation control in your implementation's documentation. It can only

be assumed that you know what you're doing, and that you are a boring date for anyone who hasn't written a garbage collector.

### 3.7.6   The `continue` and `break` Statements

The `continue` statement forces a jump to the end of the statement controlled by the innermost `while`, `do-while`, `for`, or `foreach` statement. The loop skips the rest of its controlled statement and proceeds to the next iteration.

The `break` statement forces a jump right after the innermost `while`, `do-while`, `for`, `foreach`, `switch`, or `final switch` statement, effectively ending its execution.

Both statements accept an optional label, which allows specifying which exact statement to effect. Labeled `break` and `continue` greatly simplify the expression of complex iteration patterns without state variables and without having to resort to you-know-which statement, which is described in the next section.

```
void fun(string[] strings) {
   loop: foreach (s; strings) {
      switch (s) {
      default: ...; break;   // Break the switch
      case "ls": ...; break; // Break the switch
      case "rm": ...; break; // Break the switch
      ...
      case "#": break loop;  // Ignore rest of strings (break foreach)
      }
   }
   ...
}
```

## 3.8   The `goto` Statement

In the wake of global warming, there's no point in adding any more heat to the debate around `goto`. Suffice it to say that D does provide it in the following form:

```
goto ‹label›;
```

where the symbol ‹*label*› must be visible in the function where `goto` is called. A label is defined implicitly by prefixing a statement with a symbol followed by a colon. For example:

```
int a;
...
mylabel: a = 1;
```

```
...
if (a == 0) goto mylabel;
```

There cannot be multiply-defined labels in the same function. Another restriction is that a goto cannot skip the definition point of a value that's visible at the landing point, even when that value is not used. For example:

```
void main() {
  goto target;
  int x = 10;
  target: {} // Error! goto bypasses definition of x!
}
```

Finally, a goto cannot cross an exception boundary, a restriction that § 3.11 on page 81 will explain. Other than that, goto obeys remarkably few restrictions, and that's precisely what makes it dangerous. goto can jump all over the place: forward or backward, in and out of if statements, and in and out of loops, including the infamous forward jump into the middle of a loop.

However, in D not everything bearing the goto name is dangerous. Inside a switch statement, writing

```
goto case ‹expression›;
```

jumps to the corresponding case ‹*expression*› label, and

```
goto default;
```

jumps to the default label. While these jumps are not much more structured than any other gotos, they are easier to follow because they are localized and can make switch statements substantially simpler:

```
enum Pref { superFast, veryFast, fast, accurate,
    regular, slow, slower };
Pref preference;
double coarseness = 1;
...
switch (preference) {
  case Pref.fast: ...; break;
  case Pref.veryFast: coarseness = 1.5; goto case Pref.fast;
  case Pref.superFast: coarseness = 3; goto case Pref.fast;
  case Pref.accurate: ...; break;
  case Pref.regular: goto default;
  default: ...
  ...
}
```

With labeled `break` and `continue` (§ 3.7.6 on page 78), exceptions (§ 3.11 on the next page), and the advanced flow control statement `scope` (§ 3.13 on page 84), finding good justification becomes increasingly difficult for `goto` aficionados.

## 3.9  The `with` Statement

The Pascal-inspired `with` statement allows working on a specific object comfortably. The statement

---

`with` (‹*expression*›) ‹*statement*›

---

first evaluates ‹*expression*› and then makes the resulting object's members the topmost visible symbols inside ‹*statement*›. We've met `struct` in the first chapter, so let's look at a short example involving a `struct`:

```
import std.math, std.stdio;

struct Point {
    double x, y;
    double norm() { return sqrt(x * x + y * y); }
}

void main() {
    Point p;
    int z;
    with (p) {
        x = 3;    // Assigns p.x
        p.y = 4; // It's fine to still use p explicitly
        writeln(norm()); // Writes p.norm, which is 5
        z = 1;           // z is still visible
    }
}
```

Changes to the fields are reflected directly in the object that `with` operates on—`with` recognizes and preserves the fact that p is an lvalue.

If one symbol made visible through `with` shadows a symbol defined earlier in the function, the compiler does not allow access for ambiguity reasons. Assuming the same definition of `Point`, the following code does not compile:

```
void fun() {
    Point p;
    string y = "I'm here to make a point (and a pun).";
    with (p) {
```

```
    writeln(x, ":", y); // Error!
        // p.y is not allowed to shadow y!
    }
}
```

However, the error is always signaled on *actual*, not *potential*, ambiguity. For example, if the `with` statement above did not use y at all, the code would have compiled and run, in spite of the latent ambiguity. Also, replacing `writeln(x, ":", y)` with `writeln(x, ":", p.y)` also works because the explicit qualification of y eliminates any possibility of ambiguity.

A `with` statement can mask module-level (e.g., global) symbols. Accessing the symbols masked by a `with` statement is possible with the syntax `.symbol`.

Notice that you can make multiple members implicit by writing

```
with (‹expr₁›) with (‹expr₂›) ... with (‹exprₙ›) ‹statement›
```

There is no ambiguity-related danger in using nested `with`s because the language disallows shadowing of a symbol introduced by an outer `with` by a symbol introduced by an inner `with`. In brief, in D a local symbol can never shadow another local symbol.

## 3.10 The return Statement

To immediately return a value from the current function, write

```
return ‹expression›;
```

The statement evaluates ‹*expression*› and then returns it to the caller, implicitly converted (if needed) to the function's returned type.

If the current function has type `void`, ‹*expression*› must either be omitted or consist of a call to a function that in turn has type `void`.

It is illegal for the execution flow to exit a non-`void` function without a `return`. This is hard to enforce effectively during compilation, so you might see the compiler complain unnecessarily on rare occasions.

## 3.11 The throw and try Statements

D supports error handling via exceptions. An exception is initiated by the `throw` statement and handled via the `try` statement. To throw an exception, you typically write

```
throw new SomeException("Something fishy happened");
```

The `SomeException` type must inherit the built-in class `Throwable`. D does not support throwing arbitrary types, partly because choosing a specific root type makes it easy to support chaining exceptions of different types together, as we'll see in a minute.

To handle an exception or at least be aware of it, use the `try` statement, which generally looks like this:

```
try ‹statement›
catch (‹E₁› ‹e₁›) ‹statement₁›
catch (‹E₂› ‹e₂›) ‹statement₂›
...
catch (‹Eₙ› ‹eₙ›) ‹statementₙ›
finally ‹statementf›
```

All controlled statements must be block statements; that is, they must be enclosed by braces. The `finally` clause, as well as any and all of the `catch` clauses, can be omitted, but the `try` statement must have at least one `catch` or the `finally` clause. $‹E_k›$ are types that, as mentioned, must inherit `Throwable`. The symbol names $‹e_k›$ bind to the exception object being caught and can be missing.

The semantics is as follows. First, ‹*statement*› is executed. If it throws an exception (let's call it $‹e_x›$ of type $‹E_x›$), then types $‹E_1›$, $‹E_2›$, ..., $‹E_n›$ are tentatively matched against $‹E_x›$. The first type $‹E_k›$ that is $‹E_x›$ or a class derived from it "wins." The symbol $‹e_k›$ is bound to the exception object $‹e_x›$ and ‹*statement*$_k$› is executed. The exception is considered already handled, so if ‹*statement*$_k$› throws itself an exception, that exception will not be dispatched among the current exception's `catch` blocks. If no type $‹E_k›$ matches, $‹e_x›$ continues up the call stack to find a handler.

The `finally` clause ‹*statement*$_f$›, if present, is executed in absolutely all cases, whether an exception ends up being thrown or not, and even if a `catch` clause catches an exception and then throws another. It is essentially guaranteed to be executed (barring, of course, infinite loops and system calls causing program termination). If ‹*statement*$_f$› throws an exception $‹e_f›$, that exception will be appended to the current exception chain. Chapter 9 contains full information about D's exception model.

A `goto` statement (§ 3.8 on page 78) cannot jump inside any of ‹*statement*›, ‹*statement*$_1$›, ..., ‹*statement*$_n$›, and ‹*statement*$_f$›, except if the `goto` also originates in that statement.

### 3.12   The `mixin` Statement

We saw in Chapter 2 (§ 2.3.4.2 on page 47) that `mixin` expressions allow you to transform strings known during compilation in D expressions that are compiled just like regular code. `mixin` statements take that one step further—you can use `mixin` to generate not only expressions, but also declarations and statements.

Consider, for example, that you want to compute the number of nonzero bits in a byte really fast. This count, also known as the Hamming weight, is useful in a number of applications such as encryption, distributed computing, and approximate database searches. The simplest method of counting the nonzero bits in a byte is by successively accumulating the least significant bit and shifting the input number. A faster method was first suggested by Peter Wegner [60] and popularized by Kernighan and Ritchie in their K&R classic [34]:

```
uint bitsSet(uint value) {
    uint result;
    for (; value; ++result) {
        value &= value - 1;
    }
    return result;
}
unittest {
    assert(bitsSet(10) == 2);
    assert(bitsSet(0) == 0);
    assert(bitsSet(255) == 8);
}
```

This method is faster than the naïve one because it makes only exactly as many iterations as bits are set. But `bitsSet` still has control flow; a faster method is to simply do a table lookup. For best results, let's fill the table during compilation, which is where a `mixin` declaration may greatly help. The plan is to first generate a string that looks like a declaration of a table and then use `mixin` to compile that string into regular code. The table generator may look like this:

```
import std.conv;

string makeHammingWeightsTable(string name, uint max = 255) {
    string result = "immutable ubyte["~to!string(max + 1)~"] "
        ~name~" = [ ";
    foreach (b; 0 .. max + 1) {
        result ~= to!string(bitsSet(b)) ~ ", ";
    }
    return result ~ "];";
}
```

Calling `makeHammingWeightsTable("t")` returns the string `"immutable ubyte[256] t = [ 0, 1, 1, 2, ..., 7, 7, 8, ];"`. The `immutable` qualifier (Chapter 8) states that the table never changes after the initialization. We first met the library function `to!string` on page 16—it converts anything (in this case the `uint` returned by `bitsSet`) into a string. Once we have the needed code in `string` format, defining the table is only one step away:

```
mixin(makeHammingWeightsTable("hwTable"));
unittest {
```

```
    assert(hwTable[10] == 2);
    assert(hwTable[0] == 0);
    assert(hwTable[255] == 8);
}
```

You may build tables of virtually any size, but careful testing is always recommended—too large tables may actually become slower than computation because of cache effects.

Finally, with the reluctance of an aikido trainer recommending pepper spray in class, it should be mentioned that combining string import (§ 2.2.5.1 on page 37) with mixin declarations offers the lowest form of modularity: textual inclusion. Consider:

```
mixin(import("widget.d"));
```

The import expression reads the text of file widget.d into a literal string, and immediately after that, the mixin expression transforms that string into code. Use such a trick only after you've convinced yourself that your path to glory in hacking depends on it.

## 3.13   The scope Statement

The scope statement is original to D, although its functionality can be found with slight variations in other languages, too. With scope, it is very easy to write exception-safe code in D and, most important, to also read and understand it later. The correctness of code using scope can be achieved with other means; however, the result is inscrutable except for the most trivial examples.

Writing

```
scope(exit) ‹statement›
```

allows you to plant ‹*statement*› to be executed when control flow leaves the current scope. It does what the finally clause of a try statement does, but in a much more scalable manner. Using scope(exit) comes in handy when you want to make sure you "remember" to leave something in good order as you leave a scope. For example, say you have a "verbose" flag in an application that you want to temporarily disable. Then you can write

```
bool g_verbose;
...
void silentFunction() {
    auto oldVerbose = g_verbose;
    scope(exit) g_verbose = oldVerbose;
    g_verbose = false;
    ...
```

```
}
```

The rest of silentFunction can contain arbitrary code with early returns and possibly exceptions, in full confidence that, come hell or high water, g_verbose will be properly restored when silentFunction's execution ends.

More generally, let us define a *lowering* for scope(exit), that is, a systematic means for rewriting code using scope(exit) as equivalent code containing other statements, such as try. We already used lowering informally when explaining the for statement in terms of the while statement, and then the foreach statement in terms of the for statement.

Consider a block containing a scope(exit) statement:

```
{
    ‹statements₁›
    scope(exit) ‹statement₂›
    ‹statements₃›
}
```

Let's pick the first scope in the block, so we can assume that ‹statements₁› itself does not contain scope (but ‹statement₂› and ‹statements₃› might). Lowering transforms the code into this:

```
{
    ‹statements₁›
    try {
        ‹statements₃›
    } finally {
        ‹statement₂›
    }
}
```

Following the transform, ‹statements₃› and ‹statement₂› are further lowered because they may contain additional scope statements. (The lowering always ends because the fragments are always strictly smaller than the initial sequence.) This means that code containing multiple scope(exit) statements is well defined, even in weird cases like scope(exit) scope(exit) scope(exit) writeln("?"). In particular, let's see what happens in the interesting case of two scope(exit) statements in the same block:

```
{
    ‹statements₁›
    scope(exit) ‹statement₂›
    ‹statements₃›
    scope(exit) ‹statement₄›
    ‹statements₅›
```

```
}
```

Let's assume that all statements do not contain additional `scope(exit)` statements. After lowering we obtain

```
{
    ‹statements₁›
    try {
        ‹statements₃›
        try {
            ‹statements₅›
        } finally {
            ‹statement₄›
        }
    } finally {
        ‹statement₂›
    }
}
```

The purpose of showing this unwieldy code is to figure out the order of execution of multiple `scope(exit)` statements in the same block. Following the flow shows that ‹statement₄› gets executed *before* ‹statement₂›. In general, `scope(exit)` statements execute in a stack, LIFO manner, the reverse of their order in the execution flow.

It is much easier to track the flow of the `scope` version than that of the equivalent `try/finally` code; simply reaching a `scope` statement guarantees that its controlled statement will be executed when the scope exits. This allows you to achieve exception safety in your code not through awkwardly nested `try/finally` statements, but simply by ordering straight-line statements appropriately.

The previous example also shows a very nice property of the `scope` statement: scalability. `scope` shines best when its formidable scalability is taken into account. (After all, if all we needed was one occasional `scope`, we already had the linguistic means to write its lowered equivalent by hand.) Achieving the functionality of several `scope(exit)` statements requires a linear growth in code length when using `scope(exit)` itself, and a linear growth in both length and depth of code when using the equivalent `try`-based code; the depth scales very poorly, in addition to sharing real estate with other compound statements such as `if` or `for`. C++-style destructors (also supported by D; see Chapter 7) offer a scalable solution, too, as long as you are able to discount the cost of defining new types; but if a class must be defined mostly for its destructor's sake (ever felt a need for a class like `CleanerUpper`?), then its scalability is even worse than that of inline `try` statements. In short, if classes were vacuum welding and `try/finally` were chewing gum, then `scope(exit)` would qualify as a quick-dry epoxy glue.

The `scope(success)` ‹*statement*› schedules ‹*statement*› for execution only in the case when the current scope will ultimately be exited normally, not by throwing. The lowering of `scope(success)` is as follows:

```
{
    ‹statements₁›
    scope(success) ‹statement₂›
    ‹statements₃›
}
```

becomes

```
{
    ‹statements₁›
    bool __succeeded = true;
    try {
        ‹statements₃›
    } catch(Exception e) {
        __succeeded = false;
        throw e;
    } finally {
        if (__succeeded) ‹statement₂›
    }
}
```

Again, ‹*statement₂*› and ‹*statements₃*› must undergo further lowering until they contain no more `scope` statements.

Moving on to a gloomier form, executing `scope(failure)` ‹*statement*› guarantees that ‹*statement*› will be executed if and only if the current scope is exited by throwing an exception.

The lowering of `scope(failure)` is almost identical to that of `scope(exit)`—it just negates the test of `__succeeded`. The code

```
{
    ‹statements₁›
    scope(failure) ‹statement₂›
    ‹statements₃›
}
```

becomes

```
{
    ‹statements₁›
    bool __succeeded = true;
```

```
try {
    ‹statements₃›
} catch(Exception e) {
    __succeeded = false;
    throw e;
} finally {
    if (!__succeeded) ‹statement₂›
}
}
```

followed by further lowering of ‹*statement₂*› and ‹*statements₃*›.

There are many places where scope statements can be put to good use. Consider, for example, that you want to create a file transactionally—that is, if creating the file fails, you don't want a partially created file on the disk. You could go about it like this:

```
import std.contracts, std.stdio;

void transactionalCreate(string filename) {
    string tempFilename = filename ~ ".fragment";
    scope(success) {
        std.file.rename(tempFilename, filename);
    }
    auto f = File(tempFilename, "w");
    ... // Write to f at your leisure
}
```

scope(success) sets the goal of the function early on. The equivalent scope-less code would be much more convoluted, and indeed, many programmers would be simply too busy making the blessed thing work on the normal path to put in extra work for supporting unlikely cases. That's why the language should make it as easy as possible to handle errors.

One nice artifact of this style of programming is that all error-handling code is concentrated in transactionalCreate's prologue and does not otherwise affect the main code. As simple as it stands, transactionalCreate is rock-solid: you are left with either a good file or a fragment file, but not a corrupt file claiming to be correct.

## 3.14    The synchronized Statement

The synchronized statement has the form

synchronized (‹*expression₁*›, ‹*expression₂*›...) ‹*statement*›

synchronized effects scoped locking in multithreaded programs. Chapter 13 defines the semantics of synchronized.

## 3.15 The asm Statement

D would not respect its vow to be a system-level programming language without allowing some sort of interface with assembly language. So if you enjoy getting your hands dirty, you'll be glad to hear that D has a very carefully defined embedded assembly language for Intel x86. Better yet, D's x86 assembler language is portable across virtually all D implementations working on x86 machines. Given that assembly language depends on only the machine and not the operating system, this looks like a "duh" sort of feature but you'd be surprised. For historical reasons, each operating system defines its own incompatible assembly language syntax, so, for example, you couldn't get any Windows assembler code working on Linux because the syntaxes are entirely different (arguably gratuitously). What D does to cut that Gordian knot is to not rely on a system-specific external assembler. Instead, the compiler truly parses and understands assembler language statements. To write assembler code, just go

```
asm ‹asm-statement›
```

or

```
asm { ‹asm-statements› }
```

The symbols normally visible just before `asm` are accessible inside the `asm` block as well, ensuring that the assembler can access D entities. This book does not cover D's assembler language, which should look familiar to anyone who's used any x86 assembler; consult D's assembler documentation [12] for the full story.

## 3.16 Summary and Quick Reference

D offers the usual suspects in terms of statements, plus a few interesting newcomers such as `static if`, `final switch`, and `scope`. Table 3.1 is a quick reference for all of D's statements, favoring brevity at the expense of ultimate precision and excruciating detail (for those, refer to the respective sections of this chapter).

**Table 3.1:** Statements cheat sheet (‹*s*› means statement, ‹*e*› means expression, ‹*d*› means declaration, ‹*x*› means symbol)

| Statement | Description |
| --- | --- |
| ‹*e*› ; | Evaluates ‹*e*›. Expressions that have no effect and involve only built-in types and operators are statically disallowed (§ 3.1 on page 65). |

**Table 3.1:** Statements Cheat Sheet *(continued)*

| Statement | Description |
|---|---|
| { ‹$s_1$› ... ‹$s_n$› } | Executes statements ‹$s_1$› through ‹$s_n$› in lexical order for as long as control is not explicitly transferred (e.g., via `return`) (§ 3.2 on page 66). |
| asm ‹$s$› | Machine-dependent assembler code (‹$s$› here is assembler code, not a D statement). Currently x86 assembler is supported with the same syntax across all supported operating systems (§ 3.15 on the preceding page). |
| break; | Stops the current (innermost) `switch`, `for`, `foreach`, `while`, or do statement by transferring control to right after the end of the corresponding controlled statement (§ 3.7.6 on page 78). |
| break ‹$x$›; | Stops the `switch`, `for`, `foreach`, `while`, or do statement that was immediately preceded by label ‹$x$›: by transferring control to right after the end of the corresponding controlled statement (§ 3.7.6 on page 78). |
| continue; | Continues the current (innermost) `for`, `foreach`, `while`, or do statement by skipping over the remainder of the corresponding controlled statement (§ 3.7.6 on page 78). |
| continue ‹$x$›; | Continues the `for`, `foreach`, `while`, or do statement that was immediately preceded by label ‹$x$›: by skipping over the remainder of the corresponding controlled statement (§ 3.7.6 on page 78). |
| do ‹$s$› while (‹$e$›); | Executes ‹$s$› once and then continues executing it as long as ‹$e$› is nonzero (§ 3.7.2 on page 73). |
| for (‹$s_1$› ‹$e_1$›; ‹$e_2$› ) ‹$s_2$› | Executes ‹$s_1$› which can be an expression statement, a value definition, a semicolon, or a value definition; then as long as ‹$e_1$› is nonzero, executes ‹$s$› and then evaluates ‹$e_2$› (§ 3.7.3 on page 74). |
| foreach (‹$x$›; ‹$e_1$› .. ‹$e_2$›) ‹$s$› | Executes ‹$s$› initializing ‹$x$› to ‹$e_1$› and then successively incrementing it by 1, for as long as ‹$x$› < ‹$e_2$›. No execution if ‹$e_1$› >= ‹$e_2$›. ‹$e_1$› and ‹$e_2$› are evaluated once each (§ 3.7.4 on page 74). |
| foreach (ref$_{opt}$ ‹$x$› ; ‹$e$› ) ‹$s$› | Executes ‹$s$› by declaring ‹$x$› and then binding it in turn to each element of ‹$e$›. The expression ‹$e$› must evaluate to an array type or a user-defined range type (Chapter 12). If `ref` is present, changes to ‹$x$› will be reflected back in the iterated entity (§ 3.7.5 on page 75). |

**Table 3.1:** Statements Cheat Sheet *(continued)*

| Statement | Description |
|---|---|
| foreach (‹$x_1$›, ref$_{opt}$ ‹$x_2$›; ‹$e$›) ‹$s$› | Similar to the use above but introduces the extra value ‹$x_1$›. If ‹$e$› is an associative array, ‹$x_1$› is bound to the key and ‹$x_2$› to the value being iterated. Otherwise, the value is bound to an integer counting the number of executions of the loop (starting from zero) (§ 3.7.5 on page 75). |
| goto ‹$x$›; | Transfers control to the label ‹$x$›, which must be defined with ‹$x$›: in the current function (§ 3.8 on page 78). |
| goto case ‹$x$›; | Transfers control to the case label ‹$x$› in the current switch statement (§ 3.8 on page 78). |
| goto default; | Transfers control to the default label ‹$x$› in the current switch statement (§ 3.8 on page 78). |
| if (‹$e$›) ‹$s$› | Executes ‹$s$› if ‹$e$› is nonzero (§ 3.3 on page 67). |
| if (‹$e$›) ‹$s_1$› else ‹$s_2$› | Executes statement ‹$s_1$› if ‹$e$› is nonzero, ‹$s_2$› otherwise. Trailing else binds to the last if or static if (§ 3.3 on page 67). |
| static if (‹$e$›) ‹$d/s$› | Evaluates ‹$e$› during compilation and then, if ‹$e$› is nonzero, compile declaration or statement ‹$d/s$›. One level of { and } around ‹$d/s$› is peeled away if it exists (§ 3.4 on page 68). |
| static if (‹$e$›) ‹$d/s_1$› else ‹$d/s_2$› | Similar to static if, plus an else clause. Trailing else binds to the last if or static if (§ 3.4 on page 68). |
| return ‹$e$›$_{opt}$; | Returns from the current function. The expression returned must be convertible to the declared return type. Expression ‹$e$› may be missing if the function's return type is void (§ 3.10 on page 81). |
| scope(exit) ‹$s$› | Executes ‹$s$› when the current scope is exited in any way (e.g., return, fall through, or throwing an exception). Multiple scope statements of all kinds (including failure and success below) are executed in reverse order of their definition (§ 3.13 on page 84). |
| scope(failure) ‹$s$› | Executes ‹$s$› when the current scope is exited by throwing an exception (§ 3.13 on page 84). |
| scope(success) ‹$s$› | Executes ‹$s$› when the current scope is exited normally (return or fall through) (§ 3.13 on page 84). |
| switch (‹$e$›) ‹$s$› | Evaluates ‹$e$› and jumps to the matching case label contained within ‹$s$› (§ 3.5 on page 71). |

**Table 3.1:** Statements Cheat Sheet *(continued)*

| Statement | Description |
| --- | --- |
| `final switch (‹e›) ‹s›` | Like `switch`, but works with enumerated values and enforces statically that all values are handled with `case` labels (§ 3.6 on page 72). |
| `synchronized (‹e₁›, ‹e₂›...) ‹s›` | Executes ‹s› while the objects returned by ‹$e_1$›, ‹$e_2$›, etc. are locked. Expressions ‹$e_i$› must return a `class` object (§ 3.14 on page 88). |
| `throw ‹e›;` | Evaluates ‹e› and throws it such that control is transferred to the closest matching `catch` handler. The type of ‹e› must be `Throwable` or derived (§ 3.11 on page 81). |
| `try ‹s› catch(‹T₁› ‹x₁›) ‹s₁› ... catch(‹Tₙ› ‹xₙ›) ‹sₙ› finally ‹sf›` | Executes ‹s›. If ‹s› throws an exception, attempts to match it against ‹$T_1$› to ‹$T_n$› in that order. If a match k is found, matching stops and ‹$s_k$› is executed. In all cases, executes ‹$s_f$› just before passing control out of the `try` statement (whether normally or by means of an exception). All `catch` clauses or the `finally` clause may be missing, but not both (§ 3.11 on page 81). |
| `while (‹e›) ‹s›` | Executes ‹s› as long as ‹e› is nonzero (no execution if ‹e› is zero upon the first evaluation) (§ 3.7.1 on page 73). |
| `with (‹e›) ‹s›` | Evaluates ‹e›, then executes ‹s› as if it were a member function of ‹e›'s type: all symbols used in ‹s› are first looked up as members of ‹e› (§ 3.9 on page 80). |

# Arrays, Associative Arrays, and Strings

The previous chapters indirectly acquainted us with arrays, associative arrays, and strings—an expression here, a literal there—so it's time for a closer inspection. A lot of good code can be written using only these three types, so learning about them comes in handy now that we have expressions and statements under our belt.

## 4.1 Dynamic Arrays

D offers a simple but very versatile array abstraction. For a type T, T[] is the type of contiguous regions of memory containing elements of type T. D calls T[] "array of values of type T" or, colloquially, "array of Ts."

To create a dynamic array, use a new expression (§ 2.3.6.1 on page 51) as follows:

```
int[] array = new int[20]; // Create an array of 20 integers
```

or simpler and more convenient:

```
auto array = new int[20];  // Create an array of 20 integers
```

All elements of a freshly created array of type T[] are initialized with T.init, which is 0 for integers. After creation, the array's elements are accessible through the index expression array[n]:

```
auto array = new int[20];
auto x = array[5];          // Valid indices are 0 through 19
```

```
assert(x == 0);            // Initial element values are int.init = 0
array[7] = 42;             // Elements are assignable
assert(array[7] == 42);
```

The number of elements passed to the new expression does not need to be constant. For example, the program below creates an array of random length and then fills it with random numbers, for which generation it enlists the help of the function uniform in module std.random:

```
import std.random;

void main() {
   // Anywhere between 1 and 127 elements
   auto array = new double[uniform(1, 128)];
   foreach (i;  0 .. array.length) {
      array[i] = uniform(0.0, 1.0);
   }
   ...
}
```

The foreach loop above could be rewritten to refer directly to each array element instead of using indexing (recall § 3.7.5 on page 75):

```
foreach (ref element; array) {
   element = uniform(0.0, 1.0);
}
```

The ref informs the compiler that we want to reflect assignments to element back into the original array. Otherwise, element would be a copy of each array element in turn.

If you want to initialize an array with specific contents, you may want to use an array literal:

```
auto somePrimes = [ 2, 3, 5, 7, 11, 13, 17 ];
```

Another way to create an array is by duplicating an existing one. The property array.dup yields an element-by-element copy of array:

```
auto array = new int[100];
...
auto copy = array.dup;
assert(array !is copy);          // The arrays are distinct
assert(array == copy);           //      but have equal contents
```

Finally, if you just define a variable of type T[] without initializing it or by initializing it with `null`, that's a null array. A `null` array has no elements and compares equal to `null`.

```
string[] a;            // Same as string[] a = null
assert(a is null);
assert(a == null);    // Same as above
a = new string[2];
assert(a !is null);
a = a[0 .. 0];
assert(a !is null);
```

One odd detail revealed by the last line of the snippet above is that an empty array is not necessarily `null`.

### 4.1.1  Length

Dynamic arrays remember their length. To access it, use the array's `.length` property:

```
auto array = new short[55];
assert(array.length == 55);
```

The expression `array.length` occurs frequently inside an index expression for `array`. For example, the last element of `array` is `array[array.length - 1]`. To simplify such cases, the symbol $ inside an index expression stands for "the length of the array being indexed into."

```
auto array = new int[10];
array[9] = 42;
assert(array[$ - 1] == 42);
```

Effecting changes to an array's length is discussed in § 4.1.8 on page 102, § 4.1.9 on page 103, and § 4.1.10 on page 106.

### 4.1.2  Bounds Checking

What happens if you do this?

```
auto array = new int[10];
auto invalid = array[100];
```

Given that arrays already know their own length, it is possible to insert the appropriate bounds checks, so feasibility is not an issue. The only problem is that bounds checking is one of the instances that painfully put efficiency and safety at odds.

For safety reasons, it is imperative to make sure, one way or another, that array accesses are within bounds. Out-of-bounds accesses may exhibit arbitrary behavior and expose the program to exploits and breakages.

However, thorough bounds checking still affects efficiency considerably with current compiler technology. Efficient bounds checking is the target of intensive research. One popular approach is to start with a fully checked program and remove as many checks as a static analyzer can prove redundant. In the general case that quickly becomes difficult, in particular when uses of arrays cross procedure and module boundaries. Today's approaches require a long analysis time even for modest programs and remove only a fraction of checks [58].

D is in a conflicted position regarding the bounds checking conundrum. The language is trying to offer at the same time the safety and convenience of modern languages and the ultimate unmuffled performance sought by system-level programmers. The bounds checking issue implies a choice between the two, and D allows you to make that choice instead of making it for you.

D makes two distinctions during compilation:

- Safe module versus system module (§ 11.2.2 on page 355)
- Non-release build versus release build (§ 10.6 on page 324)

D distinguishes between modules that are "safe" and modules that are "system." An intermediate safety level is "trusted," which means the module exposes a safe interface but may use system-level access in its implementation. You get to decide how to categorize each module. When compiling a safe module, the compiler statically disables all language features that could cause memory corruption, including unchecked array indexing. When compiling a system or trusted module, the compiler allows raw, unchecked access to hardware. You may choose whether a given portion of a module is safe, system, or trusted by using a command-line option or by inserting an attribute like this:

```
@safe:
```

or

```
@trusted:
```

or

```
@system:
```

From the point of insertion on, the chosen safety level is in action until another one is used or until end of file.

Chapter 11 explains in detail how module safety works, but at this point the important tidbit of information is that there are ways for you, the application developer, to choose whether a module you're working on is @safe, @trusted, or @system. Most, if not all, modules of a typical application should be @safe.

Module safety is orthogonal to choosing a *release* build for your application. You direct the D compiler to build a release version by passing it a command-line flag (-release in the reference implementation). In a safe module, array bounds are *always* checked. In a system module, bounds checks are inserted only for non-release builds. In a non-release build, the compiler also inserts other checks such as assert expressions and contract assertions (see Chapter 10 for a thorough discussion of what the release mode entails). The interaction between safe versus system modules and release versus non-release modes is summarized in Table 4.1.

**Table 4.1:** Presence of bounds checking depending on module kind and build mode

|  | Safe module | System module |
|---|:---:|:---:|
| Non-release build | ✔ | ✔ |
| Release build (-release flag on dmd) | ✔ | ☠ |

You've been warned.

### 4.1.3 Slicing

Slicing is a powerful feature that allows you to select and work with only a contiguous portion of an array. For example, say you want to print only the last half of an array:

```
import std.stdio;

void main() {
    auto array = [0, 1, 2, 3, 4, 5, 6, 7, 8, 9];
    // Print only the last half
    writeln(array[$ / 2 .. $]);
}
```

The program above prints

```
5 6 7 8 9
```

To extract a slice out of array, use the notation array[m .. n], which extracts the portion of the array starting at index m and ending with (and including) index n - 1. The slice has the same type as array itself, so you can, for example, reassign the slice back to the array it originated from:

```
array = array[$ / 2 .. $];
```

The symbol $ may participate in an expression inside either limit of the slice and—just as in the case of simple indexing—stands in for the length of the array being sliced. The situation m == n is acceptable and yields an empty slice. However, slices with m > n or n > array.length are illegal. Checking for such illegal cases obeys the bounds checking rules described previously (§ 4.1.2 on page 95).

The expression array[0 .. $] extracts a slice including the entire contents of array. That expression is encountered quite often, so the language gives a hand by making array[] equivalent to array[0 .. $].

### 4.1.4 Copying

At a minimum, an array object keeps (or can compute in negligible time) two key pieces of information, namely the upper and lower bounds of its data chunk. For example, executing

```
auto a = [1, 5, 2, 3, 6];
```

leads to a state illustrated in Figure 4.1. The array "sees" only the region between its bounds; the hashed area is inaccessible to it.

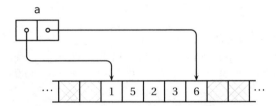

**Figure 4.1:** An array object referring to a chunk of five elements.

(Other representations are possible, for example, storing the address of the first element and the length of the block, or the address of the first element and the address just past the last element. All representations have access to the same essential information.)

Initializing one array from another (auto b = a;) or assigning one array from another (int[] b; ... b = a;) does not automatically copy data under the hood. Such operations simply make b refer to the same memory chunk as a, as shown in Figure 4.2 on the facing page.

Furthermore, taking a slice off b reduces the chunk "seen" by b, again without copying it. Starting from the state in Figure 4.2 on the next page, if we now execute

```
b = b[1 .. $ - 2];
```

then b shrinks in range, again without any data copying (Figure 4.3 on the facing page).

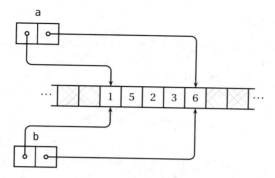

**Figure 4.2:** Executing `auto b = a;` does not copy the contents of a but creates a new array object referring to the same chunk of data.

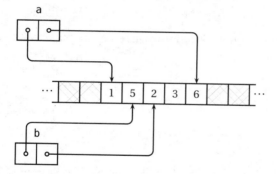

**Figure 4.3:** Executing `b = b[1 .. $ - 2];` shrinks the chunk controlled by b without copying the selected slice.

As a direct consequence of the data sharing illustrated in the figures, writing an element of one array may be reflected in others:

```
int[] array = [0, 1, 2];
int[] subarray = array[1 .. $];
assert(subarray.length == 2);
subarray[1] = 33;
assert(array[2] == 33); // Writing to subarray affected array
```

### 4.1.5   Comparing for Equality

The expression a is b (§ 2.3.4.3 on page 48) compares the bounds of the two arrays for equality and yields true if and only if a and b are bound to the same exact region of memory. No comparison of content is carried out at all.

To compare arrays a and b for element-for-element equality, use a == b or its negation a != b (§ 2.3.12 on page 56).

```
auto a = ["hello", "world"];
auto b = a;
assert(a is b);             // Pass, a and b have the same bounds
assert(a == b);             // Pass, of course
b = a.dup;
assert(a == b);             // Pass, a and b are equal although
                            //    they have different locations

assert(a !is b);            // Pass, a and b are different although
                            //    they have equal contents
```

Comparing for equality iterates in lockstep through all elements of the two arrays and compares them in turn with ==.

### 4.1.6   Concatenating

The construct

```
lhs ~ rhs
```

is a concatenation expression. The result of the concatenation is a new array with the contents of lhs followed by the contents of rhs. You may concatenate two arrays of types T[] and T[]; array with value (T[] and T); and value with array (T and T[]).

```
int[] a = [0, 10, 20];
int[] b = a ~ 42;
assert(b == [0, 10, 20, 42]);
a = b ~ a ~ 15;
assert(a.length == 8);
```

A concatenation always allocates a new array.

### 4.1.7   Array-wise Expressions

A few operations apply to arrays as a whole, without any explicit iteration. To create an array-wise expression, specify a trailing [] or [m .. n] on all slices involved in the expression, including the *left*-hand side of assignments, like this:

```
auto a = [ 0.5, -0.5, 1.5, 2 ];
auto b = [ 3.5, 5.5, 4.5, -1 ];
auto c = new double[4];            // Must be already allocated
c[] = (a[] + b[]) / 2;             // Take the average of a and b
assert(c == [ 2.0, 2.5, 3.0, 0.5 ]);
```

An array-wise expression has one of the following forms:

- A single value, such as 5
- A slice explicitly trailed with [] or [m .. n], such as a[] or a[1 .. $ - 1]
- Any valid D expression involving the two terms above, the unary operators - and ~, and the binary operators +, -, *, /, %, ^^, ^, &, |, =, +=, -=, *=, /=, %=, ^=, &=, and |=

The effect of an array-wise expression is that of a loop assigning each element of the left-hand side in turn with the corresponding index of the right-hand side. For example, the assignment

```
auto a = [1.0, 2.5, 3.6];
auto b = [4.5, 5.5, 1.4];
auto c = new double[3];
c[] += 4 * a[] + b[];
```

is the same as

```
foreach (i; 0 .. c.length) {
   c[i] += 4 * a[i] + b[i];
}
```

Bounds checking rules apply normally according to § 4.1.2 on page 95.

Using slices suffixed with [] or '[m .. n]', numbers, and the allowed operators, you may form parenthesized expressions of any depth and complexity, for example:

```
double[] a, b, c;
double d;
...
a[] = -(b[] * (c[] + 4)) + c[] * d;
```

One popular use of array-wise operations is simple filling and copying:

```
int[] a = new int[128];
int[] b = new int[128];
...
b[] = -1;                  // Fill all of b with -1
a[] = b[];                 // Copy b's data over a's data
```

**Warning** Array-wise operations are powerful, but with great power comes great responsibility. You are responsible for making sure that the lvalue and the rvalue parts of any assignment in an array-wise operation do not overlap. The compiler is free to assume that when optimizing the operations into primitive vector operations offered by the host processor. If you do have overlapping, you'll need to write the loops by hand, in which case the compiler is not allowed to make any unchecked assumptions.

### 4.1.8 Shrinking

Array shrinking means that the array should "forget" about some elements from either the left or the right end, without needing to move the rest. The restriction on moving is important; if moving elements were an option, arrays would be easy to shrink—just create a new copy containing the elements to be kept.

Shrinking an array is the easiest thing: just assign to the array a slice of itself.

```
auto array = [0, 2, 4, 6, 8, 10];
array = array[0 .. $ - 2];          // Right-shrink by two elements
assert(array == [0, 2, 4, 6]);
array = array[1 .. $];              // Left-shrink by one element
assert(array == [2, 4, 6]);
array = array[1 .. $ - 1];          // Shrink from both sides
assert(array == [4]);
```

All shrink operations take time independent of the array's length (practically they consist only of a couple of word assignments). Affordable shrinking from both ends is a very useful feature of D arrays. (Other languages allow cheap array shrinking from the right, but not from the left because the latter would involve moving over all elements of the array to preserve the location of the array's left edge.) In D you can take a copy of the array and progressively shrink it to systematically manipulate elements of the array, confident that the constant-time shrinking operations have no significant impact upon the processing time.

For example, let's write a little program that detects palindrome arrays passed via the command line. A palindrome array is left-right symmetric; for example, [5, 17, 8, 17, 5] is a palindrome, but [5, 7, 8, 7] is not. We need to avail ourselves of a few helpers. One is command line fetching, which nicely comes as an array of strings if you define main as main(string[] args). Then we need to convert arguments from strings to ints, for which we use the function aptly named to in the std.conv module. For some string str, evaluating to!int(str) parses str into an int. Armed with these features, we can write the palindrome test program like this:

```
import std.conv, std.stdio;

int main(string[] args) {
```

```
// Get rid of the program name
args = args[1 .. $];
while (args.length >= 2) {
    if (to!int(args[0]) != to!int(args[$ - 1])) {
        writeln("not palindrome");
        return 1;
    }
    args = args[1 .. $ - 1];
}
writeln("palindrome");
return 0;
}
```

First, the program must get rid of the program name from the argument list, which follows a tradition established by C. When you invoke our program (call it "palindrome") like this:

```
palindrome 34 95 548
```

then the array args contains ["palindrome", "34", "95", "548"]. Here's where shrinking from the left args = args[1 .. $] comes in handy, reducing args to ["34", "95", "548"]. Then the program iteratively compares the two ends of the array. If they are different, there's no purpose in continuing to test, so write "no palindrome" and bail out. If the test succeeds, args is reduced simultaneously from its left and right ends. Only if all tests succeed and args got shorter than two elements (the program considers arrays of zero or one element palindromes), the program prints "palindrome" and exits. Although it does a fair amount of array manipulation, the program does not allocate any memory—it just starts with the preallocated array args and shrinks it.

### 4.1.9 Expanding

On to expanding arrays. To expand an array, use the append operator '~=', for example:

```
auto a = [87, 40, 10];
a ~= 42;
assert(a == [87, 40, 10, 42]);
a ~= [5, 17];
assert(a == [87, 40, 10, 42, 5, 17]);
```

Expanding arrays has a couple of subtleties that concern possible reallocation of the array. Consider:

```
auto a = [87, 40, 10, 2];
auto b = a;                    // Now a and b refer to the same chunk
```

```
a ~= [5, 17];        // Append to a
a[0] = 15;           // Modify a[0]
assert(b[0] == 15);  // Pass or fail?
```

Does the post-append assignment to a[0] also affect b[0], or, in other words, do a and b still share data post-reallocation? The short answer is, b[0] may or may not be 15—the language makes no guarantee.

Realistically, there is no way to always have enough room at the end of a to reallocate it in place. At least sometimes, reallocation must occur. One easy way out would be to *always* reallocate a upon appending to it with ~=, thereby always making a ~= b the same exact thing as a = a ~ b, that is, "Allocate a new array consisting of a concatenated with b and then bind a to that new array." Although that behavior is easiest to implement, it has serious efficiency problems. For example, oftentimes arrays are iteratively grown in a loop:

```
int[] a;
foreach (i; 0 .. 100) {
    a ~= i;
}
```

For 100 elements, pretty much any expansion scheme would work, but when arrays become larger, only solid solutions can remain reasonably fast. One particularly unsavory approach would be to allow the convenient but inefficient expansion syntax a ~= b and encourage it for short arrays but discourage it on large arrays in favor of another, less convenient syntax. At best, the simplest and most intuitive syntax works for short and long arrays.

D leaves ~= the freedom of either expanding by reallocation or opportunistically expanding in place if there is enough unused memory at the end of the current array. The decision belongs entirely to the implementation of ~=, but client code is guaranteed good *average* performance over a large number of appends to the same array.

Figure 4.4 on the facing page illustrates the two possible outcomes of the expansion request a ~= [5, 17].

Depending on how the underlying memory allocator works, an array can expand in more ways than one:

- Often, allocators can allocate chunks only in specific sizes (e.g., powers of 2). It is therefore possible that a request for 700 bytes would receive 1024 bytes of storage, of which 324 are slack. When an expansion request occurs, the array may check whether there's slack storage and use it.
- If there is no slack space left, the array may initiate a more involved negotiation with the underlying memory allocator. "You know, I'm sitting here and could use some space to the right. Is by any chance the adjacent block available?" The allocator may find an empty block to the right of the current block and gobble it into

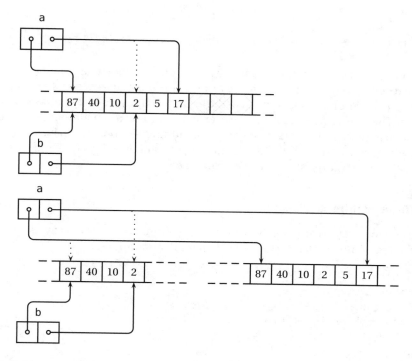

**Figure 4.4:** Two possible outcomes of an attempt to expand array a. In the first case (top), the memory chunk had available memory at its end, which is used for in-place expansion. In the second case, there was no more available room so a new chunk was allocated and a was adjusted to refer to it. Consequently, after expansion, a's and b's chunks may or may not overlap.

its own block. This operation is known as *coalescing*. Then expansion can still proceed without moving any data.

- Finally, if there is absolutely no room in the current block, the array allocates a brand-new block and copies all of its data in it. The implementation may deliberately allocate extra slack space when, for example, it detects repeated expansions of the same array.

An expanding array never stomps on an existing array. For example:

```
int[] a = [0, 10, 20, 30, 40, 50, 60, 70];
auto b = a[4 .. $];
a = a[0 .. 4];
// At this point a and b are adjacent
```

```
a ~= [0, 0, 0, 0];
assert(b == [40, 50, 60, 70]); // Pass; a got reallocated
```

The code above is carefully crafted to fool a into thinking it has room at its end: initially a received a larger size, and then b received the upper part of a and a got reduced to its lower part. Prior to appending to a, the arrays occupy adjacent chunks with a to the left of b. The post-append assert, however, confirms that a actually got reallocated, not expanded in place. The append operator appends in place only when it can prove there is no other array to the right of the expanding one and is always free to conservatively reallocate whenever the slightest suspicion is afoot.

### 4.1.10  Assigning to .length

Assigning to array.length allows you to either shrink or expand array, depending on the relation of the new length to the old length. For example:

```
int[] array;
assert(array.length == 0);
array.length = 1000;          // Grow
assert(array.length == 1000);
array.length = 500;
assert(array.length == 500);  // Shrink
```

If the array grows as a result of assigning to .length, the added elements are initialized with T.init. The growth strategy and guarantees are identical to those of the append operator ~= (§ 4.1.9 on page 103).

If the array shrinks as a result of assigning to .length, D guarantees the array is not reallocated. Practically, if n <= a.length, a.length = n is equivalent to a = a[0 .. n]. (However, that guarantee does not also imply that further expansions of the array will avoid reallocation.)

You may carry out read-modify-write operations with .length, for example:

```
auto array = new int[10];
array.length += 1000;         // Grow
assert(array.length == 1010);
array.length /= 10;
assert(array.length == 101);  // Shrink
```

Not much magic happens here; all the compiler does is to rewrite array.length ‹op›= b into array.length = array.length ‹op› b. There is some minor magic involved, though (just a sleight of hand, really): array is evaluated only once in the rewritten expression, which is relevant if array is actually some elaborate expression.

## 4.2 Fixed-Size Arrays

D offers arrays of a size known during compilation, declared, for example, like this:

```
int[128] someInts;
```

For each type T and size n, the type T[n] is distinct from any other—for example, uint[10] is distinct from uint[11] and also from int[10].

All fixed-size array values are allocated statically at the place of declaration. If the array value is defined globally, it goes in the per-thread data segment of the program. If allocated inside a function, the array will be allocated on the stack of that function upon the function call. (This means that defining very large arrays in functions may be dangerous.) If, however, you define such an array with static inside a function, the array is allocated in the per-thread data segment so there is no risk of stack overflow.

Upon creation, a fixed-size array T[n] value has all of its data initialized to T.init. For example:

```
int[3] a;
assert(a == [0, 0, 0]);
```

You can initialize a T[n] with a literal:

```
int[3] a = [1, 2, 3];
assert(a == [1, 2, 3]);
```

Beware, however: if you replace int[3] above with auto, a's type will be deduced as int[], not int[3]. Although it seems logical that the type of [1, 2, 3] should be int[3], which in a way is more "precise" than int[], it turns out that dynamically sized arrays are used much more often than fixed-size arrays, so insisting on fixed-size array literals would have been a usability impediment and a source of unpleasant surprises. Effectively, the use of literals would have prevented the gainful use of auto. As it is, array literals are T[] by default, and T[n] if you *ask* for that specific type and if n matches the number of values in the literal (as the code above shows).

If you initialize a fixed-size array of type T[n] with a single value of type T, the entire array will be filled with that value:

```
int[4] a = -1;
assert(a == [-1, -1, -1, -1]);
```

If you plan to leave the array uninitialized and fill it at runtime, just specify void as an initializer:

```
int[1024] a = void;
```

Such uninitialized arrays are particularly useful for large arrays that serve as temporary buffers. But beware—an uninitialized integral may not cause too much harm, but uninitialized values of types with indirections (such as multidimensional arrays) are unsafe.

Accessing elements of fixed-size arrays is done by using the indexing operator a[i], the same way as for dynamic arrays. Iteration is also virtually identical to that of dynamic arrays. For example, creating an array of 1024 random numbers would go like this:

```
import std.random;

void main() {
   double[1024] array;
   foreach (i;  0 .. array.length) {
      array[i] = uniform(0.0, 1.0);
   }
   ...
}
```

The loop could use `ref` values to use array elements without indexing:

```
foreach (ref element; array) {
   element = uniform(0.0, 1.0);
}
```

### 4.2.1  Length

Obviously, fixed-size arrays are aware of their length because it's stuck in their very type. Unlike dynamic arrays' length, the `.length` property is read-only and a static constant. This means you can use `array.length` for fixed-size arrays whenever a compile-time constant is required, for example, in the length of another fixed-size array definition:

```
int[100] quadrupeds;
int[4 * quadrupeds.length] legs; // Fine, 400 legs
```

Inside an index expression for array a, $ can be used in lieu of a.length and is, again, a compile-time expression.

### 4.2.2  Bounds Checking

Bounds checking for fixed-size arrays has an interesting twist. Whenever indexing is used with a compile-time expression, the compiler checks validity during compilation and refuses to compile in case of an out-of-bounds access. For example:

```
int[10] array;
array[15] = 5;  // Error!
```

```
// Array index 15 is out of bounds a[0 .. 10]!
```

If the expression is a runtime value, compile-time bounds checking is done on a best-effort basis, and runtime checking follows the same protocol as bounds checking for dynamic arrays (§ 4.1.2 on page 95).

### 4.2.3 Slicing

Taking any slice off an array of type T[n] yields an array of type T[] without an intervening copy:

```
int[5] array = [40, 30, 20, 10, 0];
auto slice1 = array[2 .. $];        // slice1 has type int[]
assert(slice1 == [20, 10, 0]);
auto slice2 = array[];              // Same as array[0 .. $]
assert(slice2 == array);
```

Compile-time bounds checking is carried out against either or both bounds when they are compile-time constants.

If you take a slice with compile-time-known limits T[a1 .. a2] off an array T[n], *and* if you request an array of type T[a2 - a1], the compiler grants the request. (The default type yielded by the slice operation—e.g., if you use auto—is still T[].) For example:

```
int[10] a;
int[] b = a[1 .. 7];   // Fine
auto c = a[1 .. 7];    // Fine, c also has type int[]
int[6] d = a[1 .. 7];  // Fine, a[1 .. 7] copied into d
```

### 4.2.4 Copying and Implicit Conversion

Unlike dynamic arrays, fixed-size arrays have value semantics. This means that copying arrays, passing them into functions, and returning them from functions all copy entire arrays. For example:

```
int[3] a = [1, 2, 3];
int[3] b = a;
a[1] = 42;
assert(b[1] == 2); // b is an independent copy of a
int[3] fun(int[3] x, int[3] y) {
   // x and y are copies of the arguments
   x[0] = y[0] = 100;
   return x;
}
```

```
auto c = fun(a, b);          // c has type int[3]
assert(c == [100, 42, 3]);
assert(b == [1, 2, 3]);      // b is unaffected by fun
```

Passing entire arrays by value may be inefficient for large arrays, but it has many advantages. One advantage is that short arrays and pass-by-value are frequently used in high-performance computing. Another advantage is that pass-by-value has a simple cure—whenever you want reference semantics, just use `ref` or automatic conversion to `T[]` (see the next paragraph). Finally, value semantics makes fixed-size arrays consistent with many other aspects of the language. (Historically, D had reference semantics for fixed-size arrays, which turned out to be a continuous source of contortions and special casing in client code.)

Arrays of type `T[n]` are implicitly convertible to arrays of type `T[]`. The dynamic array thus obtained is not allocated anew—it simply latches on to the bounds of the source array. Therefore, the conversion is considered unsafe if the source array is stack-allocated. The implicit conversion makes it easy to pass fixed-size arrays of type `T[n]` to functions expecting `T[]`. However, if a function has `T[n]` as its return type, its result cannot be automatically converted to `T[]`.

```
double[3] point = [0, 0, 0];
double[] test = point;       // Fine
double[3] fun(double[] x) {
    double[3] result;
    result[] = 2 * x[];      // Array-wise operation
    return result;
}
auto r = fun(point);         // Fine, r has type double[3]
```

You can duplicate a fixed-size array with the `.dup` property (§ 4.1 on page 93), but you don't get an object of type `T[n]` back; you get a dynamically allocated array of type `T[]` that contains a copy of the fixed-size array. This behavior is sensible given that you otherwise don't need to duplicate a fixed-size array—to obtain a duplicate of a, just say `auto copy = a`. With `.dup`, you get to make a dynamic copy of a fixed-size array.

### 4.2.5   Comparing for Equality

Fixed-size arrays may be compared with `is` and `==`, just like dynamic arrays (§ 4.1.5 on page 100). You may also transparently mix fixed-size and dynamic-size arrays in comparisons:

```
int[4] fixed = [1, 2, 3, 4];
auto anotherFixed = fixed;
assert(anotherFixed !is fixed); // Not the same (value semantics)
```

```
assert(anotherFixed == fixed);   // Same data
auto dynamic = fixed[];          // Fetches the limits of fixed
assert(dynamic is fixed);
assert(dynamic == fixed);        // Obviously
dynamic = dynamic.dup;           // Creates a copy
assert(dynamic !is fixed);
assert(dynamic == fixed);
```

### 4.2.6 Concatenating

Concatenation follows rules similar to those governing concatenation of dynamic arrays (§ 4.1.6 on page 100). There is one important difference. If you *ask* for a fixed-size array, you get a fixed-size array. Otherwise, you get a newly allocated dynamic array. For example:

```
double[2] a;
double[] b = a ~ 0.5;     // Concat double[2] with value, get double[]
auto c = a ~ 0.5;         // Same as above
double[3] d = a ~ 1.5;    // Fine, explicitly ask for fixed-size array
double[5] e = a ~ d;      // Fine, explicitly ask for fixed-size array
```

Whenever a fixed-array is requested as the result of the concatenating operator ~, there is no dynamic allocation—the result is statically allocated and the result of the concatenation is copied into it.

### 4.2.7 Array-wise Operations

Array-wise operations on static arrays work similarly to those for dynamic arrays (§ 4.1.7 on page 100). Wherever possible, the compiler performs compile-time bounds checking for arrays bearing static lengths involved in an array-wise expression. You may mix fixed-size and dynamic arrays in expressions.

## 4.3 Multidimensional Arrays

Since T[] is a dynamic array with elements of type T, and T[] itself is a type, it's easy to infer that T[][] is an array of T[]s, or, put another way, an array of arrays of Ts. Each element of the outer array is in turn an array offering the usual array primitives. Let's give T[][] a test drive.

```
auto array = new double[][5];   // Array of five arrays of double,
                                //    each initially null
// Make a triangular matrix
```

```
foreach (i, ref e; array) {
   e = new double[array.length - i];
}
```

The shape of `array` defined above is triangular: the first row has five `doubles`, the second has four, and so on to the fifth one (technically row four), which has one element. Multidimensional arrays obtained by simply composing dynamic arrays are called *jagged arrays* because their rows may assume arbitrary lengths (as opposed to the somewhat expected straight right edge obtained when all rows have the same length). Figure 4.5 illustrates `array`'s emplacement in memory.

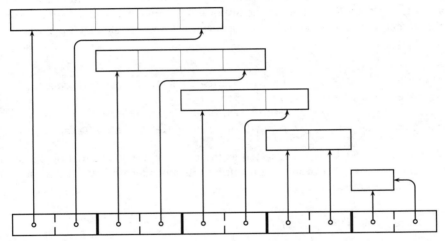

**Figure 4.5:** A jagged array storing a triangular matrix as defined in the example on the previous page.

To access an element in a jagged array, specify indices for each dimension in turn; for example, `array[3][1]` accesses the second element in the fourth row of a jagged array.

Jagged arrays are not contiguous. On the plus side, this means that jagged arrays can spread themselves in memory and require smaller amounts of contiguous memory. The ability to store rows of different lengths may save quite a bit of memory, too. On the minus side, "tall and thin" arrays with many rows and few columns incur a large size overhead as there's one array to keep per column. For example, one array with 1,000,000 rows each having only 10 integers needs to hold an array of 2,000,000 words (one array per row) plus the management overhead of 1,000,000 small blocks, which, depending on the memory allocator implementation, may be considerable relative to the small per-row payload of 10 `ints` (40 bytes).

Jagged arrays may have problems with efficiency of access and cache friendliness. Each element access requires two indirections, first through the outer array corresponding to the row, and then through the inner array corresponding to the column. Iterating row-wise is not much of a problem if you first fetch the row and then use it, but going column-wise through a jagged array is a cache miss bonanza.

If the number of columns is known during compilation, you can easily compose a fixed-size array with a dynamic array:

```
enum size_t columns = 128;
// Define a matrix with 64 rows and 128 columns
auto matrix = new double[columns][64];
// No need to allocate each row - they already exist in situ
foreach (ref row; matrix) {
    ... // Use row of type double[columns]
}
```

In the example above it is crucial to use `ref` with `foreach`. Without `ref`, the value semantics of `double[columns]` (§ 4.2.4 on page 109) would create a copy of each row being iterated, which is likely to put a damper on the speed of your code.

If you know the number of both rows and columns during compilation, you may want to use a fixed-size array of fixed-size arrays, as follows:

```
enum size_t rows = 64, columns = 128;
// Allocate a matrix with 64 rows and 128 columns
double[columns][rows] matrix;
// No need to allocate the array at all - it's a value
foreach (ref row; matrix) {
    ... // Use row of type double[columns]
}
```

To access an element at row `i` and column `j`, write `matrix[i][j]`. One small oddity is that the declaration specifies the sizes for each dimension in right-to-left order (i.e., `double[columns][rows]`), but when accessing elements, indices come in left-to-right order. This is because `[]` and `[n]` in types bind right to left, but in expressions they bind left to right.

A variety of multidimensional array shapes can be created by composing fixed-size arrays and dynamic arrays. For example, `int[5][][15]` is a three-dimensional array consisting of 15 arrays, each being a dynamically allocated array of blocks of five `int`s each.

## 4.4  Associative Arrays

An array could be thought of as a function that maps positive integers (indices) to values of some arbitrary type (the data stored in the array). The function is defined only for integers from zero to the array's length minus one and is entirely tabulated by the contents of the array.

Seen from that angle, associative arrays introduce a certain generalization of arrays. Instead of integers, an associative array may accept an (almost) arbitrary type as its domain. For each value in the domain, it is possible to map a value of a different type—similarly to an array's slot. The storage method and associated algorithms are different from those of arrays, but, much like an array, an associative array offers fast storage and retrieval of a value given its key.

The type of an associative array is suggestively denoted as V[K], where K is the key type and V is the associated value type. For example, let's create and initialize an associative array that maps strings to integers:

```
int[string] aa = [ "hello":42, "world":75 ];
```

An associative array literal (introduced in § 2.2.6 on page 39) is a comma-separated list of terms of the form key : value, enclosed in square brackets. In the case above the literal is informative enough to make the explicit type of aa redundant, so it's more comfortable to write

```
auto aa = [ "hello":42, "world":75 ];
```

### 4.4.1  Length

For an associative array aa, the property aa.length of type size_t yields the number of keys in aa (and also the number of values, given that there is a one-to-one mapping of keys to values). The type of aa.length is size_t.

A default-constructed associative array has length equal to zero and also compares equal to null.

```
string[int] aa;
assert(aa == null);
assert(aa.length == 0);
aa = [0:"zero", 1:"not zero"];
assert(aa.length == 2);
```

Unlike the homonym property for arrays, associative arrays' .length is not writable. You may, however, write null to an associative array to clear it.

### 4.4.2 Reading and Writing Slots

To write a new key/value pair into aa, or to overwrite the value currently stored for that key, just assign to aa[key] like this:

```
// Create a string-to-string associative array
auto aa = [ "hello":"salve", "world":"mundi" ];
// Overwrite values
aa["hello"] = "ciao";
aa["world"] = "mondo";
// Create some new key/value pairs
aa["cabbage"] = "cavolo";
aa["mozzarella"] = "mozzarella";
```

To read a value off an associative array given a key, just read aa[key]. (The compiler distinguishes reads from writes and invokes slightly different functions.) Continuing the example above:

```
assert(aa["hello"] == "ciao");
```

If you try to read the value for a key not found in the associative array, a range violation exception is thrown. Oftentimes, throwing an exception in case a key doesn't exist is a bit too harsh to be useful, so associative arrays offer a read with a default in the form of a two-argument get method. In the call aa.get(key, defaultValue), if key is found in the map, its corresponding value is returned and defaultValue is not evaluated; otherwise, defaultValue is evaluated and returned as the result of get.

```
assert(aa["hello"] == "ciao");
// Key "hello" exists, therefore ignore the second argument
assert(aa.get("hello", "salute") == "ciao");
// Key "yo" doesn't exist, return the second argument
assert(aa.get("yo", "buongiorno") == "buongiorno");
```

If you want to peacefully test for the existence of a key in an associative array, use the in operator:

```
assert("hello" in aa);
assert("yowza" !in aa);
// Trying to read aa["yowza"] would throw
```

### 4.4.3 Copying

Associative arrays are sheer references with shallow copying: copying or assigning associative arrays just creates new aliases for the same underlying slots. For example:

```
auto a1 = [ "Jane":10.0, "Jack":20, "Bob":15 ];
auto a2 = a1;                    // a1 and a2 refer to the same data
a1["Bob"] = 100;                 // Changing a1...
assert(a2["Bob"] == 100);        // ...is the same as changing a2...
a2["Sam"] = 3.5;                 // ...and vice
assert(a2["Sam"] == 3.5);        //     versa
```

### 4.4.4   Comparing for Equality

The operators is, ==, and != work the expected way. For two associative arrays of the same type a and b, the expression a is b yields true if and only if a and b refer to the same associative array (e.g., one was initialized as a copy of the other). The expression a == b compares the key/value pairs of two arrays with == in turn. For a and b to be equal, they must have equal key sets and equal values associated with each key.

```
auto a1 = [ "Jane":10.0, "Jack":20, "Bob":15 ];
auto a2 = [ "Jane":10.0, "Jack":20, "Bob":15 ];
assert(a1 !is a2);
assert(a1 == a2);
a2["Bob"] = 18;
assert(a1 != a2);
```

### 4.4.5   Removing Elements

To remove a key/value pair from the map, pass the key to the remove method of the associative array.

```
auto aa = [ "hello":1, "goodbye":2 ];
aa.remove("hello");
assert("hello" !in aa);
aa.remove("yowza");              // Has no effect: "yowza" was not in aa
```

The remove method returns a bool that is true if the deleted key was in the associative array, or false otherwise.

### 4.4.6   Iterating

You can iterate an associative array by using the good old foreach statement (§ 3.7.5 on page 75). The key/value slots are iterated in an unspecified order:

```
import std.stdio;
```

```
void main() {
    auto coffeePrices = [
        "french vanilla" : 8.75,
        "java" : 7.99,
        "french roast" : 7.49
    ];
    foreach (kind, price; coffeePrices) {
        writefln("%s costs $%s per pound", kind, price);
    }
}
```

The program above will print

```
french vanilla costs $8.75 per pound
java costs $7.99 per pound
french roast costs $7.49 per pound
```

To fetch a copy of all keys in an array, use the .keys property. For an associative array aa of type V[K], the type returned by aa.keys is K[].

```
auto gammaFunc = [-1.5:2.363, -0.5:-3.545, 0.5:1.772];
double[] keys = gammaFunc.keys;
assert(keys == [ -1.5, 0.5, -0.5 ]);
```

Similarly, for aa of type V[K], the aa.values property yields the values stored in aa as an array of type V[]. Generally, it is preferable to iterate with foreach instead of fetching keys of values because the properties allocate a new array, which may be a considerable size for large associative arrays.

Two methods offer iteration through the keys and the values of an associative array without creating new arrays: aa.byKey() spans only the keys of the associative array aa, and aa.byValue() spans the values. For example:

```
auto gammaFunc = [-1.5:2.363, -0.5:-3.545, 0.5:1.772];
// Write all keys
foreach (k; gammaFunc.byKey()) {
    writeln(k);
}
```

### 4.4.7  User-Defined Types as Keys

Internally, associative arrays use hashing and sorting for keys to ensure fast retrieval of values given keys. For a user-defined type to be used as a key in an associative array, it must define two special methods, opHash and opCmp. We haven't yet learned how to define user-defined types and methods, so for now let's defer that discussion to Chapter 6.

## 4.5  Strings

Strings receive special treatment in D. Two decisions made early in the definition of the language turned out to be winning bets. First, D embraces Unicode as its standard character set. Unicode is today's most popular and comprehensive standard for defining and representing textual data. Second, D chose UTF-8, UTF-16, and UTF-32 as its native encodings, without favoring any and without preventing your code from using other encodings.

In order to understand how D deals with text, we need to acquire some knowledge of Unicode and UTF. For an in-depth treatment, *Unicode Explained* [36] is a useful resource; the Unicode Consortium Standard document, currently in the fifth edition corresponding to version 5.1 of the Unicode standard [56], is the ultimate reference.

### 4.5.1  Code Points

One important fact about Unicode that, once understood, dissipates a lot of potential confusion is that Unicode separates the notion of abstract character, or *code point*, from the notion of representation, or *encoding*. This is a nontrivial distinction that often escapes the unwary, particularly because the well-known ASCII standard has no notion of separate representation. Good old ASCII maps each character commonly used in English text, plus a few "control codes," to a number between 0 and 127—that is, 7 bits. Since at the time ASCII got introduced most computers already used the 8-bit byte (octet) as a unit of addressing, there was no question about "encoding" ASCII text at all: use 7 bits off an octet; that was the encoding. (The remaining bit left the door open for creative uses, which led to a Cambrian explosion of mutually incompatible extensions.)

Unicode, in contrast, first defines code points, which are, simply put, numbers assigned to abstract characters. The abstract character "A" receives number 65, the abstract character € receives number 8364, and so on. Deciding which symbols deserve a place in the Unicode mapping and how to assign numbers to them is one important task of the Unicode Consortium, and that's great because the rest of us can use the mapping without worrying about the minutiae of defining and documenting it.

As of version 5.1, Unicode code points lie between 0 and 1,114,111 (the upper limit is more often expressed in hexadecimal: `0x10FFFF` or, in Unicode's specific spelling, `U+10FFFF`). A common misconception about Unicode is that 2 bytes are enough to represent any Unicode character, perhaps because some languages standardized on 2-byte characters originating in earlier versions of the Unicode standard. In fact, there are exactly 17 times more Unicode symbols than the 65,536 afforded by a 2-byte representation. (Truth be told, most of the higher code points are seldom used or not yet allocated.)

Anyhow, when discussing code points, representation should not necessarily come to mind. At the highest level, code points are a giant tabulated function mapping integers from 0 to 1,114,111 to abstract character entities. There are many details on how that numeric range is allocated, but that does not diminish the correctness of our highest-level description. Exactly how to put Unicode code points in sequences of bytes is something that *encodings* need to worry about.

### 4.5.2 Encodings

If Unicode simply followed ASCII's grand tradition, it would have just rounded the upper limit `0x10FFFF` to the next byte, obtaining a simple 3-byte representation for each code point. This potential representation has an issue, however. Most text in English or other Latin-derived writing systems would use a statistically very narrow range of code points (numbers), which leads to wasted space. The storage for the typical Latin text would just blow up in size by a factor of three. Richer alphabets such as Asian writing systems would make better use of the three bytes, and that's fine because there would be fewer total symbols in the text (each symbol is more informative).

To address the issue of wasting space, Unicode adopted several *variable-length* encoding schemes. Such schemes use one or more narrow codes to represent the full range of Unicode code points. The narrow codes (usually 8- or 16-bit) are known as *code units*. Each code point is represented by one or more code units.

UTF-8 is the first encoding that was standardized. UTF-8, invented by Ken Thompson in one evening inside a New Jersey diner [47], is an almost canonical example of solid, ingenious design. The basic idea behind UTF-8 is to use 1 to 6 bytes for encoding any given character, and to add control bits to disambiguate between encodings of different lengths. UTF-8 is identical to ASCII for the first 127 code points. That instantly makes any ASCII text also valid UTF-8 text, which in and of itself was a brilliant move. For code points beyond the ASCII range, UTF-8 uses a variable-length encoding, shown in Table 4.2.

**Table 4.2:** UTF-8 encodings. The choice of control bits allows midstream synchronization, error recovery, and backward iteration.

| Code point (hex) | Codes (binary) |
| --- | --- |
| 00000000–0000007F | 0xxxxxxx |
| 00000080–000007FF | 110xxxxx 10xxxxxx |
| 00000800–0000FFFF | 1110xxxx 10xxxxxx 10xxxxxx |
| 00010000–001FFFFF | 11110xxx 10xxxxxx 10xxxxxx 10xxxxxx |
| 00200000–03FFFFFF | 111110xx 10xxxxxx 10xxxxxx 10xxxxxx 10xxxxxx |
| 04000000–7FFFFFFF | 1111110x 10xxxxxx 10xxxxxx 10xxxxxx 10xxxxxx 10xxxxxx |

Since today the range of defined Unicode code points stops at `0x10FFFF`, the last two sequences are reserved for future use; only up to 4-byte encodings are currently valid.

The control bit patterns chosen have two interesting properties:

1. A non-leading byte is never equal to a leading byte.
2. The first byte unambiguously determines the length of an encoding.

The first property is crucial because it enables two important applications. One is simple synchronization—if you pick up a UTF-8 transmission somewhere in midstream, you can easily figure out where the next code point starts: just look for the next byte with anything but 10 as its most significant bits. The other application is backward iteration—it is easy to go backward in a UTF-8 string without ever getting confused. Backward iteration opens UTF-8 strings to a host of algorithms (e.g., finding the last occurrence of a string in another can be implemented efficiently). The second property is not essential but simplifies and accelerates string processing.

Ideally, frequent code points should have small values and infrequent ones should have large values. If that condition is fulfilled, UTF-8 acts as a good statistical encoder by encoding more frequent symbols in fewer bits. This is certainly the case for Latin-derived languages, where most code units fit in 1 byte and the occasional accented characters fit in 2.

UTF-16 is also a variable-length encoding but uses a different (and arguably less elegant) approach to encoding. Code points between 0 and 0xFFFF are encoded as a sole 16-bit code unit and code points between 0x10000 and 0x10FFFF are represented by a pair in which the first code unit is in the range 0xD800 through 0xDBFF and the second code unit is in the range 0xDC00 through 0xDFFF. To support this encoding, Unicode allocates no valid characters to numbers in the range 0xD800 through 0xDBFF. The two ranges are called *high surrogate area* and *low surrogate area*, respectively.

One criticism commonly leveled against UTF-16 is that it makes the statistically rare cases also the most complicated and the ones deserving the most scrutiny. Most—but alas, not all—Unicode characters (the so-called Basic Multilingual Plane) *do* fit in one UTF-16 code unit, and therefore a lot of UTF-16 code tacitly assumes one code unit per character and is effectively untested for surrogate pairs. To further the confusion, some languages initially centered their string support around UCS-2, a precursor of UTF-16 with exactly 16 bits per code point, to later add UTF-16 support, subtly obsoleting older code that relied on a one-to-one mapping between characters and codes.

Finally, UTF-32 uses 32 bits per code unit, which allows a true one-to-one mapping of code points to code units. This means UTF-32 is the simplest and easiest-to-use representation, but it's also the most space-consuming. A common recommendation is to use UTF-8 for storage and UTF-32 temporarily during processing if necessary.

### 4.5.3 Character Types

D defines three character types: char, wchar, and dchar, representing code units for UTF-8, UTF-16, and UTF-32, respectively. Their .init values are intentionally invalid encodings: char.init is 0xFF, wchar.init is 0xFFFF, and dchar.init is 0x0000FFFF.

Table 4.2 on page 119 clarifies that `0xFF` may not be part of any valid UTF-8 encoding, and also Unicode deliberately assigns no valid code point for `0xFFFF`.

Used individually, the three character types mostly behave like unsigned integers and can occasionally be used to store invalid UTF code points (the compiler does not enforce valid encodings throughout), but the intended meaning of `char`, `wchar`, and `dchar` is as UTF code points. For general 8-, 16-, and 32-bit unsigned integers, or for using encodings other than UTF, it's best to use `ubyte`, `ushort`, and `uint`, respectively. For example, if you want to use pre-Unicode 8-bit code pages, you may want to use `ubyte`, not `char`, as your building block.

### 4.5.4 · Arrays of Characters + Benefits = Strings

When assembling any of the character types in an array—as in `char[]`, `wchar[]`, or `dchar[]`—the compiler and the runtime support library "understand" that you are working with UTF-encoded Unicode strings. Consequently, arrays of characters enjoy the power and versatility of general arrays, plus a few extra goodies as Unicode denizens.

In fact, D already defines three string types corresponding to the three character widths: `string`, `wstring`, and `dstring`. They are not special types at all; in fact, they are aliases for character array types, with a twist: the character type is adorned with the `immutable` qualifier to disallow arbitrary changes of individual characters in strings. For example, type `string` is a synonym for the more verbose type `immutable(char)[]`. We won't get to discussing type qualifiers such as `immutable` until Chapter 8, but for strings of all widths the effect of `immutable` is very simple: a `string`, aka an `immutable(char)[]`, is just like a `char[]` (and a `wstring` is just like a `wchar[]`, etc.), except you can't assign new values to individual characters in the string:

```
string a = "hello";
char h = a[0];        // Fine
a[0] = 'H';           // Error!
                      // Cannot assign to immutable(char)!
```

To change one individual character in a `string`, you need to create another `string` via concatenation:

```
string a = "hello";
a = 'H' ~ a[1 .. $]; // Fine, makes a == "Hello"
```

Why such a decision? After all, in the case above it's quite a waste to allocate a whole new `string` (recall from § 4.1.6 on page 100 that ~ always allocates a new array) instead of just modifying the existing one. There are, however, a few good reasons for disallowing modification of individual characters in strings. One reason is that `immutable` simplifies situations when `string`, `wstring`, and `dstring` objects are copied and then changed. Effectively `immutable` ensures no undue aliasing between strings. Consider:

```
string a = "hello";
string b = a;          // b is also "hello"
string c = b[0 .. 4];  // c is "hell"
// If this were allowed, it would change a, b, and c
// a[0] = 'H';
// The concatenation below leaves b and c unmodified
a = 'H' ~ a[1 .. $];
assert(a == "Hello" && b == "hello" && c == "hell");
```

With `immutable` characters, you know you can have several variables refer to the same string, without fearing that modifying one would also modify the others. Copying `string` objects is very cheap because it doesn't need to do any special copy management (such as eager copy or copy-on-write).

An equally strong reason for disallowing changes in strings at code unit level is that such changes don't make much sense anyway. Elements of a `string` are variable-length, and most of the time you want to replace logical characters (code points), not physical `chars` (code units), so you seldom want to do surgery on individual `chars`. It's much easier to write correct UTF code if you forgo individual `char` assignments and you focus instead on manipulating entire strings and fragments thereof. D's standard library sets the tone by fostering manipulation of strings as whole entities instead of focusing on indices and individual characters. However, UTF code is not trivially easy to write; for example, the concatenation `'H' ~ a[1 .. $]` above has a bug in the general case because it assumes that the first code point in a has exactly 1 byte. The correct way to go about it is

```
a = 'H' ~ a[stride(a, 0) .. $];
```

The function `stride`, found in the standard library module `std.utf`, returns the length of the code starting at a specified position in a string. (To use `stride` and related library artifacts, insert the line

```
import std.utf;
```

near the top of your program.) In our case, the call `stride(a, 0)` returns the length of the encoding for the first character (aka code point) in a, which we pass to select the offset marking the beginning of the second character.

A very visible artifact of the language's support for Unicode can be found in string literals, which we've already looked at (§ 2.2.5 on page 35). D string literals understand Unicode code points and automatically encode them appropriately for whichever encoding scheme you choose. For example:

```
import std.stdio;
```

```
void main() {
    string a = "No matter how you put it, a \u03bb costs \u20AC20.";
    wstring b = "No matter how you put it, a \u03bb costs \u20AC20.";
    dstring c = "No matter how you put it, a \u03bb costs \u20AC20.";
    writeln(a, '\n', b, '\n', c);
}
```

Although the internal representations of a, b, and c are very different, you don't need to worry about that because you express the literal in an abstract way by using code points. The compiler takes care of all encoding details, such that in the end the program prints three lines containing the same exact text:

```
No matter how you put it, a λ costs €20.
```

The encoding of the literal is determined by the context in which the literal occurs. In the cases above, the compiler has the literal morph without any runtime processing into the encodings UTF-8, UTF-16, and UTF-32 (corresponding to types string, wstring, and dstring), in spite of it being spelled the exact same way throughout. If the requested literal encoding is ambiguous, suffixing the literal with one of c, w, or d (something "like that"d) forces the encoding of the string to UTF-8, UTF-16, and UTF-32, respectively (refer to § 2.2.5.2 on page 37).

### 4.5.4.1 foreach with Strings

If you iterate a string str of any width like this:

```
foreach (c; str) {
    ... // Use c
}
```

then c will iterate every *code unit* of str. For example, if str is an array of char (immutable or not), c takes type char. This is expected from the general behavior of foreach with arrays but is sometimes undesirable for strings. For example, let's print each character of a string enclosed in square brackets:

```
void main() {
    string str = "Hall\u00E5, V\u00E4rld!";
    foreach (c; str) {
        write('[', c, ']');
    }
    writeln();
}
```

The program above ungainly prints

[H][a][l][l][ ? ][ ? ][,][ ][V][ ? ][ ? ][r][l][d][!]

The reverse video ? (which may vary depending on system and font used) is the console's mute way of protesting against seeing an invalid UTF code. Of course, trying to print alone a char that would make sense only in combination with other chars is bound to fail.

The interesting part starts when you specify a different character type for c. For example, specify dchar for c:

```
... as above, just add "dchar" ...
foreach (dchar c; str) {
   write('[', c, ']');
}
```

In this case, the compiler automatically inserts code for transcoding on the fly each code unit in str in the representation dictated by c's type. The loop above prints

[H][a][l][l][å][,][ ][v][ä][r][d][!]

which indicates that the double-byte characters å and ä were converted correctly to one dchar each and subsequently printed correctly. The same exact result would be printed if c had type wchar because the two non-ASCII characters used fit in one UTF-16 unit each, but not in the most general case (surrogate pairs would be wrongly processed). To be on the safe side, it is of course best to use dchar with loops over strings.

In the case above, the transcoding performed by foreach went from a narrow to a wide representation, but it could go either way. For example, you could start with a dstring and iterate it one (encoded) char at a time.

## 4.6  Arrays' Maverick Cousin: The Pointer

An array object tracks a chunk of typed objects in memory by storing the lower and upper bound. A pointer is "half" an array—it tracks only one object. As such, the pointer does not have information on whether the chunk starts and ends. If you have that information from the outside, you can use it to move the pointer around and make it point to neighboring elements.

A pointer to an object of type T is denoted as type T*, with the default value null (i.e., a pointer that points to no actual object). To make a pointer point to an object, use the address-of operator &, and to use that object, use the dereference operator * (§ 2.3.6.2 on page 52). For example:

```
int x = 42;
int* p = &x;       // Take the address of x
*p = 10;           // Using *p is the same as using x
++*p;              // Regular operators also apply
```

```
assert(x == 11); // x was modified through p
```

Pointers allow arithmetic that makes them apt as cursors inside arrays. Increment-ing a pointer makes it point to the next element of the array; decrementing it moves it to the previous element. Adding an integer n to a pointer yields a pointer to an object situated n positions away in the array, to the right if n is positive and to the left if n is negative. To simplify indexed operations, p[n] is equivalent to *(p + n). Finally, taking the difference between two pointers p2 - p1 yields an integral n such that p1 + n == p2.

You can fetch the address of the first element of an array with a.ptr. It follows that a pointer to the last element of a non-empty array arr can be obtained with arr.ptr + arr.length - 1, and a pointer just past the last element with arr.ptr + arr.length. To exemplify all of the above:

```
auto arr = [ 5, 10, 20, 30 ];
auto p = arr.ptr;
assert(*p == 5);
++p;
assert(*p == 10);
++*p;
assert(*p == 11);
p += 2;
assert(*p == 30);
assert(p - arr.ptr == 3);
```

Careful, however: unless you have access to array bounds information from out-side the pointer, things could go awry very easily. All pointer operations go completely unchecked—the implementation of the pointer is just a word-long memory address and the corresponding arithmetic just blindly does what you ask. That makes pointers blaz-ingly fast and also appallingly ignorant. Pointers aren't even smart enough to realize they are pointing at individual objects (as opposed to pointing inside arrays):

```
auto x = 10;
auto y = &x;
++y;            // Huh?
```

Pointers also don't know when they fall off the limits of arrays:

```
auto x = [ 10, 20 ];
auto y = x.ptr;
y += 100;               // Huh?
*y = 0xdeadbeef;        // Russian roulette
```

Writing through a pointer that doesn't point to valid data is essentially playing Rus-sian roulette with your program's integrity: the writes could land anywhere, stomping the most carefully maintained data or possibly even code. Such operations make pointers a *memory-unsafe* feature.

For these reasons, you should consistently avoid pointers and prefer using arrays, `class` references (Chapter 6), `ref` function parameters (§ 5.2.1 on page 135), and automatic memory management. All of these are safe, can be effectively checked, and do not undergo significant efficiency loss in most cases.

In fact, arrays are a very useful abstraction, and they were very carefully designed to hit a narrow target: *the fastest thing beyond pointers that can be made memory-safe.* Clearly a bald pointer does not have access to enough information to figure out anything on its own; arrays, on the other hand, are aware of their extent so they can cheaply verify that all operations are within range.

From a high-level perspective, it could be argued that arrays are rather low-level and that they could have aimed at implementing an abstract data type. On the contrary, from a low-level perspective, it could be argued that arrays are unnecessary because they can be implemented by using pointers. The answer to both arguments is a resounding "Let me explain."

Arrays are needed as the lowest-level abstraction that is still safe. If only pointers were provided, the language would have been unable to provide any kind of guarantee regarding various higher-level user-defined constructs built on top of pointers. Arrays also should not be a too-high-level feature because they are built in, so everything else comes on top of them. A good built-in facility is low-level and fast such that high-level and perhaps not-as-fast abstractions can be built on top of it. Abstraction never flows the other way.

D offers a proper subset known as SafeD (Chapter 11), and compilers offer a switch that enforces use of that subset. Naturally, most pointer operations are not allowed in SafeD. Built-in arrays are an important enabler of powerful, expressive SafeD programs.

## 4.7   Summary and Quick Reference

Table 4.3 on the facing page summarizes dynamic array operations; Table 4.4 on page 128 summarizes operations on fixed-size arrays; and Table 4.5 on page 129 summarizes operations available for associative arrays.

**Table 4.3:** Dynamic array operations (a and b are two values of type T[], t, $t_1$, ..., $t_k$ are values of type T, and n is a value convertible to type size_t)

| Name | Type | Description |
|---|---|---|
| new T[n] | T[] | Creates an array (§ 4.1 on page 93) |
| [$t_1$, $t_2$, ..., $t_k$] | T[] | Array literal; T is deduced as the type of $t_1$ (§ 2.2.6 on page 39, § 4.1 on page 93) |
| a = b | T[] | Assigns an array to another (§ 4.1.4 on page 98) |
| a[‹e›] | ref T | Accesses an element by index ($ is replaced in ‹e› with a.length, ‹e› must be convertible to size_t, and ‹e› < a.length) (§ 4.1 on page 93) |
| a[‹$e_1$› .. ‹$e_2$›] | T[] | Takes a slice off a ($ is replaced in ‹$e_1$› and ‹$e_2$› with a.length, ‹$e_1$› and ‹$e_2$› must be convertible to size_t, and ‹$e_1$› <= ‹$e_2$› && ‹$e_2$› <= a.length) (§ 4.1.3 on page 97) |
| a[] | T[] | Participate in array-wise expressions (§ 4.1.7 on page 100), otherwise just the identity operation a[0 .. $] |
| a.dup | T[] | Duplicates the array (§ 4.1 on page 93) |
| a.length | size_t | Reads array's length (§ 4.1.10 on page 106) |
| a.length = n | size_t | Changes array's length (§ 4.1.1 on page 95) |
| a is b | bool | Compares arrays for identity (§ 4.1.5 on page 100, § 2.3.4.3 on page 48) |
| a !is b | bool | Same as !(a is b) |
| a == b | bool | Compares arrays for element-for-element equality (§ 4.1.5 on page 100, § 2.3.12 on page 56) |
| a != b | bool | Same as !(a == b) |
| a ~ t | T[] | Concatenates an array with a value (§ 4.1.6 on page 100) |
| t ~ a | T[] | Concatenates one value with an array (§ 4.1.6 on page 100) |
| a ~ b | T[] | Concatenates two arrays (§ 4.1.6 on page 100) |
| a ~= t | T[] | Appends an element to an array (§ 4.1.6 on page 100) |
| a ~= b | T[] | Appends an array to another (§ 4.1.6 on page 100) |
| a.ptr | T* | Yields the address of a's first element (unsafe) (§ 4.6 on page 124) |

**Table 4.4:** Fixed-size array operations (a and b are two values of type T[], t, $t_1$, ..., $t_k$ are values of type T, and n is a statically known value convertible to type size_t)

| Name | Type | Description |
|------|------|-------------|
| [$t_1$,..., $t_k$] | T[k] | Array literal, but only if type T[k] is explicitly requested; T is deduced as the type of $t_1$ (§ 2.2.6 on page 39, § 4.1 on page 93) |
| a = b | ref T[n] | Copies contents over (§ 4.2.4 on page 109) |
| a[‹*e*›] | ref T | Accesses an element by index ($ is replaced in ‹*e*› with a.length, ‹*e*› must be convertible to size_t, and ‹*e*› < a.length) (§ 4.1 on page 93) |
| a[‹$e_1$› .. ‹$e_2$›] | T[]/T[k] | Takes a slice off a ($ is replaced in ‹$e_1$› and ‹$e_2$› with a.length, ‹$e_1$› and ‹$e_2$› must be convertible to size_t, and ‹$e_1$› <= ‹$e_2$› && ‹$e_2$› <= a.length) (§ 4.2.3 on page 109) |
| a[] | T[] | Participate in array-wise expressions (§ 4.1.7 on page 100) or just convert a to a dynamic array, same as a[0 .. $] |
| a.dup | T[] | Duplicates the array (§ 4.2.4 on page 109) |
| a.length | size_t | Reads the array's length (§ 4.2.1 on page 108) |
| a is b | bool | Compares arrays for identity (§ 4.2.5 on page 110, § 2.3.4.3 on page 48) |
| a !is b | bool | Same as !(a is b) |
| a == b | bool | Compares arrays for element-for-element equality (§ 4.2.5 on page 110, § 2.3.12 on page 56) |
| a != b | bool | Same as !(a == b) |
| a ~ t | T[] | Concatenates an array with a value (§ 4.2.6 on page 111) |
| t ~ a | T[] | Concatenates a value with an array (§ 4.2.6 on page 111) |
| a ~ b | T[] | Concatenates two arrays (§ 4.2.6 on page 111) |
| a.ptr | T* | Yields the address of a's first element (unsafe) |

**Table 4.5:** Associative array operations (a and b are two values of type V[K], k, $k_1$, ..., $k_i$ are values of type K, and v, $v_1$, ..., $v_k$ are values of type V)

| Name | Type | Description |
|---|---|---|
| [$t_1$:$v_1$, ..., $t_i$:$v_i$] | V[K] | Associative array literal; K is deduced as the type of $k_1$ and V is deduced as the type of $v_1$ (§ 2.2.6 on page 39, § 4.4 on page 114) |
| a = b | V[K] | Assigns b to a (§ 4.4.3 on page 115) |
| a[k] | V | Accesses an element by index (if k is not found, throws an exception) (§ 4.4.2 on page 115) |
| a[k] = v | V | Associates value v with key k (overwrites the previous association, if any) (§ 4.4.2 on page 115) |
| k in a | V* | Looks up k in a, returns null if absent or a pointer to the value associated to k if present (§ 4.4.2 on page 115) |
| k !in a | bool | Same as !(k in a) |
| a.length | size_t | Reads the number of elements in a (§ 4.4.1 on page 114) |
| a is b | bool | Compares associative arrays for identity (§ 4.4.4 on page 116, § 2.3.4.3 on page 48) |
| a !is b | bool | Same as !(a is b) |
| a == b | bool | Compares arrays for element-for-element equality (§ 4.4.4 on page 116, § 2.3.12 on page 56) |
| a != b | bool | Same as !(a == b) |
| a.remove(k) | bool | Removes the association of k, if any; returns true if and only if k existed in a (§ 4.4.5 on page 116) |
| a.get(k, v) | V | Returns the value in a corresponding to key k, with v as default (§ 4.4.2 on page 115) |

# Data and Functions. Functional Style

Talking about data and functions today when even objects are old news—that's so 1970s. Yet, sadly, the days when we'll just tell the computer what we want to do and let it figure out ways to do it are still ahead of us. Until then, functions are an essential component of all major programming disciplines. Fundamentally, any program consists of computations pushing data around; all of the elaborate scaffolding we build—types, objects, modules, frameworks, design patterns—just add interesting properties to the computation, such as modularity, error isolation, or ease of maintenance. A good language allows its user to hit a golden ratio of code that's there for "doing" to code that's there for "being." The ideal ratio depends on a number of factors, program size being an obvious one: a short script should be dedicated mostly to doing things, whereas a large application will inevitably be concerned with specifying non-executable things such as interfaces, protocols, and modular constraints.

D allows creation of sizable programs so it has powerful modeling abilities; however, it strives to reduce, within reason, code dedicated to "being," thus allowing you to concentrate on the "doing" part. Well-written D functions tend to be compact and general, packing a sometimes disconcerting power-to-weight ratio. So get ready to burn some tire.

## 5.1  Writing and `unittesting` a Simple Function

It could reasonably be argued that what computers do most of the time (save for uninteresting things such as waiting for input) is *searching*. Database programs search. Artificial Intelligence programs search. (That annoying automated telephone bank teller

131

making chitchat with you? Search.) Internet search engines ... well, you know. And
as you no doubt know from direct experience, at their core, many programs that have
ostensibly nothing to do with searching actually do quite a bit of it. Wherever there's a
problem to be solved, searching is involved in the solution. Conversely, many ingenious
solutions to problems hinge on searching intelligently and on setting things up such
that searching is easy to do. Naturally, the computing world is full of searching-related
memes: pattern matching, relational algebra, binary searching, hashtables, binary trees,
tries, red-black trees, skip lists ... well, we can't pretend to look at them all here, so for
the moment let's aim for a more modest goal—defining a few simple searching functions in D, starting with linear search, the simplest search there is. So without further
ado, let's write a function that tells whether a slice of ints contains some particular int.

```d
bool find(int[] haystack, int needle) {
   foreach (v; haystack) {
      if (v == needle) return true;
   }
   return false;
}
```

Great. Now since this is the first D function under our belt, let's describe what it really does in minute detail. When the compiler sees the definition of find, it compiles the
function down to binary code. At runtime, when find is invoked, haystack and needle
are passed into the function by value. Now, "by value" does not mean that if you pass
in a million-element array that will be copied; as discussed in Chapter 4, the type int[]
(aka a slice of an array of integers) is what's called a *fat pointer*, really a pointer + length
pair or a pointer + pointer pair that stores only the limits of a given portion of an array. Passing a slice of a million-element array into find really means passing enough
information to get to the beginning and the end of the slice, as explained in § 4.1.4 on
page 98. (Dealing with a container through a small, bounded representative that knows
how to crawl the container is pervasive in the D language and standard library. That
representative is generally called a *range*.) So at the end of the day, three machine words
need to make it from the caller side into find. Once find gets control, it does its deed
and returns a Boolean value (usually in a processor register), at which point the caller is
ready to pick it up. And—as they encouragingly say at the end of a home improvement
show after having completed an incredibly complicated task—that's all there is to it.

To be frank, find's design is quite a bit lacking. Returning bool is terribly uninforma-
tive; often, position information is also needed, for example, for continuing the search.
We could return an integer (and some special value such as -1 for "not found"), but although integers are great for referring elements in contiguous storage, they are terribly
inefficient for most other containers (such as linked lists). Getting to the $n^{th}$ element of a
linked list after find returns n requires walking the list node by node all the way from its

head—almost as much work as the `find` operation itself! So returning an integer would port terribly to most anything but arrays.

One idea that would work for a variety of `haystacks`—arrays, linked lists, and even files and sockets—is to have `find` simply nibble one element (straw?) off `haystack` until the searched value is found and return what's left of `haystack`. (If the value is never found, `find` naturally returns the emptied `haystack`.) That's a simple and general specification: "`find(haystack, needle)` reduces `haystack` from the left until it starts with `needle` or until `haystack` is exhausted and then returns the balance of `haystack`." Let's implement that design for `int[]`.

```
int[] find(int[] haystack, int needle) {
    while (haystack.length > 0 && haystack[0] != needle) {
        haystack = haystack[1 .. $];
    }
    return haystack;
}
```

Note how `find` accesses only the first element of `haystack` and repeatedly reassigns `haystack` to a shorter subset of it. These primitives should be easily replaced later with, for example, list-specific primitives, but let's worry about that generalization in a few minutes. For now let's kick `find`'s tires a bit.

Recent years have seen increased attention paid to proper software testing in virtually all development methodologies. That's a good trend because proper testing does have a huge positive impact on bug management. Let us, then, be in keeping with the times and write a short unit test for `find`. Simply follow (if you're like yours truly) or precede (if you're a true test-driven developer) `find`'s definition with this:

```
unittest {
    int[] a = [];
    assert(find(a, 5) == []);
    a = [ 1, 2, 3 ];
    assert(find(a, 0) == []);
    assert(find(a, 1).length == 3);
    assert(find(a, 2).length == 2);
    assert(a[0 .. $ - find(a, 3).length] == [ 1, 2 ]);
}
```

All we have to do to obtain a working module is to put together the function and the unit test in a file `searching.d` and then run

```
$ rdmd --main -unittest searching.d
```

If you pass the `-unittest` flag, unit tests will be compiled and set up to run before the main program. Otherwise, the compiler ignores the `unittest` blocks, which is

useful if you're interested in running already tested code without startup latencies. The
`--main` flag instructs `rdmd` to add a do-nothing `main` function. (If you forget about
`--main`, don't worry; the linker will fluently and baroquely remind you of that in its
native language, encrypted Klingon.) The surrogate `main` is useful to us because we're
interested in running only the unit test, not an actual program. Presumably there will
be hordes of interested developers who will take our little file and use it in their projects,
each defining its own `main`.

## 5.2   Passing Conventions and Storage Classes

As mentioned, the two arguments to `find` (one `int` plus one fat pointer representing an
`int[]`) are copied into `find`'s private state. When `find` returns, a fat pointer is copied
back to the caller. This is easily recognizable as straight call by value. In particular,
changes to the arguments are not "seen" by the caller after the function returns. But beware of indirection: given that the *content* of the slice is not copied, changing individual
elements of the slice *will* be seen by the caller. Consider:

```
void fun(int x) { x += 42; }
void gun(int[] x) { x = [ 1, 2, 3 ]; }
void hun(int[] x) { x[0] = x[1]; }
unittest {
    int x = 10;
    fun(x);
    assert(x == 10);                    // Unchanged
    int[] y = [ 10, 20, 30 ];
    gun(y);
    assert(y == [ 10, 20, 30 ]); // Unchanged
    hun(y);
    assert(y == [ 20, 20, 30 ]); // Changed!
}
```

What happened? In the first two cases, `fun` and `gun` changed only their own copies of
the parameters. In particular, the second case rebinds the fat pointer to point elsewhere,
leaving the original array intact. In the third case, however, `hun` chose to change one element of the array, a change reflected in the original array. It is easy to imagine why when
we think that the slice y is in a different place from the three integers that y manages. So
if you assign a slice wholesale à la x = [ 1, 2, 3 ], then the slice that x previously held is
left alone as x starts a new life; but if you change some particular element x[i] of a slice,
other slices seeing that element (in our case, the caller of hun) will see the change.

### 5.2.1 ref Parameters and Returns

Sometimes we do want to make a change visible in the caller. In that case, the `ref` storage class comes to the rescue:

```
void bump(ref int x) { ++x; }
unittest {
   int x = 1;
   bump(x);
   assert(x == 2);
}
```

If a function expects a `ref`, it accepts only "real" data, not temporaries; anything that's not an lvalue is rejected during compilation; for example:

```
bump(5); // Error! Cannot bind an rvalue to a ref parameter
```

This preempts silly mistakes when people believe work is being done but in fact the call has no visible effect.

You can also attach `ref` to the result of a function. In that case, the result of the function is an lvalue itself. For example, let's modify bump as follows:

```
ref int bump(ref int x) { return ++x; }
unittest {
   int x = 1;
   bump(bump(x)); // Two increments
   assert(x == 3);
}
```

The inner call to `bump` returns an lvalue, which is then a legit argument for the outer call. Had the definition of bump looked like this:

```
int bump(ref int x) { return ++x; }
```

the compiler would have rejected the call `bump(bump(x))` as an illegal attempt to bind the rvalue resulting from `bump(x)` to the `ref` parameter of the outer call to bump.

### 5.2.2 in Parameters

If you specify `in` with a parameter, then that parameter is considered read-only so you cannot change it in any way. For example:

```
void fun(in int x) {
   x = 42; // Error! Cannot modify 'in' parameter
}
```

The code above does not compile, revealing that in is quite strict. Even though fun already owns a copy of its argument, it is unable to change it.

Having an effectively constant parameter inside a function may certainly be helpful when reviewing its implementation, but the more interesting effect is *outside* the function. An in parameter disallows even indirect changes to the parameter, changes that would be reflected in the object after the function has returned. This makes in parameters extremely useful because they give guarantees to the caller, not only to the function implementation itself. Consider:

```
void fun(in int[] data) {
    data = new int[10]; // Error! Cannot modify 'in' parameter
    data[5] = 42;       // Error! Cannot modify 'in' parameter
}
```

The first error is not surprising because it is of the same kind as the error involving an int alone. The second error is much more interesting. Somehow the compiler has magically extended the reach of in from data itself to each of data's slots—in is sort of "deep."

The restriction actually goes to any depth, not only one level. Let's exemplify that with a multidimensional array:

```
// An array of arrays of int has two indirections
void fun(in int[][] data) {
    data[5] = data[0];        // Error! Cannot modify 'in' parameter
    data[5][0] = data[0][5]; // Error! Cannot modify 'in' parameter
}
```

So in protects its data from modification *transitively*, all the way down through indirections. This behavior is not specific to arrays and applies to all of D's data types. In fact, in in a parameter context is a synonym for the type qualifier const. Chapter 8 discusses in detail how const works.

### 5.2.3   out Parameters

Sometimes a ref parameter is meant only for the function to deposit something in. In such cases, you may want to use the out storage class, which is much like ref, except that it initializes the argument to its default value upon entry into the function:

```
// Computes divisor and remainder of a and b
// Returns divisor by value, remainder in the 'rem' parameter
int divrem(int a, int b, out int rem) {
    assert(b != 0);
    rem = a % b;
    return a / b;
```

```
}
unittest {
    int r;
    int d = divrem(5, 2, r);
    assert(d == 2 && r == 1);
}
```

The code above could have used `ref` instead of `out` without a hitch; however, using `out` clarifies to the caller that the function `divrem` does not expect `rem` to contain anything interesting upon entry.

### 5.2.4 `static` Data

Although `static` is not related to passing arguments to functions, discussing it here is appropriate because, just like `ref`, `static` applied to data is a *storage class*, meaning an indication about a detail regarding how data is stored.

Any variable declaration may be amended with `static`, which means that the data has *one copy per execution thread*. This is different from the C-established tradition of allocating one copy of the data for the entire application, and Chapter 13 discusses the rationale and consequences of D's decision.

Static data being shared, it preserves its value across function calls, whether it sits inside or outside the function. The choice of placing `static` data inside various scopes concerns only visibility, but not storage. At module level, `static` is really handled the same way `private` is.

```
static int zeros; // Practically the same as private int zeros;

void fun(int x) {
    static int calls;
    ++calls;
    if (!x) ++zeros;
    ...
}
```

Static data must be initialized with compile-time constants. To initialize function-level `static` data upon first pass through a function, you may want to use a simple trick that uses a companion `bool static` variable:

```
void fun(double x) {
    static double minInput;
    static bool minInputInitialized;
    if (!minInputInitialized) {
        minInput = x;
```

```
        minInputInitialized = true;
    } else {
        if (x < minInput) minInput = x;
    }
    ...
}
```

## 5.3   Type Parameters

Let's get back to the `find` function defined on page 132, because it has more than a few issues. For starters, `find` has a pretty narrow usefulness, so it's worth looking into ways to make it more general. Let's start with a simple observation. The presence of `int` in `find` is hard coding, pure and simple. There's nothing different in the code shape when it comes to finding `double` values in `double[]` slices or `string` values in `string[]` slices. What we'd like, then, is to transform `int` into a placeholder—a parameter of `find` that describes the type, not the value, of the entities involved. To do so, we need to change our definition to

```
T[] find(T)(T[] haystack, T needle) {
    while (haystack.length > 0 && haystack[0] != needle) {
        haystack = haystack[1 .. $];
    }
    return haystack;
}
```

As expected, there is no change in the body of `find`, only in its signature. The signature now has two pairs of parenthesized items. The first one lists the type parameters of the function, and the second one is the regular parameter list, which now can make use of the just-defined type parameters. Now we can handle not only slices of `int`, but slices of *everything*, be they other built-in types or user-defined types. To top it off, our previous `unittest` continues to work because the compiler deduces `T` automatically from the argument types. Neat. But instead of resting on our laurels let's add a unit test to confirm these extraordinary claims:

```
unittest {
    // Testing generic capabilities
    double[] d = [ 1.5, 2.4 ];
    assert(find(d, 1.0) == null);
    assert(find(d, 1.5) == d);
    string[] s = [ "one", "two" ];
    assert(find(s, "two") == [ "two" ]);
}
```

Now what happens when the compiler sees the improved definition of `find`? The compiler faces a tougher challenge compared to the `int[]` case because now `T` is not known yet—it could be just about any type. And different types are stored differently, passed around differently, and sport different definitions of `==`. Dealing with this challenge is important because type parameters really open up possibilities and multiply reusability of code. When it comes to generating code for type parameterization, two schools of thought are prevalent today [43]:

- *Homogeneous translation:* Bring all data to a common format, which allows compiling only one version of `find` that will work for everybody.
- *Heterogeneous translation:* Invoking `find` with various type arguments (e.g., `int` versus `double` versus `string`) prompts the compiler to generate as many specialized versions of `find`.

In homogeneous translation, the language must offer a uniform access interface to data as a prerequisite to presenting it to `find`. Heterogeneous translation is pretty much as if you had an assistant writing one special `find` for each data format you may come up with, all built from the same mold. Clearly the two approaches have relative advantages and disadvantages, which are often the subject of passionate debates in various languages' communities. Homogeneous translation favors uniformity, simplicity, and compact generated code. For example, traditional functional languages favor putting everything in list format, and many traditional object-oriented languages favor making everything an object that offers uniform access to its features. However, the disadvantages of homogeneous translation may include rigidity, lack of expressive power, and inefficiency. In contrast, heterogeneous translation favors specialization, expressive power, and speed of generated code. The costs may include bloating of generated code, increases in language complexity, and an awkward compilation model (a frequently aired argument against heterogeneous approaches is that they're glorified macros [gasp]; and ever since C gave such a bad reputation to macros, the label evokes quite a powerful negative connotation).

A detail worth noting is an inclusion relationship: heterogeneous translation includes homogeneous translation for the simple reason that "many formats" includes "one format," and "many implementations" includes "one implementation." Therefore it can be argued (all other issues left aside) that heterogeneous translation is more powerful than homogeneous translation. If you have heterogeneous translation means at your disposal, at least in principle there's nothing stopping you from choosing one unified data format and one unified function when you so wish. The converse option is simply not available under a homogeneous approach. However, it would be oversimplifying to conclude that heterogeneous approaches are "better" because aside from expressive power there are, again, other arguments that need to be taken into consideration.

D uses heterogeneous translation with (warning, incoming technical terms flak) statically scoped symbol lookup and deferred typechecking. This means that when the D compiler sees the generic `find` definition, it parses and saves the body, remembers where the function was defined, and does nothing else until `find` gets called. At that point, the compiler fetches the parsed definition of `find` and attempts to compile it with the type that the caller chose in lieu of T. When the function uses symbols, they are looked up in the context in which the function was defined.

Should the compiler fail to generate `find` for your particular type, an error message is generated. This can actually be annoying because the error may be due to a bug in `find` that went undetected. This, in fact, provides the perfect motivation for the next section because `find` has two bugs—not functional bugs, but generality bugs: as it stands now, `find` is at the same time too general and not general enough. Let's see how that Zen claim works.

## 5.4 Signature Constraints

Say we have an array of `double` and we want to look for an integer in it. It should go over rather smoothly, right?

```
double[] a = [ 1.0, 2.5, 2.0, 3.4 ];
a = find(a, 2); // Error! 'find(double[], int)' undefined
```

Yes, you were ambushed. What happens is that the function `find` expects a T[] in the first position and a T in the second. However, `find` receives a `double[]` and an `int`, which are claiming T = double and T = int, respectively. If we squint hard enough, we do see that the intent of the caller in this case was to have T = double and benefit from the nice implicit conversion from `int` to `double`. However, having the language attempt combinatorially at the same time implicit conversions and type deduction is a dicey proposition in the general case, so D does not attempt to do all that. If you said T[] and T, you can't pass a `double[]` and an `int`.

It seems like our implementation of `find` lacks generality because it asks for the type of the slice to be identical to the type of the searched value. In fact, for a given slice type, we need to accept *any* value that can be compared using == against a slice element.

Well, if one type parameter is good, two can only be better:

```
T[] find(T, E)(T[] haystack, E needle) {
    while (haystack.length > 0 && haystack[0] != needle) {
        haystack = haystack[1 .. $];
    }
    return haystack;
}
```

Now the test passes with flying colors. However, `find` is technically lying because it declares it accepts any T and E, including pairings that make no sense! To illustrate why that is a problem, consider the call

```
assert(find([1, 2, 3], "Hello")); // Error!
   // Comparison haystack[0] != needle is invalid
   //     for int[] and string
```

The compiler does find a problem; however, it finds it in the comparison situated inside `find`'s body. This can get rather confusing to the unwitting user, because it's unclear whether the error lies at the call site or in the implementation of `find`. (In particular, the file and line reported by the compiler point straight inside `find`'s definition.) If the problem is at the end of a long chain of invocations, it gets all the more confusing, so we'd like to fix this. Now, what is the root of the problem? If you allow a little wordplay, `find` puts its signature on checks that its body can't cash.

In its signature (i.e., the part just before the first {), `find` solemnly states it accepts a slice of any type `T` and a value of any type `E`. The compiler gladly acknowledges that, dispatches the nonsensical arguments to `find`, deduces `T = int` and `E = string`, and is about to call it a day. However, as soon as `find`'s body comes into the discussion, the compiler embarrassingly realizes it is unable to generate sensible code for the comparison `haystack[0] != needle` and reports an error tantamount to "`find` bit off more than it can chew." Only a few combinations of all possible `T`s and `E`s are really accepted by `find`'s body, namely, those that accept comparison for equality.

Building some sort of back-off mechanism would be possible. Another solution, chosen by D, is to allow `find`'s implementor to systematically limit the applicability of the function, and the right place to specify that constraint is `find`'s signature, right where `T` and `E` appear for the first time. D allows that via a *signature constraint*:

```
T[] find(T, E)(T[] haystack, E needle)
   if (is(typeof(haystack[0] != needle) == bool))
{
   ... // Implementation remains the same
}
```

The `if` clause in the signature advertises that `find` accepts `haystack` of type `T[]` and `needle` of type `E` only if the type of the expression `haystack[0] != needle` is `bool`. This has several important consequences. First, the `if` clause clarifies to the writer, the compiler, and the reader what expectations `find` has of its parameters, without having to inspect the body at all (which most of the time is longer than what we now have). Second, with the `if` clause in tow, `find` is now able to elegantly decline commitment when incompatible arguments are passed to it, which in turn allows other features like function overloading to work smoothly. Third, the new definition makes for better compiler error messages because the error becomes evident in the call, not the body, of `find`.

Note that the expression under `typeof` is never evaluated at runtime; its purpose is merely to tell what type it would have if the expression compiled. (If the expression under `typeof` does not compile, that is no compilation error, just mere information that it has no type at all, and "no type at all" is not `bool`.) In particular, you shouldn't be worried that `haystack[0]` is under the test even if `haystack`'s length is zero. Conversely, you cannot put runtime-evaluated conditions in a signature constraint; for example, you could not specify that you limit the charter of `find` to `needle > 0`.

## 5.5   Overloading

We defined `find` for a slice and an element. Let's now set out to write a version of `find` that tells whether a slice can be found within another slice. A common approach is a brute-force search using two nested loops. That algorithm is not very efficient—its runtime is proportional to the product of the two slices' lengths. Let's not worry about algorithmic efficiency for the time being; for now let's focus on defining a good signature for the newly added function. The previous section equipped us with most everything we need. Indeed, the implementation writes itself:

```
T1[] find(T1, T2)(T1[] longer, T2[] shorter)
   if (is(typeof(longer[0 .. 1] == shorter) : bool))
{
   while (longer.length >= shorter.length) {
      if (longer[0 .. shorter.length] == shorter) break;
      longer = longer[1 .. $];
   }
   return longer;
}
```

Aha! You see, this time we didn't fall again into the trap of making the function unduly particular. An inferior definition would have been

```
// No! This signature is severely limiting!
bool find(T)(T[] longer, T[] shorter) {
   ...
}
```

which, agreed, is a bit terser but plenty more limiting. Our implementation can tell whether a slice of `int` includes a slice of `long`, or whether a slice of `double` includes a slice of `float`, without copying any data around. These options were simply inaccessible to the simplistic signature. You would have to either copy data around to ensure the right types are in place or give up on using the function altogether and roll your search by hand. And what kind of function is one that looks cute in toy examples and fails for serious use?

As far as the implementation goes, note (in the outer loop) the now familiar reduction of `longer` by one element from the left end. The inner loop is implicit in the bulk comparison `longer[0 .. shorter.length] == shorter`, which compares the first `shorter.length` elements of `longer` with `shorter`.

D supports function overloading—several functions may share the same name as long as they differ in the number of parameters or the type of at least one parameter. Language rules decide during compilation where actual calls should go. Overloading builds on our innate linguistic ability to disambiguate the meaning of words by using context and is very helpful for providing ample functionality without a corresponding growth in the vocabulary that callers must remember. The converse risk is that if the call disambiguation rules are too lax, people may think they are calling one function and call another instead, or if said rules are too tight, people would need to contort their code to explain to the compiler which version they meant to call. D strives to keep the rules simple, and in this particular case the rule in effect is a no-brainer: if a function's signature constraint (the `if` clause) evaluates to `false`, the function simply vanishes from the overload set—it's not considered as a candidate at all. For our two `find` versions, the corresponding `if` clauses are never true for the same arguments. So for any possible call to `find`, at least one of the two overloads will make itself invisible; there's never an ambiguity to solve. So let's follow these thoughts with a `unittest`.

```
unittest {
    // Test the newly introduced overload
    double[] d1 = [ 6.0, 1.5, 2.4, 3 ];
    float[] d2 = [ 1.5, 2.4 ];
    assert(find(d1, d2) == d1[1 .. $]);
}
```

The two versions of `find` may live in the same file or in different files; there is no competition between them because their `if` clauses are never true at the same time. Now, to discuss overloading rules further, let's assume we work with `int[]` a lot so we want to define an optimized `find` for that type:

```
int[] find(int[] longer, int[] shorter) {
    ...
}
```

As written, this overload of `find` has no type parameters. Also, it is rather clear that some competition is going on between the general `find` we defined before and the specialized `find` for integers. What is the relative position of the two functions in the overloading food chain, and which of them will succeed in grabbing the call below?

```
int[] ints1 = [ 1, 2, 3, 5, 2 ];
int[] ints2 = [ 3, 5 ];
auto test = find(ints1, ints2); // Correct or error?
                                // General or specialized?
```

D's approach to the matter is very simple: its choice is consistently biased in favor of the more specialized function. Now, in the general case the notion of "more specialized" demands some explanation; it suggests there's a sort of specialization order, a "less-than" for functions. Indeed there is, and that relation is called *partial ordering of functions.*

### 5.5.1 Partial Ordering of Functions

Although it sounds like it would demand a lot of math-fu, partial ordering is a very simple notion. Think of generalizing the familiar numeric relation $\leq$ to other sets, in our case functions. Given two functions $foo_1$ and $foo_2$, we want to tell whether $foo_1$ is any less fit than $foo_2$ for a call (let's denote "$foo_1$ is less fit than $foo_2$" as $foo_1 \leq foo_2$). If we define such a relation, we then have a criterion for deciding which of them should be called in an overloading contest: upon a call to foo, sort the possible foos by $\leq$ and choose the "largest" foo found. To be worth its salt, a partial order must be reflexive ($a \leq a$), antisymmetric (if $a \leq b$ and $b \leq a$ then $a$ and $b$ are considered equivalent), and transitive (if $a \leq b$ and $b \leq c$ then $a \leq c$).

D defines a simple partial ordering relation for functions: if $foo_1$ can be called with the parameter types of $foo_2$, then $foo_1 \leq foo_2$. It is possible that $foo_1 \leq foo_2$ and $foo_2 \leq foo_1$ simultaneously, in which case we say that the two are *equally specialized.* For example

```
// Three equally specialized functions: either could be called
//     with another's parameter type
void sqrt(real);
void sqrt(double);
void sqrt(float);
```

are equally specialized because any of them could be called with either a float, a double, or a real (paradoxically sensible in spite of the lossy conversion, as discussed in § 2.3.2 on page 42).

It's also possible that neither function is $\leq$ the other, in which case we say that $foo_1$ and $foo_2$ are *unordered.*[1] There are plenty of examples, such as

```
// Two unordered functions: neither could be called with
//     the other's parameter type
void print(double);
void print(string);
```

In the most interesting case, exactly one of $foo_1 \leq foo_2$ and $foo_2 \leq foo_1$ is true—for example, the first, in which case we say that $foo_1$ is *less specialized* than $foo_2$. To wit:

---

1. This situation puts the "partial" in "partial ordering." Under a total order (e.g., $\leq$ for real numbers), there are no unordered elements.

```
// Two ordered functions: write(double) is less specialized than
//     write(int) because the former can be called with an int, but
//     the latter cannot be called with a double
void write(double);
void write(int);
```

Using this partial order, D performs the following simple algorithm for making a decision in an overloaded call `foo(arg1, ..., argn)`:

1. If there's one exact match (same types and same number of parameters as the arguments), take that.
2. Select a set of candidates { $foo_1$, ... $foo_k$ } that would accept the call if no other overloads are present. Here is where type deduction deduces types and `if` clauses are evaluated.
3. If the set has size zero, issue "no match" error.
4. If all functions are not in the same module, issue "attempt at cross-module overloading" error.
5. From that set eliminate all functions that are less specialized than any others in the set, that is, keep only the most specialized functions.
6. If the remaining set has size greater than one, issue "ambiguous call" error.
7. The sole element of the set is the winner.

That's about it. Consider a first example:

```
void transmogrify(uint) {}
void transmogrify(long) {}

unittest {
    transmogrify(42); // Calls transmogrify(uint)
}
```

There is no exact match and both functions could apply, so partial ordering kicks in. It dictates that, although both functions would accept the call, the first is more specialized so it is entitled to win. (For better or worse, `int` converts automatically to `uint`.) Now let's throw a generic function into the mix:

```
// As above, plus ...
void transmogrify(T)(T value) {}

unittest {
    transmogrify(42);      // Still calls transmogrify(uint)
    transmogrify("hello"); // Calls transmogrify(T), T=string
}
```

```
    transmogrify(1.1);       // Calls transmogrify(T), T=double
}
```

Now, what happens when `transmogrify(int)` is compared for ordering against the generic function `transmogrify(T)(T)`? Well, even though it was decided T = uint, when comparing for ordering, T is not replaced with `uint` but preserved in all its genericity. Could `transmogrify(int)` accept some arbitrary type T? It couldn't. Could `transmogrify(T)(T)` accept an int? Sure it could. It follows that `transmogrify(T)(T)` is less specialized than `transmogrify(int)`, so it is eliminated from the candidate set. So non-generic functions are generally preferred to generic functions, even when the non-generic functions need an implicit conversion.

### 5.5.2   Cross-Module Overloading

Step 4 in the overloading algorithm on the preceding page deserves particular attention. Consider a slightly modified example with overloads for uint and long, just with more files involved:

```
// In module calvin.d
void transmogrify(long) { ... }

// In module hobbes.d
void transmogrify(uint) { ... }

// Module client.d
import calvin, hobbes;
unittest {
    transmogrify(42);
}
```

The `transmogrify(uint)` overload in **calvin.d** is more specialized; however, the compiler refuses to call it by claiming ambiguity. D staunchly refuses to overload across different modules. If such overloading were allowed, then the meaning of the call would depend on the interplay of various modules included (and in general there could be many modules, many overloads, and more complicated calls in the fray). Imagine adding one new `import` to a working program and having its behavior change in unpredictable ways! Conversely, if cross-module overloading were allowed, the burden on the code reader would increase enormously: now, in order to figure out where a call goes, they don't need to know what one module contains, but instead what all included modules contain because one of them might define a better match. Worse, if the order of top-level declarations mattered, the call `transmogrify(5)` could actually end up calling different functions depending on its position in the file. This is an endless source of problems because it essentially means that the reader of a piece of code must keep a large moving context in mind at all times.

A module can define a bunch of overloads that implement functionality for a variety of types. Another module cannot just barge in with its own addenda to that functionality. However, the second module can define its own bunch of overloads. As long as a function in one module does not hijack calls that would otherwise go to a function in another module, there's no ambiguity. The decision on whether there's a conflict or not is made on a per-call basis. Consider:

```d
// In module calvin.d
void transmogrify(long) { ... }
void transmogrify(uint) { ... }

// In module hobbes.d
void transmogrify(double) { ... }

// In module susie.d
void transmogrify(int[]) { ... }
void transmogrify(string) { ... }

// Module client.d
import calvin, hobbes, susie;

unittest {
   transmogrify(5);           // Error! cross-module overloading
                              //    across calvin and hobbes
   calvin.transmogrify(5); // Fine, explicit resolution
                              // calvin.transmogrify(uint) called
   transmogrify(5.5);         // Fine, only hobbes could take it
   transmogrify("hi");        // Hello from Susie
}
```

Calvin, Hobbes, and Susie interact in interesting ways. Note how ambiguities are very fine-grained; the fact that there's a conflict between `calvin.d` and `hobbes.d` in the first call does not render the modules mutually incompatible—the third call still goes through because no function in other modules was able to take it. Finally, `susie.d` defines its own overloads and is never in conflict with the other two (unlike the eponymous comic strip characters).

**Guiding Overloading** Whenever there is ambiguity between modules, there are two main ways in which you can guide the workings of overloading. One is to qualify the function name with the module name, as shown in the second call calvin.transmogrify(5). Doing this restricts lookup to only `calvin.d`. Inside that module, overloading rules are still at work. A more transparent way is to use a *local alias* for the symbol in question, which goes like this:

```
// Inside calvin.d
alias hobbes.transmogrify transmogrify;
```

This directive does something very interesting: it wheelbarrows all of the overloads of `transmogrify` in module `hobbes.d` into the current module, `calvin.d`. So if `calvin.d` contains the directive above, it's as if it defined all overloads of `transmogrify` that `hobbes.d` defined, in addition to its own overloads. That's very nice of `calvin.d`—it democratically consults `hobbes.d` whenever the important decision of calling `transmogrify` is to be made. Alternatively, if `calvin.d` and `hobbes.d` have had a misadventure and choose to ignore each other's existence, `client.d` can still call `transmogrify`, taking all overloads into account by aliasing both `calvin.transmogrify` and `hobbes.transmogrify`:

```
// Inside client.d
alias calvin.transmogrify transmogrify;
alias hobbes.transmogrify transmogrify;
```

Now any call to `transmogrify` issued from `client.d` will resolve overloads as if the definitions in both `calvin.d` and `hobbes.d` were present in `client.d`.

## 5.6  Higher-Order Functions. Function Literals

So far we know how to find an element or a slice inside a slice. However, finding is not always about searching a given item. Consider a task such as "Find the first negative element in an array of numbers." For all its might, our `find` library cannot solve that problem.

Fundamentally, `find` looks to fulfill some Boolean condition, a predicate; so far, the predicate has always been a comparison using == against a given value. A more flexible `find` would receive a predicate from the user and assemble the linear search logic around it. If it could amass such power, `find` would become a *higher-order function*, meaning a function that can take other functions as arguments. This is a quite powerful approach to doing things because higher-order functions compound their own functionality with the functionality provided by their arguments, reaching a range of behaviors inaccessible to simple functions. To have `find` take a predicate, we can use an *alias parameter*.

```
T[] find(alias pred, T)(T[] input)
   if (is(typeof(pred(input[0])) == bool))
{
```

```
    for (; input.length > 0; input = input[1 .. $]) {
        if (pred(input[0])) break;
    }
    return input;
}
```

This new overload of `find` takes only one "classic" parameter but adds the mysterious `alias pred` parameter. An alias parameter can match any argument: a value, a type, a function name—anything that can be expressed symbolically. Let's now see how to invoke this new overload of `find`.

```
unittest {
    int[] a = [ 1, 2, 3, 4, -5, 3, -4 ];
    // Find the first negative number
    auto b = find!(function bool(int x) { return x < 0; })(a);
}
```

This time `find` takes two argument lists. The first list is distinguished by the syntax `!(...)` and consists of generic arguments. The second list consists of the classic arguments. Note that although `find` declares two generic parameters (`alias pred` and `T`), the calling code specifies only one. That's because deduction works as usual by binding `T = int`. In our use of `find` so far, we've never needed to specify any generic arguments because the compiler deduced them for us. This time around, there's no deduction for `pred` so we specified it as a function literal. The function literal is

```
function bool(int x) { return x < 0; }
```

where `function` is a keyword and the rest is a regular function definition, just without a name.

Function literals (also known as anonymous functions or lambda functions) turn out to be very useful in a variety of situations, but their syntax is a bit heavy. The literal used above is 41 characters long, of which only about 5 do actual work. To help with that, D allows you to trim the syntax quite a bit. The first shortcut is to eliminate either or both return type and parameter types; the compiler is smart enough to infer them all because by its very definition, the body of the anonymous function is right there.

```
auto b = find!(function(x) { return x < 0; })(a);
```

The second shortcut is to simply eliminate the keyword `function` itself. You can combine the two shortcuts like this, leading to a rather terse notation:

```
auto b = find!((x) { return x < 0; })(a);
```

That looks easily recognizable to the initiated, which you just became as of a couple of seconds ago.

### 5.6.1 Function Literals versus Delegate Literals

One important requirement of a lambda function facility is to allow access to the context in which the lambda was defined. Consider a slightly modified invocation:

```
unittest {
    int[] a = [ 1, 2, 3, 4, -5, 3, -4 ];
    int z = -2;
    // Find the first number less than z
    auto b = find!((x) { return x < z; })(a);
    assert(b == a[4 .. $]);
}
```

This modified example works, which apparently answers the question. However, if, just for kicks, we prepend `function` to the literal, the code mysteriously stops working!

```
auto b = find!(function(x) { return x < z; })(a);
// Error! function cannot access frame of caller function!
```

What's happening, and what's with that complaint about a frame? Clearly there must be some underlying mechanism through which the function literal gets access to z—it can't divine its location from thin air. That mechanism is encoded as a hidden parameter, called a *frame pointer*, that the literal takes. The compiler uses the frame pointer to wire access to outer variables such as z. However, a function literal that does *not* use any local variable wouldn't need that extra parameter. D being statically typed, it must distinguish between the two, and indeed it does. Aside from `function` literals, there are also `delegate` literals, which can be created like this:

```
unittest {
    int z = 3;
    auto b = find!(delegate(x) { return x < z; })(a); // OK
}
```

Delegates have access to the enclosing frame, whereas functions do not. If both `function` and `delegate` are absent from the literal, the compiler automatically detects which is necessary. Type deduction comes to the rescue again by making the tersest, most convenient code also do the right thing automagically.

```
auto f = (int i) {};
assert(is(f == function));
```

## 5.7 Nested Functions

We can now invoke `find` with an arbitrary function literal, which is quite neat. However, if the literal grows pretty large or if we want to reuse it, it becomes clumsy to write its body at the invocation place (potentially several times, too). We'd like to invoke `find` with a named function, as opposed to an anonymous one; furthermore, we'd want to preserve the right to access local variables if we so wish. For that kind of activity and many others, D has nested functions.

A nested function definition looks exactly like a regular one, except that it appears inside another function. Consider:

```d
void transmogrify(int[] input, int z) {
    // Nested function
    bool isTransmogrifiable(int x) {
        if (x == 42) {
            throw new Exception("42 cannot be transmogrified");
        }
        return x < z;
    }
    // Find the first transmogrifiable element in the input
    input = find!(isTransmogrifiable)(input);
    ...
    // ... and again
    input = find!(isTransmogrifiable)(input);
    ...
}
```

Nested functions can come in very handy in a variety of situations. Although they don't do anything that regular functions can't do, nested functions enhance convenience and modularity because they sit right inside the function using them, and they have intimate access to the context of the nesting function. The latter advantage is very important; in the example above, if nesting were not an option, accessing z would have been much more problematic.

The nested function `isTransmogrifiable` uses the same trick (a hidden parameter) to get access to its parent's stack frame, and z in particular. Sometimes you may want to actively prevent that from happening and make `isTransmogrifiable` just an absolutely regular function, save for its definition sitting inside `transmogrify`. To effect that, simply prepend `static` (what else?) to `isTransmogrifiable`'s definition:

```d
void transmogrify(int[] input, int z) {
    static int w = 42;
    // Nested regular function
    static bool isTransmogrifiable(int x) {
        if (x == 42) {
            throw new Exception("42 cannot be transmogrified");
        }
        return x < w; // Accessing z would be an error
```

```
    }
    ...
}
```

With `static` in tow, `isTransmogrifiable` can access only module-level and `static` data defined inside `transmogrify` (as shown in the example with `w`). Any transitory data such as function parameters or non-static variables is not accessible (but of course could be explicitly passed).

## 5.8  Closures

As mentioned, `alias` is a purely symbolic device; all it does is to make a symbol mean the same thing as another. In our examples above, `pred` is not a real value, as much as any function name is not a value; you can't assign something to `pred`. If you want to create an array of functions (e.g., a sequence of commands), `alias` won't help you a bit. Definitely something extra is needed here, and that something is the ability to have a palpable function object that can be stored and retrieved, much like a pointer to a function in C.

Consider, for example, the following challenge: "Given a value x of type T, return a function that finds the first value equal to x in an array of Ts." This alembicated, indirect definition is typical of a higher-order function: you don't *do* something, you just return something that will do it. So we need to write a function that in turn (careful here) returns a function that in turn (we're on a roll!) takes a `T[]` and returns a `T[]`. So the type returned is `T[] delegate(T[])`. Why `delegate` and not `function`? Well, as discussed above, the `delegate` gets to access its own state in addition to its arguments, whereas `function` cannot. And our function must have some state because it has to save that value x.

This is a very important point, so it is worth emphasizing. Imagine the type `T[] function(T[])` as the sheer address of a function: one machine word. That function has access only to its parameters and the program globals. If you take two pointers to the same function and pass them the same arguments, they will have access to the same program state. Anyone who has tried to deal with C callbacks—for example, for windowing systems or thread launching—knows about this perennial problem: pointers to functions can't have access to private state. The way C callbacks get around it is usually by taking a `void*` (an untyped address) that passes state information around. Other callback systems—such as the old and crotchety MFC library—store additional state in a global associative array, and yet others, such as the Active Template Library (ATL), use assembler code to create new functions dynamically. The cross-platform Qt library uses an advanced mechanism called signals/slots to effect the same thing. Wherever there's interfacing with C callbacks, there's some involved solution that allows callbacks to access state; it's not a simple problem.

With `delegate`, all of these issues vanish. Delegates achieve that by taking a size penalty: a `delegate` holds a pointer to a function and a pointer to that function's environment. That may be larger and sometimes slower, but it also is considerably more powerful, so you should prefer using `delegate` to using `function` objects for your own designs. (Of course, `function` is irreplaceable when interfacing with C via callbacks.)

That being said, let's take a stab at writing the new `finder` function. Remember that we need to return a `T[] delegate(T[])`.

```
import std.algorithm;

T[] delegate(T[]) finder(T)(T x)
    if (is(typeof(x == x) == bool))
{
    return delegate(T[] a) { return find(a, x); };
}

unittest {
    auto d = finder(5);
    assert(d([1, 3, 5, 7, 9]) == [ 5, 7, 9 ]);
    d = finder(10);
    assert(d([1, 3, 5, 7, 9]) == []);
}
```

Agreed, things like two `return` statements on the same line are bound to look odd to the uninitiated, but then many higher-order functions are liable to seem bizarre at first. So, line by line: `finder` is parameterized by a type `T`, takes a `T` and returns a `T[] delegate(T[])`; `finder` imposes a condition on `T`: you must be able to compare two values of type `T` and get a `bool`. (Again, the silly comparison `x == x` is there just for the sake of types, not particular values.) Then, `finder` cleverly does its deed by returning a delegate literal. That literal has a short body that calls our previously defined `find`, which fulfills the contract. The returned delegate is called a *closure*.

Usage is as expected—calling `finder` returns a delegate that you can later call or reassign. The variable d defined by the `unittest` has type `T[] delegate(T[])`, but thanks to `auto` there's no need for us to write that type explicitly. In fact, to be completely honest, `auto` can serve as a shortcut in defining `finder` as well; the presence of all types was intended as training wheels and exposition helpers. A considerably briefer definition of `finder` could look like this:

```
auto finder(T)(T x) if (is(typeof(x == x) == bool)) {
    return (T[] a) { return find(a, x); };
}
```

Note the use of auto as the result type of the function and also the omission of the delegate keyword; the compiler will gladly take care of those for us. However, the T[] in front of delegate parameter a must be specified. This is because the compiler must have a starting point to make the auto magic happen: the type returned by the delegate is inferred from the type of find(a, x), which in turn is inferred from the type of a and that of x; from there, the type of the delegate is inferred as T[] delegate(T[]), which is also the return type of finder. Without knowing the type of a, all this chain of reasoning could not be carried out.

### 5.8.1    OK, This Works. Wait, It Shouldn't. Oh, It Does!

The unittest supplied probes the behavior of finder, but of course that's not a proof that it works correctly. There's one advanced question that lurks in the background: the delegate returned by finder uses x. After finder has returned, where does x sit? In fact, given that D uses the regular call stack for calling functions, the question even suggests that something very dangerous is going on: a caller invokes finder, x is deposited onto the call stack, finder returns, the stack is popped back to its position just before the call ... which implies that the delegate returned by finder accesses a defunct stack location!

Persistence of local environment (in our case the environment consists only of x, but it could be arbitrarily large) is a classic problem in implementing closures, and each language that supports closures must address it somehow. D uses the following approach:[2] Ordinarily, all calls use a simple stack. When the compiler detects the presence of a closure, it automatically copies the used context onto heap-allocated memory and wires the delegate to use the heap-allocated data. That heap is garbage-collected.

The disadvantage is that every call to finder will issue a memory allocation request. However, closures are very expressive and enable a host of interesting programming paradigms, so in most cases the cost is more than justified.

## 5.9    Beyond Arrays. Ranges. Pseudo Members

The end of § 5.3 on page 138 enigmatically claimed: "find is at the same time too general and not general enough." We then saw how find is too general and fixed that by restricting its accepted types. It is time now to figure out why find is still not general enough.

What's the essence of linear search? You go through the searched elements one by one looking for a specific value, or to fulfill a predicate. The problem is that so far we've been working on contiguous arrays (slices aka T[]) exclusively, but contiguity is never, ever of relevance to the notion of linear searching. (It is relevant only to the mechanics of carrying out the walk.) By limiting ourselves to T[], we robbed find of access to a host of other data structures with various topologies that could be searched linearly. A

---

2. Similar to the approach of ML and other functional language implementations.

language that, for example, makes `find` a method of some type `Array` rightly deserves your scornful eye. That's not to say you can't get work done in that language; you'd sure be busy doing work, actually quite a bit more than you should.

It's time to clean the slate and reevaluate our basic `find` implementation, copied below for convenience:

```
T[] find(T)(T[] haystack, T needle) {
    while (haystack.length > 0 && haystack[0] != needle) {
        haystack = haystack[1 .. $];
    }
    return haystack;
}
```

What are the primitive operations we're using against `haystack`, and what are their respective meanings?

1. `haystack.length > 0` tells whether there are elements left in `haystack`.
2. `haystack[0]` accesses the first element of `haystack`.
3. `haystack = haystack[1 .. $]` eliminates the first element of `haystack`.

The particular manner in which arrays implement these operations is not easy to generalize to other containers. For example, it would be Darwin-awards-worthy to ask whether a singly linked list has elements in it by evaluating `haystack.length > 0`. Unless the list consistently caches its length (problematic in more ways than one), evaluating a list's length takes time proportional to the actual length of the list, whereas a quick look at the head node in the list takes only a few machine instructions. Using indexed access with lists is an equally losing proposition. So let's distill the primitives as three named functions and leave it to `haystack`'s type to figure out their implementation. The syntax of the primitives could be

1. `haystack.empty` for testing whether `haystack` is done
2. `haystack.front` for getting the first element of `haystack`
3. `haystack.popFront()` for eliminating the first element of `haystack`

Note how the first two operations do not modify `haystack` so they don't use parentheses, whereas the third does affect `haystack`, which is reinforced syntactically by the use of `()`. Let's redefine `find` to use the new shiny syntax:

```
R find(R, T)(R haystack, T needle)
    if (is(typeof(haystack.front != needle) == bool))
{
    while (!haystack.empty && haystack.front != needle) {
        haystack.popFront();
```

```
    }
    return haystack;
}
```

It would be great now to bask a little in the glow of this generous definition, but the failing `unittests` are an unpleasant reality check. Well, of course: the built-in slice type `T[]` has no idea that we were suddenly enlightened to opt for a new set of primitives bearing arbitrary names such as `empty`, `front`, and `popFront`. We need to define them for all `T[]`s. Sure, they will have trivial implementations, but we need those to have our nice abstraction work again with the type we started from.

### 5.9.1   Pseudo Members and the @property Attribute

One syntactic problem is that function invocations so far have looked like `fun(argument)`, whereas now we'd like to define calls that look like `argument.fun()` and `argument.fun`. The latter syntaxes are called *method invocation* syntax and *property access* syntax, respectively. We'll learn in the next chapter that they're rather easy to define for user-defined types, but `T[]` is a built-in type. What to do?

D recognizes this as a purely syntactic issue and allows pseudo-member notation: if `a.fun(b, c, d)` is seen but `fun` is not a member of a's type, D rewrites that as `fun(a, b, c, d)` and tries that as well. (The opposite path is never taken, though: if you write `fun(a, b, c, d)` and it does not make sense, `a.fun(b, c, d)` is not tried.) The intent of pseudo methods is to allow you to call regular functions with the send-message-to-object syntax that is familiar to some of us. Without further ado, let's implement `empty`, `front`, and `popFront` for built-in arrays. Three lines and we're done:

```
@property bool empty(T)(T[] a) { return a.length == 0; }
@property ref T front(T)(T[] a) { return a[0]; }
void popFront(T)(ref T[] a) { a = a[1 .. $]; }
```

The `@property` notation introduces an *attribute* called "property." Attributes, always introduced with `@`, are simple adornments specifying certain features for the symbol being defined. Some attributes are recognized by the compiler; some are defined and used by the programmer alone. In particular, "property" is recognized by the compiler and signals the fact that the function bearing such an attribute must be called without the trailing `()`.

Also note the use of `ref` (§ 5.2.1 on page 135) in two places. One is `front`'s return type, the intent being to allow you to modify elements in the array if you want to. Also, `popFront` uses `ref` to make sure it effects its change on the slice directly.

With the help of the three simple definitions, the modified `find` compiles and runs smoothly, which is deeply satisfying; we generalized `find` to work against any type that defines `empty`, `front`, and `popFront` and then completed the circle having the general version work with the concrete case that motivated generalization in the first place. If the three primitives are inlined, the general `find` stays just as efficient as the previous implementation that was crippled to work only for slices.

Now, if `empty`, `front`, and `popFront` were useful only for defining `find`, the abstraction would be distinctly underwhelming. All right, we pulled it off with `find`, but when we define another function, will the `empty-front-popFront` troika be of any use, or will we have to start all over again with some different primitives? Fortunately, an extensive body of experience shows that there is something distinctly fundamental about the notion of a one pass access to a collection of data. The notion is so useful, it has been enshrined as the Iterator pattern in the famous *Design Patterns* book [27]; C++'s STL [51] refines the notion further and defines a conceptual hierarchy of iterators: input, forward, bidirectional, and random-access iterators.

In D's nomenclature, the abstract data type that allows traversal of a collection of elements is called a *range*. (*Iterator* would have been a good name choice as well, but different preexisting libraries ascribe different meanings to the term, leading to possible confusion.) D's ranges are more akin to the Iterator pattern than STL iterators (a D range can be modeled roughly by a pair of STL iterators) but do inherit STL's categorical taxonomy. The troika `empty-front-popFront` in particular defines an *input range*, so our quest for a good `find` function revealed the inextricable relationship between linear searching and input ranges: you can't linearly search anything less capable than an input range, and it would be a mistake to gratuitously require more than input range capabilities from your collection (e.g., you shouldn't need arrays with indexed access). A near-identical implementation of our `find` can be found in the `std.algorithm` module of the standard library.

### 5.9.2 `reduce`—Just Not *ad Absurdum*

How about a challenging task that uses only input ranges: Define a function `reduce` that, given an input range `r`, an operation `fun`, and a seed `x`, repeatedly computes `x = fun(x, e)` for each element `e` in `r`, and then returns `x`. The `reduce` higher-order function is mightily powerful because it can express a variety of interesting accumulations. Many languages capable of higher-order functions define `reduce` as a staple facility, possibly under names such as `accumulate`, `compress`, `inject`, or `foldl`. Let's start to define `reduce` in the undying spirit of test-driven development with a few unit tests:

```
unittest {
    int[] r = [ 10, 14, 3, 5, 23 ];
    // Compute the sum of all elements
    int sum = reduce!((a, b) { return a + b; })(0, r);
    assert(sum == 55);
    // Compute minimum
    int min = reduce!((a, b) { return a < b ? a : b; })(r[0], r);
    assert(min == 3);
```

```
}
```

As you can see, reduce is quite flexible and useful, of course if we ignore the minor detail that it doesn't exist yet. Let's set out to implement reduce such that it fulfills the tests above. We now have the knowledge to write a true industry-strength reduce from scratch: we know from § 5.3 on page 138 how to pass type parameters into a function; § 5.4 on page 140 taught us how to restrict reduce such that it accepts only sensible arguments; we saw in § 5.6 on page 148 how function literals can be passed into a function as alias parameters; and we just zeroed in on a nice, simple input range interface.

```
V reduce(alias fun, V, R)(V x, R range)
   if (is(typeof(x = fun(x, range.front)))
      && is(typeof(range.empty) == bool)
      && is(typeof(range.popFront())))
{
   for (; !range.empty; range.popFront()) {
      x = fun(x, range.front);
   }
   return x;
}
```

Compile, run unittests, and all pass. The definition of reduce would be, however, a bit more likable if the constraints weren't about as bulky as the implementation itself. Besides, nobody wants to write the tedious tests that ensure R is an input range. Such verbose constraints are a subtle form of duplication. Fortunately, we have the tests for ranges nicely packaged in the standard module std.range, which simplifies reduce's implementation to

```
import std.range;

V reduce(alias fun, V, R)(V x, R range)
   if (isInputRange!R && is(typeof(x = fun(x, range.front))))
{
   for (; !range.empty; range.popFront()) {
      x = fun(x, range.front);
   }
   return x;
}
```

which is distinctly more palatable. With reduce you can compute not only sum and minimum, but a variety of other aggregate functions such as the closest number to a given one, the largest number in absolute value, and standard deviation. The standard library defines reduce in std.algorithm pretty much as above, except that it accepts multiple functions to compute; that makes for very efficient computation of multiple aggregate functions because it makes only one pass through the input.

## 5.10 Variadic Functions

The traditional "Hello, world!" program on page 1 used the standard library function writeln to print its greeting to the standard output. One interesting detail about writeln is that it accepts any number and types of arguments. There are several ways to define variadic functions in D, catering to different needs; let's start with the simplest.

### 5.10.1 Homogeneous Variadic Functions

A homogeneous variadic function accepts any number of arguments of the same type and is defined like this:

```
import std.algorithm, std.array;

// Computes the average of a set of numbers,
//     passable directly or via an array.
double average(double[] values...) {
    if (values.empty) {
        throw new Exception("Average of zero elements is undefined");
    }
    return reduce!((a, b) { return a + b; })(0.0, values)
        / values.length;
}

unittest {
    assert(average(0) == 0);
    assert(average(1, 2) == 1.5);
    assert(average(1, 2, 3) == 2);
    // Passing arrays and slices works as well
    double[] v = [1, 2, 3];
    assert(average(v) == 2);
}
```

(Notice the reuse of reduce at its best.) The distinguishing trait of average is the presence of the ellipsis ... following the values parameter, in conjunction with the fact that values has slice type. (If it didn't, or if values were not the last parameter of average, the ellipsis would have been in error.)

If you invoke average with a slice of double, it's business as usual, as shown in the unittest's last line. But thanks to the ellipsis, you can also invoke average with any number of arguments, as long as each is convertible to `double`. The compiler will automatically arrange all arguments in a slice and will pass it to `average`.

You could consider that this feature is little more than syntactic sugar rewriting `average(a, b, c)` into `average([a, b, c])`. But because of its invocation syntax, a homogeneous variadic function overloads others in its scope. For example:

```
// For the sake of argument
double average() {}
double average(double) {}
// Homogeneous variadic function
double average(double[] values...) { /* as above */ ... }
unittest {
    average(); // Error! Ambiguous call to overloaded function!
}
```

The presence of the first two overloads of `average` effectively renders zero- and one-argument calls to the variadic version of `average` ambiguous. You can disambiguate the calls by explicitly passing a slice to `average`, for example, `average([1, 2])`.

If a non-variadic function and a variadic one coexist in the same scope for the same slice type, the non-variadic function is preferred for calls that pass an actual slice:

```
import std.stdio;

void average(double[]) { writeln("non-variadic"); }
void average(double[]...) { writeln("variadic"); }
void main() {
    average(1, 2, 3);   // Writes "variadic"
    average([1, 2, 3]); // Writes "non-variadic"
}
```

### 5.10.2　Heterogeneous Variadic Functions

Getting back to `writeln`, clearly it must be doing something other than what `average` did because `writeln` accepts arguments of different types. To match an arbitrary number and types of arguments, you'd use a heterogeneous variadic function, which is defined like this:

```
import std.conv;

void writeln(T...)(T args) {
    foreach (arg; args) {
        stdout.rawWrite(to!string(arg));
    }
}
```

```
    stdout.rawWrite('\n');
    stdout.flush();
}
```

This implementation is a bit crude and inefficient, but it does work. Inside writeln, T is a *parameter type tuple*—a type that packs together several types—and args is a *parameter tuple*. The foreach statement detects that args is a type tuple, so it generates radically different code from that of a usual foreach invocation (such as one for iterating an array). For example, consider the call

```
writeln("Writing integer: ", 42, " and array: ", [ 1, 2, 3 ]);
```

For this call, the code generated by foreach would look like this:

```
// Approximation of generated code
void writeln(string a0, int a1, string a2, int[new] a3) {
    stdout.rawWrite(to!string(arg0));
    stdout.rawWrite(to!string(arg1));
    stdout.rawWrite(to!string(arg2));
    stdout.rawWrite(to!string(arg3));
    stdout.rawWrite('\n');
    stdout.flush();
}
```

The module std.conv defines to!string for all types (including string itself, for which to!string is the identity function), so the function works by converting each argument in turn to a string and writing it as raw bytes to the standard output.

You don't need to use foreach to access the types or the values in a parameter tuple. If n is a compile-time constant integral, T[n] yields the $n^{th}$ type and args[n] yields the $n^{th}$ value in the parameter tuple. To get the number of arguments, use T.length or args.length (both are compile-time constants). If you noticed a resemblance to arrays, you won't be surprised to find out that T[$ - 1] accesses the last type in T (and args[$ - 1] is an alias for the last value in args). For example:

```
import std.stdio;

void testing(T...)(T values) {
    writeln("Called with ", values.length, " arguments.");
    // Access each index and each value
    foreach (i, value; values) {
        writeln(i, ": ", typeid(T[i]), " ", value);
    }
}
```

```
void main() {
   testing(5, "hello", 4.2);
}
```

The program prints

```
Called with 3 arguments.
0: int 5
1: immutable(char)[] hello
2: double 4.2
```

### 5.10.2.1   The Type without a Name

The writeln function does too many specific things to be general—it always prints '\n' at the end and then flushes the stream. We'd like to define writeln in terms of a primitive write that just writes each argument in turn:

```
import std.conv;

void write(T...)(T args) {
   foreach (arg; args) {
      stdout.rawWrite(to!string(arg));
   }
}

void writeln(T...)(T args) {
   write(args, '\n');
   stdout.flush();
}
```

Note how writeln forwards args plus '\n' to write. When forwarding a parameter tuple, it is automatically expanded, so the call writeln(1, "2", 3) forwards four, not two, arguments to write. This behavior is a tad irregular and potentially puzzling because pretty much anywhere else in D mentioning one symbol means one value. Here's an example that could surprise even the prepared:

```
void fun(T...)(T args) {
   gun(args);
}

void gun(T)(T value) {
   writeln(value);
}
```

```
unittest {
    fun(1);       // Fine
    fun(1, 2.2); // Error! Cannot find 'gun' taking two arguments!
}
```

The first call goes through, but the second call does not. You'd expect it would, because any value has a type, so `args` must have some type that is then inferred by `gun`. What is happening?

The answer is that indeed all values do have a type that is correctly tracked by the compiler. The culprit is the call `gun(args)` because wherever a parameter tuple is passed to a function as an argument, the compiler expands it automatically. So even though you wrote `gun(args)`, the compiler *always* expands that to `gun(args[0]`, `args[1], ..., args[$ - 1])`. In the second call that means `gun(args[0], args[1])`, which looks for a two-parameter `gun` and doesn't find it—hence the error.

To investigate the matter further, let's have `fun` print out the type of `args`:

```
void fun(T...)(T args) {
    writeln(typeof(args).stringof);
}
```

The `typeof` construct is not a function call; it just yields the type of `args`, so we needn't worry about automatic expansion. The `.stringof` property of any type yields its name, so let's compile and run the program again. It prints

```
(int)
(int, double)
```

So indeed it seems like the compiler tracks the type of parameter tuples and has a string representation for them. However, you cannot explicitly define a parameter tuple—there is no type called `(int, double)`:

```
// No avail
(int, double) value = (1, 4.2);
```

This is because tuples are unique that way: they are types that the compiler uses internally but cannot be expressed. There is no way you can sit down and write a parameter tuple type. For that matter, there is no literal value that would yield a parameter tuple (if there were, `auto` would obviate the need for a type name).

### 5.10.2.2  Tuple and tuple

Types without a name and values without a literal may seem an interesting concept for a thrill seeker, but quite crippling for a practical programmer. Fortunately (finally! a "fortunately" was due sooner or later), that's not really a limitation as much as a way to save on syntax. You can eminently express parameter tuple types by using the standard library type Tuple, and parameter tuple values with tuple. Both are to be found in the standard module std.typecons. So a parameter tuple containing an int and a double could be written as

```
import std.typecons;
unittest {
    Tuple!(int, double) value = tuple(1, 4.2); // Whew
}
```

or equivalently, given that tuple(1, 4.2) returns a value of type Tuple!(int, double):

```
auto value = tuple(1, 4.2); // Double whew
```

Tuple!(int, double) being a type like any other, it doesn't do the automatic expansion trick, so if you want to expand it into its constituents you must do so explicitly by using Tuple's expand property. For example, let's scrap our fun/gun program and rewrite it like this:

```
import std.stdio, std.typecons;

void fun(T...)(T args) {
    // Create a Tuple to pack all arguments together
    gun(tuple(args));
}

void gun(T)(T value) {
    // Expand the tuple back
    writeln(value.expand);
}

void main() {
    fun(1);        // Fine
    fun(1, 2.2); // Fine
}
```

Notice how fun packs all of its arguments inside a Tuple and passes it to gun, which expands the received tuple into whatever it contains. The expression value.expand is automatically rewritten into an arguments list containing whatever you put in the Tuple.

The implementation of Tuple has a couple of subtleties but uses means available to any programmer. Checking its definition in the standard library is a useful exercise.

## 5.11   Function Attributes

D functions allow attachment of a number of *attributes*—specific features that advertise certain characteristics of a function to the programmer and the compiler. Function attributes are checked, so all the user has to do to figure out important information about a function's behavior is to look at its signature, with the assurance that the guarantee is much more than just a comment or a convention.

### 5.11.1   Pure Functions

Purity of functions is a notion borrowed from mathematics that has quite a few theoretical and practical advantages. In D, a function is considered pure if returning a result is its only effect and the result depends only on the function's arguments.

In classic mathematics, all functions are pure because classic mathematics does not use state and mutation. What's $\sqrt{2}$? Well, 1.4142 something, same as yesterday, tomorrow, or really at any point in time. It could even be argued that $\sqrt{2}$ had the same value even before humankind discovered roots, algebra, numbers, or even before there even *was* a humankind to appreciate the beauty of mathematics, and will be the same long after the universe dies of heat exhaustion. Mathematical results are forever.

Purity is good for functions, at least sometimes and with qualifications, just as in life. (Also as in life, functional purity is not easy to achieve. Plus, at least according to some, too much of either kind of purity could get really annoying.) But looking at the bright side, a pure function is easier to reason about. You know you can call it at any time and only look at the call to see what effect it's supposed to have. You can substitute equivalent function calls for values and values for equivalent function calls. You know that bugs in pure functions never cause "shrapnel"—bugs can never affect more than the result of the function itself.

Also, pure functions can run literally in parallel because they don't interact with the rest of the program except through their result. In contrast, mutation-intensive functions are prone to step on each other's toes when running in parallel. Even when being run in sequence, their effect may subtly depend on the order in which you call them. Many of us got so used to this way of doing things, we consider the difficulties a part of the job so we hardly raise an eyebrow. But it can be very refreshing and very useful if at least parts of an application obey purity.

You can define a pure function by prefixing its definition with `pure`:

```
pure bool leapYear(uint y) {
    return (y % 4) == 0 && (y % 100 || (y % 400) == 0);
}
```

The function's signature is

```
pure bool leapYear(uint y);
```

and gives the user a guarantee that, for example, leapYear doesn't write to the standard output. In addition, just by seeing the signature it's clear that leapYear(2020) returns the same value now or ever.

The compiler is keenly aware of pure, too, and it actually guards against anything that would render leapYear less than pristine. Consider the following change:

```
pure bool leapYear(uint y) {
    auto result = (y % 4) == 0 && (y % 100 || (y % 400) == 0);
    if (result) writeln(y, " is a leap year!"); // Error!
        // Cannot call impure function writeln from pure function!
    return result;
}
```

The writeln function is not, and cannot be, pure. If it claimed to be, the compiler would have disabused it of such a pretense. The compiler makes sure a pure function never calls an impure one. That's why the modified leapYear does not compile. On the other hand, the compiler can successfully verify a function such as daysInYear:

```
// Certified pure
pure uint daysInYear(uint y) {
    return 365 + leapYear(y);
}
```

### 5.11.1.1    pure Is as pure Does

Traditionally, functional languages require absolutely no mutation in order to allow programs to claim purity. D relaxes that requirement by allowing functions to mutate their own private and transitory state. That way, even if mutation is present inside, from the outside the function is still spotless.

Let's see how that relaxation works. Consider, for example, a naïve implementation of the functional-style Fibonacci function:

```
ulong fib(uint n) {
    return n < 2 ? n : fib(n - 1) + fib(n - 2);
}
```

No computer science teacher should ever teach such an implementation of Fibonacci. fib takes *exponential* time to complete and as such promotes nothing but ignorance of complexity and of the costs of computation, a "cute excuses sloppy" attitude, and SUV driving. You know how bad exponential is? fib(10) and fib(20) take negligible time on a contemporary machine, whereas fib(50) takes 19 minutes. In all likelihood, evaluating fib(1000) will outlast humankind (just not in a good way like $\sqrt{2}$ does).

Fine, so then what does a "green" functional Fibonacci implementation look like?

```
ulong fib(uint n) {
  ulong iter(uint i, ulong fib_1, ulong fib_2) {
    return i == n
      ? fib_2
      : iter(i + 1, fib_1 + fib_2, fib_1);
  }
  return iter(0, 1, 0);
}
```

The revised version takes negligible time to compute `fib(50)`. The implementation now takes $\mathcal{O}(n)$ time, and tail call elimination (§ 1.4.2 on page 12) takes care of the space complexity. (It should be mentioned that in fact there are $\mathcal{O}(\log n)$-time algorithms that compute Fibonacci.)

The problem is that the new `fib` kind of lost its glory. Essentially the revised implementation maintains two state variables in the disguise of function parameters, so we might as well come clean and write the straight loop that `iter` made unnecessarily obscure:

```
ulong fib(uint n) {
  ulong fib_1 = 1, fib_2 = 0;
  foreach (i; 0 .. n) {
    auto t = fib_1;
    fib_1 += fib_2;
    fib_2 = t;
  }
  return fib_2;
}
```

But, alas, this is not functional anymore. Look at all that mutation going on in the loop. One mistaken step, and we fell all the way from the peak of mathematical purity down to the unsophisticatedness of the unwashed masses.

But if we sit for a minute and think, the iterative `fib` is not *that* unwashed. If you think of it as a black box, `fib` always outputs the same thing for a given input, and after all, pure is as pure does. The fact that it uses private mutable state may make it less functional in letter, but not in spirit. Pulling carefully on that thread, we reach a very interesting conclusion: as long as the mutable state in a function is entirely *transitory* (i.e., allocated on the stack) and *private* (i.e., not passed along by reference to functions that may taint it), then the function can be considered pure.

And that's how D defines functional purity: you can use mutation in the implementation of a pure function, as long as it's transitory and private. You can then put `pure` in that function's signature and the compiler will compile it without a hitch:

```
pure ulong fib(uint n) {
    ... // Iterative implementation
}
```

The way D relaxes purity is pretty cool because you're getting the best of both worlds: ironclad functional purity guarantees, and comfortable implementation when mutation is the preferred method.

### 5.11.2   The nothrow Function Attribute

The nothrow attribute specified with a function conveys the information that that function will never throw an exception. Just like pure, nothrow is compile-time-checked. For example:

```
import std.stdio;

nothrow void tryLog(string msg) {
    try {
        stderr.writeln(msg);
    } catch (Exception) {
        // Ignore exception
    }
}
```

The tryLog function does a best-effort attempt at logging a message. If an exception is thrown, it is silently ignored. This makes tryLog usable in critical sections of code. In some circumstances it would be silly for some important transaction to fail just because a log message couldn't be written. Code with transactional semantics relies critically on certain portions never throwing, and nothrow is the way you can ensure such facts statically.

The semantic checking of nothrow functions ensures an exception may never leak out of the function. Essentially any statement in that function must never throw (e.g., is a call to another nothrow function) or is nested inside a try statement that swallows the exception. To illustrate the former case:

```
nothrow void sensitive(Widget w) {
    tryLog("Starting sensitive operation");
    try {
        w.mayThrow();
        tryLog("Sensitive operation succeeded");
    } catch (Exception) {
        tryLog("Sensitive operation failed");
    }
```

```
}
```

The first call to `tryLog` needn't be inside a `try` statement because the compiler already knows it can't throw. Similarly, the call inside the `catch` clause does not need to be protected by an extra `try` statement.

What is the relationship between `pure` and `nothrow`? It might appear that they are entirely orthogonal, but there may be a certain degree of correlation. At least in the standard library, many mathematical functions are both `pure` and `nothrow`, for example, most transcendental functions (`exp`, `sin`, `cos`, etc.).

## 5.12  Compile-Time Evaluation

In keeping with the saying that good things come to those who wait (or read patiently), this last section discusses a very interesting feature of D. The best part is, you don't even need to learn much to use this feature gainfully.

Let's use an example that's large enough to be meaningful. Suppose you want to define the ultimate random number generator library. There are many random number generators out there, among them the fast and well-studied linear congruential generators [35, § 3.2.1, pages 10–26]. Such generators have three integral parameters: the modulus $m > 0$, the multiplier $0 < a < m$, and the increment[3] $0 < c < m$. Starting from an arbitrary seed $0 \le x_0 < m$, the linear congruential generator yields pseudorandom numbers using the following recurrence formula:

$$x_{n+1} = (ax_n + c) \bmod m$$

Coding such an algorithm is simple—all you need is to keep the state defined by $m$, $a$, $c$, and $x_n$ and define a `getNext` function that changes $x_n$ into $x_{n+1}$ and returns it.

But there is a rub. Not all combinations of $m$, $a$, and $c$ lead to good random number generators. For starters, if $a = 1$ and $c = 1$, the generator gives the sequence $0, 1, \ldots, m-1, 0, 1, \ldots, m-1, 0, 1, \ldots$ which is admittedly quite non-random.

With larger values of $a$ and $c$ such obvious risks are avoided, but a subtler problem appears: periodicity. Because of the modulus operator the generated number is always between 0 and $m-1$, so it's good to make $m$ as large as possible (usually it's a power of 2 to match the machine word size, in which case the mod comes for free). The problem is that the generated sequence may have a period much smaller than $m$. Say we operate with `uint` and choose $m = 2^{32}$ so we don't even need a modulus operation; then $a = 210$, $c = 123$, and some crazy value for $x_0$, such as $1,780,588,661$. Let's run this program:

```
import std.stdio;

void main() {
```

---

3. The case $c = 0$ is also allowed, but the associated theory is more difficult so here we require $c > 0$.

```d
    enum uint a = 210, c = 123, x0 = 1_780_588_661;
    auto x = x0;
    foreach (i; 0 .. 100) {
        x = a * x + c;
        writeln(x);
    }
}
```

Instead of a colorful random display of digits, we see something rather surprising:

```
 1  261464181
 2  3367870581
 3  2878185589
 4  3123552373
 5  3110969461
 6  468557941
 7  3907887221
 8  317562997
 9  2263720053
10  2934808693
11  2129502325
12  518889589
13  1592631413
14  3740115061
15  3740115061
16  3740115061
17  ...
```

The generator starts with great aplomb. At least to the untrained eye, it does a good job of generating random numbers. But it doesn't take more than 14 steps to stall in a fixed point: through one of those strange coincidences that only math is capable of, 3740115061 is (and was and will be) exactly equal to $(3740115061 * 210 + 123) \bmod 2^{32}$. That's a period of one, the worst possible!

So we need to make sure that $m$, $a$, and $c$ are chosen such that the generator has a large period. Investigating the matter further, it turns out that the conditions for generating a sequence of period $m$ (the largest period possible) are the following:

1. $c$ and $m$ are relatively prime.
2. $a - 1$ is divisible by all prime factors of $m$.
3. If $a - 1$ is a multiple of 4, then $m$ is a multiple of 4, too.

The relative primality of c and m can be easily checked by comparing their greatest common divisor against 1. To compute the greatest common divisor, we use Euclid's algorithm:[4]

```
// Implementation of Euclid's algorithm
ulong gcd(ulong a, ulong b) {
    while (b) {
        auto t = b;
        b = a % b;
        a = t;
    }
    return a;
}
```

Euclid expressed his algorithm by using subtraction instead of modulus. The modulus version takes fewer iterations, but on today's machines, % can be quite slow, something that Euclid might have had in mind.

The second test is a tad more difficult to implement. We could write a function `factorize` that returns all prime factors of a number with their powers and then use it, but `factorize` is more than the bare necessity. Going with the simplest design that could possibly work, probably a simple choice is to write a function `primeFactorsOnly(n)` that returns the product of n's prime factors, but without the powers. Then the requirement boils down to checking `(a - 1) % primeFactorsOnly(m) == 0`. So let's implement `primeFactorsOnly`.

There are many ways to go about getting the prime factors of some number n. A simple one would be to generate prime numbers $p_1, p_2, p_3, \ldots$ and check in turn whether $p_k$ divides n, in which case $p_k$ is multiplied to an accumulator r. When $p_k$ has become greater than n, the accumulator contains the desired answer: the product of all of n's prime factors, each taken once.

(I know you are asking yourself what this has to do with compile-time evaluation. It does. Please bear with me.)

A simpler version would be to do away with generating prime numbers and simply evaluate n mod k for increasing values of k starting at 2: 2, 3, 5, 7, 9, ... Whenever k divides n, the accumulator is multiplied by k and then n is "depleted" of all powers of k, that is, n is reassigned n/k for as long as k divides n. That way, we recorded the divisor k, and we also reduced n until it became irreducible by k. That seems like a wasteful method, but note that generating prime numbers would probably entail comparable work, at least in a straightforward implementation. An implementation of this idea would look like this:

```
ulong primeFactorsOnly(ulong n) {
```

---

4. Somehow, Euclid's algorithm always manages to make its way into good (ahem) programming books.

```
    ulong accum = 1;
    ulong iter = 2;
    for (; n >= iter * iter; iter += 2 - (iter == 2)) {
        if (n % iter) continue;
        accum *= iter;
        do n /= iter; while (n % iter == 0);
    }
    return accum * n;
}
```

The update `iter += 2 - (iter == 2)` bumps `iter` by 2 except when `iter` is 2, in which case the update brings `iter` to 3. That way `iter` spans 2, 3, 5, 7, 9, and so on. It would be wasteful to check any even number such as 4 because 2 has been tested already and all powers of 2 have been extracted out of `n`.

Why does the iteration go on while `n >= iter * iter` as opposed to `n >= iter`? The answer is a bit subtle. If `iter` is greater than $\sqrt{n}$ and different from `n` itself, then we can be sure `iter` can't be a divisor of `n`: if it were, there would need to be some multiplier `k` such that `n == k * iter`, but all divisors smaller than `iter` have been tried already, so `k` must be greater than `iter` and consequently `k * iter` is greater than `n`, which makes the equality impossible.

Let's `unittest` the `primeFactorsOnly` function:

```
unittest {
    assert(primeFactorsOnly(100) == 10);
    assert(primeFactorsOnly(11) == 11);
    assert(primeFactorsOnly(7 * 7 * 11 * 11 * 15) == 7 * 11 * 15);
    assert(primeFactorsOnly(129 * 2) == 129 * 2);
}
```

To conclude, we need a small wrapper that performs the three checks against the three candidate linear congruential generator parameters:

```
bool properLinearCongruentialParameters(ulong m, ulong a, ulong c) {
    // Bounds checking
    if (m == 0 || a == 0 || a >= m || c == 0 || c >= m) return false;
    // c and m are relatively prime
    if (gcd(c, m) != 1) return false;
    // a - 1 is divisible by all prime factors of m
    if ((a - 1) % primeFactorsOnly(m)) return false;
    // If a - 1 is multiple of 4, then m is a multiple of 4, too.
    if ((a - 1) % 4 == 0 && m % 4) return false;
    // Passed all tests
    return true;
```

```
}
```

Let's `unittest` a few popular values of `m`, `a`, and `c`:

```d
unittest {
    // Our broken example
    assert(!properLinearCongruentialParameters(
        1UL << 32, 210, 123));
    // Numerical Recipes book [48]
    assert(properLinearCongruentialParameters(
        1UL << 32, 1664525, 1013904223));
    // Borland C/C++ compiler
    assert(properLinearCongruentialParameters(
        1UL << 32, 22695477, 1));
    // glibc
    assert(properLinearCongruentialParameters(
        1UL << 32, 1103515245, 12345));
    // ANSI C
    assert(properLinearCongruentialParameters(
        1UL << 32, 134775813, 1));
    // Microsoft Visual C/C++
    assert(properLinearCongruentialParameters(
        1UL << 32, 214013, 2531011));
}
```

It looks like `properLinearCongruentialParameters` works like a charm, so we're done with all the details of testing the soundness of a linear congruential generator. It's about time to stop stalling and fess up. What does all that primality and factorization stuff have to do with compile-time evaluation? Where's the meat? Where are the templates, macros, or whatever they call them? The clever `static if`s? The mind-blowing code generation and expansion?

Well, here's the truth: you just saw everything there is to be seen about compile-time function evaluation. Given any constant numbers `m`, `a`, and `c`, you can evaluate `properLinearCongruentialParameters` *during compilation* without any change in that function or the functions it calls. The D compiler embeds an interpreter that evaluates D functions during compilation—with arithmetic, loops, mutation, early returns, arrays, and even transcendental functions.

All you need to do is to clarify to the compiler that the evaluation must be performed at compile time. There are several ways to do that:

```d
unittest {
    enum ulong m = 1UL << 32, a = 1664525, c = 1013904223;
    // Method 1: use static assert
```

```
    static assert(properLinearCongruentialParameters(m, a, c));
    // Method 2: assign the result to an enum
    enum proper1 = properLinearCongruentialParameters(m, a, c);
    // Method 3: assign the result to a static value
    static proper2 = properLinearCongruentialParameters(m, a, c);
}
```

We haven't looked closely at `struct`s and `class`es yet, but just to anticipate a little, the typical way you'd use `properLinearCongruentialParameters` would be inside a `struct` or a `class` that defines a linear congruential generator, for example:

```
struct LinearCongruentialEngine(UIntType,
    UIntType a, UIntType c, UIntType m) {
    static assert(properLinearCongruentialParameters(m, a, c),
        "Incorrect instantiation of LinearCongruentialEngine");
    ...
}
```

In fact, the lines above were copied from the eponymous `struct` found in the standard module `std.random`.

There are two interesting consequences of moving the test from runtime to compile time. First, `LinearCongruentialEngine` could have deferred the test to runtime, for example, by placing it in its constructor. As a general rule, however, it is better to discover errors sooner rather than later, particularly in a library that has little control over how it is being used. The static test does not make erroneous instantiations of `LinearCongruentialEngine` signal the error; it makes them nonexistent. Second, the code using compile-time constants has a good chance to be faster than code that uses regular variables for `m`, `a`, and `b`. On most of today's processors, literal constants can be made part of the instruction stream so loading them causes no extra memory access at all. And let's face it—linear congruential engines aren't the most random out there, so the primary reason you'd want to use one is speed.

The interpretation process is slower than generating code by a couple of orders of magnitude, but that is already much faster and more scalable than traditional metaprogramming carried out with C++ templates. Besides, within reason, compile-time activity is in a way "free."

At the time of this writing, the interpreter has certain limitations. Allocating class objects and memory in general is not allowed (though built-in arrays work). Static data, inline assembler, and unsafe features such as `union`s and certain `cast`s are also disallowed. But the limits of what can be done during interpretation form an envelope under continuous pressure. The plan is to allow everything in the safe subset of D to be interpretable during compilation. All in all, the ability to interpret code during compilation is recent and opens very exciting possibilities that deserve further exploration.

# Classes. Object-Oriented Style

Object-oriented programming (OOP) has evolved through the years from an endearing child to an annoying pimple-faced adolescent to the well-adjusted individual of today. Nowadays we have a better understanding of not only the power but also the inherent limitations of object technology. This in turn made the programming community aware that a gainful approach to creating solid designs is to combine the strengths of OOP with the strengths of other paradigms. That trend is quite visible—increasingly, today's languages either adopt more eclectic features or are designed from the get-go to foster OOP in conjunction with other programming styles. D is in the latter category, and, at least in the opinion of some, it has done a quite remarkable job of keeping different programming paradigms in harmony. This chapter explores D's object-oriented features and how they integrate with the rest of the language. For an in-depth treatment of object orientation, a good starting point is Bertrand Meyer's classic *Object-Oriented Software Construction* [40] (for a more formal treatment, see Pierce's *Types and Programming Languages* [46, Chapter 18]).

## 6.1   Classes

The unit of object encapsulation in D is the class. A class defines a cookie cutter for creating objects, defining how they look and feel. A class may specify constants, per-class state, per-object state, and methods. For example:

```
class Widget {
    // A constant
    enum fudgeFactor = 0.2;
    // A shared immutable value
```

```
static immutable defaultName = "A Widget";
// Some state allocated for each Widget object
string name = defaultName;
uint width, height;
// A static method
static double howFudgy() {
   return fudgeFactor;
}
// A method
void changeName(string another) {
   name = another;
}
// A non-overridable method
final void quadrupleSize() {
   width *= 2;
   height *= 2;
}
}
```

Creation of an object of type `Widget` is achieved with the new expression new
Widget (§ 2.3.6.1 on page 51), which you'd usually invoke to store its result in a named
object. To access a symbol defined inside `Widget`, you need to prefix it with the object
you want to operate on, followed by a dot. In case the accessed member is `static`, the
class name suffices. For example:

```
unittest {
   // Access a static method of Widget
   assert(Widget.howFudgy() == 0.2);
   // Create a Widget
   auto w = new Widget;
   // Play with the Widget
   assert(w.name == w.defaultName); // Or Widget.defaultName
   w.changeName("My Widget");
   assert(w.name == "My Widget");
}
```

Note a little twist. The code above used `w.defaultName` instead of `Widget.default-`
`Name`. Wherever you access a `static` member, an object name is as good as the class
name. This is because the name to the left of the dot guides name lookup first and
(if needed) object identification second. `w` is evaluated whether it ends up being used
or not.

## 6.2 Object Names Are References

Let's conduct a little experiment:

```
import std.stdio;

class A {
    int x = 42;
}

unittest {
    auto a1 = new A;
    assert(a1.x == 42);
    auto a2 = a1;
    a2.x = 100;
    assert(a1.x == 100);
}
```

This experiment succeeds (all `assertions` pass), revealing that `a1` and `a2` are not distinct objects: changing `a2` in fact went back and changed `a1` as well. The two are only two distinct names for the same object, and consequently changing `a2` affected `a1`. The statement `auto a2 = a1;` created no extra object of type A; it only made the existing object known by another name. Figure 6.1 illustrates this fact.

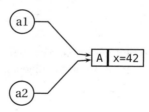

**Figure 6.1:** The statement `auto a2 = a1;` only adds one extra name for the same underlying object.

This behavior is consistent with the notion that all `class` objects are *entities*, meaning that they have "personality" and are not supposed to be duplicated without good reason. In contrast, value objects (e.g., built-in numbers) feature full copying; to define new value types, `struct` (Chapter 7) is the way to go.

So in the world of `class` objects there are *objects*, and then there are *references* to them. The imaginary arrows linking references to objects are called *bindings*—we say, for example, that `a1` and `a2` are bound to the same object, or have the same binding. The only way you can work on an object is to use a reference to it. As far as the object itself is concerned, once you have created it, it will live forever in the same place. What you

can do if you get bored with some object is to bind your reference to another object. For
example, consider that you want to swap two references:

```
unittest {
    auto a1 = new A;
    auto a2 = new A;
    a1.x = 100;
    a2.x = 200;
    // Let's swap a1 and a2
    auto t = a1;
    a1 = a2;
    a2 = t;
    assert(a1.x == 200);
    assert(a2.x == 100);
}
```

Instead of the last three lines we could have availed ourselves of the universal routine swap found in the module std.algorithm by calling swap(a1, a2), but doing the
rewiring explicitly makes what's going on clearer. Figure 6.2 illustrates the bindings before and after swapping.

**Figure 6.2:** The bindings before and after swapping two references. The swapping process changes the way references are wired to the objects; the objects themselves stay in
the same place.

The objects themselves stay put, that is, their locations in memory never change
after creation. Just as remarkably, the object never goes away—once it's created, you
can count on it being there forever. (A garbage collector recycles in the background
memory of objects that are not used anymore.) The references to the objects (in this
case a1 and a2) can be convinced to "look" elsewhere by rebinding them. When the
runtime system figures out that an object has no more references bound to it, it can
recycle the object's memory, an activity known as garbage collection. Such a behavior is
fundamentally different from *value semantics* (e.g., int), in which there is no indirection
and no rebinding—each name is stuck directly to the value it manipulates.

A reference that is not bound to any object is a null reference. Upon default initialization with .init, class references are null. A reference can be compared to null and
assigned from null. The following assertions succeed:

```
unittest {
    A a;
    assert(a is null);
    a = new A;
    assert(a !is null);
    a = null;
    assert(a is null);
    a = A.init;
    assert(a is null);
}
```

Accessing a member of an unbound (`null`) reference results in a hardware fault that terminates the application (or, on some systems and under certain conditions, starts the debugger). If you try to access a non-`static` member of a reference and the compiler can prove statically that the reference would definitely be `null`, it will refuse to compile the code.

```
A a;
a.x = 5;            // Error! a is null!
```

```
class A { int x; }
A a;
assert(!__traits(compiles, a.x = 5));
```

In an attempt to not annoy you too much, the compiler is conservative—if a reference may be `null` but not always, the compiler lets the code go through and defers any errors to runtime. For example:

```
A a;
if (‹condition›) {
    a = new A;
}
...
if (‹condition›) {
    a.x = 43;       // Fine
}
```

The compiler lets such code go through even though it's possible that ‹*condition*› changes value between the two evaluations. In the general case it would be very difficult to verify proper object initialization, so the compiler assumes you know what you're doing except for the simplest cases where it can vouch that you are trying to use a `null` reference in a faulty manner.

D's reference semantics approach to handling class objects is similar to that found
in many object-oriented languages.  Using reference semantics and garbage collection
for class objects has both positive and negative consequences, including the following:

+ ***Polymorphism.*** The level of indirection brought by the consistent use of references enables support for polymorphism.  All references have the same size, but
  related objects can have different sizes even though they have ostensibly the same
  type (through the use of inheritance, which we'll discuss shortly).  Because references have the same size regardless of the size of the object they refer to, you
  can always substitute references to derived objects for references to base objects.
  Also, arrays of objects work properly even when the actual objects in the array
  have different sizes.  If you've used C++, you sure know about the necessity of using pointers with polymorphism, and about the various lethal problems you encounter when you forget to.

+ ***Safety.*** Many of us see garbage collection as just a convenience that simplifies
  coding by relieving the programmer of managing memory.  Perhaps surprisingly,
  however, there is a very strong connection between the infinite lifetime model
  (which garbage collection makes practical) and memory safety.  Where there's infinite lifetime, there are no dangling references, that is, references to some object that has gone out of existence and has had its memory reused for an unrelated object.  Note that it would be just as safe to use value semantics throughout (have `auto a2 = a1;` duplicate the `A` object that `a1` refers to and have `a2` refer
  to the copy).  That setup, however, is hardly interesting because it disallows creation of any referential structure (such as lists, trees, graphs, and more generally
  shared resources).

– ***Allocation cost.*** Generally, class objects must reside in the garbage-collected
  heap, which generally is slower and eats more memory than memory on the stack.
  The margin has diminished quite a bit lately but is still nonzero.

– ***Long-range coupling.*** The main risk with using references is undue aliasing.  Using reference semantics throughout makes it all too easy to end up with references
  to the same object residing in different—and unexpected—places.  In Figure 6.1 on
  page 177, `a1` and `a2` may be arbitrarily far from each other as far as the application
  logic is concerned, and additionally there may be many other references hanging
  off the same object.  Interestingly, if the referred object is immutable, the problem
  vanishes—as long as nobody modifies the object, there is no coupling.  Difficulties arise when one change effected in a certain context affects surprisingly and
  dramatically the state as seen in a different part of the application.  Another way
  to alleviate this problem is explicit duplication, often by calling a special method
  `clone`, whenever passing objects around.  The downside of that technique is that
  it is based on discipline and that it could lead to inefficiency if several parts of an
  application decide to conservatively clone objects "just to be sure."

Contrast reference semantics with value semantics à la `int`. Value semantics has advantages, notably equational reasoning: you can always substitute equals for equals in expressions without altering the result. (In contrast, references that use method calls to modify underlying objects do not allow such reasoning.) Speed is also an important advantage of value semantics, but if you want the dynamic generosity of polymorphism, reference semantics is a must. Some languages tried to accommodate both, which earned them the moniker of "impure," in contrast to pure object-oriented languages that foster reference semantics uniformly across all types. D is impure and up-front about it. You get to choose at design time whether you use OOP for a particular type, in which case you use `class`; otherwise, you go with `struct` and forgo the particular OOP amenities that go hand in hand with reference semantics.

## 6.3   It's an Object's Life

Now that we have a general notion of objects' whereabouts, let's look in detail at their life cycle. To create an object, you use a `new` expression:

```
import std.math;

class Test {
    double a = 0.4;
    double b;
}

unittest {
    // Use a new expression to create an object
    auto t = new Test;
    assert(t.a == 0.4 && isnan(t.b));
}
```

Issuing `new Test` constructs a *default-initialized* `Test` object, which is a `Test` with each field initialized to its default value. Each type `T` has a statically known default value, accessible as `T.init` (see Table 2.1 on page 30 for the `.init` values of basic types). If you'd prefer to initialize some member variables to something other than their types' `.init` value, you can specify a statically known initializer when you define the member, as shown in the example above for `a`. The `unittest` above passes because `a` is explicitly initialized with `0.4`, and `b` is left alone so it is implicitly initialized with `double.init`, which is "Not a Number" (NaN).

### 6.3.1   Constructors

Of course, most of the time initializing fields with some statically known values is not enough. To execute code upon the creation of an object, you can use special functions

called *constructors*. A constructor is a function with the name `this` that declares no
return type:

```
class Test {
   double a = 0.4;
   int b;
   this(int b) {
      this.b = b;
   }
}
unittest {
   auto t = new Test(5);
}
```

As soon as a class defines at least one constructor, the implicit default constructor is
not available anymore. With `Test` defined as above, trying

```
auto t = new Test;
```

does not work anymore. This interdiction was intended to help avoiding a common bug:
a designer carefully defines a number of constructors with parameters but forgets all
about the default constructor. As is often the case in D, such protection for the forgetful
is easy to avoid by simply telling the compiler that yes, you did remember:

```
class Test {
   double a = 0.4;
   int b;
   this(int b) {
      this.b = b;
   }
   this() {} // Default constructor,
             //    all fields implicitly initialized
}
```

Inside a method—except `static` ones; see § 6.5 on page 196—the reference `this` is
implicitly bound to the object receiving the call. That reference is occasionally useful, as
in the example above that illustrates a common naming convention in constructors: if a
parameter is meant to initialize a member, give it the same name and disambiguate the
member from the parameter by prefixing the former with an explicit reference to `this`.
Without the prefix `this`, a parameter hides the homonym members.

Although you can modify `this.field` for any field, you can never rebind `this` itself,
which effectively behaves like an rvalue:

```
class NoGo {
```

```
void fun() {
    // Let's just rebind this to a different object
    this = new NoGo; // Error! Cannot modify 'this'!
}
}
```

The usual function overloading rules (§ 5.5 on page 142) apply to constructors: a `class` may define any number of constructors as long as they have distinct signatures (different in the number of parameters or in the type of at least one parameter).

### 6.3.2 Forwarding Constructors

Consider a class `Widget` that defines two constructors:

```
class Widget {
    this(uint height) {
        this.width = 1;
        this.height = height;
    }
    this(uint width, uint height) {
        this.width = width;
        this.height = height;
    }
    uint width, height;
    ...
}
```

The code above is quite repetitive and gets only worse for larger classes, but fortunately one constructor may defer to another:

```
class Widget {
    this(uint height) {
        this(1, height); // Defer to the other constructor
    }
    this(uint width, uint height) {
        this.width = width;
        this.height = height;
    }
    uint width, height;
    ...
}
```

There are certain limitations when it comes to calling constructors explicitly à la
`this(1, h)`. First, you can issue such a call only from within another constructor. Second, if you decide to make such a call, you must convince the compiler that you're making exactly one such call throughout your constructor, no matter what.  For example,
this constructor would be invalid:

```
this(uint h) {
   if (h > 1) {
      this(1, h);
   }
   // Error! One path skips constructor
}
```

In the case above, the compiler figures there are cases in which another constructor
is not called and flags that situation as an error. The intent is to have a constructor either
carry the construction itself or forward the task to another constructor. The situations in
which a constructor may or may not choose to defer to another constructor are rejected.

Invoking the same constructor twice is incorrect as well:

```
this(uint h) {
   if (h > 1) {
      this(1, h);
   }
   this(0, h);
}
```

You don't want a doubly initialized object any more than one you forgot to initialize,
so this case is also flagged as a compile-time error.  In short, a constructor is allowed
to call another constructor either exactly zero times or exactly one time.  This claim is
verified during compilation by using simple flow analysis.

### 6.3.3  Construction Sequence

In all languages, object construction is a bit tricky. The construction process starts with
a chunk of untyped memory and deposits in it information that makes that chunk look
and feel like a class object. A certain amount of magic is always needed.

In D, object construction takes the following steps:

1. *Allocation.*  The runtime allocates on the heap a chunk of raw memory large
   enough to store the non-`static` fields of the object. All class-based objects are
   dynamically allocated—unlike in C++, there is no way to allocate a class object on
   the stack. If allocation fails, construction is abandoned by throwing an exception.

2. *Field initialization.* Each field is initialized to its default value. As discussed above, the default field value is the one specified in the field declaration with = `value` or, absent that, the `.init` value of the field's type.
3. *Branding.* After default field initialization has taken place, the object is branded as a full-fledged `T`, even *before* the actual constructor gets called. The branding process is implementation-dependent and usually consists of initializing one or more hidden fields with type-dependent information.
4. *Constructor call.* Finally, the compiler issues a call to the applicable constructor. If the class defines no constructor, this step is skipped.

Since the object is considered alive and well right after the default field initialization, it is highly recommended that the field initializers always put the object in a meaningful state. Then, the actual constructor does adjustments that put the object in an interesting state (which is, of course, also meaningful).

In case your constructor reassigns some fields, the double assignment should not be an efficiency problem. Most of the time, if the body of the constructor is simple enough, the compiler should be able to figure out that the first assignment is redundant and perform the dark-humored "dead assignment elimination" optimization.

If efficiency is an absolutely essential concern, you may specify = `void` as a field initializer for certain fields, in which case you must be very careful to initialize that member in the constructor. You might find = `void` useful with fixed-size arrays. It is difficult for the compiler to optimize double initialization of all array elements, so you can give it a hand. The code below efficiently initializes a fixed-size array with `0.0`, `0.1`, `0.2`, ..., `1.28`:

```
class Transmogrifier {
    double[128] alpha = void;
    this() {
        foreach (i, ref e; alpha) {
            e = i * 0.1;
        }
    }
    ...
}
```

Sometimes, a design may ask for certain fields to be left deliberately uninitialized. For example, `Transmogrifier` may track the already used portion of `alpha` in a separate variable `usedAlpha`, initially zero. The object primitives know that only the portion of `alphas` from zero up to a size `usedAlpha` are actually initialized:

```
class Transmogrifier {
    double[128] alpha = void;
    size_t usedAlpha;
```

```
this() {
    // Leave usedAlpha = 0 and alpha uninitialized
}
...
}
```

Initially usedAlpha is zero, which is all the initialization that Transmogrifier needs. As usedAlpha grows, the code must never read elements in the interval alpha[usedAlpha .. $] before writing them. This is, of course, stuff that you, not the compiler, must ensure—which illustrates the inevitable tension that sometimes exists between efficiency and static verifiability. Although such optimizations are often frivolous, there are cases in which unnecessary compulsive initializations could sensibly affect bottom-line results, so having an opt-in escape hatch is reassuring.

### 6.3.4   Destruction and Deallocation

D maintains a garbage-collected heap for all class objects. Once an object is successfully allocated, it may be considered to live forever as far as the application is concerned. The garbage collector recycles the memory used by an object only when it can prove there are no more accessible references to that object. This setup makes for clean, safe class-based code.

For certain classes, it is important to have a hook on the termination process so they can free additional resources that they might have acquired. Such classes may define a *destructor*, introduced as a special function with the name ~this:

```
import core.stdc.stdlib;

class Buffer {
    private void* data;
    // Constructor
    this() {
        data = malloc(1024);
    }
    // Destructor
    ~this() {
        free(data);
    }
    ...
}
```

The example above illustrates an extreme situation—a class maintaining its own raw memory buffer. Most of the time a class would use properly encapsulated resources, so there is little need for defining destructors.

### 6.3.5 Tear-Down Sequence

Like construction, tearing an object down follows a little protocol:

1. Right after branding (step 3 in the construction process) the object is considered alive and put under the scrutiny of the garbage collector. Note that this happens even if the user-defined constructor throws an exception later. Given that default initialization and branding cannot fail, it follows that an object that was successfully allocated is considered a full-fledged object as far as the garbage collector is concerned.
2. The object is used throughout the program.
3. All accessible references to the object are gone; no code could possibly reach the object anymore.
4. At some implementation-dependent point, the system acknowledges that the object's memory may be recycled and invokes its destructor.
5. At a later point in time (either immediately after calling the destructor or later on) the system reuses the object's memory.

One important detail regarding the last two steps is that the garbage collector makes sure that an object's destructor can never access an already deallocated object. It is possible to access an already destroyed object, just not deallocated; in D, destroyed objects hold their memory for a short while, until their peers get destroyed. If that were not the case, destroying and deallocating objects that refer to each other in a cycle (e.g., circular lists) would be impossible to implement safely.

The life cycle described above may be amended in several ways. First, it is very possible that an application ends before ever reaching step 4. This is often the case for small applications running on systems with enough memory. In that case, D assumes that exiting the application will *de facto* free all resources associated with it, so it does not invoke any destructor.

Another way to amend the life cycle of an object is to explicitly invoke its destructor. This is accomplished by calling the `clear` function defined in module `object` (the standard library module that is `imported` automatically in any compilation).

```
unittest {
    auto b = new Buffer;
    ...
    clear(b); // Get rid of b's extra state
    ... // b is still usable here
}
```

By calling `clear(b)`, the user expresses the intent to explicitly invoke b's destructor (if any), obliterate that object's state with `Buffer.init`, and call `Buffer`'s default constructor. However, unlike in C++, `clear` does not dispose of the object's own memory

and there is no `delete` operator. (D used to have a `delete` operator, but it was depre-
cated.) You still can free memory manually if you really, *really* know what you're doing
by calling the function `GC.free()` found in the module `core.memory`. Freeing memory
is unsafe, but calling `clear` is safe because no memory goes away so there's no risk of
dangling pointers. After `clear(obj)`, the object `obj` remains eminently accessible and
usable for any purpose, even though it does not contain any interesting state. For example, the following is correct D code:

```
unittest {
   auto b = new Buffer;
   auto b1 = b;              // Extra alias for b
   clear(b);
   assert(b1.data is null); // The extra alias still refers to
                            //   the (valid) chassis of b
}
```

So after you invoke `clear`, the object is still alive and well, but its destructor has been
called and the object is now carrying its default-constructed state. Interestingly, during
the next garbage collection, the destructor of the object is called *again*. This is because,
obviously, the garbage collector has no idea in what state you have left the object.

Why this behavior? The answer is simple—divorcing object tear-down from memory
deallocation gives you manual control over expensive resources that the object might
control (such as files, sockets, mutexes, and system handles) while at the same time ensuring memory safety. You will never create dangling pointers by using `new` and `clear`.
(Of course, if you get your hands greasy by using C's `malloc` and `free` or the aforementioned `GC.free`, you do expose yourself to the dangers of dangling pointers.) Generally,
it is wise to separate resource disposal (safe) with memory recycling (unsafe). Memory
is fundamentally different from any other resource because it is the physical support of
the type system. Deallocate it unwittingly, and you are liable to break any guarantee that
the type system could ever make.

### 6.3.6 Static Constructors and Destructors

Inside a class and essentially anywhere in D, `static` data must always be initialized with
compile-time constants. To allow for an orderly means to execute code during thread
startup, the compiler allows defining the special function `static this()`. The code doing module-level and class-level initialization is collected together, and the runtime support library proceeds with static initialization in an orderly fashion.

Inside a class you can define one or more default constructors prefixed by `static`:

```
class A {
   static A a1;
   static this() {
```

```
      a1 = new A;
   }
   ...
   static this() {
      a2 = new A;
   }
   static A a2;
}
```

Such functions are called *static class constructors*. When loading the application and before executing `main`, the compiler executes each static class constructor in turn, in the order they appeared in the source code. In the example above, `a1` will be initialized before `a2`. The order of execution of static class constructors in distinct classes inside the same module is again dictated by the lexical order. Static class constructors in unrelated modules are executed in an unspecified order. Finally and most interestingly, static class constructors of classes that are in interdependent modules are ordered to eliminate the possibility of a `class` ever being used before its `static this()` has run.

initialization orderHere's how the ordering works. Consider class `A` defined in module `MA` and class `B` defined in module `MB`. The following situations may occur:

- At most one of `A` and `B` defines a static class constructor. Then there is no ordering to worry about.
- Neither `MA` nor `MB` imports the other. Then the ordering is unspecified—any order works because the two modules don't depend on each other.
- `MA` imports `MB`. Then `A`'s static class constructors run before `B`'s.
- `MB` imports `MA`. Then `B`'s static class constructors run before `A`'s.
- `MA` imports `MB` and `MB` imports `MA`. Then a "cyclic dependency" error is signaled and execution is abandoned during program loading.

This reasoning does not really depend on classes `A` and `B`, just on the modules themselves and their `import` relationships. Chapter 11 discusses the matter in detail.

If any static class constructor fails by throwing an exception, the program is terminated. If all succeed, classes are also given a chance to clean things up during thread shutdown by defining static class destructors, which predictably look like this:

```
class A {
   static A a1;
   static ~this() {
      clear(a1);
   }
   ...
   static A a2;
```

```
    static ~this() {
        clear(a2);
    }
}
```

Static destructors are run during thread shutdown. Within each module they are run in *reverse* order of their definition. In the example above, a2's destructor will get called before a1's. When multiple modules are involved, the order of modules invoking static class destructors is the exact reverse of the order in which the modules were given a chance to call their static class constructor. It's reversed turtles, all the way up.

## 6.4   Methods and Inheritance

We're now experts in creating and obliterating objects, so let's take a look at using them. Most of the interaction with an object is carried out by calling its methods. (In some languages that activity is known as "sending messages" to the object.) A method definition looks much like a regular function definition, the only difference being that it occurs inside a class. To focus the description on an example, say you build a Rolodex application that allows you to store and display contact information. The unit of information—one virtual business card—could then be a class Contact. Among other things, it might define a method specifying the background color used when displaying the contact:

```
class Contact {
    string bgColor() {
        return "Gray";
    }
}
unittest {
    auto c = new Contact;
    assert(c.bgColor() == "Gray");
}
```

The interesting part starts when you decide that a class should *inherit* another. For example, certain contacts are friends, and for those we use a different background color:

```
class Friend : Contact {
    string currentBgColor = "LightGreen";
    string currentReminder;
    override string bgColor() {
        return currentBgColor;
    }
    string reminder() {
        ...
```

```
      return currentReminder;
   }
}
```

By declaring inheritance from `Contact` through the notation `: Contact`, an instance of class `Friend` will contain everything that a `Contact` has, plus `Friend`'s additional state (in this case, `currentBgColor`) and methods (in this case, `reminder`).

We call `Friend` a subclass of `Contact` and `Contact` a superclass of `Friend`. By virtue of subclassing, you can substitute a `Friend` value wherever a `Contact` value is expected:

```
unittest {
   Friend f = new Friend;
   Contact c = f;            // Substitute a Friend for a Contact
   auto color = c.bgColor(); // Call a Contact method
}
```

If the substituted `Friend` would behave *precisely* like a `Contact`, there would be little if any impetus to use `Friend`s. One key feature of object technology is that it allows a derived class to override functions in the base class and therefore customize behavior in a modular manner. Predictably, overriding is introduced with the `override` keyword (in `Friend`'s definition of `bgColor`), which indicates that calling `c.bgColor()` against an object of type `Contact` that was actually substituted with an object of type `Friend` will always invoke `Friend`'s version of the method. `Friend`s will always be `Friend`s, even when the compiler thinks they're simple `Contact`s.

### 6.4.1 A Terminological Smörgåsbord

Object technology has had a long and successful history in both academia and industry. Consequently, it has been the focus of much work and has spawned a fair amount of terminology, which can get confusing at times. Let's stop for a minute to review the nomenclature.

If a class `D` directly inherits a class `B`, `D` is called a *subclass* of `B`, a *child class* of `B`, or a class *derived* from `B`. Conversely, `B` is called a *superclass*, *parent class*, or *base class* of `D`.

A class `X` is a descendant of class `B` if and only if either `X` is a child of `B`, or `X` is a descendant of a child of `B`. This definition is recursive, which, put another way, means that if you walk up `X`'s parent and then `X`'s parent's parent and so on, at some point you'll meet `B`.

This book uses the notions of *parent/child* and *ancestor/descendant* throughout because these phrases distinguish the notion of direct versus possibly indirect inheritance more precisely than the terms superclass/subclass.

Oddly enough, although classes are types, subtype is not the same thing as subclass (and supertype is not the same thing as superclass). Subtyping is a more general notion that means a type `S` is a subtype of type `T` if a value of type `S` can be safely used in all contexts where a value of type T is expected. Note that this definition does not require or mention inheritance. Indeed, inheritance is but one way of achieving subtyping, but there are other means in general (and in D). The relationship between subtyping and inheritance is that the descendants of a class C plus C itself are all subtypes of C. A subtype of C that is different from C is a *proper subtype*.

### 6.4.2  Inheritance Is Subtyping. Static and Dynamic Type

Let's exemplify how inheritance induces subtyping. As mentioned, an object of the derived class is always substitutable for an object of the base class:

```
class Contact { ... }
class Friend : Contact { ... }
void fun(Contact c) {  ... }
unittest {
    auto c = new Contact;    // c has type Contact
    fun(c);
    auto f = new Friend;     // f has type Friend
    fun(f);
}
```

Although fun expects a Contact object, passing f is fair game because Friend is a subclass (and therefore a subtype) of Contact.

When subtyping is in effect, it is very often possible that the actual type of an object is partially "forgotten." Consider:

```
class Contact { string bgColor() { return ""; } }
class Friend : Contact {
   override string bgColor() { return "LightGreen"; }
}
```

```
unittest {
    Contact c = new Friend; // c has type Contact
                            //    but really refers to a Friend
    assert(c.bgColor() == "LightGreen");
                            // It's a friend indeed!
}
```

Given that c has type Contact, it could be used only in ways any Contact object could be used, even though it has been bound to an object of type Friend. For example, you can't call c.reminder because that method is specific to Friend and not present in Contact. However, the assert above shows that friends will always be friends: calling c.bgColor reveals that the Friend-specific method gets called. As discussed in the section on construction (§ 6.3 on page 181), once an object is constructed it will just live forever, so the Friend object created with new never goes away. The interesting twist that occurs is that the *reference* c bound to it has type Contact, not Friend. In that case we say that c has static type Contact and dynamic type Friend. An unbound (null) reference has no dynamic type.

Teasing out the Friend that's hiding under the disguise of a Contact—or in general a descendant from an ancestor—is a bit more elaborate. For one thing, the operation may fail: what if this contact didn't really refer to a Friend? Most of the time, the compiler wouldn't be able to tell. To do such extraction you'd need to rely on a cast:

```
unittest {
    auto c = new Contact;    // c has static and dynamic type Contact
    auto f = cast(Friend) c;
    assert(f is null);       // f has static type Friend and is unbound
    c = new Friend;          // Static: Contact, dynamic: Friend
    f = cast(Friend) c;      // Static: Friend, dynamic: Friend
    assert(f !is null);      // Passes!
}
```

### 6.4.3 Overriding Is Only Voluntary

The override keyword in the signature of Friend.bgColor is required, which at first sight is a bit annoying. After all, the compiler could figure out that overriding is in effect all by itself and wire things appropriately. So why was override deemed necessary?

The answer is related to maintainability. Indeed, the compiler has no trouble figuring out automatically which methods you wanted to override. The problem is, it has no means to determine which methods you did *not* mean to override. Such a situation may occur when you change the base class after having defined the derived class. Imagine, for example, that class Contact initially defines only the bgColor method and you derive Friend from it and override bgColor as shown in the snippet above. You may also define another method in Friend, such as Friend.reminder, which allows you to retrieve reminders about that particular friend. If later on someone else (including you three months later) defines a reminder method for Contact with some other meaning, you now have the odd bug that calls to Contact.reminder get routed through Friend.reminder when passed to a Contact or a Friend, something that Friend was unprepared for.

The converse situation is just as pernicious, if not more so. Say, for example, that after the initial design, Contact decides to remove a method or change its name. The designer would have to manually go through all of Contact's derived classes and decide what to do with the now orphaned methods. This is a highly error-prone activity and is sometimes impossible to carry out in its entirety when parts of a hierarchy are not writable by the base class designer.

So requiring `override` allows you to modify base classes without risking unexpected harm to derived classes.

### 6.4.4   Calling Overridden Methods

Sometimes, an overriding method wants to call the very method it is overriding. Consider, for example, a graphical widget `Button` that inherits a `Clickable` class. The `Clickable` class knows how to dispatch button presses to listeners but is not concerned with visual effects at all. To introduce visual feedback, `Button` overrides the `onClick` method defined by `Clickable` and introduces the visual effects part but also wants to invoke `Clickable.onClick` to carry out the dispatch part.

```
class Clickable {
    void onClick() { ... }
}
class Button : Clickable {
    void drawClicked() { ... }
    override void onClick() {
        drawClicked();    // Introduce graphical effect
        super.onClick();  // Dispatch click to listeners
    }
}
```

To call the overridden method, use the predefined alias `super`, which instructs the compiler to access a method as it was defined in the parent class. You are free to call any method, not only the method being currently overridden (for example, you can issue `super.onDoubleClick()` from within `Button.onClick`). To be entirely honest, the accessed symbol doesn't even have to be a method name; it could be a field name as well, or really any symbol. For example:

```
class Base {
    double number = 5.5;
}
class Derived : Base {
    int number = 10;
    double fun() {
        return number + super.number;
    }
}
```

`Derived.fun` accesses its own member and also the member in its base class, which incidentally has a different type.

The general means to access members in ancestors is to use `Classname.membername`. In fact, `super` is nothing but an `alias` for whatever name the current base class has. In the example above, writing `Base.number` is entirely equivalent to writing `super.number`. The obvious difference is that `super` leads to more maintainable code: if you change the base of a class, you don't need to search and replace names.

With explicit class names, you can jump more than one inheritance level. Explicitly qualifying a method name with `super` or a class name is also a tad faster because the compiler knows exactly which function to dispatch to. If the symbol involved is anything but an overridable method, the explicit qualification affects only visibility but not speed.

Although destructors (§ 6.3.4 on page 186) are just methods, destructor call handling is a bit different. You cannot issue a call to `super`'s destructor, but when calling a destructor (either during a garbage collection cycle or in response to a `clear(obj)` request), D's runtime support always calls all destructors all the way up in the hierarchy.

### 6.4.5 Covariant Return Types

Continuing the example with `Widget`, `TextWidget`, and `VisibleTextWidget`, consider that you want to add code that duplicates a `Widget`. In that case, if the duplicated object is a `Widget`, the copy will also be a `Widget`; if it is a `TextWidget`, the copy will be a `TextWidget` as well; and so on. A way to achieve proper duplication is by defining a method `duplicate` in the base class and by requiring every derived class to implement it:

```
class Widget {
   ...
   this(Widget source) {
      ... // Copy state
   }
   Widget duplicate() {
      return new Widget(this); // Allocates memory
                               //    and calls this(Widget)
   }
}
```

So far, so good. Let's look at the corresponding override in the `TextWidget` class:

```
class TextWidget : Widget {
   ...
   this(TextWidget source) {
      super(source);
      ... // Copy state
   }
   override Widget duplicate() {
      return new TextWidget(this);
   }
```

```
}
```

Everything is correct, but there is a notable loss of static information: `TextWidget.duplicate` actually returns a `Widget` object, not a `TextWidget` object. But the result type of `TextWidget.duplicate` is `TextWidget` as long as we look *inside* that function. However, that information is lost as soon as `TextWidget.duplicate` returns because the return type of `TextWidget.duplicate` is `Widget`—the same as `Widget.duplicate`'s return type. Therefore, the following code does not work, although in a perfect world it should:

```
void workWith(TextWidget tw) {
   TextWidget clone = tw.duplicate(); // Error!
      // Cannot convert a Widget to a TextWidget!
   ...
}
```

To maximize the availability of static type information, D defines a feature known as *covariant return types*. As snazzy as it sounds, covariance of return types is rather simple: if a base type returns some class type C, an overriding function is allowed to return not only C, but any class derived from C. With this feature, you can declare `TextWidget.duplicate` to return `TextWidget`. Just as important, sneaking "covariant return types" into a conversation makes you sound pretty cool. (Kidding. Really. Do not attempt.)

## 6.5   Class-Level Encapsulation with `static` Members

Sometimes it's useful to encapsulate not only fields and methods, but regular functions and (gasp) global data inside a class. Such functions and data should have no special property aside from being scope inside the class. To share regular functions and data among all objects of a class, introduce them with the `static` keyword:

```
class Widget {
   static Color defaultBgColor;
   static Color combineBackgrounds(Widget bottom, Widget top) {
      ...
   }
}
```

Inside a `static` method, there is no `this` reference. This is because, again, `static` methods are regular functions scoped inside a class. It logically follows that you don't need an object to access `defaultBgColor` or call `combineBackgrounds`—you just prefix them with the class's name:

```
unittest {
   auto w1 = new Widget, w2 = new Widget;
   auto c = Widget.defaultBgColor;
   // This works too: w1.defaultBgColor;
   c = Widget.combineBackgrounds(w1, w2);
   // This works too: w2.combineBackgrounds(w1, w2);
}
```

If you use an object instead of the class name when accessing a `static` member, that's fine, too. Note that the object value is still computed even though it's not really needed:

```
// Creates a Widget and throws it away
auto c = (new Widget).defaultBgColor;
```

## 6.6   Curbing Extensibility with final Methods

There are times when you actively want to disallow subclasses from overriding a certain method. This is a common occurrence because some methods are not meant as customization points. Such methods may call customizable methods, but there may often be cases when you want to keep certain control flows unchanged. (The Template Method design pattern [27] comes to mind.) To prevent inheriting classes from overriding a method, prefix its definition with `final`.

For example, consider a stock ticker application that wants to make sure it updates the on-screen information whenever a stock price has changed:

```
class StockTicker {
   final void updatePrice(double last) {
      doUpdatePrice(last);
      refreshDisplay();
   }
   void doUpdatePrice(double last) { ... }
   void refreshDisplay() { ... }
}
```

The methods `doUpdatePrice` and `refreshDisplay` are overridable and therefore offer customization points to subclasses of `StockTicker`. For example, some stock tickers may introduce triggers and alerts upon certain changes in price or display themselves in specific colors. But `updatePrice` cannot be overriden, so the caller can be sure that no stock price gets updated without an accompanying update of the display. In fact, just to be sticklers for correctness, let's define `updatePrice` as follows:

```
final void updatePrice(double last) {
  scope(exit) refreshDisplay();
  doUpdatePrice(last);
}
```

With `scope(exit)` in tow, the display is properly refreshed even if `doUpdatePrice` throws an exception. This approach really ensures that the display reflects the latest and greatest state of the object.

There is a perk associated with `final` methods that is almost dangerous to know, because it could easily lure you toward the dark side of premature optimization. The truth is, `final` methods may be more efficient. This is because non-`final` methods go through one indirection step for each call, a step that ensures the flexibility brought about by `override`. For some `final` methods that indirection is still necessary. For example, a `final` override of a method is normally still subject to indirect calls when invoked via a base class object; in general the compiler still wouldn't know where the call goes. But if the `final` method is also a first introduced method (not an override of a base class' method), then whenever you call it, the compiler is 100% sure where the call will land. So `final` non-`override` methods are never subjected to indirect calls; instead, they enjoy the same calling convention, low overhead, and inlining opportunities as regular functions. It would appear that `final` non-`override` methods are much faster than others, but this margin is eroded by two factors.

First, the baseline call overhead is assessed against a function that does nothing. To assess the overhead that matters, the actual time spent inside the function must be considered in addition to the invocation overhead. If the function is very short, the relative overhead can be considerable, but if the function does some nontrivial work, the relative overhead decreases quickly until it falls into the noise. Second, a variety of compiler, linker, and runtime optimization techniques work aggressively to minimize or eliminate the dispatch overhead. You're definitely much better off starting with flexibility and optimizing sparingly, instead of crippling your design from day one by making it unduly rigid for the sake of a potential future performance issue.

If you've used Java and C#, `final` is immediately recognizable because it has the same semantics in those languages. If you compare the state of affairs with C++, you'll notice an interesting change of defaults: in C++ methods are `final` by default if you don't use any annotation, and non-`final` if you explicitly annotate them with `virtual`. Again, at least in this case it was deemed that it is better to default on the side of flexibility. You may want to use `final` primarily in support of a design decision, and only seldom as a means to shave off some extra cycles.

### 6.6.1 final Classes

Sometimes you want a class to be the final word on a subject. You can achieve that by marking an entire class as final:

```
class Widget { ... }
final class UltimateWidget : Widget { ... }
class PostUltimateWidget : Widget { ... } // Error!
            // Cannot inherit from a final class
```

A final class cannot be inherited from—it is a leaf in the inheritance hierarchy. This can sometimes be an important design device. Obviously, all of a final class' methods are implicitly final because no overriding would ever be possible.

An interesting secondary effect of final classes is a strong implementation guarantee. Client code that uses a final class can be sure that said class' methods have known implementations with guaranteed effects that cannot be tweaked by some subclass.

## 6.7 Encapsulation

One hallmark of object-oriented design, and of other design techniques as well, is *encapsulation*. Objects encapsulate their implementation details and expose only well-defined interfaces. That way, objects reserve the freedom to change a host of implementation details without disrupting clients. This leads to more decoupling and consequently fewer dependencies, confirming the adage that every design technique is, at the end of the day, aimed at dependency management.

In turn, encapsulation is a manifestation of *information hiding*, a general philosophy in designing software. Information hiding prescribes that various modular elements in an application should focus on defining and using abstract interfaces for communicating with one another, while hiding the details of how they implement the interfaces. Often, the details are related to data layout, for which reason "data hiding" is a commonly encountered notion. Focusing on data hiding alone, however, misses part of the point because a component may hide a variety of information, such as design decisions or algorithmic strategies.

Today, encapsulation sounds quite attractive and perhaps even obvious, but much of that is the result of accumulated collective experience. Things weren't that clear-cut in the olden times. After all, information is ostensibly a good thing and the more you have of it the better off you are, so why would you want to hide it?

Back in the 1960s, Fred Brooks (author of the seminal book *The Mythical Man-Month*) was an advocate of a transparent, white-box, "everybody knows everything" approach to designing software. Under his management, the team building the OS/360 operating system received documentation of all design details of the project on a regular basis through a sophisticated hard copy annotation method [13, Chapter 7]. The project enjoyed qualified success, but it would be tenuous to argue that transparency was a positive contributor; more plausibly, it was a risk minimized by intensive management. It took a revolutionary paper by David L. Parnas [44] to forever establish the notion of information hiding in the community lore. Brooks himself commented in 1995 that his advocacy of transparency was the only major element of *The Mythical Man-Month* that hadn't withstood the test of time. But the information hiding concept was quite controversial back in 1972, as witnessed by this comment by a reviewer of Parnas' revolutionary paper: "Obviously Parnas does not know what he is talking about because nobody does it this way." Funnily enough, only a decade later the tide had reversed so radically, the same paper almost got trivialized: "Parnas only wrote down what all good programmers did anyway" [32, page 138].

Getting back to encapsulation as enabled by D, you can prefix the declaration of any type, data, function, or method with one of five access specifiers. Let's start from the most reclusive specifier and work our way up toward notoriety.

### 6.7.1  private

The label `private` can be specified at `class` level, outside all `classes` (module-level), or inside a `struct` (Chapter 7). In all contexts, `private` has the same power: it restricts symbol access to the current module (file).

This behavior is unlike that in other languages, which limit access to `private` symbols to the current class only. However, making `private` module-level is consistent with D's general approach to protection—the units of protection are identical to the operating system's unit of protection (file and directory). The advantage of file-level protection is that it facilitates collecting together small, tightly coupled entities that have a given responsibility. If `class`-level protection is needed, simply put the `class` in its own file.

### 6.7.2  package

The label `package` can be specified at `class` level, outside all `classes` (module-level), or inside a `struct` (Chapter 7). In all contexts, `package` introduces directory-level protection: all files within the same directory as the current module have access to the symbol. Subdirectories or the parent directory of the current module's directory have no special privileges.

### 6.7.3  protected

The `protected` access specifier makes sense only inside a `class`, not at module level. When used inside of some class C, the `protected` access specifier means that access to the declared symbol is reserved to the module in which C is defined and also to C's descendants, regardless of which modules they're in. For example:

```
class C {
    // x is accessible only inside this file
    private int x;
    // This file plus all classes inheriting C directly or
    //    indirectly may call setX()
    protected void setX(int x) { this.x = x; }
    // Everybody may call getX()
    public int getX() { return x; }
}
```

Again, the access `protected` grants is transitive—it goes not only to direct children, but to all descendants that ultimately inherit from the class using `protected`. This makes `protected` quite generous in terms of giving access away.

### 6.7.4 public

Public access means that the declared symbol is accessible freely from within the application. All the application has to do is gain visibility to the symbol, most often by `importing` the module that defines it.

In D, `public` is also the default access level throughout. Since the order of declarations is ineffectual, a nice style is to put the visible interface of a module or class toward the beginning, then restrict access by using (for example) `private:` and continue with definitions. That way, the client only needs to look at the top of a file or class to learn about its accessible entities.

### 6.7.5 export

It would appear that `public` is the rock bottom of access levels, the most permissive of all. However, D defines an even more permissive access: `export`. When using `export` with a symbol, the symbol is accessible even from *outside* the program it's defined in. This is the case with shared libraries that expose interfaces to the outside world. The compiler carries out the system-dependent steps required for a symbol to be exported, often including a special naming convention for the symbol. At this time, D does not define a sophisticated dynamic loading infrastructure, so `export` is to some extent a stub waiting for more extensive support.

### 6.7.6 How Much Encapsulation?

One interesting question we should ask ourselves is: How do the five access specifiers compare? For example, assuming we have already agreed that information hiding is a good thing, it is reasonable to infer that `private` is "better" than `protected` because it is more restrictive. Continuing along that line of thought, we might think that `protected` is better than `public` (heck, `public` sets the bar pretty low, not to mention `export`). It is unclear, however, how to rate `protected` in comparison to `package`. Most important, such a qualitative analysis does not give an idea of how much of a hit the design takes if, for example, it decides to loosen the restrictiveness of a symbol. Is `protected` closer to `private`, closer to `public`, or smack in the middle of the scale? And what's the scale after all?

Back in December 1999, when everybody else was worried about Y2K, Scott Meyers was worried about encapsulation, or more exactly, about coding techniques that could maximize it. In his subsequent article [41], Meyers proposes a simple criterion for devising the "amount" of encapsulation of an entity: if we were to change that entity, how much code would be affected? The less code is affected, the more encapsulation has been achieved.

Having a means to measure the degree of encapsulation clarifies things a lot. Without a metric, a common assessment is that `private` is good, `public` is bad, and `protected` is sort of halfway in between. As people are optimistic by nature, `protected` has been for many of us a feel-good-within-bounds protection level, kind of like drinking responsibly.

Another aspect we can use in assessing the degree of encapsulation is *control*, that is, the influence you can exercise over the code that may be affected by a change. Do you know (or can you cheaply find) the code affected by a change? Do you have the rights to modify that code? Can others add to that code? The answers to these questions define degrees of control.

For starters, consider `private`. Modifying a `private` symbol affects exactly one file. A source file has on the order of a thousand lines; smaller files are common, whereas much larger files (e.g., 10,000 lines) would become difficult to manage. You have control over that file by the sheer fact that you're changing it, and you could easily restrict others' access to it by the use of file attributes, version control, or team coding standards. So `private` offers excellent encapsulation: little code affected and good control over that code.

When you use package-level access, all files within the same directory would be affected by the change. We can estimate that the files grouped in a package have about one order of magnitude more lines (for example, it's reasonable to think of a package containing on the order of ten modules). Correspondingly, it costs to mess with package symbols: a change affects an order of magnitude more code than a similar change against a `private` symbol. Fortunately, however, you have good control over the affected code because, again, the operating system and various version control tools allow directory-level control over adding and changing files.

Sadly, `protected` protects much less than it would appear. First off, `protected` marks a definite departure from the confines of `private` and `package`: any class situated anywhere in a program can gain access to a `protected` symbol by simply inheriting a descendant of the class defining it. You don't have fine-grained control over inheritance, except through the all-or-none attribute `final`. It follows that if you mess with a `protected` symbol, you affect an unbounded amount of code. To add insult to injury, not only do you have no ability to limit who inherits from your class, but you could also break code that you yourself don't have the right to fix. (Think, for example, of changing a library symbol that affects applications elsewhere.) The reality is as grim as it is crisp: as soon as you step outside `private` and `package`, you're out in the wild. Using `protected` offers hardly any protection.

How much code do you need to inspect when changing a `protected` symbol? That would be all of the descendants of the class defining the symbol. A reasonable ballpark is one order of magnitude above a package size, or a few hundreds of thousands of lines. Tools that index source code and track a class' descendants can help a lot here, but at the end of the day, a change of a `protected` symbol potentially affects large amounts of code.

Using `public` does not change much in terms of control, but it does add one extra order of magnitude to the bulk of the code potentially affected. Now it's not only a class' descendants, it's the entire code of the application. And finally, `export` adds one interesting twist to the situation—it's all binary applications using your code as a binary library, so you're not only looking at code that you can't modify, it's code you can't even look at because it may not be available in source form.

Figure 6.3 on the following page illustrates these ballpark approximations by plotting the potentially affected lines of code for each access specifier. Of course, the amounts are guesstimates and could vary wildly, but the rough proportions should not be affected too much. The vertical axis uses logarithmic scale and the steps suggest a linear trend, so each time you give up one iota of access protection, you must work about ten times harder to keep things in sync. The upward-pointing arrows suggest loss of control over the affected code. One corollary is that `protected` is not smack in between `private` and `public`—it's much more like `public` so you should treat it as such (that is, with atavistic fear).

## 6.8   One Root to Rule Them All

Some languages define a root class for all other classes, and D is among them. The root of everything is called `Object`. If you define a class like this:

```
class C {
    ...
}
```

to the compiler things are exactly as if you wrote

```
class C : Object {
    ...
}
```

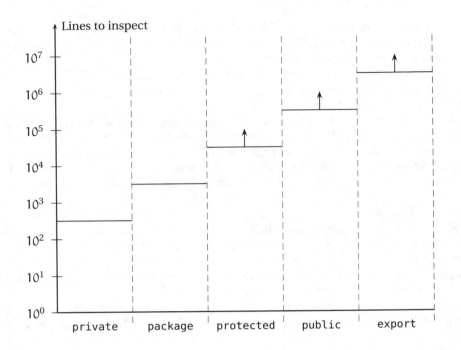

**Figure 6.3:** Ballpark estimates of lines of codes potentially affected by altering a symbol for each protection level. The vertical axis uses logarithmic scale, so each relaxation of encapsulation makes things worse by an order of magnitude. The upward-pointing arrows symbolize the fact that the amount of code affected by `protected`, `public`, and `export` is not under the control of the coder who maintains the symbol.

Other than the automatic rewrite above, `Object` is not very special—it's a class like any other. Your implementation defines it in a module called `object.di` or `object.d`, which is `imported` automatically in every module you compile. You should easily find and inspect that module by navigating around the directory in which your D implementation resides.

There are several advantages to having a root for all classes. An obvious boon is that `Object` can introduce a few universally useful methods. Below is a slightly simplified definition of the `Object` class:

```
class Object {
   string toString();
   size_t toHash();
   bool opEquals(Object rhs);
```

```
    int opCmp(Object rhs);
    static Object factory(string classname);
}
```

Let's look closer at the semantics of each of these symbols.

### 6.8.1 `string toString()`

This returns a textual representation of the object. By default it returns the class name:

```
// File test.d
class Widget {}
unittest {
    assert((new Widget).toString() == "test.Widget");
}
```

Note that the name of the class comes together with the name of the module the class is defined in. By default, the module name is the same as the file name, a default that can be changed with a `module` declaration (§ 11.1.8 on page 348).

### 6.8.2 `size_t toHash()`

This returns a hash of the object as an unsigned integral value (32 bits on 32-bit machines, 64 bits on 64-bit machines). By default, the hash is computed by using the bitwise representation of the object. The hash value is a concise but inexact digest of the object. One important requirement is *consistency:* If `toHash` is called twice against a reference without an intervening change to the state of the object, it should return the same value. Also, the hashes of two equal objects must be equal, and the hash values of two distinct (non-equal) objects are unlikely to be equal. The next section discusses in detail how object equality is defined.

### 6.8.3 `bool opEquals(Object rhs)`

This returns `true` if `this` considers that `rhs` is equal to it. This odd formulation is intentional. Experience with Java's similar function `equals` has shown that there are some subtle issues related to defining equality in the presence of inheritance, for which reason D approaches the problem in a relatively elaborate manner.

First off, one notion of equality for objects already exists: when you compare two references to class objects `a1` and `a2` by using the expression `a1 is a2` (§ 2.3.4.3 on page 48), you get `true` if and only if `a1` and `a2` refer to the same object, just as in Figure 6.1 on page 177. This notion of object equality is sensible, but too restrictive to be useful. Often, two actually distinct objects should be considered equal if they hold the same state. In D, logical equality is assessed by using the `==` and `!=` operators. Here's how they work.

Let's say you write ‹*lhs*› == ‹*rhs*› for expressions ‹*lhs*› and ‹*rhs*›. Then, if at least one of ‹*lhs*› and ‹*rhs*› has a user-defined type, the compiler rewrites the comparison as `object.opEquals(`‹*lhs*›`, `‹*rhs*›`)`. Similarly, ‹*lhs*› != ‹*rhs*› is rewritten as `!object.opEquals(`‹*lhs*›`, `‹*rhs*›`)`. Recall from earlier in this section that `object` is a core module defined by your D implementation and implicitly `import`ed in any module that you build. So the comparisons are rewritten into calls to a free function provided by your implementation and residing in module `object`.

The equality relation between objects is expected to obey certain invariants, and `object.opEquals(`‹*lhs*›`, `‹*rhs*›`)` goes a long way toward ensuring correctness. First, `null` references must compare equal. Then, for any three non-`null` references x, y, and z, the following assertions must hold true:

```
// The null reference is singular; no non-null object equals null
assert(x != null);
// Reflexivity
assert(x == x);
// Symmetry
assert((x == y) == (y == x));
// Transitivity
if (x == y && y == z) assert(x == z);
// Relationship with toHash
if (x == y) assert(x.toHash() == y.toHash());
```

A more subtle requirement of `opEquals` is *consistency*: evaluating equality twice against the same references without an intervening mutation to the underlying objects must return the same result.

The typical implementation of `object.opEquals` eliminates a few simple or degenerate cases and then defers to the member version. Here's what `object.opEquals` may look like:

```
// Inside system module object.d
bool opEquals(Object lhs, Object rhs) {
    // If aliased to the same object or both null => equal
    if (lhs is rhs) return true;
    // If either is null => non-equal
    if (lhs is null || rhs is null) return false;
    // If same exact type => one call to method opEquals
    if (typeid(lhs) == typeid(rhs)) return lhs.opEquals(rhs);
    // General case => symmetric calls to method opEquals
    return lhs.opEquals(rhs) && rhs.opEquals(lhs);
}
```

First, if the two references refer to the same object or are both null, the result is trivially `true` (ensuring reflexivity). Then, once it is established that the objects are distinct, if one of them is `null`, the comparison result is `false` (ensuring singularity of `null`). The third test checks whether the two objects have exactly the same type and, if they do, defers to `lhs.opEquals(rhs)`. And a more interesting part is the double evaluation on the last line. Why isn't one call enough?

Recall the initial—and slightly cryptic—description of the `opEquals` method: "returns `true` if `this` considers that `rhs` is equal to it." The definition cares only about `this` but does not gauge any opinion `rhs` may have. To get the complete agreement, a handshake must take place—each of the two objects must respond affirmatively to the question: Do you consider that object your equal? Disagreements about equality may appear to be only an academic problem, but they are quite common in the presence of inheritance, as pointed out by Joshua Bloch in his book *Effective Java* [9] and subsequently by Tal Cohen in an article [17]. Let's restate that argument.

Getting back to an example related to graphical user interfaces, consider that you define a graphical widget that could sit on a window:

```
class Rectangle { ... }
class Window { ... }
class Widget {
   private Window parent;
   private Rectangle position;
   ... // Widget-specific functions
}
```

Then you define a class `TextWidget`, which is a widget that displays some text.

```
class TextWidget : Widget {
   private string text;
   ...
}
```

How do we implement `opEquals` for these two classes? As far as `Widget` is concerned, another `Widget` that has the same state is equal:

```
// Inside class Widget
override bool opEquals(Object rhs) {
   // The other must be a Widget
   auto that = cast(Widget) rhs;
   if (!that) return false;
   // Compare all state
   return parent == that.parent
      && position == that.position;
}
```

The expression `cast(Widget) rhs` attempts to recover the `Widget` from `rhs`. If `rhs` is `null` or `rhs`'s actual, dynamic type is not `Widget` or a subclass thereof, the `cast` expression returns `null`.

The `TextWidget` class has a more discriminating notion of equality because the right-hand side of the comparison must also be a `TextWidget` and carry the same text.

```
// Inside class TextWidget
override bool opEquals(Object rhs) {
    // The other must be a TextWidget
    auto that = cast(TextWidget) rhs;
    if (!that) return false;
    // Compare all relevant state
    return super.opEquals(that) && text == that.text;
}
```

Now consider a `TextWidget` `tw` superimposed on a `Widget` `w` with the same position and parent window. As far as `w` is concerned, `tw` is equal to it. But from `tw`'s viewpoint, there is no equality because `w` is not a `TextWidget`. If we accepted that `w == tw` but `tw != w`, that would break reflexivity of the equality operator. To restore reflexivity, let's consider making `TextWiget` less strict: inside `TextWidget.opEquals`, if comparison is against a `Widget` that is not a `TextWidget`, the comparison just agrees to go with `Widget`'s notion of equality. The implementation would look like this:

```
// Alternate TextWidget.opEquals -- BROKEN
override bool opEquals(Object rhs) {
    // The other must be at least a Widget
    auto that = cast(Widget) rhs;
    if (!that) return false;
    // Do they compare equal as Widgets? If not, we're done
    if (!super.opEquals(that)) return false;
    // Is it a TextWidget?
    auto that2 = cast(TextWidget) rhs;
    // If not, we're done comparing with success
    if (!that2) return true;
    // Compare as TextWidgets
    return text == that.text;
}
```

Alas, `TextWidget`'s attempts at being accommodating are ill advised. The problem is that now transitivity of comparison is broken: it is easy to create two `TextWidgets` `tw1` and `tw2` that are different (by containing different texts) but at the same time equal with a simple `Widget` object `w`. That would create a situation where `tw1 == w` and `tw2 == w`, but `tw1 != tw2`.

So in the general case, comparison must be carried out both ways—each side of the comparison must agree on equality. The good news is that the free function object.opEquals(Object, Object) avoids the handshake whenever the two involved objects have the same exact type, and even any other call in a few other cases.

### 6.8.4 `int opCmp(Object rhs)`

This implements a three-way ordering comparison, which is needed for using objects as keys in associative arrays. It returns an unspecified negative number if this is less than rhs, an unspecified positive number if rhs is less than this, and 0 if this is considered unordered with rhs. Similarly to opEquals, opCmp is seldom called explicitly. Most of the time, you invoke it implicitly by using one of a < b, a <= b, a > b, and a >= b.

The rewrite follows a protocol similar to opEquals, by using a global object.opCmp definition that intermediates communication between the two involved objects. For each of the operators <, <=, >, and >=, the D compiler rewrites the expression a ‹*op*› b as object.opCmp(a, b) ‹*op*› 0. For example, a < b becomes object.opCmp(a, b) < 0.

Implementing opCmp is optional. The default implementation Object.opCmp throws an exception. In case you do implement it, opCmp must be a "strict weak order," that is it must satisfy the following invariants for any non-null references x, y, and z.

```
// 1. Reflexivity
assert(x.opCmp(x) == 0);
// 2. Transitivity of sign
if (x.opCmp(y) < 0 && y.opCmp(z) < 0) assert(x.opCmp(z) < 0);
// 3. Transitivity of equality with zero
if ((x.opCmp(y) == 0 && y.opCmp(z) == 0) assert(x.opCmp(z) == 0);
```

The rules above may seem a bit odd because they express axioms in terms of the less familiar notion of three-way comparison. If we rewrite them in terms of <, we obtain the familiar properties of strict weak ordering in mathematics:

```
// 1. Irreflexivity of '<'
assert(!(x < x));
// 2. Transitivity of '<'
if (x < y && y < z) assert(x < z);
// 3. Transitivity of '!(x < y) && !(y < x)'
if (!(x < y) && !(y < x) && !(y < z) && !(z < y))
    assert(!(x < z) && !(z < x));
```

The third condition is necessary for making < a strict weak ordering. Without it, < is called a *partial order*. You might get away with a partial order, but only for restricted uses; most interesting algorithms require a strict weak ordering. If you want to define a partial order, you're better off giving up all syntactic sugar and defining your own named functions distinct from opCmp.

Note that the conditions above focus only on < and not on the other ordering comparisons because the latter are just syntactic sugar (x > y is the same as y < x, x <= y is the same as !(y > x), and so on).

One property that derives from irreflexivity and transitivity, but is sometimes confused with an axiom, is antisymmetry: x < y implies !(y < x). It is easy to verify by *reductio ad absurdum* that there can never be x and y such that x < y and y < x are simultaneously true: if that were the case, we could replace z with x in the transitivity of < above, obtaining

```
if (x < y && y < x) assert(x < x);
```

The tested condition is true by the hypothesis, so the `assert` will be checked. But it can never pass because of irreflexivity, thus contradicting the hypothesis.

In addition to the restrictions above, `opCmp` must be consistent with `opEquals`:

```
// Relationship with opEquals
if (x == y) assert(x <= y && y <= x);
```

The relationship with `opEquals` is relaxed: it is possible to have classes for which x <= y and y <= x are simultaneously true, so common sense would dictate they are equal. However, it is not necessary that x == y. A simple example would be a class that defines equality in terms of case-sensitive string matching, but ordering in terms of case-insensitive string matching.

### 6.8.5  `static Object factory(string className)`

This is an interesting method that allows you to create an object given the name of its class. The class involved must accept construction without arguments; otherwise, `factory` throws an exception. Let's give `factory` a test drive.

```
// File test.d
import std.stdio;

class MyClass {
    string s = "Hello, world!";
}

void main() {
    // Create an Object
    auto obj1 = Object.factory("object.Object");
    assert(obj1);
    // Now create a MyClass
    auto obj2 = cast(MyClass) Object.factory("test.MyClass");
    writeln(obj2.s); // Writes "Hello, world!"
```

```
    // Attempting factory against nonexistent classes returns null
    auto obj3 = Object.factory("Nonexistent");
    assert(!obj3);
}
```

Having the ability to create an object from a string is very useful for a variety of idioms, such as the Factory design pattern [27, Chapter 23] and object serialization. On the face of it, there's nothing wrong with

```
void widgetize() {
    Widget w = new Widget;
    ... use w ...
}
```

However, it is possible that later on you will change your mind and decide a derived class TextWidget is better for the task at hand, so you need to change the code above to

```
void widgetize() {
    Widget w = new TextWidget;
    ... use w ...
}
```

The problem is that you need to *change the code*. Doing surgery on code for new functionality is bad because it is liable to break existing functionality. Ideally you'd only need to add code to add functionality, thus remaining confident that existing code continues to work as usual. That's when overridable functions are most useful—they allow you to customize code without actually changing it, by tweaking specific and well-defined customization points. Meyer nicely dubbed this notion the Zen-sounding *Open/Closed Principle* [40]: a class (and more generally a unit of encapsulation) should be open for extension, but closed for modification. The new operator works precisely against all that because it requires you to change the initializer of w if you want to tweak its behavior. A better solution would be to pass the name of the class to be created from the outside, thus decoupling widgetize from the choice of the exact widget to use:

```
void widgetize(string widgetClass) {
    Widget w = cast(Widget) Object.factory(widgetClass);
    ... use w ...
}
```

Now widgetize is relieved of the responsibility for choosing which concrete Widget to use. There are some other ways of achieving flexible object construction that explore the design space in different directions. For a thorough discussion of the matter, you may want to peruse the dramatically entitled "Java's new considered harmful" [4].

## 6.9   Interfaces

Most often, `class` objects contain state and define methods that work with that state. As such, a given object acts at the same time as an interface to the outside world (through its `public` methods) and as an encapsulated implementation of that interface.

Sometimes, however, it is very useful to separate the notion of interface from that of implementation. Doing so is particularly useful when you want to define communication among various parts of a large program. A function trying to operate on a `Widget` is solely preoccupied with `Widget`'s interface—`Widget`'s implementation is irrelevant by the very definition of encapsulation. This brings to the fore the notion of a completely abstract interface, consisting only of the methods that a `class` *must* implement, but devoid of any implementation. That entity is called an *interface*.

D's interface definitions look like restricted class definitions. In addition to replacing the keyword `class` with `interface`, an interface definition needs to obey certain restrictions. You cannot define any non-`static` data in an interface, and you cannot specify an implementation for any overridable function. It is legal to define `static` data and `final` functions with implementation inside an interface. For example:

```
interface Transmogrifier {
   void transmogrify();
   void untransmogrify();
   final void thereAndBack() {
      transmogrify();
      untransmogrify();
   }
}
```

This is everything a function using `Transmogrifier` needs to compile. For example:

```
void aDayInLife(Transmogrifier device, string mood) {
   if (mood == "play") {
      device.transmogrify();
      play();
      device.untransmogrify();
   } else if (mood == "experiment") {
      device.thereAndBack();
   }
}
```

Of course, given that at the moment there is no definition for `Transmogrifier`'s primitives, there is no sensible way to call `aDayInLife`. So let's create an implementation of the interface:

```
class CardboardBox : Transmogrifier {
```

```
  override void transmogrify() {
    // Get in the box
    ...
  }
  override void untransmogrify() {
    // Get out of the box
    ...
  }
}
```

The implementation of an interface uses the same syntax as regular inheritance. With a `CardboardBox` at hand, we can now issue a call such as

```
aDayInLife(new CardboardBox, "play");
```

Any implementation of an interface is a subtype of that interface, so it converts automatically to it. We used that by simply passing a `CardboardBox` object in lieu of the `Transmogrifier` expected by `aDayInLife`.

### 6.9.1  The Non-Virtual Interface (NVI) Idiom

One presence that may seem unfamiliar is the `final` function in the `Transmogrifier` interface. What happened to waxing poetic about abstract, unimplemented functionality? If the interface is abstract, it behooves it to define no implementation.

In 2001, Herb Sutter wrote an article [52] that put forward an interesting observation, which he later resumed in a book [55, Item 39]. Overridable methods defined by an interface (such as `transmogrify` and `untransmogrify` in our example) fulfill a double role. First, they are elements of the interface itself, that is, what calling code uses in order to get things done. Second, such methods are also customization points because that's what inheriting classes define directly. It may be useful, Sutter argued, to distinguish between the two categories: an interface may define some low-level abstract methods that are to be implemented later, *plus* higher-level, visible, non-overridable methods that client code may use. The two sets may or may not overlap, but it would be a net loss to consider them equal.

There are many benefits to making a distinction between what the client sees and what the implementor defines. The approach allows you to design interfaces that are at the same time implementation-friendly and client-friendly. An interface that conflates the needs of the implementation and the needs of clients must compromise between serving the needs of the two. Too much focus on implementation leads to overly pedestrian, verbose, and low-level interfaces that invite code duplication in client code, whereas too much focus on client code leads to large, loose, redundant interfaces that specify convenience functions in addition to essential primitives. With the Non-Virtual

Interface (NVI) idiom, you can afford to make life easier for both. For example, `Transmo-grifier.thereAndBack` offers callers a convenience function that is specified in terms of primitive operations.

The then-nascent idiom was in keeping with the Template Method pattern that prescribes fixed high-level operations with customized intermediate steps, but it seemed particular enough to receive its own name, which came out to be Non-Virtual Interface (NVI). Unfortunately, although NVI has since become a widely used pattern, it has remained a convention among good designers more than a language-assisted means to enforce design consistency. Language support for NVI has been lacking, mostly because the definition of some popular OOP languages has predated (and conditioned) the better understanding of OOP design that led to NVI. So Java does not support NVI at all, C# supports it scarcely (yet uses it extensively as a design guideline), and C++ allows good convention-helped support but, however, no strong guarantees to callers or implementors.

D fully supports NVI by providing specific guarantees when `interfaces` use access specifiers. Consider, for example, that the author of `Transmogrifier` is worried about incorrect use—what if people call `transmogrify` and then forget to `untransmogrify`? Let's expose only `thereAndBack` to clients, while still requiring implementations to define `transmogrify` and `untransmogrify`:

```
interface Transmogrifier {
   // Client interface
   final void thereAndBack() {
      transmogrify();
      untransmogrify();
   }
   // Implementation interface
private:
   void transmogrify();
   void untransmogrify();
}
```

The `Transmogrifier` interface made the two primitives `private`. This setup makes for a very interesting design: a `class` that implements `Transmogrifier` must define `transmogrify` and `untransmogrify` but is unable to call them. In fact, nobody outside `Transmogrifier`'s module could ever call the two primitives. The only way to call them is indirectly, by using the high-level routine `thereAndBack`, which is the very point of the design: well-defined access points and a well-structured flow around the calls through said access points. The language thwarts casual attempts at breaking this guarantee. For example, an implementing class may not relax the protection level of `transmogrify` and `untransmogrify`:

```
class CardboardBox : Transmogrifier {
```

```
    override private void transmogrify() { ... } // Fine
    override void untransmogrify() { ... }       // Error!
        // Cannot change protection of untransmogrify
        //    from private to public!
}
```

Of course, since after all it's your implementation, you can make a primitive public if you so want, but you'd have to give it a different name:

```
class CardboardBox : Transmogrifier {
    override private void transmogrify() { ... } // Fine
    override private void untransmogrify() {     // Fine
        doUntransmogrify();
    }
    override void doUntransmogrify() { ... }      // Fine
}
```

Now users of `CardboardBox` can call `doUntransmogrify`, which does the same thing as `untransmogrify`. But the important point is that `void untransmogrify()` with that specific name and signature could not be directly exposed by an implementing class. So client code would never access the `private` functionality specified under the `private` name. If an implementation wishes to define and document an alternate function, that's its decision.

A second way in which D enforces consistency of NVI is by disabling hijacking of `final` methods: no implementor of `Transmogrifier` can define a method that effectively hijacks `thereAndBack`. For example:

```
class Broken : Transmogrifier {
    void thereAndBack() {
        // Why not do it twice?
        this.Transmogrifier.thereAndBack();
        this.Transmogrifier.thereAndBack();
    }
    // Error! Cannot hijack final method Transmogrifier.thereAndBack
    ...
}
```

If such hiding were allowed, a client with knowledge that `Broken` implements `Transmogrifier` cannot assuredly call `obj.thereAndBack()` against an `obj` of type `Broken`; there would be no confidence that `thereAndBack` does what it is supposed to do as prescribed and documented by `Transmogrifier`. Of course, client code could call `obj.Transmogrifier.thereAndBack()` to make sure that the call is routed properly, but such attention-driven designs are never too appealing. After all, a good design doesn't wait for you to lower your guard to strike you with puzzling behavior. Bottom line—if an interface defines a `public` function, that stays visible as it is through all of its implementations. If the implementation is also `final`, there is no way for an implementing class to intercept such a call to it. An implementation, however, could define a function with the same name as long as there is no potential conflict. For example:

```
class Good : Transmogrifier {
   void thereAndBack(uint times) {
      // Why not do it multiple times?
      foreach (i; 0 .. times) {
         thereAndBack();
      }
   }
   ...
}
```

The case above is allowed because there is never a risk of confusion: a call is either spelled as `obj.thereAndBack()` and goes to `Transmogrify.thereAndBack`, or as `obj.thereAndBack(n)` and goes to `Good.thereAndBack`. To wit, the implementation of `Good.thereAndBack` does not need to qualify its internal call to the homonym interface function.

### 6.9.2   `protected` Primitives

Making an overridable function `private` in an interface is sometimes more restrictive than needed. For example, it prevents an implementation from calling the `super` function, as shown here:

```
class CardboardBox : Transmogrifier {
private:
   override void transmogrify() { ... }
   override void untransmogrify() { ... }
}
class FlippableCardboardBox : CardboardBox {
private:
   bool flipped;
   override void transmogrify() {
      enforce(!flipped, "Can't transmogrify: "
         "box is in time machine mode");
      super.transmogrify(); // Error! Cannot invoke private
                            //    method CardboardBox.transmogrify!
   }
}
```

When the cardboard box is flipped, it can't function as a transmogrifier—as we all know, in that case it's a boring ol' time machine. FlippableCardboardBox enforces that fact, but on the normal path it is unable to call its parent's version. What to do?

One solution would be to use the renaming trick illustrated above with doUntransmogrify, but that gets repetitive if you need to do it for several methods. A simpler solution is to relax the access of the two overridables in Transmogrifier from private to protected:

```
interface Transmogrifier {
   final void thereAndBack() { ... }
protected:
   void transmogrify();
   void untransmogrify();
}
```

With protected access, an implementation is now able to call its parent's implementation. Note that strengthening protection is also illegal. If an interface defined a method, an implementation cannot lay stronger protection claims on that method. For example, given the Transmogrifier that defines both transmogrify and untransmogrify as protected, this code would be in error:

```
class BrokenInTwoWays {
   public void transmogrify() { ... }      // Error!
   private void untransmogrify() { ... }  // Error!
}
```

It would be technically feasible to allow both relaxation and strengthening of an interface's requirements in an implementation, but that would hardly serve any good design purposes. An interface expresses an intent, and a reader should only absorb the definition of the interface to fully use it, whether or not the static type of the implementor is available.

### 6.9.3   Selective Implementation

It is sometimes possible that two interfaces define ambiguous public final methods:

```
interface Timer {
   final void run() { ... }
   ...
}
interface Application {
   final void run() { ... }
   ...
}
```

```
class TimedApp : Timer, Application {
    ... // Cannot define run()
}
```

In cases like these, `TimedApp` is unable to define its own `run()` because it would actually hijack two methods, and in all likelihood two hijacks are worse than one. Eliminating one `final` in either `Timer` or `Application` would not help the situation because one hijack remains active. If both were non-`final`, we're in good shape—`TimedApp.run` implements `Timer.run` and `Application.run` *simultaneously.*

To access those methods for app of type `TimedApp`, you'd have to write `app.Timer.run()` and `app.Application.run()` for `Timer`'s and `Application`'s version, respectively. `TimedApp` could define its own functions that forward to these as long as they do not hijack `run()`.

## 6.10   Abstract Classes

Often, a base class is unable to provide any sensible implementation for some or all of its methods. A thought would be to convert that class to an interface, but sometimes it would be very helpful to have that class define some state and non-`final` methods, privileges not allowed to `interfaces`. Here's where `abstract classes` come to the rescue: they are almost like regular classes, with the liberty to leave functions unimplemented by declaring them using the `abstract` keyword as prefix.

As illustration, consider the time-honored example featuring a hierarchy of shape objects that participate in a vector-oriented drawing program. The hierarchy is rooted in class `Shape`. Any shape has a bounding rectangle, so `Shape` may want to define it as a member variable (something that an `interface` would not be able to do). On the other hand, `Shape` must leave some methods, such as `draw`, undefined because it is unable to implement them sensibly. Those methods are supposed to be implemented by `Shape`'s descendants.

```
class Rectangle {
    uint left, right, top, bottom;
}
```

```
class Shape {
    protected Rectangle _bounds;
    abstract void draw();
    bool overlaps(Shape that) {
        return _bounds.left <= that._bounds.right &&
            _bounds.right >= that._bounds.left &&
            _bounds.top <= that._bounds.bottom &&
            _bounds.bottom >= that._bounds.top;
```

```
      }
   }
```

Method `draw` is `abstract`, which means three things. First, the compiler does not expect that `Shape` implements `draw`. Second, the compiler disallows instantiation of `Shape`. Third, the compiler disallows instantiation of any descendant of `Shape` that does not implement (directly or indirectly in an ancestor) the `draw` method. The "directly or indirectly" part means that the implementation requirement is not transitive; for example, if you define a class `RectangularShape` inheriting `Shape` that implements `draw`, you are not required to reimplement it in `RectangularShape`'s descendants.

If the compiler does not *expect* an implementation for an `abstract` method, that doesn't mean you can't provide one if you so wish. You could provide, for example, an implementation for `Shape.draw`. Clients can call it by explicitly qualifying the call as in `this.Shape.draw()`.

The `overlaps` method is at the same time implemented and overridable, an interesting detail. By default, `overlaps` approximates the intersection of two shapes as the intersection of their bounding rectangles. This is inaccurate for most non-rectangular shapes; for example, two circles may not overlap, even though their bounding boxes do.

A class that has at least one `abstract` method is itself called an *abstract class*. If class `RectangularShape` inherits abstract class `Shape` without overriding all of `Shape`'s `abstract` methods, `RectangularShape` is also abstract and passes the requirement of implementing those abstract methods down to `RectangularShape`'s descendants. In addition, `RectangularShape` is allowed to introduce new `abstract` methods. For example:

```
class Shape {
   // As above
   abstract void draw();
   ...
}
class RectangularShape : Shape {
   // Inherits one abstract method from Shape
   //    and introduces one more
   abstract void drawFrame();
}
class Rectangle : RectangularShape {
   override void draw() { ... }
   // Rectangle is still an abstract class
}
class SolidRectangle : Rectangle {
   override void drawFrame() { ... }
   // SolidRectangle is concrete:
   //    no more abstract functions to implement
```

```
}
```

Most interestingly, a class may decide to reintroduce a function as abstract, even though it was previously overriden and implemented! The code below introduces an abstract class, derives a concrete class from it, and then derives an abstract class from the concrete class, all on account on a single method.

```
class Abstract {
   abstract void fun();
}
class Concrete : Abstract {
   override void fun() { ... }
}
class BornAgainAbstract : Concrete {
   abstract override void fun();
}
```

You can finalize an implementation of an abstract method ...

```
class UltimateShape : Shape {
   // This is the last word about method draw
   override final void draw() { ... }
}
```

... but for obvious reasons you can't define a method that is at the same time abstract and final.

If you want to introduce a bunch of abstract methods, you can reuse the abstract keyword in a manner similar to a protection specifier (§ 6.7.1 on page 200):

```
class QuiteAbstract {
   abstract {
      // Everything in this scope is abstract
      void fun();
      int gun();
      double hun(string);
   }
}
```

There's no way to turn off abstract inside an abstract scope, so this definition is incorrect:

```
class NiceTry {
   abstract {
      void fun();
      final int gun(); // Error!
```

```
            // Cannot define a final abstract function!
    }
}
```

You can use abstract as a label:

```
class Abstractissimo {
abstract:
    // Everything below is abstract
    void fun();
    int gun();
    double hun(string);
}
```

Once you introduce abstract:, it's impossible to turn it off.

Finally, you can label an entire class as abstract:

```
abstract class AbstractByName {
    void fun() {}
    int gun() {}
    double hun(string) {}
}
```

In light of the crescendo of abstract uses above, it might appear that making an entire class abstract really pulls the big guns by making every single method in that class abstract. Nope. That would actually be too coarse to be of any use. What abstract does in front of a class is to simply prevent client code from instantiating it—you can instantiate only non-abstract classes derived from it. Continuing the AbstractByName example above:

```
unittest {
    auto obj = new AbstractByName; // Error! Cannot instantiate
        // Abstract class AbstractByName!
}
class MakeItConcrete : AbstractByName {
}
unittest {
    auto obj = new MakeItConcrete; // OK
}
```

## 6.11   Nested Classes

Nested classes are an interesting feature that deserves special attention. They are useful as building blocks for important idioms, such as multiple subtyping (discussed in the next section).

A class may define another class right inside of it:

```
class Outer {
   int x;
   void fun(int a) { ... }
   // Define an inner class
   class Inner {
      int y;
      void gun() {
         fun(x + y);
      }
   }
}
```

A nested class is just an ordinary ... wait a *minute!* How come Inner.gun has access to Outer's non-static member variables and methods? If Outer.Inner were simply a classic class definition scoped inside Outer, it could not possibly fetch data and call methods of the Outer object. In fact, where does that object come from? Let's just create an object of type Outer.Inner and see what happens:

```
unittest {
   // Nagonna work
   auto obj = new Outer.Inner;
   obj.gun(); // This should crash the world because there's no
      // Outer.x or Outer.fun in sight - there's no Outer at all!
}
```

Since this code creates only an Outer.Inner but not an Outer, the only allocated data is whatever Outer.Inner defines (i.e., y) but not what Outer defines (i.e., x).

However, surprisingly, the class definition does compile, and the unittest does not. What is happening?

First off, you can never create an Inner object without an Outer object, a limitation that makes a lot of sense since Inner has magical access to Outer's state and methods. Here's how you correctly create an Outer.Inner object:

```
unittest {
   Outer obj1 = new Outer;
   auto obj = obj1.new Inner; // Aha!
}
```

The very syntax of new is indicative of what's happening: creating an object of type Outer.Inner necessitates the preexistence of an object of type Outer. A reference to that object (in our case obj1) is surreptitiously stored in the Inner object as a language-defined property called outer. Then, whenever you use a member of Outer such as x, the access is rewritten as this.outer.x. Initialization of the hidden back reference stored in the inner object occurs right before that inner object's constructor gets called, so the constructor itself has immediate access to the outer object's members. Let's actually test all that by making a few changes to the Outer/Inner example:

```
class Outer {
    int x;
    class Inner {
        int y;
        this() {
            x = 42;
            // x or this.outer.x are the same thing
            assert(this.outer.x == 42);
        }
    }
}
unittest {
    auto outer = new Outer;
    auto inner = outer.new Inner;
    assert(outer.x == 42); // inner changed outer
}
```

If you create the Outer.Inner object from within a non-static member function of Outer, there is no need to prefix the new expression with this. because that's implicit. For example:

```
class Outer {
    class Inner { ... }
    Inner _member;
    this() {
        _member = new Inner;           // Same as this.new Inner
        assert(_member.outer is this); // Check the link
    }
}
```

## 6.11.1 Classes Nested in Functions

Nesting a class inside a function works surprisingly similarly to nesting a class inside another class. A class planted inside a function can access that function's parameters and local variables:

```
void fun(int x) {
    string y = "Hello";
    class Nested {
        double z;
        this() {
            // Access to parameter
            x = 42;
            // Access to local variable
            y = "world";
            // Access to own members
            z = 0.5;
        }
    }
    auto n = new Nested;
    assert(x == 42);
    assert(y == "world");
    assert(n.z == 0.5);
    ...
}
```

Classes nested inside functions are particularly useful when you have a function that returns a class type and you want to inherit that type and tweak its behavior. Consider:

```
class Calculation {
    double result() {
        double n;
        ...
        return n;
    }
}

Calculation truncate(double limit) {
    assert(limit >= 0);
    class TruncatedCalculation : Calculation {
        override double result() {
            auto r = super.result();
            if (r < -limit) r = -limit;
            else if (r > limit) r = limit;
            return r;
        }
    }
```

```
    return new TruncatedCalculation;
}
```

The `truncate` function overrides the `result` method of a `Calculation` class to truncate it within limits. There's a very subtle aspect to the workings of `truncate`: note how the override of `result` uses the `limit` parameter. That's not too odd as long as TruncatedCalculation is used within `truncate`, but `truncate` returns a `TruncatedCalculation` to the outside world. A simple question would be: Where does `limit` lie after `truncate` returns? Normally a function's parameters and local variables live on the stack and disappear when the function returns. In this case `limit` gets used *after* `truncate` has long returned, so `limit` had better sit somewhere; otherwise, the entire code would fall apart by unsafely accessing disposed stack memory.

The example does work properly, with a little help from the compiler. Whenever compiling a function, the compiler searches and detects non-local escapes—situations when a parameter or a local variable remains in use after the function has returned. If such an escape is detected, the compiler switches that function's allocation of local state (parameters plus local variables) from stack allocation to dynamic allocation. That way the `limit` parameter of `truncate` successfully survives the return of `truncate` and can be used by `TruncatedCalculation`.

### 6.11.2 `static` Nested Classes

Let's face it: nested classes are not quite what they seem to be. They would appear to simply be regular classes defined inside classes or functions, but they clearly aren't regular: the particular new syntax and semantics, the magic `.outer` property, the modified lookup rules—nested `classes` are definitely unlike regular `classes`.

What if you do want to define a bona fide class inside another class or in a function? Overuse of the `static` keyword comes to the rescue: just prefix the `class` definition with `static`. For example:

```
class Outer {
   static int s;
   int x;
   static class Ordinary {
      void fun() {
         writeln(s); // Fine, access to static value is allowed
         writeln(x); // Error! Cannot access non-static member x!
      }
   }
}
unittest {
   auto obj = new Outer.Ordinary; // Fine
```

```
}
```

A `static` inner class being just a regular class, it does not have access to the outer object simply because there isn't any. However, by virtue of its scoping, the `static` inner class does have access to the `static` members of the enclosing class.

### 6.11.3  Anonymous Classes

A `class` definition that omits the name and the `:` in its superclass specification introduces an *anonymous class*. Such classes must always be nested (non-`statically`) inside functions, and the only use you can make of them is to create a new one right away:

```
class Widget {
   abstract uint width();
   abstract uint height();
}

Widget makeWidget(uint w, uint h) {
   return new class Widget {
      override uint width() { return w; }
      override uint height() { return h; }
      ...
   };
}
```

The feature works a lot like anonymous functions. Creating an anonymous class is equivalent to creating a new named class and then instantiating it. The two steps are merged into one. This may seem an obscure feature with minor savings, but it turns out many designs use it extensively to connect observers to subjects [7].

## 6.12   Multiple Inheritance

D models single inheritance of `classes` and multiple inheritance of interfaces. This is a stance similar to Java's and C#'s, but different from the path that languages such as C++ and Eiffel took.

An interface can inherit any number of interfaces. Since it is unable to implement any overridable function, an inheriting interface is simply an enhanced interface that requires the sum of primitives of its base interfaces, plus potentially some of its own. Consider:

```
interface DuplicativeTransmogrifier : Transmogrifier {
   Object duplicate(Object whatever);
}
```

The interface DuplicativeTransmogrifier inherits Transmogrifier, so anyone implementing DuplicativeTransmogrifier must also implement all of Transmogrifier's primitives, in addition to the newly introduced duplicate. The inheritance relationship works as expected—you can pass around a DuplicativeTransmogrifier wherever a Transmogrifier is expected, but not vice versa.

Generally, an interface may inherit any number of interfaces, with the expected accumulation of required primitives. Also, a class may implement any number of interfaces. For example:

```
interface Observer {
   void notify(Object data);
   ...
}
interface VisualElement {
   void draw();
   ...
}
interface Actor {
   void nudge();
   ...
}
interface VisualActor : Actor, VisualElement {
   void animate();
   ...
}
class Sprite : VisualActor, Observer {
   void draw() { ... }
   void animate() { ... }
   void nudge() { ... }
   void notify(Object data) { ... }
   ...
}
```

Figure 6.4 on the next page displays the inheritance hierarchy coded above. Interfaces are encoded as ovals, and classes are encoded as rectangles.

Let's now define a class Sprite2. Sprite2's author has forgotten that VisualActor is an Actor, so Sprite2 inherits Actor directly in addition to Observer and VisualActor. Figure 6.5 on the following page shows the resulting hierarchy.

A redundant path in a hierarchy is immediately recognizable as a direct connection with an interface that you also inherit indirectly. Redundant paths do not pose particular problems, but in most implementations they add to the size of the final object, in this case Sprite2.

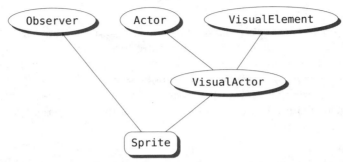

**Figure 6.4:** A simple inheritance hierarchy featuring multiple inheritance of interfaces.

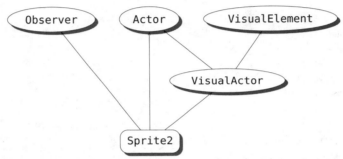

**Figure 6.5:** An inheritance hierarchy featuring a redundant path (in this case the link from Sprite2 to Actor). Redundant paths are not a liability, but eliminating them is often trivial and leads to a cleaner design and a reduction in object size.

There are cases in which you inherit the same interface through two paths, but it's impossible to remove either of the paths. Consider that we first add an ObservantActor interface that inherits Observer and Actor:

```
interface ObservantActor : Observer, Actor {
    void setActive(bool active);
}
interface HyperObservantActor : ObservantActor {
    void setHyperActive(bool hyperActive);
}
```

Then we define Sprite3 to implement ObservantActor and VisualActor:

```
class Sprite3 : HyperObservantActor, VisualActor {
    override void notify(Object) { ... }
```

```
    override void setActive(bool) { ... }
    override void setHyperActive(bool) { ... }
    override void nudge() { ... }
    override void animate() { ... }
    override void draw() { ... }
    ...
}
```

This setup changes things quite a bit (Figure 6.6). If `Sprite3` wants to implement both `HyperObservantActor` and `VisualActor`, it ends up implementing `Actor` twice, through different paths, and there is no way to eliminate that. Fortunately, however, the compiler does not have a problem with that—repeated inheritance of the same interface is allowed. However, repeated inheritance of the same `class` is *not* allowed, and for that reason D disallows any multiple inheritance of `classes` altogether.

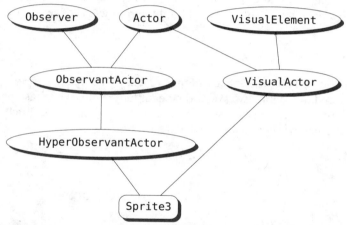

**Figure 6.6:** A hierarchy with multiple paths between nodes (in this case `Sprite3` and `Actor`). This setup is usually known as a "diamond inheritance hierarchy" because, in the absence of `HyperObservantActor`, the two paths between `Sprite3` and `Actor` would describe a diamond shape. In the general case, such hierarchies may have a variety of shapes. The indicative feature is the presence of multiple indirect paths from one node to another.

Why the discrimination? What is so special about interfaces that makes them more amenable to multiple inheritance than classes? The full explanation would be quite elaborate, but in short, the essential difference between an interface and a class is that the latter may contain state. More to the point, a class may contain modifiable state. In contrast, an interface does not hold its own state; there is some bookkeeping associated with each implemented interface (in many implementations, a pointer to a "virtual table"—an array of pointers to functions) but that pointer is identical for all occurrences of an interface inside a class, never changes, and is under the compiler's control. Taking advantage of these restrictions, the compiler actually plants multiple copies of that bookkeeping information in the class, but the class could never tell.

Historically, there has been a huge amount of debate about the merits and demerits of multiple inheritance. That debate has not converged and probably won't converge any time soon, but one thing that is generally agreed upon is that it's difficult to implement multiple inheritance in a way that's at the same time simple, efficient, and useful. Some languages do not have efficiency as a prime concern so they opt for the extra expressiveness brought about by multiple inheritance. Some others want to achieve some basic performance premises, such as contiguous objects or rapid function dispatch, and consequently limit the flexibility of possible designs. One interesting design that shares most advantages of multiple inheritance without its woes is Scala's mixins, which essentially are interfaces packaged with default implementations. D's approach is to allow multiple *subtyping*—that is, subtyping without inheritance. Let's see how that works.

## 6.13   Multiple Subtyping

Let's continue building on the Shape example and say we'd like to define Shape objects that can be stored in a database. We find a beautifully crafted database persistence library that seems to suit our purposes very well, with only one small hitch—it requires each storable object to inherit a class called DBObject.

```
class DBObject {
private:
    ... // State
public:
    void saveState() { ... }
    void loadState() { ... }
    ...
}
```

This situation could be modeled in a number of ways, but let's face it—if language limitations were not an issue, a quite natural approach would be to define a class StorableShape that "is a" Shape and a DBObject at the same time. The shapes hierarchy would be rooted in StorableShape. Then, when you need to draw a StorableShape, it would look and feel like a Shape; when you want to maneuver it in and out of a database, it will behave like a DBObject all right. That would mean multiple inheritance of classes, which is *verboten* in D, so we need to look for alternative solutions.

Fortunately, the language comes to the rescue with a general and very useful mechanism: multiple subtyping. A class can specify that it is a subtype of any other class, without needing to inherit from it. All you'd need to do is specify an `alias this` declaration. The simplest example would go like this:

```
class StorableShape : Shape {
   private DBObject _store;
   alias _store this;
   this() {
      _store = new DBObject;
   }
   ...
}
```

`StorableShape` inherits and "is a" `Shape`, but is also a `DBObject`. Whenever conversion from `StorableShape` to `DBObject` is requested, or whenever a member of `StorableShape` is looked up, the member `_store` also has a say in the matter. Requests that match `DBObject` are automatically redirected from `this` to `this._store`. For example:

```
unittest {
   auto s = new StorableShape;
   s.draw();        // Calls a Shape method
   s.saveState();   // Calls a DBObject method
                    // Gets rewritten as s._store.saveState()
   Shape sh = s;    // Normal upcast derived -> base
   DBObject db = s; // Rewritten as DBObject db = s._store
}
```

Effectively, a `StorableShape` is a subtype of `DBObject`, and the `_store` member is the `DBObject` subobject of the `StorableShape` object.

A class could introduce any number of `alias this` declarations, thus subtyping any number of types.

### 6.13.1 Overriding Methods in Multiple Subtyping Scenarios

Things couldn't be so simple, could they? They aren't, because `StorableShape` was cheating all along. Yes, with the `alias _store this` declaration in tow, a `StorableShape` is nominally a `DBShape`, but it cannot directly override any of its methods. Clearly `Shape`'s methods can be overridden as usual, but where's the place where `DBObject.saveState` could be overridden? Returning `_store` as a pseudo subobject is a copout—in fact, there isn't much about `_store` that's linked to its `StorableShape` outer object, at least not unless we do something about it. Let's see what that something consists of.

The exact point where the original `StorableShape` definition cheated was at the initialization of `_store` with `new DBObject`. That completely disconnects the subobject `_store` from the `StorableShape` outer object that is supposed to override methods in `DBObject`. So what we need to do is to define a new class `MyDBObject` inside `StorableShape`. That class would store a back reference to the `StorableObject` outer object and would `override` whichever methods need overriding. Finally, inside the overriden methods, `MyDBObject` has access to the full `StorableObject`, and everything can be done as if full-fledged multiple inheritance were in action. Cool!

If the phrase "outer object" rang a bell from upstream in this chapter, you have noticed one of the most serendipitous occurrences in the annals of computing. Nested classes (§ 6.11 on page 222) fit the need for multiple subtyping so well, you'd think they're a *deus ex machina* trick. In fact, nested classes (inspired by Java) predate the `alias this` feature by years.

Using a nested class makes overriding with `alias this` extremely simple. All you need to do in this case is define a nested class that inherits `DBObject`. Inside that class, you override any method of `DBObject` you wish, and you have full access to `DBObject`'s `public` and `protected` definitions *and* all definitions of `StorableShape`. If it were any easier, it'd be illegal in at least a few states.

```
class StorableShape : Shape {
    private class MyDBObject : DBObject {
        override void saveState() {
            // Access DBObject and StorableShape
            ...
        }
    }
    private MyDBObject _store;
    alias _store this;
    this() {
        // Here's the crucial point where the link is made
        _store = this.new MyDBObject;
    }
    ...
}
```

Crucially, `_store` has access to the outer `StorableShape` object. As discussed in § 6.11 on page 222, creating a nested class will surreptitiously store the outer object (in our case `this`) inside the nested class. The notation `this.new MyDBObject` just attempted to make it very clear that `this` conditions the creation of the new `MyDBObject` object. (In fact, `this.`, being implicit, is not required in that case.)

The only rub is that members of `DBObject` would mask members of `StorableShape`. For example, let's say both `DBObject` and `Shape` defined a member variable called `_name`:

```
class Shape {
    protected string _name;
    abstract void draw();
```

```
    ...
}
class DBObject {
   protected string _name;
   void saveState() { ... }
   void loadState() { ... }
   ...
}
```

When using multiple subtyping with class MyDBObject nested inside StorableShape, the member DBObject._name hides StorableShape._name. So if code inside MyDBObject simply uses _name, that will refer to DBObject._name:

```
class StorableShape : Shape {
   private class MyDBObject : DBObject {
      override void saveState() {
         // Modify Shape._name for the outer Shape object
         this.outer._name = "A";
         // Modify DBObject._name for the base object
         _name = "B";
         // Just to make the point clear
         assert(super._name == "B");
      }
   }
   private MyDBObject _store;
   alias _store this;
   this() {
      _store = new MyDBObject;
   }
   ...
}
```

## 6.14 Parameterized Classes and Interfaces

Sometimes you need to parameterize a class or an interface with a statically known entity. Consider, for example, defining a stack interface. The interface should be parameterized with the type stored in the stack so we avoid duplication (StackInt, StackDouble, StackWidget ...). To define a parameterized interface in D you go like this:

```
interface Stack(T) {
   @property bool empty();
```

```
  @property ref T top();
  void push(T value);
  void pop();
}
```

The syntax (T) introduces a type parameter to Stack. Inside Stack, you use T as you'd use any type. To use Stack in client code, you need to specify an argument, much as you'd have to pass an argument to a one-parameter function when you call it. You pass the argument by using the binary operator ! like this:

```
unittest {
  alias Stack!(int) StackOfInt;
  alias Stack!int SameAsAbove;
  ...
}
```

Where there's only one argument (as is the case with Stack), the parentheses around it can be omitted.

A logical next step would be to implement the interface in a class. The implementation should ideally also be generic (not specialized for a particular element type), so we define a parameterized class StackImpl that takes type parameter T, passes it to Stack, and uses it inside the implementation. Let's actually implement a stack using an array as back end:

```
class StackImpl(T) : Stack!T {
  private T[] _store;
  @property bool empty() {
    return _store.empty;
  }
  @property ref T top() {
    assert(!empty);
    return _store.back;
  }
  void push(T value) {
    _store ~= value;
  }
  void pop() {
    assert(!empty);
    _store.popBack();
  }
}
```

Using StackImpl is as much fun as implementing it:

```
unittest {
    auto stack = new StackImpl!int;
    assert(stack.empty);
    stack.push(3);
    assert(stack.top == 3);
    stack.push(5);
    assert(stack.top == 5);
    stack.pop();
    assert(stack.top == 3);
    stack.pop();
    assert(stack.empty);
}
```

Once you instantiate a parameterized class, it is a class all right, so `StackImpl!int` is a class like any other. This particular class implements `Stack!int` because the cookie cutter `StackImpl(T)` pasted `int` in lieu of `T` everywhere in its definition.

### 6.14.1 Heterogeneous Translation, Again

Now that we talked about hatching actual types out of parameterized types, let's take a closer look at instantiation mechanics. We first discussed the notion of heterogeneous translation (as opposed to homogeneous translation) in § 5.3 on page 138, in the context of type-parameterized functions. To recap, in homogeneous translation the language infrastructure adopts a common format for all values (e.g., everything is an `Object`) and then adjusts generic (type-parameterized) code to that common format under the hood. Adjustments may include casting types back and forth and "boxing" some types to make them obey the common value format, then "unboxing" them when user code asks for them. The process is typesafe and entirely transparent. Java and C# use heterogeneous translation for their parameterized types.

Under a homogeneous approach, all `StackImpl`s for all types would share the same code for their method implementations. More important, there's no distinction at the type level—the dynamic types of `StackImpl!int` and `StackImpl!double` are the same. The translator essentially defines *one* interface for all `Stack!T` and *one* class for all `StackImpl!T`. These types are called *erased* types because they erase any T-specific information. Then, the translator skillfully replaces code using `Stack` and `StackImpl` with various Ts to use only those erased types. The static information about whatever types client code uses with `Stack` and `StackImpl` is not preserved; that information is used for static typechecking and then promptly forgotten—or better put, erased. This process comes with its problems on account of the simple fact that there is some loss of information. A simple example is that you cannot overload a function on `Stack!int` versus Stack!double—they have the same type. Then there are deeper soundness issues that are discussed and partially addressed in the research literature [14, 1, 49].

A heterogeneous translator (such as C++'s template mechanism) approaches things differently. To a heterogeneous translator, Stack is not a type; it's a means to create a type. (Extra indirection for the win: a type is a blueprint of a value, and a parameterized type is a blueprint of a type.) Each instantiation of Stack!int, Stack!string, or whatever types you need throughout your application, will generate a distinct type. The heterogeneous translator generates all of these types by copying and pasting Stack's body while replacing T with whatever type you are using Stack with. This approach is liable to generate more code, but it's also more powerful because it preserves static type information in full. Besides, given that heterogeneous translation generates specialized code for each case, it may generate faster code.

D uses heterogeneous translation throughout, which means that Stack!int and Stack!double are distinct interfaces, and also that StackImpl!int is a distinct type from StackImpl!double. Apart from originating in the same parameterized type, the types are unrelated. (You could, of course, relate them somehow by, for example, having all Stack instantiations inherit a common interface.) Given that StackImpl generates one battery of methods for each type it's instantiated with, there is quite some binary code duplication, which is jarring particularly since the generated code may often be, in fact, identical. A clever compiler could merge all of the identical functions into one (at the time of this writing, the official D compiler does not do that, but such merging is a proven technology in the more mature C++ compilers).

A class may have, of course, more than one type parameter, so let's showcase this with an interesting twist in StackImpl's implementation. Instead of tying the storage to an array, we could hoist that decision outside of StackImpl. Of all an array's capabilities, StackImpl uses only empty, back, ~=, and popBack. Let's then make the container decision an implementation detail of StackImpl:

```d
class StackImpl(T, Backend) : Stack!T {
    private Backend _store;
    @property bool empty() {
        return _store.empty;
    }
    @property ref T top() {
        assert(!empty);
        return _store.back;
    }
    void push(T value) {
        _store ~= value;
    }
    void pop() {
        assert(!empty);
```

```
        _store.popBack();
    }
}
```

## 6.15 Summary

Classes are the primary mechanism for implementing object-oriented design in D. They consistently use reference semantics and are garbage-collected.

Inheritance is the enabler of dynamic polymorphism. Only single inheritance of state is allowed, but a `class` may inherit many `interface` types, which have no state but may define `final` methods.

Protection rules follow operating system protection (directories and files).

All classes inherit class `Object` defined in module `object` provided by the implementation. `Object` defines a few important primitives, and the module `object` defines pivotal functions for object comparison.

A class may define nested classes that automatically store a reference to their parent class, and `static` nested classes that do not.

D fully supports the Non-Virtual-Interface idiom and also a semi-automated mechanism for multiple subtyping.

# Other User-Defined Types

Much good software can be written by using classes, primitive types, and functions. Classes and functions parameterized with types and values make things even better. But oftentimes it becomes painfully obvious that classes are not the ultimate type abstraction device, for a few reasons.

First, classes obey reference semantics, which may force them to represent many designs poorly and with considerable overhead. An entity as simple as a Point with 2-D or 3-D coordinates becomes practically difficult to model with a class if there are more than a few million of them, which puts the designer in the dreaded position of choosing between good abstraction and reasonable efficiency. Also, in linear algebra, aliasing is a huge hassle. You'd have a difficult time convincing a mathematician or a scientific programmer that assigning two matrices by using a = b should make a and b refer to the same actual matrix instead of making a an independent copy of b. Even a type as simple as an array would incur overhead to model as a class when compared to D's lean and mean abstraction (Chapter 4). Sure, arrays could be "magic," but experience has shown time and again that offering many magic types that are unattainable to user code is a frustrating proposition and a sign of poor language design. The payload of an array is two words, so allocating a class object and using an extra indirection would mean large space and time overheads for all of arrays' primitives. Even a type as simple as int cannot be expressed as a class in a cheap and elegant manner, even if we ignore the issue of operator convenience. A class such as BigInt faces again the issue that a = b does something very different from the corresponding assignment for ints.

Second, classes have an infinite lifetime, which means they make it difficult to model resources with an emphatically *finite* lifetime and in relatively scarce supply, such as file handles, graphics handles, mutexes, sockets, and such. Dealing with such resources with classes puts a permanent strain on your attention because you must remember to

239

free the encapsulated resources in a timely manner by using a method such as `close` or `dispose`. The `scope` statement (§ 3.13 on page 84) often helps, but it is very useful to encapsulate such scoped semantics once and for all in a type.

Third, classes are a relatively heavy and high-level abstraction mechanism, so they aren't particularly convenient for expressing lightweight abstractions such as enumerated types or alternate names for a given type.

D wouldn't be true to form as a system-level programming language if it offered classes as the sole abstraction mechanism. In addition to classes, D has in store `structs` (value types wielding most of classes' power, but with value semantics and without polymorphism), `enums` (lightweight enumerated types and simple constants), `unions` (low-level overlapped storage for unrelated types), and ancillary type definition mechanisms such as `alias`. This chapter looks at each of these in turn.

## 7.1  structs

`struct` allows defining simple, encapsulated value types. A good model to keep in mind is `int`: an `int` value consists of 4 bytes supporting certain operations. There is no hidden state and no indirection in an `int`, and two `ints` always refer to distinct values.[1] The charter of `structs` precludes dynamic polymorphism, `override` for functions, inheritance, and infinite lifetime. A `struct` is but a glorified `int`.

Recall that `classes` have reference semantics (§ 6.2 on page 177), meaning that you always manipulate an object via a reference to it, and that copying references around actually just adds more references to the same object, without duplicating the actual object. In contrast, `structs` are value types, meaning essentially they behave "like `int`": names are stuck to the values they represent, and copying `struct` values around actually copies entire objects, not only references.

Defining a `struct` is very similar to defining a `class`, with the following differences:

- `struct` replaces `class`.
- Inheritance of classes and implementation of interfaces are not allowed, so a `struct` cannot specify `: BaseType, Interface`, and obviously there's no `super` to refer to inside a `struct`.
- `override` is not allowed for `struct` methods—all methods are `final` (you may redundantly specify `final` with a `struct`'s method).
- You cannot use `synchronized` with a `struct` (see Chapter 13).
- A `struct` is not allowed to define the default constructor `this()` (an issue that deserves an explanation, to come in § 7.1.3.1 on page 244).
- Inside a `struct` you can define the *postblit constructor* `this(this)` (we'll get to that in § 7.1.3.4 on page 245).

---

1. Barring simple name equivalence created with `alias`, which we'll look at later in this chapter (§ 7.4 on page 276).

- The `protected` access specifier is not allowed (it would imply there exist derived `struct`s).

Let's define a simple `struct`:

```
struct Widget {
    // A constant
    enum fudgeFactor = 0.2;
    // A shared immutable value
    static immutable defaultName = "A Widget";
    // Some state allocated for each Widget object
    string name = defaultName;
    uint width, height;
    // A static method
    static double howFudgy() {
        return fudgeFactor;
    }
    // A method
    void changeName(string another) {
        name = another;
    }
}
```

## 7.1.1  Copy Semantics

The few surface differences between `struct`s and `class`es are consequences of deeper semantic differences. Let's reenact an experiment we first carried out with `class`es in § 6.2 on page 177. This time we create a `class` and a `struct` containing the same fields, and we experiment with the copy behavior of the two types:

```
class C {
    int x = 42;
    double y = 3.14;
}

struct S {
    int x = 42;
    double y = 3.14;
}

unittest {
    C c1 = new C;
```

```
    S s1;              // No new for S: stack allocation
    auto c2 = c1;
    auto s2 = s1;
    c2.x = 100;
    s2.x = 100;
    assert(c1.x == 100); // c1 and c2 refer to the same object...
    assert(s1.x == 42);  // ...but s2 is a true copy of s1
}
```

With `struct` there are no references that you bind and rebind by using initialization and assignment. Any name of a `struct` value is associated with a distinct value. Defining `auto s2 = s1;` copies the entire `struct` object wholesale, field by field. As discussed, `struct` objects have *value semantics* and `class` object have *reference semantics*. Figure 7.1 shows the state of affairs after having just defined c2 and s2.

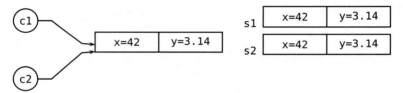

**Figure 7.1:** Evaluating `auto c2 = c1;` for a `class` object c1 and `auto s2 = s1;` for a `struct` object s1 has very different effects because of the reference nature of `classes` and the value nature of `structs`.

Unlike c1 and c2, which have the ability to bind to any object, s1 and s2 are simply inextricable names given to existing objects. There is no way two names could refer to the same `struct` object (unless you use `alias`, which defines simple equivalent symbols; see § 7.4 on page 276) and you cannot have a name without a `struct` attached to it—the comparison `s1 is null` is nonsensical and a compile-time error.

### 7.1.2  Passing `struct` Objects to Functions

Because of value semantics, `struct` objects are copied into functions by value.

```
struct S {
    int a, b, c;
    double x, y, z;
}
void fun(S s) {    // fun receives a copy
    ...
}
```

To pass a `struct` object by reference, use `ref` arguments (§ 5.2.1 on page 135):

```d
void fun(ref S s) {     // fun receives a reference
    ...
}
```

Speaking of `ref`, `this` is passed inside the methods of a `struct S` as a hidden `ref` S parameter.

### 7.1.3  Life Cycle of a `struct` Object

Unlike `class` objects, `struct` objects do not have an infinite lifetime. They obey very precise scoped lifetime semantics, akin to the lifetime of transitory function (stack) objects.

To create a `struct` object, just use its name as you'd use a function:

```d
import std.math;

struct Test {
    double a = 0.4;
    double b;
}

unittest {
    // Use the struct name as a function to create an object
    auto t = Test();
    assert(t.a == 0.4 && isnan(t.b));
}
```

Calling `Test()` creates a `struct` object with all fields default-initialized. In our case, that means `t.a` is `0.4` and `t.b` is left as `double.init`.

The calls `Test(1)` and `Test(1.5, 2.5)` are also allowed and initialize the object's fields in the order of their declarations. Continuing the previous example:

```d
unittest {
    auto t1 = Test(1);
    assert(t1.a == 1 && isnan(t1.b));
    auto t2 = Test(1.5, 2.5);
    assert(t2.a == 1.5 && t2.b == 2.5);
}
```

The syntactic difference between the expression creating a `struct` object—`Test(‹args›)`—and the expression creating a `class` object—`new Test(‹args›)`—may be jarring at first. D could have dropped the new keyword entirely when creating class objects, but that new reminds the programmer that a memory allocation operation (i.e., nontrivial work) takes place.

### 7.1.3.1   Constructors

You may define constructors for structs in a manner similar to class constructors (§ 6.3.1 on page 181):

```
struct Test {
   double a = 0.4;
   double b;
   this(double b) {
      this.b = b;
   }
}
unittest {
   auto t = Test(5);
}
```

The presence of at least one constructor disables all of the field-oriented constructors discussed above:

```
auto t1 = Test(1.1, 1.2);        // Error!
   // No constructor matches Test(double, double)
static Test t2 = { 0.0, 1.0 };  // Error!
   // No constructor matches Test(double, double)
```

There is an important exception: the compiler always defines the no-arguments constructor.

```
auto t2 = Test(); // Fine, create a default-filled object
```

Also, user code is unable to define the no-arguments constructor:

```
struct Test {
   double a = 0.4;
   double b;
   this() { b = 0; }  // Error!
      // A struct cannot define the default constructor!
}
```

Why this limitation? It all has to do with T.init, the default value that every type defines. T.init must be statically known, which contradicts the existence of a default constructor that executes arbitrary code. (For classes, T.init is the null reference, not a default-constructed object.) For all `structs`, the default constructor initializes an object with each field default-initialized.

### 7.1.3.2 Forwarding Constructors

Let's copy the example from § 6.3.2 on page 183 and change `class` to `struct`.

```
struct Widget {
   this(uint height) {
      this(1, height); // Defer to the other constructor
   }
   this(uint width, uint height) {
      this.width = width;
      this.height = height;
   }
   uint width, height;
   ...
}
```

The code runs without other modification. Just like `classes`, `structs` allow one constructor to forward to another, and with the same restrictions.

### 7.1.3.3 Construction Sequence

Classes need to worry about allocating dynamic memory and initializing their base subobject (§ 6.3.3 on page 184). Things are considerably simpler for `structs` because the memory allocation step is not implicit in the construction sequence. The steps taken toward constructing a `struct` object of type `T` are

1. Copy `T.init` over the memory that will contain the object by using raw memory copying (à la `memcpy`).
2. Call the constructor, if applicable.

If some or all of a `struct`'s fields are initialized with = `void`, the work in the first step can be reduced, but that is seldom a concern and often just a way to introduce subtle bugs into your code (however, do refer to the `Transmogrifier` example on page 185 for a plausible case).

### 7.1.3.4 The Postblit Constructor `this(this)`

Let's say we want to define an object that holds a `private` array inside and exposes a limited API for that array:

```
struct Widget {
   private int[] array;
   this(uint length) {
      array = new int[length];
   }
   int get(size_t offset) {
      return array[offset];
   }
   void set(size_t offset, int value) {
      array[offset] = value;
   }
}
```

There is a problem with Widget as defined: copying Widget objects creates a long-distance dependency between copies. Consider:

```
unittest {
   auto w1 = Widget(10);
   auto w2 = w1;
   w1.set(5, 100);
   w2.set(5, 42);            // Sets w1.array[5] as well!
   assert(w1.get(5) == 100); // Fails!?!
}
```

Where's the problem? Copying w1 into w2 is "shallow," that is, field-by-field, without transitively copying whatever memory may be indirectly referenced by each field. Copying an array does not allocate a new array; it only copies the bounds of the array (§ 4.1.4 on page 98). After the copy, w1 and w2 do contain distinct array fields, but they refer to the same region of memory. Such objects that are value types but contain indirect shared references could jokingly be called "clucts": a hybrid of structs with their value semantics and classes with their reference semantics.[2]

Oftentimes, structs want to define real value semantics, which means that a copy becomes entirely independent from its source. To do so, define a postblit constructor like this:

```
struct Widget {
   private int[] array;
   this(uint length) {
      array = new int[length];
   }
   // Postblit constructor
```

---

2. The term *clucts* was coined by Bartosz Milewski.

```
this(this) {
    array = array.dup;
}
// As before
int get(size_t offset) { return array[offset]; }
void set(size_t offset, int value) { array[offset] = value; }
}
```

A postblit constructor intervenes during object copying. When initializing a `struct` object `tgt` from another object `src` of the same type, the compiler takes the following steps:

1. Copy the raw memory of `src` over the memory of `tgt`.
2. For each transitive field (i.e., field of field of . . .) that defines method `this(this)`, call it bottom up (innermost fields first).
3. Call method `this(this)` against `tgt`.

The name *postblit* comes from *blit*, a popular abbreviation of "*BL*ock *T*ransfer," which meant raw memory copying. The language does the courtesy of raw copying objects upon initialization and offers a hook right after that. In the example above, the postblit constructor takes the now aliased array and makes it into a full-blown copy, ensuring that from here on the source and the target `Widget` objects have nothing in common. With the postblit constructor in effect, this test now passes:

```
unittest {
    auto w1 = Widget(10);
    auto w2 = w1;              // this(this) invoked here against w2
    w1.set(5, 100);
    w2.set(5, 42);
    assert(w1.get(5) == 100);  // Pass
}
```

The postblit constructor calls are consistently inserted whenever you copy objects, whether or not a named variable is explicitly created. For example, passing a `Widget` by value to a function also involves creating a copy.

```
void fun(Widget w) {           // Pass by value
    w.set(2, 42);
}

void gun(ref Widget w) {       // Pass by reference
    w.set(2, 42);
}
```

```
unittest {
    auto w1 = Widget(10);
    w1.set(2, 100);
    fun(w1);                        // A copy is created here
    assert(w1.get(2) == 100);  // Pass
    gun(w1);                        // No copy
    assert(w1.get(2) == 42);   // Pass
}
```

The second step (the part with "transitive field") of the postblit copy process deserves a special mention. The rationale for that behavior is *encapsulation*—the postblit constructor of a struct object must be called even when the struct is embedded in another struct object. Consider, for example, that we make Widget a member of another struct, which in turn is a member of yet another struct:

```
struct Widget2 {
    Widget w1;
    int x;
}

struct Widget3 {
    Widget2 w2;
    string name;
    this(this) {
        name = name ~ " (copy)";
    }
}
```

Now, if you want to copy around objects that contain Widgets, it would be pretty bad if the compiler forgot to properly copy the Widget subobjects. That's why when copying objects of type Widget2, a call to this(this) is issued for the w subobject, even though Widget2 does not intercept copying at all. Also, when copying objects of type Widget3, again this(this) is invoked for the field w of field w2. To clarify:

```
unittest {
    Widget2 a;
    a.w1 = Widget(10);                  // Allocate some data
    auto b = a;                         // this(this) called for b.w
    assert(a.w1.array !is b.w1.array);  // Pass

    Widget3 c;
    c.w2.w1 = Widget(20);
```

```
    auto d = c;                             // this(this) for d.w2.w
    assert(c.w2.w1.array !is d.w2.w1.array);  // Pass
}
```

In brief, if you define the postblit constructor this(this) for a struct type, the compiler makes sure that the postblit is invoked consistently whenever the object is copied, be it stand-alone or part of a larger struct object.

### 7.1.3.5  The *Why*s of this(this)

What was the rationale behind the postblit constructor? There is no precedent for this(this) in other languages. Why not just pass the source object to the target object (the way C++ does it)?

```
// This is not D
struct S {
    this(S another) { ... }
// Or
    this(ref S another) { ... }
}
```

Experience with C++ has shown that excessive copying of objects is a prime source of inefficiency in C++ programs. To mitigate that loss in efficiency, C++ established cases in which calls to the copy constructor could be elided by the compiler. The elision rules have quickly gotten fairly complicated and still do not cover all cases, leaving the problem unsolved. The upcoming C++ standard addresses those issues by defining a new type "rvalue reference," which allows user-controlled copy elision at the cost of even more language complication.

Because of postblit, D's approach to copy elision is simple and largely automated. First off, D objects must be *relocatable*, that is, location-independent: an object can be moved around memory by using raw memory move without its integrity being affected. The restriction, however, means that objects may not embed so-called *internal pointers*, addresses of sub-parts of the object. This is a technique that is never indispensable, so D simply rules it out. It is illegal to create objects with internal pointers in D, and the compiler and runtime subsystem are free to assume observance of this rule. Relocatable objects give the compiler and the runtime subsystem (for example, the garbage collector) great opportunities to make programs faster and more compact.

With relocatable objects in place, object copying becomes a logical extension of object moving: the postblit constructor this(this) makes copying equivalent to a move plus an optional user-defined hook. That way, user code does not have the opportunity to change the fields of the source object, which is good because copying should not affect the source, but it does have the opportunity to fix up fields that should not indirectly share state with the source object. To elide copies, the compiler is free to not insert the call to `this(this)` whenever it can prove the source of the copy will not be used after the copying process. Consider, for example, a function that returns a `Widget` (as defined above) by value:

```
Widget hun(uint x) {
    return Widget(x * 2);
}


unittest {
    auto w = hun(1000);
    ...
}
```

A naïve approach would be to simply create a `Widget` object inside `hun` and then copy it into `w` by using a bitwise copy followed by a call to `this(this)`. But this is wasteful because D assumes objects to be relocatable, so then why not simply move the moribund temporary created by `hun` into `w`? Nobody could really tell because there's no use of the temporary after `hun` returns. If a tree falls in the forest and nobody hears it, there should be no problem with moving the tree instead of copying it. A similar but not identical example is shown here:

```
Widget iun(uint x) {
    auto result = Widget(x * 2);
    ...
    return result;
}


unittest {
    auto w = iun(1000);
    ...
}
```

In this case, again, `result` is gone after `iun` returns, so a call to `this(this)` is unnecessary. Finally, a subtler case is the following:

```
void jun(Widget w) {
    ...
}


unittest {
    auto w = Widget(1000);
    ... // ‹code₁›
    jun(w);
    ... // ‹code₂›
```

```
}
```

This case is tricky to rid of a call to this(this). It is possible that ‹*code₂*› continues using w, in which case moving it out from the unittest into jun would be incorrect.[3]

In view of all of the considerations above, D takes the following stance on copy elision:

- All anonymous rvalues are moved, not copied. A call to this(this) is never inserted when the source is an anonymous rvalue (i.e., a temporary as featured in the function hun above).
- All named temporaries that are stack-allocated inside a function and then returned elide a call to this(this).
- There is no guarantee that other potential elisions are observed.

Sometimes, however, we actively want to order the compiler to perform a move. This is in fact doable via the move function defined in the standard library module std.algorithm:

```
import std.algorithm;

void kun(Widget w) {
   ...
}

unittest {
   auto w = Widget(1000);
   ... // ‹code₁›
   // Call to move inserted
   kun(move(w));
   assert(w == Widget.init); // Passes
   ... // ‹code₂›
}
```

Using move ensures that w will be moved, and that an empty, default-constructed Widget replaces w's contents. By the way, this is one place where the existence of a stateless non-throwing default constructor (§ 7.1.3.1 on page 244) called Widget.init comes in really handy. Without that, there might be no way to put the source of a move in a well-defined, empty state.

---

3. In addition, ‹*code₁*› may save a pointer to w that ‹*code₂*› uses.

### 7.1.3.6    Destruction and Deallocation

A `struct` may define a destructor, spelled like `~this()`:

```d
import std.stdio;

struct S {
    int x = 42;
    ~this() {
        writeln("An S with payload ", x, " is going away. Bye!");
    }
}

void main() {
    writeln("Creating an object of type S.");
    {
        S object;
        writeln("Inside object's scope");
    }
    writeln("After object's scope.");
}
```

The program above reliably prints

```
Creating an object of type S.
Inside object's scope
An S with payload 42 is going away. Bye!
After object's scope.
```

Any `struct` object obeys *scoped lifetime*, meaning that its lifetime effectively ends at the end of the object's scope. More specifically:

- The lifetime of a non-`static` object defined inside a function ends at the end of the current scope, before all `struct` objects defined before it.
- The lifetime of an object defined as a member inside another `struct` ends immediately after the enclosing object's lifetime.
- The lifetime of an object defined at module scope is infinite. If you want to call that object's destructor, you must do so in a module destructor (§ 11.3 on page 356).
- The lifetime of an object defined as a member inside a `class` ends at the point the enclosing object's memory is collected.

The language guarantees calling `~this` automatically at the end of a `struct` object's lifetime, which is very handy if you want to automatically carry out operations like closing files and freeing any sensitive resources.

The source of a copy that uses this(this) obeys its normal lifetime rules, but the source of an elided copy that is moved through memory does not have its destructor called.

Deallocation of a struct object is conceptually carried out immediately after destruction.

### 7.1.3.7  Tear-Down Sequence

By default, struct objects are destroyed in the exact opposite order of their creation. For example, the last struct object defined in a scope is the first to be destroyed:

```
import std.conv, std.stdio;

struct S {
   private string name;
   this(string name) {
      writeln(name, " checking in.");
      this.name = name;
   }
   ~this() {
      writeln(name, " checking out.");
   }
}

void main() {
   auto obj1 = S("first object");
   foreach (i; 0 .. 3) {
      auto obj = S(text("object ", i));
   }
   auto obj2 = S("last object");
}
```

The program above prints

```
first object checking in.
object 0 checking in.
object 0 checking out.
object 1 checking in.
object 1 checking out.
object 2 checking in.
object 2 checking out.
last object checking in.
last object checking out.
first object checking out.
```

As expected, the first object created is the last object to be destroyed. A loop enters and exits the scope of the controlled statement at each pass through the loop.

You can invoke a `struct` object's destructor explicitly by calling `clear(obj)`. We got acquainted with the `clear` function on page 187. There, `clear` was useful for resetting `class` objects to their default-constructed state. For `struct` objects, `clear` does a similar deed: it invokes the destructor and then copies `.init` over the bits of the object. The result is a valid object, just one that doesn't hold any interesting state.

### 7.1.4 Static Constructors and Destructors

A `struct` may define any number of static constructors and destructors. This feature is virtually identical to the homonym feature we introduced for `classes` in § 6.3.6 on page 188.

```d
import std.stdio;

struct A {
    static ~this() {
        writeln("First static destructor");
    }
    ...
    static this() {
        writeln("First static constructor");
    }
    ...
    static this() {
        writeln("Second static constructor");
    }
    ...
    static ~this() {
        writeln("Second static destructor");
    }
}

void main() {
    writeln("This is main speaking");
}
```

No pairing is needed between `static` constructors and `static` destructors. Before evaluating `main`, the runtime support boringly executes all `static` constructors in the order of their definition. After `main` terminates, the runtime support just as boringly executes all `static` destructors in the opposite order of their definition. The program above writes

```
First static constructor
Second static constructor
This is main speaking
Second static destructor
First static destructor
```

The order of execution of `static` constructors and destructors is well defined (as above) within a module, but not always across modules. The order of execution of `static` constructors and destructors across modules is defined on page 189.

### 7.1.5 Methods

`struct`s may define member functions, also known as methods. Since there is no inheritance and no overriding for `struct`s, `struct` methods are only little more than regular functions.

For a `struct` type S, non-`static` methods take a hidden parameter `this` by reference (equivalent to a `ref S` parameter). Inside a method, name lookup proceeds as with `class`es: parameters hide homonym member names, and member names hide homonym module-level names.

```
void fun(int x) {
    assert(x != 0);
}

// Illustrating name lookup rules
struct S {
    int x = 1;
    static int y = 324;

    void fun(int x) {
        assert(x == 0);        // Fetch parameter x
        assert(this.x == 1);   // Fetch member x
    }

    void gun() {
        fun(0);                // Call method fun
        .fun(1);               // Call module-level fun
    }

    // unittests may be struct members
    unittest {
        S obj;
        obj.gun();
```

```
        assert(y == 324); // "Member" unittests see static data
    }
}
```

Also featured above is a `unittest` defined inside a `struct`. Such member `unittests` have no special status but are very convenient to insert after each method definition. Code inside a member `unittest` enjoys the same name visibility as regular `static` methods—for example, the `unittest` above does not have to prefix the `static` member y with S, just as a static method wouldn't.

A few special methods are worth a closer investigation. They are the assignment operator `opAssign` used for =, the equality operator `opEquals` used for == and !=, and the ordering operator `opCmp` used for <, <=, >=, and >. This topic really belongs in Chapter 12 because it concerns operator overloading, but these operators are special because the compiler may generate them automatically with a specific behavior.

### 7.1.5.1 The Assignment Operator

By default, if you say

```
struct Widget { ... } // Defined as in § 7.1.3.4 on page 245
Widget w1, w2;
...
w1 = w2;
```

then the assignment is done member by member. This may cause trouble with the type `Widget` discussed in § 7.1.3.4 on page 245. Recall that `Widget` holds a private `int[]` member that was supposed to be distinct for each `Widget` object. Assigning w2 to w1 field by field assigns `w2.array` to `w1.array`—a simple assignment of array bounds, without actually copying the array contents. This needs fixing because what we want is to create a *duplicate* of the array in the source `Widget` and assign that duplicate to the target `Widget`.

User code can intercept assignment by defining the method `opAssign`. Essentially, an assignment `lhs = rhs` is translated into `lhs.opAssign(rhs)` if `lhs` defines `opAssign` with a compatible signature (otherwise, it performs the default field-by-field assignment if `lhs` and `rhs` have the same type). Let's define `Widget.opAssign`:

```
struct Widget {
    private int[] array;
    ... // this(uint), this(this), etc.
    ref Widget opAssign(ref Widget rhs) {
        array = rhs.array.dup;
        return this;
    }
}
```

```
}
```

The assignment operator returns a reference to `this` to allow chained assignments
à la `w1 = w2 = w3`, which the compiler rewrites into `w1.opAssign(w2.opAssign(w3))`.

There is one problem left. Consider the assignment

```
Widget w;
...
w = Widget(50);   // Error!
    // Cannot bind an rvalue of type Widget to ref Widget!
```

The problem is that `opAssign` as defined expects a `ref Widget`, that is, an lvalue of
type `Widget`. To accept assignment from rvalues in addition to lvalues, `Widget` must
define *two* assignment operators:

```
import std.algorithm;

struct Widget {
    private int[] array;
    ... // this(uint), this(this), etc.
    ref Widget opAssign(ref Widget rhs) {
        array = rhs.array.dup;
        return this;
    }
    ref Widget opAssign(Widget rhs) {
        swap(array, rhs.array);
        return this;
    }
}
```

There's no more `.dup` in the version taking an rvalue. Why? Well, the rvalue (with
its `array` in tow) is practically owned by the second `opAssign`: it was copied prior to
entering the function and will be destroyed just before the function returns. This means
there's no more need to duplicate `rhs.array` because nobody will miss it. Swapping
`rhs.array` with `this.array` is enough. When `opAssign` returns, `rhs` goes away with
`this`'s old `array`, and `this` stays with `rhs`'s old `array`—perfect conservation of state.

We now could remove the first overload of `opAssign` altogether: the one taking
`rhs` by value takes care of everything (lvalues are automatically converted to rvalues).
But keeping the lvalue version allows for a useful optimization: instead of `.dup`ing the
source, `opAssign` can check whether the current `array` has space for accommodating
the new contents, in which case an overwrite is enough.

```
// Inside Widget ...
ref Widget opAssign(ref Widget rhs) {
```

```
    if (array.length < rhs.array.length) {
        array = rhs.array.dup;
    } else {
        // Adjust length
        array.length = rhs.array.length;
        // Copy array contents (§ 4.1.7 on page 100)
        array[] = rhs.array[];
    }
    return this;
}
```

### 7.1.5.2   Comparing `structs` for Equality

Objects of `struct` type can be compared for equality out of the box with `==` and `!=`. Comparison is carried out member by member and yields `false` if at least two corresponding members in the compared objects are not equal, and `true` otherwise.

```
struct Point {
    int x, y;
}
unittest {
    Point a, b;
    assert(a == b);
    a.x = 1;
    assert(a != b);
}
```

To define a custom comparison routine, define the `opEquals` method:

```
import std.math, std.stdio;

struct Point {
    float x = 0, y = 0;
    // Added
    bool opEquals(ref const Point rhs) const {
        // Perform an approximate comparison
        return approxEqual(x, rhs.x) && approxEqual(y, rhs.y);
    }
}

unittest {
    Point a, b;
```

```
    assert(a == b);
    a.x = 1e-8;
    assert(a == b);
    a.y = 1e-1;
    assert(a != b);
}
```

Compared to opEquals for classes (§ 6.8.3 on page 205), opEquals for structs is much simpler because it doesn't need to worry about correctness in the presence of inheritance. The compiler simply rewrites a comparison of struct objects into a call to opEquals. Of course, structs must still define a meaningful opEquals: reflexive, symmetric, and transitive. It must be said that, although Point.opEquals looks quite sensible, it fails the transitivity test. A better test would compare two Points truncated to their most significant bits; that test could be made transitive more easily.

When a struct contains members that define opEquals but it does not itself define opEquals, comparison will still invoke opEquals for the members that define it. Continuing the Point example above:

```
struct Rectangle {
    Point leftBottom, rightTop;
}

unittest {
    Rectangle a, b;
    assert(a == b);
    a.leftBottom.x = 1e-8;
    assert(a == b);
    a.rightTop.y = 5;
    assert(a != b);
}
```

Given two Rectangles a and b, evaluating a == b is equivalent to evaluating

```
a.leftBottom == b.leftBottom && a.rightTop == b.rightTop
```

which in turn is rewritten as

```
a.leftBottom.opEquals(b.leftBottom) &&
    a.rightTop.opEquals(b.rightTop)
```

The example also reveals that comparison is carried out in field declaration order (i.e., leftBottom before rightTop) and stops early if two fields are not equal because of the short-circuit evaluation of &&.

### 7.1.6  `static` Members

A `struct` may define `static` data and `static` member functions. Save for their scoped visibility and observance of access rules (§ 7.1.7 on the next page), `static` member functions have the same regime as regular functions. There is no hidden `this` parameter and no other special mechanism involved.

Similarly, `static` data members have a regime much like `module`-level global data (§ 5.2.4 on page 137), save for visibility and access imposed by the `struct` defining them.

```d
import std.stdio;

struct Point {
    private int x, y;

    private static string formatSpec = "(%s %s)\n";

    static void setFormatSpec(string newSpec) {
        ... // Check the format spec for correctness
        formatSpec = newSpec;
    }

    void print() {
        writef(formatSpec, x, y);
    }
}

void main() {
    auto pt1 = Point(1, 2);
    pt1.print();
    // Call static member by prefixing it with either Point or pt1
    Point.setFormatSpec("[%s, %s]\n");
    auto pt2 = Point(5, 3);
    // The new spec affects all Point objects
    pt1.print();
    pt2.print();
}
```

The program above predictably prints

```
(1 2)
[1, 2]
[5, 3]
```

### 7.1.7    Access Specifiers

struct types obey the access specifiers private (§ 6.7.1 on page 200), package (§ 6.7.2 on page 200), public (§ 6.7.4 on page 201), and export (§ 6.7.5 on page 201) the same way as class types do. For structs, protected does not make sense because structs have no inheritance.

You may want to refer to the respective sections for the full story. Here, let's just briefly recap the meaning of each access specifier:

```
struct S {
    private int a;   // Accessible within this file and S's methods
    package int b;   // Accessible within this file's directory
    public int c;    // Accessible from within the application
    export int d;    // Accessible outside the application
                     //    (where applicable)
}
```

Again, export, although syntactically allowed anywhere an access specifier is allowed, has semantics that are at the discretion of the implementation.

### 7.1.8    Nesting structs and classes

Often, it is convenient for a struct to internally define other structs or classes. For example, a tree container may choose to expose a struct shell with a simple searching interface but use polymorphism inside to define the nodes of the tree.

```
struct Tree {
private:
  class Node {
    int value;
    abstract Node left();
    abstract Node right();
  }
  class NonLeaf : Node {
    Node _left, _right;
    override Node left() { return _left; }
    override Node right() { return _right; }
  }
  class Leaf : Node {
    override Node left() { return null; }
    override Node right() { return null; }
  }
  // Data
  Node root;
```

```
public:
   void add(int value) { ... }
   bool search(int value) { ... }
}
```

Similarly, structs may be nested inside other structs ...

```
struct Widget {
private:
   struct Field {
      string name;
      uint x, y;
   }
   Field[] fields;
public:
   ...
}
```

... and, finally, structs may be nested within classes:

```
class Window {
   struct Info {
      string name;
      Window parent;
      Window[] children;
   }
   Info getInfo();
   ...
}
```

Unlike classes nested within classes, nested structs and nested classes within structs don't contain any hidden member outer—there is no special code generated. The main design goal of nesting such types is to enforce the desired access control.

### 7.1.9  Nesting structs inside Functions

Recall from § 6.11.1 on page 223 that nested classes enjoy special, unique properties. A nested class gets to access the enclosing function's parameters and local variables. If you return a nested class object, the compiler even creates a dynamically allocated function frame such that the function's locals and parameters survive beyond the end of the function.

For conformity and consistency, D offers similar amenities to structs nested inside functions. A nested struct can access the enclosing function's parameters and locals:

```
void fun(int a) {
   int b;
   struct Local {
      int c;
      int sum() {
         // Access parameter, variable, and Local's own member
         return a + b + c;
      }
   }
   Local obj;
   int x = obj.sum();
   assert(Local.sizeof == 2 * size_t.sizeof);
}
unittest {
   fun(5);
}
```

Nested structs embed the magic "frame pointer" that allows them to access outer values such as a and b in the example above. Because of that extra state, the size of a Local object is not 4 as one might expect, but 8 (on a 32-bit machine) to account for the frame pointer. If you want to define a nested struct without that baggage, just prefix struct with static in the definition of Local, which makes Local a regular struct and consequently prevents it from accessing a and b.

Aside from avoiding a gratuitous limitation when compared with nested classes, nested structs are of little use. Nested struct objects cannot be returned from functions because the caller doesn't have access to their type. If a design gets to use sophisticated nested structs, it implicitly fosters complex functions, which should at best be avoided in the first place.

### 7.1.10  Subtyping with structs. The @disable Attribute

Although structs don't feature inheritance and polymorphism, they still support the alias this feature, first introduced in § 6.13 on page 230. By using alias this, you can have a struct subtype any other type. For example, let's define a simple type called Final that behaves much like a class reference—except you can never rebind it! Here's an example of using Final:

```
import std.stdio;

class Widget {
   void print() {
      writeln("Hi, I'm a Widget. Well, that's about it.");
```

```
    }
}

unittest {
    auto a = Final!Widget(new Widget);
    a.print();        // Fine, just print a
    auto b = a;       // Fine, a and b are bound to the same Widget
    a = b;            // Error!
                      // opAssign(Final!Widget) is disabled!
    a = new Widget;   // Error!
                      // Cannot assign to rvalue returned by get()!
}
```

The purpose of `Final` is to be a special kind of `class` reference that first binds to some object and then never lets go of it. Such "faithful" references are useful in many designs.

The first step is to get rid of assignment. The problem is, the assignment operator is automatically generated if missing, so `Final` must kindly instruct the compiler to not do that. To effect that, use the `@disable` attribute:

```
struct Final(T) {
    // Disable assignment
    @disable void opAssign(Final);
    ...
}
```

You may use `@disable` to remove other generated functions, such as comparison.

So far, so good. To implement `Final!T`, we need to make sure that the type subtypes T by using `alias this` but not offer an lvalue. A mistaken design looks like this:

```
// Mistaken design
struct Final(T) {
    private T payload;
    this(T bindTo) {
        payload = bindTo;
    }
    // Disable assignment
    @disable void opAssign(Final);
    // Subclass T
    alias payload this;
}
```

`Final` holds its value in the `payload` member and initializes it in the constructor. It also effectively disables assignment by declaring `opAssign` but never defining it. That way, clients attempting to assign to objects of type `Final!T` will either have no access (because of `private`) or encounter a link-time error.

The mistake of `Final` is to introduce `alias payload this`. Here's a `unittest` that accomplishes something it's not supposed to:

```
class A {
    int value = 42;
    this(int x) { value = x; }
}
unittest {
    auto v = Final!A(new A(42));
    void sneaky(ref A ra) {
        ra = new A(4242);
    }
    sneaky(v);                              // Hmm...
    assert(v.value == 4242);                // Passes?!?
}
```

The workings of `alias payload this` are quite simple. Whenever a value `obj` of type `Final!T` is used in a context that would be illegal for its type, the compiler rewrites `obj` as `obj.payload`. (In other words, it makes `obj.payload` an *alias* of `obj`, hence the name and syntax of the feature.) But `obj.payload` is direct access to a field of `obj` and as such it's an lvalue. That lvalue is bound to `sneaky`'s `ref` parameter and therefore allows `sneaky` to overwrite `v`'s field directly.

To fix that, we need to alias the object to an rvalue. That way, we get full functionality, but the reference stored in `payload` is impossible to touch. Binding to an rvalue is very easy by using a `@property` that returns `payload` by value:

```
struct Final(T) {
    private T payload;
    this(T bindTo) {
        payload = bindTo;
    }
    // Disable assignment by leaving opAssign undefined
    private void opAssign(Final);
    // Subclass T, but do not allow rebinding
    @property T get() { return payload; }
    alias get this;
}
```

The crucial new element is that `get` returns a `T`, not a `ref T`, so `payload` cannot be rebound. Of course, the object that `payload` refers to can be modified (for ways to prevent that, refer to `const` and `immutable` in Chapter 8 on page 287). The charter of `Final` is now fulfilled. First, `Final!T` behaves like a `T` for any class type `T`. Second, once you bind a `Final!T` to some object in the constructor, there is no way to rebind it to any other object. To wit, the killer `unittest` does not compile anymore because the call `sneaky(v)` is now illegal: an rvalue of type `A` (obtained from `v` implicitly via `v.get`) cannot be bound to `ref A` as sneaky needs for its dirty deeds.

There is one little fly left in this ointment—really just a small *Drosophila melanogaster*—that we ought to remove. Whenever a type such as `Final` uses `alias get this`, extra attention must be paid to `Final`'s own symbols masking homonym symbols defined by the aliased type. For example, say we use `Final!Widget` and `Widget` itself defines a property called `get`:

```
class Widget {
    private int x;
    @property int get() { return x; }
}
unittest {
    auto w = Final!Widget(new Widget);
    auto x = w.get;  // Gets the Widget in Final,
                     // Not the int in Widget
}
```

To avoid such collisions, we need to use a naming convention, and a solid one is to simply use the name of the type in the name of the transparent property:

```
struct Final(T) {
    private T Final_payload;
    this(T bindTo) {
        Final_payload = bindTo;
    }
    // Disable assignment
    @disable void opAssign(Final);
    // Subclass T, but do not allow rebinding
    @property T Final_get() { return Final_payload; }
    alias Final_get this;
}
```

With this convention in action, the risk of unintended collisions is diminished. (Of course, on occasion you actively want to intercept certain methods and carry them in the intercepter.)

### 7.1.11  Field Layout. Alignment

How are fields laid out in a `struct` object? D is very conservative with `struct`s—it lays their contents in the same order as that specified in the `struct` definition but is still free to insert *padding* between fields. Consider:

```
struct A {
   char a;
   int b;
   char c;
}
```

If the compiler were to lay fields exactly with the sizes prescribed by A, b would sit at the object's address plus 1 (a char occupies exactly 1 byte). This is problematic because most contemporary computer systems fetch data in 4- or 8-byte increments, with the restriction that they can fetch only from addresses that are multiples of 4 or 8, respectively. Let's assume an object of type A sits at a "good" address, for example, a multiple of 8. Then b's address would definitely be in a bad part of town. What the processor needs to do to fetch b is quite onerous—stitch the value of b by assembling byte-size pieces of it. To add insult to injury, depending on the compiler and the underlying hardware architecture, the entire operation may be performed in response to a "misaligned memory access" kernel trap, which has its own (and way larger) overhead [28]. This is definitely not a beans-counting matter—the extra gymnastics could easily dampen access speed by many orders of magnitude.

For that reason, today's compilers lay out structures with *padding*. The compiler inserts additional bytes into the object to ensure that all fields are situated at advantageous offsets. Then, allocating objects at addresses that are multiple of the word size ensures fast access to all of their members. Figure 7.2 illustrates the padded layout of A.

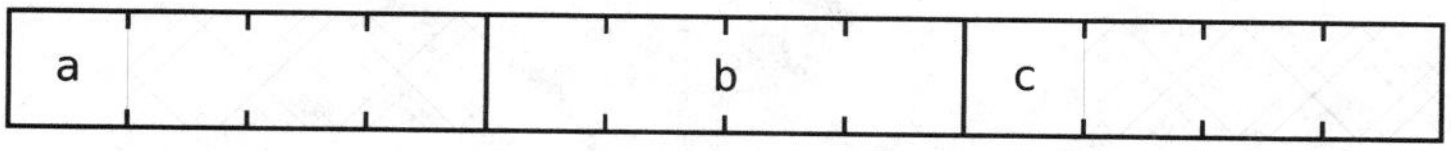

**Figure 7.2:** Padded layout for an object of type A. The hashed areas are paddings inserted for proper alignment. The compiler inserts two holes into the object adding 6 bytes of slack space, or 50% of the total object size.

The resulting layout has quite a bit of padding (the hashed bytes). In the case of a class, the compiler has the freedom to reorder fields, but with a struct you may want to pay attention to the layout of data if memory consumption is important. A better choice of field ordering would be to place the int first, followed by the two chars, which would fit in 64 bits including 2 bytes of padding.

Each field of an object has a compile-time-known offset from the starting address of the object. That offset is always the same for all objects of the same type within a given program (it may change from one compilation to the next, but not from one run to the next). The offset is user-accessible as the .offsetof property implicitly defined for any field in a class or struct:

```
import std.stdio;

struct A {
    char a;
    int b;
    char c;
}

void main() {
    A x;
    writefln("%s %s %s", x.a.offsetof, x.b.offsetof, x.c.offsetof);
}
```

The reference implementation prints 0  4  8, revealing the layout in Figure 7.2 on the previous page. It is a bit awkward that you need to create an object of type A just to access some static information about it, but the syntax A.a.offsetof does not compile. A trick that can be used, however, is to use A.init.a.offsetof, which is enough to fetch the offset associated with each member as a compile-time constant.

```
import std.stdio;

struct A {
    char a;
    int b;
    char c;
}

void main() {
    // Access field offsets without an object
    writefln("%s %s %s", A.init.a.offsetof,
        A.init.b.offsetof, A.init.c.offsetof);
}
```

D guarantees that all of the padding bytes are consistently filled with zeros.

### 7.1.11.1  The align Attribute

If you want to override the compiler's choice of alignment, which influences the padding inserted, you can use an `align` modifier with your field declaration.  Such a necessity may occur when you want to interact with a piece of hardware or a binary protocol that specifies a specific alignment. Here's what an `align` specifier looks like:

```
class A {
```

```
    char a;
    align(1) int b;
    char c;
}
```

With the specification above, the fields of A are laid out without gaps between them. (There may still be a gap at the end of the object.) The argument of `align` is the *maximum* alignment of the field, so the effective alignment will likely not go beyond the natural alignment of the field's type. To get the natural alignment of a type T, use the compiler-defined property `T.alignof`. So if you specify, for example, `align(200)` instead of `align(1)` for b above, the effective alignment obtained is 4, the same as for `int.alignof`.

You may use `align` with an entire `class` definition:

```
align(1) struct A {
    char a;
    int b;
    char c;
}
```

When specified with a `struct`, `align` sets the default alignment to a specific value. You may override that default with individual `align` attributes inside the `struct` definition. If you specify only `align` without a number for a field of type T, that counts as `align(T.alignof)`—in other words, it resets the alignment of that field to its natural alignment.

`align` is not supposed to be used with pointers and references. The garbage collector assumes that all references and pointers are aligned at `size_t` size. The compiler does not enforce this restriction because generally you could have pointers and references that are not garbage-collected. So this definition is highly dangerous because it compiles warning-free:

```
struct Node {
    short value;
    align(2) Node* next; // Avoid
}
```

If the code above assigns `obj.next = new Node` (i.e., fills `obj.next` with a garbage-collected reference), then chaos is bound to occur: the misaligned reference goes under the radar of the garbage collector, memory gets recycled, and `obj.next` is a dangling reference.

## 7.2  unions

C-style unions are also accepted in D, though it should be mentioned that they should be used rarely and with extreme care.

A union is akin to a `struct` in which all members start at the same address. This makes their storage overlap, meaning that it's your responsibility as the union's user to always read the same exact type you wrote. At any given time, only one member of a union value is valid.

```d
union IntOrFloat {
    int _int;
    float _float;
}

unittest {
    IntOrFloat iof;
    iof._int = 5;
    // Read only iof._int, but not iof._float
    assert(iof._int == 5);
    iof._float = 5.5;
    // Read only iof._float, not iof._int
    assert(iof._float == 5.5);
}
```

Since `int` and `float` both have the same exact size (4 bytes), they will precisely overlap inside `IntOrFloat`. The details of their layout, however, are not specified—for example, `_int` and `_float` may use different endianness: `_int`'s most significant byte might be at the lowest address and `_float`'s most significant byte (the one containing the sign and most of the exponent) may be at the highest address.

unions are not tagged, meaning that the union object itself does not contain a "tag," that is a means to distinguish which member is the good one. The responsibility of correct use falls straight on the user's shoulders, which makes unions quite an unpleasant means to build any kind of larger abstraction.

Upon definition without initialization, a union object has its first field initialized with its `.init` value, so after default construction the first member is readable. To initialize the first field with something other than `.init`, specify the desired initializer in brackets:

```d
unittest {
    IntOrFloat iof = { 5 };
    assert(iof._int == 5);
}
```

A static union object may have another field initialized by using the following syntax:

```
unittest {
    static IntOrFloat iof = { _float : 5 };
    assert(iof._float == 5);
}
```

Truth be told, many uses of union actually use it to read different types from those written in the first place, in order to achieve certain system-dependent manipulation of representation. Because of that, the compiler will not denounce even the detectable misuses of unions. For example, the code below passes compilation and even the assert on an Intel 32-bit machine:

```
unittest {
    IntOrFloat iof;
    iof._float = 1;
    assert(iof._int == 0x3F80_0000);
}
```

A union may define member functions and generally any members a struct may define but cannot define constructors and destructors.

The most frequent (or, better put, least infrequent) use of union is as an anonymous member inside a struct, as shown here:

```
import std.contracts;

struct TaggedUnion {
    enum Tag  { _tvoid, _tint, _tdouble, _tstring, _tarray }
    private Tag _tag;
    private union {
        int _int;
        double _double;
        string _string;
        TaggedUnion[] _array;
    }

public:
    void opAssign(int v) {
        _int = v;
        _tag = Tag._tint;
    }
    int getInt() {
        enforce(_tag == Tag._tint);
        return _int;
    }
```

```
    ...
}

unittest {
    TaggedUnion a;
    a = 4;
    assert(a.getInt() == 4);
}
```

(Details on enum are forthcoming in this chapter; refer to § 7.3.)

The example above is the absolute classic use of union as a helper in defining a so-called *discriminated union*, aka tagged union or algebraic type. TaggedUnion encapsulates an unsafe union within a safe box that keeps track of the last type assigned. Upon initialization, the value of Tag is Tag._void, meaning that the object is effectively uninitialized. When you assign to the union, opAssign kicks in and sets the type of the object appropriately. To complete the implementation, you may want to define opAssign(double), opAssign(string), and opAssign(TaggedUnion[]) as well, together with the corresponding getXxx() functions.

The union member is anonymous, meaning that it is at the same time a type definition and a member definition. The anonymous union is allocated as a regular member inside the struct, and its members are directly visible inside the struct (as the methods of TaggedUnion illustrate). Generally you may define both anonymous structs and anonymous unions and nest them as you want.

Finally, you should know that union is not as evil as it may seem. Using a union instead of type punning with cast is often good communication etiquette between you and the compiler. A union of a pointer and an integral clarifies to the compiler that it should be conservative and not collect that pointer. If you store the pointer in an integral and cast it occasionally back to the pointer's type, the results are undefined because the garbage collector might have collected the memory associated with that surreptitious pointer.

## 7.3  Enumerated Values

Types that can take only a few discrete values turn out to be very useful—so useful, in fact, that Java ended up adding enumerated types to the core language after heroically trying for years to emulate them with an idiom [8]. Good enumerated types are not easy to define, either—enum has a fair share of oddities in C++ and (particularly) C. D tried to leverage the advantage of hindsight in defining a simple and useful enum facility.

Let's start at the beginning. The simplest use of enum is just "Let me enumerate some symbolic values," without associating them with a new type:

enum

```
mega = 1024 * 1024,
pi = 3.14,
euler = 2.72,
greet = "Hello";
```

Type deduction works for `enum` as it does for `auto`, so in the example above `pi` and `euler` have type `double` and `greet` has type `string`. If you want to define one or more enums of a specific type, specify one right after the enum keyword:

```
enum float verySmall = 0.0001, veryBig = 10000;
enum dstring wideMsg = "Wide load";
```

Enumerated values are constant; using them is essentially equivalent to using the literals they stand for. In particular, the supported operations are the same—for example, you cannot take the address of `pi` much as you cannot take the address of `3.14`:

```
auto x = pi;            // Fine, x has type double
auto y = pi * euler;    // Fine, y has type double
euler = 2.73;           // Error!
                        //    Cannot modify enum value!
void f(ref double x) {
    ...
}
fun(pi);                // Error!
                        //    Cannot take the address of 3.14!
```

As shown above, the type of an enum value is not limited to `int` but also encompasses `double` and `string`. Exactly what types can be used with enum? The answer is simple: any primitive and `struct` type may be used with enum. There are only two requirements for an enum value initializer:

- The initializer must be computable during compilation.
- The type of the initializer must allow copying, that is, not `@disable this(this)` (§ 7.1.3.4 on page 245).

The first requirement ensures the enum value does not depend on any runtime parameter. The second requirement makes sure that you can actually create copies of the value; a copy will be created whenever you use the enum.

You may not define an enumerated value of `class` type because `class` objects must always be created with `new` (aside from the uninteresting `null` value), and `new` is not computable during compilation. It wouldn't be a surprise if that restriction were lifted or relaxed in the future.

Let's create and use an enum of `struct` type:

```
struct Color {
   ubyte r, g, b;
}

enum
   red = Color(255, 0, 0),
   green = Color(0, 255, 0),
   blue = Color(0, 0, 255);
```

Whenever you use, for example, green, the code will behave as if you pasted
Color(0, 255, 0) instead of the symbolic name.

### 7.3.1  Enumerated Types

You can give a collection of enumerated values a named type:

```
enum OddWord { acini, alembicated, prolegomena, aprosexia }
```

Once you ascribe a name to a collection of enums, they may not be of different types;
all must share the same type because users may subsequently define and use values of
that type. For example:

```
OddWord w;
assert(w == OddWord.acini);     // Default initializer is
                                //    the first value in the set: acini
w = OddWord.aprosexia;          // Always use type name to qualify the
                                //    value name
                                //    (it's not what you might think btw)
int x = w;                      // OddWord is convertible to int
                                //    but not vice versa
assert(x == 3);                 // Values are numbered 0, 1, 2, ...
```

The type of a named enum is automatically deduced as int. Assigning a different type
is done like this:

```
enum OddWord : byte { acini, alembicated, prolegomena, aprosexia }
```

With the new definition (byte is called the *base type* of OddWord), the enum symbols
still have the same values, just a different storage. You may make the type double or
real as well, and the values ascribed to the symbols are still 0, 1, and so on. But if you
make the base type of OddWord a non-numeric type such as string, you must specify
initializers for all values because the compiler does not have a natural succession to
follow.

Returning to numeric enums, if you assign a specific value to any value, that resets the internal step counter used by the compiler to assign values to symbols. For example:

```
enum E { a, b = 2, c, d = -1, e, f }
assert(E.c == 3);
assert(E.e == 0);
```

There is no conflict if two enum symbols end up having the same value (as is the case with E.a and E.e). You may actually create equal values without even meaning to, because of floating-point types' unwavering desire to surprise the unwary:

```
enum F : float { a = 1E30, b, c, d }
assert(F.a == F.d);              // Passes
```

The problem illustrated above is that the largest int that can be precisely represented by a float is 16_777_216, and going beyond that will have increasingly large ranges of integers represented by the same float number.

### 7.3.2   enum Properties

Each enumerated type E defines three properties: E.init is equal to the first value that E defines, E.min is the smallest value defined by E, and E.max is the largest value defined by E. The last two values are defined only if E has as base type a type that allows comparison with < during compilation.

You are free to define your own min, max, and init values inside an enum, but that is unrecommended: generic code often counts on such values having specific semantics.

One commonly asked question is: Would it be possible to get to the name of an enumerated value? It is indeed possible and actually easy, but the mechanism used is not built in but instead relies on compile-time reflection. The way compile-time reflection works is to expose, for some enumerated type Enum, a compile-time constant __traits(allMembers, Enum) that contains all members of Enum as a tuple of strings. Since strings can be manipulated at compile time as well as runtime, this approach gives considerable flexibility. For example, at the expense of anticipating just a bit, let's write a function toString that returns the string corresponding to an enumerated value. The function is parameterized on the type of the enum.

```
string toString(E)(E value) if (is(E == enum)) {
   foreach (s; __traits(allMembers, E)) {
      if (value == mixin("E." ~ s)) return s;
   }
   return null;
}

enum OddWord { acini, alembicated, prolegomena, aprosexia }
```

```
void main() {
    auto w = OddWord.alembicated;
    assert(toString(w) == "alembicated");
}
```

The not-yet-introduced element above is `mixin("E." ~ s)`, which is a *mixin expression*. A mixin expression takes a string known during compilation and simply evaluates it as an ordinary expression within the current context. In our case, we build such an expression from the name of the enum `E`, the member selector `.`, and the name of the enum value iterated by `s`. In our case, `s` will successively take the values `"acini"`, `"alembicated"`, ..., `"aprosexia"`. The constructed string will therefore be `"E.acini"` and so on, evaluated by `mixin` to the actual values corresponding to those symbols. As soon as the passed-in `value` is equal to one of those values, the function returns. Upon passing an illegal `value`, `toString` may throw; to simplify matters we chose to just return the `null` string.

The function `toString` featured above is already implemented by the standard library module `std.conv`, which deals with general conversion matters. The name is a bit different—you'd have to write `to!string(w)` instead of `toString(w)`, which is a sign of flexibility (you may also call `to!dstring(w)` or `to!byte(w)`, etc.). The same module defines the reciprocal function that converts a string to an enum; for example, `to!OddWord("acini")` returns `OddWord.acini`.

### 7.4  alias

We've met `size_t`—the type of an unsigned integral large enough to hold the size of any object—on a few occasions already. The type `size_t` is not defined by the language; it simply morphs into one of `uint` or `ulong`, depending on the host machine's address space (32 versus 64 bits, respectively).

If you opened the installation-provided file `object.d` (or `object.di`) that is included with your D installation, you'd find a declaration that may look like this:

```
alias typeof(int.sizeof) size_t;
```

The `.sizeof` property gauges the size in bytes of a type, in this case `int`. Any other type could replace `int` above; it's not that type that matters, but instead the type of its size, fetched with `typeof`. The compiler measures object sizes using `uint` on 32-bit architectures, and `ulong` on 64-bit architectures. Consequently, the `alias` statement introduces `size_t` as a synonym for either `uint` or `ulong`.

The general syntax of the `alias` declaration is not any more complex than is shown above:

```
alias ‹existingSymbol› ‹newSymbol›;
```

‹*existingSymbol*› may be anything that has a *name*. It could be a type, a variable, a module—if something has a symbolic name, it can be aliased. For example:

```d
import std.stdio;

void fun(int) {}
void fun(string) {}
int var;
enum E { e }
struct S { int x; }
S s;

unittest {
    alias object.Object Root;         // Root of all classes
    alias std            phobos;      // Package name
    alias std.stdio      io;          // Module name
    alias var            sameAsVar;   // Variable
    alias E              MyEnum;      // Enumerated type
    alias E.e            myEnumValue; // Value of that type
    alias fun            gun;         // Overloaded function
    alias S.x            field;       // Field of a struct
    alias s.x            sfield;      // Field of an object
}
```

The rules for using an alias are simple: use the alias wherever the aliased symbol would make sense. That's what the compiler does—it conceptually rewrites the name of the alias into the aliased symbol. Even the error messages or the debugged program may "see through" aliases and show the original symbols, which may seem surprising. An example is that you may see immutable(char)[] instead of string in some error messages or debug symbols, but showing one or the other is up to the implementation.

An alias may "double-alias" something that was aliased before, for example:

```d
alias int Int;
alias Int MyInt;
```

Nothing special there, just the usual rules: at the point of MyInt's definition, Int is replaced with the symbol it aliases, which is int.

alias is frequently used to give shorter names to complex symbol chains, or in conjunction with overloaded functions from different modules (§ 5.5.2 on page 146).

Another frequent use of alias is with parameterized structs and classes. For example:

```d
// Define a container class
class Container(T) {
```

```
    alias T ElementType;
    ...
}

unittest {
    Container!int container;
    Container!int.ElementType element;
    ...
}
```

Here, if `Container` hadn't exposed the `alias ElementType`, there would have been no reasonable way for the outside world to access the argument bound to `Container`'s `T` parameter. `T` is visible only inside `Container`, but not from the outside—`Container!int.T` does not compile.

Finally, `alias` is very helpful in conjunction with `static if`. For example:

```
// This is object.di
// Define the type of the difference between two pointers
static if (size_t.sizeof == 4) {
    alias int ptrdiff_t;
} else {
    alias long ptrdiff_t;
}
// Use ptrdiff_t ...
```

The `alias` declaration of `ptrdiff_t` binds it to different types depending on which branch of the `static if` was taken. Had there been no possibility of doing the binding, code that needed such a type would have had to stay inside the two branches of the `static if`.

## 7.5  Parameterized Scopes with `template`

The entities introduced so far that facilitate compile-time parameterization (akin to C++ templates or Java and C# generics) are functions (§ 5.3 on page 138), parameterized `class`es (§ 6.14 on page 233), and parameterized `struct`s, which follow the same rules as parameterized classes. Sometimes, however, you want to do some compile-time type manipulation that does not result in defining a function, `struct`, or `class`. One such entity (widely used in C++) selects one type or another depending on a statically known Boolean condition. There is no new type being defined and no function being called, only an `alias` for one of two existing types.

For situations in which compile-time parameterization is needed without defining a new type or function, D defines parameterized scopes. Such a parameterized scope is introduced like this:

```
template Select(bool cond, T1, T2) {
    ...
}
```

The above is actually the skeleton for the compile-time selection mechanism just discussed. We'll get to the implementation shortly, but before that let's focus on the declaration proper. A `template` declaration introduces a scope with a name (`Select` in this case) and compile-time parameters (in this case, a Boolean and two types). A `template` declaration may occur at module level, inside a `class` definition, inside a `struct` definition, and inside another `template` declaration, but not inside a function definition.

Inside the body of the parameterized scope, any normally accepted declaration is allowed, and parameter names may be used. From the outside, whatever declarations are inside the scope may be accessed by prefixing them with the name of the scope and a `.`, for example, `Select!(true, int, double).foo`. In fact, let's complete the definition of `Select` right away so we can play with it:

```
template Select(bool cond, T1, T2) {
    static if (cond) {
        alias T1 Type;
    } else {
        alias T2 Type;
    }
}

unittest {
    alias Select!(false, int, string).Type MyType;
    static assert(is(MyType == string));
}
```

Note that we might have used a `struct` or a `class` to achieve the same effect. After all, such types may define an `alias` inside, which is accessible with the usual dot syntax:

```
struct /* or class */ Select2(bool cond, T1, T2) { // Or class
    static if (cond) {
        alias T1 Type;
    } else {
        alias T2 Type;
    }
}

unittest {
    alias Select2!(false, int, string).Type MyType;
    static assert(is(MyType == string));
```

```
}
```

Arguably that would be an unsavory solution. For example, imagine the documentation of Select2: "Do not create objects of type Select2! It is defined only for the sake of the alias inside of it!" Having a specialized mechanism for defining parameterized scopes clarifies intent and does not leave any room for confusion and misuse.

A template scope may introduce not only an alias, but really any declaration whatsoever. Let's define another useful template, this time one that yields a Boolean telling whether a given type is a string of any width or not.

```
template isSomeString(T) {
    enum bool value = is(T : const(char[]))
        || is(T : const(wchar[])) || is(T : const(dchar[]));
}

unittest {
    // Non-strings
    static assert(!isSomeString!(int).value);
    static assert(!isSomeString!(byte[]).value);
    // Strings
    static assert(isSomeString!(char[]).value);
    static assert(isSomeString!(dchar[]).value);
    static assert(isSomeString!(string).value);
    static assert(isSomeString!(wstring).value);
    static assert(isSomeString!(dstring).value);
    static assert(isSomeString!(char[4]).value);
}
```

Parameterized scopes may be recursive; for example, here's one possible implementation of the factorial exercise:

```
template factorial(uint n) {
    static if (n <= 1)
        enum ulong value = 1;
    else
        enum ulong value = factorial!(n - 1).value * n;
}
```

Although perfectly functional, factorial above is not the best approach in this case. When computing values during compilation, you may want to consider compile-time evaluation, described in § 5.12. Unlike the factorial template above, a factorial function is more flexible because it can be evaluated during compilation as well as run-time. The template facility is best used only for manipulating types the way Select and isSomeString do.

### 7.5.1 Eponymous templates

A template may define any number of symbols, but as the examples shown above suggest, most of the time it defines exactly one. A template is usually defined to do one thing exactly, and to expose the result of its labor as a sole symbol, such as Type in the case of Select or value in the case of isSomeString.

The need to remember and always mention that symbol at the end of instantiation can become jarring. Commonly people would simply forget to append .Type and would wonder why Select!(cond, A, B) yields a mysterious error message.

D helps here with a simple rule that has come to be known as "the eponymous template trick": if a template defines a symbol of the same name as the template itself, any subsequent use of the template name will automatically append that symbol to any use of the template. For example:

```
template isNumeric(T) {
    enum bool isNumeric = is(T : long) || is(T : real);
}

unittest {
  static assert(isNumeric!(int));
  static assert(!isNumeric!(char[]));
}
```

Now whenever some code uses isNumeric!(T), the compiler automatically rewrites that as isNumeric!(T).isNumeric and saves the user the tedium of appending some redundant symbol to the name of the template.

A template using the eponymous trick may define other names inside, but those are simply inaccessible from the outside. This is because the compiler does the rewrite very early in the name lookup process. The only way to access such symbols is from within the template itself. For example:

```
template isNumeric(T) {
    enum bool test1 = is(T : long);
    enum bool test2 = is(T : real);
    enum bool isNumeric = test1 || test2;
}

unittest {
  static assert(isNumeric!(int).test1); // Error!
    // Type bool does not define a property called test1!
}
```

The error message is caused by the eponymous rule: the compiler expands isNumeric!(int) into isNumeric!(int).isNumeric before doing anything else. Then the user code tries to fetch `isNumeric!(int).isNumeric.test1`, which is tantamount to fetching member `test1` off a `bool` value, hence the error message. Long story short, use eponymous templates if and only if you want the `template` to expose exactly one symbol. That is the case more often than not, which makes eponymous `templates` very popular and convenient.

## 7.6 Injecting Code with `mixin templates`

Certain designs require adding boilerplate code (such as data definitions and method definitions) to one or more `class` implementations. Typical examples include support for serialization, the Observer design pattern [27], and event passing in windowing systems.

Inheritance could be used for such endeavors, but the single inheritance of implementation model makes it impossible for a given `class` to save on more than one source of boilerplate. Sometimes it is best to have a mechanism that simply dumps some predefined code into a class, pretty much as if it were written by hand.

Here's where `mixin templates` come to the rescue. It is worth noting that as of today, this feature is mainly experimental. It is possible that a more general AST macro facility will replace `mixin templates` in a future revision of the language.

A `mixin template` is defined much like the parameterized scope (`template`) just discussed. For example, a `mixin template` that introduces a variable, a getter, and a setter may look like this:

```
mixin template InjectX() {
   private int x;
   int getX() { return x; }
   void setX(int y) {
      ... // Checks
      x = y;
   }
}
```

Once defined, the `mixin template` can be inserted in several places:

```
// Inject at module scope
mixin InjectX;

class A {
   // Inject into a class
   mixin InjectX;
   ...
}
```

```d
void fun() {
    // Inject into a function
    mixin InjectX;
    setX(10);
    assert(getX() == 10);
}
```

The code above now defines the variable and the two associated functions at module level, inside `class A`, and inside `fun`, pretty much as if the body of `InjectX` were pasted by hand. In particular, descendants of A can `override getX` and `setX` as if A itself defined them. Copy and paste without the unpleasant duplication.

Of course, the next logical step is to reckon that `InjectX` takes no compile-time parameters but has the air of someone who could—and indeed it does:

```d
mixin template InjectX(T) {
    private T x;
    T getX() { return x; }
    void setX(T y) {
        ... // Checks
        x = y;
    }
}
```

Now usage of `InjectX` passes the argument like this:

```d
mixin InjectX!int;
mixin InjectX!double;
```

which actually brings us to the ambiguity—what if you have the two instantiations above, and then you want to use `getX`? There are two functions with that name, so clearly there is an ambiguity problem. To solve that, D allows you to introduce *scope names* with `mixin` instantiation:

```d
mixin InjectX!int MyInt;
mixin InjectX!double MyDouble;
```

With these definitions in hand, you get to unambiguously access members introduced by the two `mixins` by using regular scope resolution:

```d
MyInt.setX(5);
assert(MyInt.getX() == 5);
MyDouble.setX(5.5);
assert(MyDouble.getX() == 5.5);
```

So `mixin templates` are only *almost* like copy and paste; you get to copy and paste multiple times and specify which instance you are referring to.

### 7.6.1   Symbol Lookup inside a `mixin`

The biggest difference between a `mixin` `template` and a regular `template` (as defined in § 7.5 on page 278), and potentially the most prone to confusion, is lookup.

Templates are entirely modular: code inside a `template` looks up symbols at the `template`'s *definition* site. This is a desirable property because it means you can absorb and understand a `template` by just analyzing its definition.

In contrast, a `mixin` `template` looks up symbols at the *instantiation* site, which means that you need an understanding of the context in which you use the `mixin` `template` to figure out what its behavior will be.

To illustrate the difference, consider the example below, which offers symbols with the same name at both the definition site and the instantiation site:

```d
import std.stdio;

string lookMeUp = "Found at module level";

template TestT() {
    string get() { return lookMeUp; }
}

mixin template TestM() {
    string get() { return lookMeUp; }
}

void main() {
    string lookMeUp = "Found at function level";
    alias TestT!() asTemplate;
    mixin TestM!() asMixin;
    writeln(asTemplate.get());
    writeln(asMixin.get());
}
```

The output is

```
Found at module level
Found at function level
```

The propensity of `mixin` `templates` to pick up local symbols confers on them some expressiveness but also makes them difficult to follow.  Such behavior makes `mixin` `templates` of limited applicability; you may want to think twice before reaching for this particular tool in your toolbox.

## 7.7  Summary and Reference

Not all abstraction needs can be satisfactorily covered by `classes`, in particular fine-grained objects, scoped resources, and value types. `structs` fill that void. In particular, constructors and destructors allow easy definition of scoped resource types.

`unions` are a low-level feature that allows you to keep the compiler in known overlapped storage for various types.

Enumerations are simple user-defined discrete values. An `enum` may be assigned a new type, which strengthens the typechecking for the values defined within that type.

`alias` is a very useful means to associate one symbol with another. Oftentimes the `aliased` symbol is long and complicated or is computed within a nested entity and must be exposed as a simple name.

Parameterized scopes using `template` are very useful for defining compile-time computations such as type introspection and type traits. Eponymous `templates` allow you to offer abstractions in a highly convenient, encapsulated form.

Parameterized scopes are also offered in the form of experimental `mixin templates`, which behave much like simple macros. A full AST macro feature might replace `mixin templates`.

# 8

# Type Qualifiers

Type qualifiers capture important assertions about types in a language. Such assertions are highly useful to programmers and compilers alike but are difficult to capture by using conventions, regular subtyping (§ 6.4.2 on page 192), or type parameterization (§ 6.14 on page 233).

The canonical example of a type qualifier is const (introduced by C and refined by C++), which, when attached to a type T, expresses the assertion that T values can be initialized and read but never written to. The compiler ensures that the assertion is observed. The const qualifier is quite useful at module boundaries because it gives callers guarantees about functions. For example, the signature

```
// C standard function
int printf(const char * format, ...);
```

makes a promise to printf's clients that printf will not try to alter the characters in the format parameter. In turn, such a guarantee is useful for large-scale development because it reduces the dependencies created by non-modular mutation. Such guarantees could be defined and maintained by means of convention, but such conventions are clumsy and difficult to keep up.

D defines three type qualifiers:

- const expresses contextual immutability. A value of a const-qualified type cannot be changed directly. However, other entities in the program may have write access to that data, just as a caller of printf may have write access to format although printf itself doesn't.

- `immutable` expresses absolute, context-dependent immutability. A value of an `immutable`-qualified type cannot under any circumstances change after initialization by any code in the program. This is a much stronger guarantee than `const`.
- `shared` expresses value sharing across threads.

These qualifiers complement one another. `const` and `immutable` are important for large-scale development. `immutable` also enables functional-style programming, and `const` facilitates interfacing functional-style with object-oriented and procedural code. `immutable` and `shared` are instrumental in concurrency. We leave it to Chapter 13 to discuss concurrency and explain `shared` in depth. Here, we focus on `const` and `immutable`.

## 8.1   The `immutable` Qualifier

An `immutable` value is cast in stone: as soon as it's been initialized, you may as well consider it has been burned forever into the memory storing it. It will never change throughout the execution of the program.

A qualified type is spelled ‹*qualifier*›(T), where ‹*qualifier*› is one of `immutable`, `const`, and `shared`. For example, let's define an `immutable` integer:

```
immutable(int) forever = 42;
```

Attempting to change `forever` in any way will result in a compile-time error. Moreover, `immutable(int)` is a type like any other (it is distinct from `int`). You may, for example, `alias` it to a symbol:

```
alias immutable(int) StableInt;
StableInt forever = 42;
```

Defining a copy of `forever` with `auto` will propagate the type `immutable(int)` to the copy, so the copy itself will be `immutable(int)`. That's nothing special, but it does mark a difference between type qualifiers and simple storage classes such as `static` (§ 5.2.4 on page 137) or `ref` (§ 5.2.1 on page 135).

```
unittest {
    immutable(int) forever = 42;
    auto andEver = forever;
    ++andEver; // Error! Cannot change an immutable value!
}
```

An `immutable` value doesn't need to be initialized with a compile-time constant:

```
void fun(int x) {
    immutable(int) xEntry = x;
    ...
```

```
}
```

Using `immutable` as above is very useful to `fun`'s readers. They will know at a glance that `xEntry` is the entry value of `x` throughout `fun`'s body.

In declarations, you don't need to specify a type with `immutable`—it deduces its type the same way `auto` does:

```
immutable pi = 3.14, val = 42;
```

The compiler deduces `pi`'s type as `immutable(double)` and `val`'s type as `immutable(int)`.

### 8.1.1 Transitivity

You may qualify any type with `immutable`. For example:

```
struct Point { int x, y; }
auto origin = immutable(Point)(0, 0);
```

Since `immutable(T)` is a type like any other for all types `T`, it follows that `immutable(Point)(0, 0)` is a `struct` literal the same way `Point(0, 0)` is.

Immutability transfers naturally to the members of an object. After all, we'd expect that assigning to `origin.x` or `origin.y` is disallowed as well as assigning to `origin` as a whole. Otherwise, the entire `immutable` promise would be quite easy to break.

```
unittest {
    auto anotherOrigin = immutable(Point)(1, 1);
    origin = anotherOrigin; // Error!
    origin.x = 1;           // Error!
    origin.y = 1;           // Error!
}
```

In fact, `immutable` *propagates* to each and every field of `Point`, qualifying the field's type with `immutable` as well. For example, the `assertion` below passes:

```
static assert(is(typeof(origin.x) == immutable(int))); // Pass
```

Things are bound to get much more interesting. Let's now consider a `struct` that contains some indirection, such as an array field:

```
struct DataSample {
    int id;
    double[] payload;
}
```

Clearly, the fields of an `immutable(DataSample)` cannot be modified. How about changing an element of `payload`, however?

```
unittest {
    auto ds = immutable(DataSample)(5, [ 1.0, 2.0 ]);
    ds[1] = 4.5; // ?
}
```

One of two decisions could be made here, leading to different trade-offs. One is to make the qualifier *shallow*, that is, posit that making `DataSample` `immutable` does make its *direct* fields also `immutable` but has no effect on data that is indirectly accessed through those fields.[1] The other choice would be to make immutability *transitive*, which means that making an object `immutable` makes any data reachable from it `immutable` as well. D chose this second option.

Transitive immutability is much more restrictive than its non-transitive version. If you define an `immutable` value, the entire web of data connected to that value (via references, arrays, and pointers) must also be `immutable`. As such, it is more difficult to define transitively immutable values than shallow immutable ones. But the reward is commensurate with the investment. D chose transitive immutability for two fundamental reasons:

- *Functional programming:* Functional style means many things to many people, but most would admit that the absence of side effects is an important tenet. Keeping such a promise by convention does not scale. Transitive immutability gives the coder the opportunity to use a functional style for a well-defined fragment of a program, and the compiler the ability to verify that functional code does not inadvertently modify data.
- *Concurrent programming:* Concurrency is a huge and hugely complex topic that has precious few strong guarantees and unamended truths. Immutable sharing is such a beam of certainty: sharing immutable data across threads is correct, safe, and efficient. To allow the compiler to verify that shared data is indeed immutable, immutabilty must be transitive; otherwise, a thread having access to an immutable piece of data can easily transgress into mutable sharing simply by following indirect fields of that data.

Truly and thoroughly, as soon as you are in possession of a value of type `immutable(T)`, you know that anything you could ever reach from that value is also `immutable`. Moreover, *nobody* can ever mutate that data—`immutable` data is as good as data hardwired with a soldering iron. This is a very solid guarantee that allows you, for example, to share `immutable` data across threads without so much as thinking about it.

---

1. This is the approach taken by C++'s `const`.

## 8.2 Composing with `immutable`

Given that qualifiers use parentheses to precisely select what type they qualify, and that a qualified type is a type like any other, it follows that quite complex data structures can be created by combining `immutable` with other type constructors. For example, let's compare these two types:

```
alias immutable(int[]) T1;
alias immutable(int)[] T2;
```

In the first definition, the parentheses engulf the entire array type; in the second, only `int` is affected but not the array. If no parentheses occur with the use of `immutable`, it applies to the entire type, so an equivalent definition for T1 is spelled like this:

```
alias immutable int[] T1;
```

T1 is quite simple-minded—an immutable array of `int`. The spelling of the type says as much. By virtue of transitivity, it follows that you can't modify the array as a whole (e.g., by assigning to it) and you also can't modify any element of the array in particular:

```
T1 a = [ 1, 3, 5 ];
T1 b = [ 2, 4 ];
a = b;         // Error!
a[0] = b[1];   // Error!
```

The second definition seems more subtle, but it's really simple if we mentally consider `immutable(int)` a type of its own. Then, `immutable(int)[]` is simply an array of that type and that's all there is to it. The properties of that array are then easy to infer. You can assign the array as a whole, but you can't assign or otherwise modify individual elements of the array:

```
T2 a = [ 1, 3, 5 ];
T2 b = [ 2, 4 ];
a = b;          // Fine
a[0] = b[1];    // Error!
a ~= b;         // Fine (and subtly so)
```

It may appear odd at first, but appending to an array of `immutable` elements is legit. Why? Simply because appending to an array does not involve changing what's already in it. (It might entail copying data if the array is reallocated, which is fine.)

As already mentioned (§ 4.5 on page 118), `string` is really an `alias` for `immutable(char)[]`. The `immutable` qualifier is really to be credited for the many useful properties of `string` that previous chapters have relied upon.

The composition works the same way when you use `immutable` with parameterized types. For example, consider that you have a `Container!T` generic type.  Then `immutable(Container!T)` would qualify the entire container, whereas `Container!(immutable(T))` would qualify only individual elements in the container.

## 8.3   `immutable` Parameters and Methods

In a function signature, `immutable` is very informative. Consider a most trivial function:

```
string process(string input);
```

That really is just a concise notation for

```
immutable(char)[] process(immutable(char)[] input);
```

`process` guarantees it won't change individual characters in `input`, so the caller of `process` knows for sure that the string is the same before and after the call:

```
string s1 = "blah";
string s2 = process(s1);
assert(s1 == "blah");        // Never fails
```

Furthermore, the caller may count on a never-changing result coming out of `process`: there is no hidden aliasing, no chance that some function later on can ever change `s2`. Again: `immutable` means immutable.

A `struct` or `class` may define `immutable` methods. In that case, the qualifier applies to `this` and is spelled as follows:

```
class A {
    int[] fun();            // Regular method
    int[] gun() immutable;  // Callable only for immutable objects
    immutable int[] hun();  // Same as above
}
```

The third syntax may look confusing because it may appear that `immutable` applies to `int[]` when in fact it applies to `this`. If you want to define an `immutable` method returning an `immutable int[]`, you need to stutter a little:

```
immutable immutable(int[]) iun();
```

which is better spelled with the `immutable` at the end:

```
immutable(int[]) iun() immutable;
```

The reason for allowing the confusing `immutable` in the leading position is consistency with other method properties such as `final` or `static`. In particular, you can write

```
class A {
   immutable {
      int foo();
      int[] bar();
      void baz();
   }
}
```

to define several immutable methods in one shot. You may also use immutable as a label:

```
class A {
immutable:
   int foo();
   int[] bar();
   void baz();
}
```

Naturally, immutable methods can be called only against immutable objects:

```
class C {
   void fun() {}
   void gun() immutable {}
}

unittest {
   auto c1 = new C;
   auto c2 = new immutable(C);
   c1.fun(); // Fine
   c2.gun(); // Fine
            // No other calls would work
}
```

## 8.4  immutable Constructors

Dealing with an immutable object is not too difficult, but constructing one is a rather delicate process. This is because during construction there are two conflicting needs to satisfy: one is the need to assign fields, and the other is the need to establish their immutability. For that reason, D handles immutable constructors with extra care.

The way an immutable constructor is typechecked is simple and conservative. The compiler allows field assignment only inside the constructor, and reading fields (including passing this to a method call) is prohibited. As soon as the immutable constructor terminates, the object is "frozen"—no more changes to the fields can ever be exacted. Calling a non-static method counts as a read because the method has access to this and may potentially read any field. (The compiler does not check whether the method actually reads fields—it conservatively assumes the method does read some field.)

This rule is more restrictive than necessary; the only need is to not assign to a field after that particular field has been read. But the more restrictive rule does not impair expressiveness significantly and is simple and easy to understand. For example:

```
class A {
    int a;
    int[] b;
    this() immutable {
        a = 5;
        b = [ 1, 2, 3 ];
        // Calling fun() wouldn't be allowed
    }
    void fun() immutable {
        ...
    }
}
```

Inside an immutable constructor it is OK to call the super constructor as long as the call goes to another immutable constructor. It is also legal to forward the call to another immutable constructor. Such calls do not put the integrity of immutable in jeopardy.

You will often find that using recursion is very helpful in initializing elaborate immutable objects. For example, consider a singly linked list class that is initialized from an array:

```
class List {
    private int payload;
    private List next;
    this(int[] data) immutable {
        enforce(data.length);
        payload = data[0];
        if (data.length == 1) return;
        next = new immutable(List)(data[1 .. $]);
    }
}
```

To properly initialize the tail of the list, the constructor recurses to itself with a shorter array. Attempting to initialize the list in a loop would not compile because walking the list being created involves reading its fields, which is verboten. Recursion elegantly solves this problem.[2]

## 8.5 Conversions involving `immutable`

Consider this code:

```
unittest {
    int a = 42;
    immutable(int) b = a;
    int c = b;
}
```

If the type system were to be a stickler, it would not accept that code. It involves two conversions—first from `int` to `immutable(int)` and then back from `immutable(int)` to `int`. After all, in general such conversions are not legal. For example, if we replace `int` with `int[]` in the code above, neither conversion would be correct:

```
int[] a = [ 42 ];
immutable(int[]) b = a;  // No!
int[] c = b;             // No!
```

If such conversions were allowed, `immutable` would not be respected because then `immutable` arrays would share their content with mutable ones.

The compiler, however, does detect and allow certain automatic conversions between `immutable` and mutable data. Specifically, it allows bidirectional conversion between `T` and `immutable(T)` if `T` has "no mutable indirection." No mutable indirection intuitively means that indirectly accessed data is not writable and is defined recursively as follows:

- Built-in value types such as `int` have no mutable indirection.
- Fixed-size arrays of types with no mutable indirection have, in turn, no mutable indirection.
- Arrays and pointers that refer to types that have no mutable indirection have no mutable indirection.
- `struct` types with all fields having no mutable indirection have no mutable indirection.

For example, `S1` below has no mutable indirection, but `S2` does:

---

2. Solution suggested by Simon Peyton-Jones.

```
struct S1 {
   int a;
   double[3] b;
   string c;
}

struct S2 {
   int x;
   float[] y;
}
```

The field `S2.y` makes `S2` have mutable indirections, so conversions `immutable(S2)` ↔ `S2` are not allowed. If they were, data stored in y would become unduly shared across mutable and `immutable` objects, which would break `immutable`'s guarantee.

Getting back to the first example of this section, `int` has no mutable indirection so the compiler takes the liberty of allowing conversions from `int` to `immutable(int)` and back.

If you want to define such conversions for a `struct`, you need to do a little manual work to guide the process. You provide the appropriate constructors and the compiler makes sure your code is correct. The easiest way to do the conversion heavy lifting is to enlist the help of the universal conversion routine `std.conv.to`, which understands all the vagaries of qualifier conversions and always takes the appropriate action.

```
import std.conv;

struct S {
   private int[] a;
   // Conversion from immutable to mutable
   this(immutable(S) source) {
      // Duplicate the array into a non-immutable array
      a = to!(int[])(source.a);
   }
   // Conversion from mutable to immutable
   this(S source) immutable {
      // Duplicate the array into an immutable array
      a = to!(immutable(int[]))(source.a);
   }
   ...
}

unittest {
   S a;
```

```
    auto b = immutable(S)(a);
    auto c = S(b);
}
```

The conversion is not implicit but is possible and safe.

## 8.6 The `const` Qualifier

It doesn't take much experimentation with `immutable` to notice that it's too harsh to be widely useful. Yes, as long as you're committed to not change certain data throughout an entire program, `immutable` works great. But often immutability is a modular property: you want to reserve the right to mutate certain data, while at the same time preventing others from doing so. That data is not `immutable` because `immutable` means "See this carved stone? That's your data." You need a means to express the restriction "You can't mutate this data, but someone else could." Or, put the Alan Perlis way: "One man's constant is another man's variable." Let's see how a type system can observe Perlis' adage without falling for the irony.

A simple use case is a function such as `print` that prints some data. The `print` function does not change the data passed in, so it should work with `immutable`:

```
void print(immutable(int[]) data) { ... }
unittest {
    immutable(int[]) myData = [ 10, 20 ];
    print(myData); // Fine
}
```

Perfect. Now say we have an `int[]` that we just computed and we want to print it. That won't work because `int[]` is not convertible to `immutable(int)[]`—if it were, there would be undue sharing between mutable and ostensibly immutable data. So `print` is unable to print `int[]` data. That's quite a gratuitous limitation because `print` doesn't touch its input anyway, so it should work with `immutable` and mutable data alike.

What's needed is a sort of common type "may or may not be mutable," in which case `print` could declare

```
void print(mayormaynotbemutable(int[]) data) { ... }
```

Well, just because `mayormaynotbemutable` was a bit too long, the term `const` was introduced to denote it. The meaning is exactly the same: a `const(T)` value cannot be modified by the current code but there is the possibility that some other code may. This ambiguity reflects the fact that `const(T)` may originate in a `T` or an `immutable(T)`. This ability of `const` makes it the perfect qualifier for interfacing functional code with regular, procedural code. Continuing the example above:

```
void print(const(int[]) data) { ... }
unittest {
    immutable(int[]) myData = [ 10, 20 ];
    print(myData); // Fine
    int[] myMutableData = [ 32, 42 ];
    print(myMutableData); // Fine
}
```

The example suggests that mutable and immutable data both convert implicitly to const, which suggests some sort of subtyping relationship. Indeed, that is exactly the case: const(T) is a supertype of both T and immutable(T), as shown in Figure 8.1.

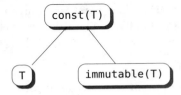

**Figure 8.1:** For all types T, const(T) is a supertype of both T and immutable(T). This implies that code manipulating const(T) values accepts both mutable and immutable Ts.

The const qualifier obeys the same transitivity and conversion rules as the immutable qualifier. Constructors of const objects, unlike immutable constructors, are unrestricted: inside a const constructor, the object is considered mutable.

## 8.7   Interaction between const and immutable

Often it happens that one qualifier attempts to affect a type that is already under the influence of another qualifier. For example:

```
struct A {
    const(int[]) c;
    immutable(int[]) i;
}

unittest {
    const(A) ca;
    immutable(A) ia;
}
```

What types do `ca.i` and `ia.c` have? If qualifiers would apply blindly, the types would come respectively as `const(immutable(int[]))` and `immutable(const(int[]))`, and clearly there's something redundant about that—not to mention the types of `ca.c` and `ia.i` that apply the same qualifier twice!

When two qualifiers are superimposed, D uses simple composition rules. If the qualifiers are identical, they are collapsed into one. Otherwise, `const(immutable(T))` and `immutable(const(T))` are both collapsed into `immutable(T)` because that is the most informative type. These rules apply to propagation inside array types; for example, the elements of an array `const(immutable(T)[])` have type `immutable(T)`, not `const(immutable(T))`. However, the type of the array itself is irreducible.

## 8.8 Propagating a Qualifier from Parameter to Result

C and C++ define a shallow `const` qualifier that has exhibited an annoying problem: functions that return a parameter must repeat their definition for `const` and non-`const` data or commit to a dangerous life. The canonical example is the C standard library function `strchr`, which C defines like this:

```
char* strchr(const char* input, int c);
```

This function is laundering types: although `input` is a `const` value that is not supposed to change naïvely, the output, which returns a pointer derived from `input`, has removed that promise. `strchr` is facilitating code that modifies immutable data without a cast in sight. C++ fixed that problem by introducing two definitions of `strchr`:

```
char* strchr(char* input, int c);
const char* strchr(const char* input, int c);
```

The functions do the same thing but can't be collapsed together because C++ has no means of saying "Please transport this qualifier, if present, from this argument to the return type."

To solve the problem, D offers a "wildcard" qualifier symbol called `inout`. With `inout`, the declaration of `strchr` would look like this:

```
inout(char)* strchr(inout(char)* input, int c);
```

(Of course, D code would prefer to use arrays instead of pointers.) The compiler understands that `inout` may be replaced with `immutable`, `const`, or nothing (the latter in case of mutable input). It typechecks the body of `strchr` to ensure it works on all of these possible inputs safely.

A qualifier may be transported from a method to its result, for example:

```
class X { ... }
```

```
class Y {
    private Y _another;
    inout(Y) another() inout {
        enforce(_another !is null);
        return _another;
    }
}
```

The method `another` works for objects with any qualifier. The method is overridable, which is remarkable because `inout` can be thought of as a generic parameter, and generic methods are ordinarily not overridable. The compiler is able to make the method overridable because it makes sure that the underlying code is the same for all qualifiers.

## 8.9  Summary

Type qualifiers express useful properties of types that are not expressible with other abstraction mechanisms. The central qualifier discussed is `immutable`, which offers a very strong guarantee—an `immutable` value can never be changed, transitively, throughout its lifetime. This is a very useful property for ensuring pure functional semantics and most important for safely sharing data across threads.

The strength of `immutable` is also its weakness—it disallows many data manipulation patterns that divide responsibility between writers and readers. The `const` qualifier addresses that issue by expressing contextual immutability—data is not modifiable by the owner of a `const` value, but other parts of the program may have write access to that data.

Finally, to avoid repetition of identical code for functions with unqualified and qualified parameters, the `inout` wildcard qualifier was introduced. `inout` can saliently stand in for `immutable`, `const`, and no qualifier at all.

# Error Handling

Error handling is a loosely formalized field of software engineering concerned with treating error situations that are possible and expected but prevent the normal functioning of a system. Exception handling is the current common approach to error handling in many of today's languages (D included) and has spawned a large lore of guidelines, techniques, and even controversy.

Exceptions are a language feature dedicated to error handling via out-of-band, dedicated control paths. A function unable to return a meaningful result to its caller may throw an exception object that encodes the cause of the error. Throwing is a "get out of jail" card that relieves the function of its normal duties. The exception skips all callers that are not prepared to handle it and lands at a *catch site* that takes contingency action. In a well-designed program, there are many fewer catch sites than throw sites, implying centralized and reusable error handling, which would be difficult with traditional techniques based on pervasive error codes.

## 9.1 throwing and catching

D uses a popular model for exceptions. A function may initiate an exception by using the throw statement (§ 3.11 on page 81), which throws a class object. To enter into possession of that object, code must use the try statement (§ 3.11 on page 81) and fetch the object in that statement's catch clause. Paraphrasing an adage, one code sample is worth 1024 words, so let's look at the following example:

```
import std.stdio;

void main() {
```

```
try {
    auto x = fun();
} catch (Exception e) {
    writeln(e);
}
}

int fun() {
    return gun() * 2;
}

int gun() {
    throw new Exception("Going straight back to main");
}
```

Function gun chooses to not return an int but instead to throw an exception, which in the case above is an object of the Exception class. The thrown object can be used to transport an arbitrary amount of information about what happened. The exceptional path relieves the initiating function and all of its callers from returning and passes control to a caller that is prepared to handle the error—the catch block.

Upon executing the throw, fun is skipped entirely because it is not prepared to handle the exception. This marks a crucial difference between old-school error handling that must propagate errors manually through all invocation levels, and the relatively newfangled exception handling that cleverly transfers control straight from the error locus (gun) to the spot qualified to handle that error (the catch in main). This approach promises simplified, centralized error handling by relieving many functions of the chore of propagating errors around; fun may stay blissfully unaware of the subband communication between gun and main.

Unfortunately, the direct transfer of control flow from the throw site to the catch site is also a weakness of exception handling: that blissful unawareness is in fact just a pipe dream. In reality, functions traversed by an exception must mind the additional hidden exit points and make sure that program invariants remain satisfied for all possible control flows. D offers solid mechanisms to ensure invariant preservation when exceptions are in effect, which we'll discuss in good order in this chapter.

## 9.2  Types

D's basic exception hierarchy (Figure 9.1 on the facing page) is simple.

A throw statement cannot throw just any value, only class objects, and more specifically objects rooted in class Throwable. In the overwhelming majority of cases, code actually throws a class rooted in the Exception subclass of Throwable. These are normal, recoverable exceptions and recognized by the language as such. Exceptions inheriting

`Throwable` but not `Exception` (such as `AssertError`, which we'll discuss in Chapter 10) are unrecoverable and should be used in normal code extremely sparingly if at all. (More detail on what the language guarantees and doesn't guarantee for unrecoverable errors is coming in § 9.4 on page 307.)

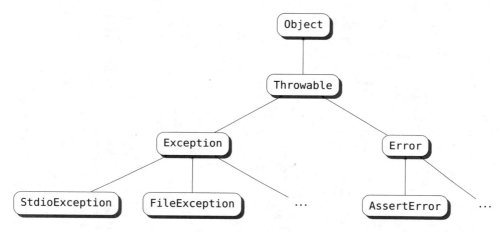

**Figure 9.1:** Regular exceptions inherit the `Exception` class and therefore can be caught with `catch (Exception)`. The `Error` class inherits class `Throwable` directly. Normal code should catch only `Exception` and its descendants—the others are meant to assure orderly shutdown when an error is found in the logic of the program.

A `try` statement may define more than one `catch` block, for example:

```
try {
    ...
} catch (SomeException e) {
    ...
} catch (SomeOtherException e) {
    ...
}
```

Exceptions propagate from the `throw` site to the most recent `catch` site following a *first match* rule: as soon as a `catch` handler is found that catches the thrown class or a base of it, that `catch` is activated and passed the thrown exception. Here is an example that throws and catches two different types of exceptions:

```
import std.stdio;

class MyException : Exception {
```

```
    this(string s) { super(s); }
}

void fun(int x) {
    if (x == 1) {
        throw new MyException("");
    } else {
        throw new StdioException("");
    }
}

void main() {
    foreach (i; 1 .. 3) {
        try {
            fun(i);
        } catch (StdioException e) {
            writeln("StdioException");
        } catch (Exception e) {
            writeln("Exception");
        }
    }
}
```

The program above prints

```
Exception
StdioException
```

The first call to fun throws a MyException object that's not matched by the first catch handler but is matched by the second because MyException inherits Exception. The exception thrown by the second throw gets matched straightaway by the first catch handler.  This first-match process can go through not one but several function layers, as shown in the following more elaborate example:

```
import std.stdio;

class MyException : Exception {
    this(string s) { super(s); }
}

void fun(int x) {
    if (x == 1) {
        throw new MyException("");
    } else if (x == 2) {
```

```
        throw new StdioException("");
    } else {
        throw new Exception("");
    }
}

void funDriver(int x) {
    try {
        fun(x);
    }
    catch (MyException e) {
        writeln("MyException");
    }
}

unittest {
    foreach (i; 1 .. 4) {
        try {
            funDriver(i);
        } catch (StdioException e) {
            writeln("StdioException");
        } catch (Exception e) {
            writeln("Just an Exception");
        }
    }
}
```

The program above prints

```
MyException
StdioException
Just an Exception
```

because the handlers are conceptually tried as the control flow bubbles up the call stack.

One obvious fallout of the first-match rule is that, if a catch for exception type E1 is followed by a catch handler for exception type E2, and E2 is a subtype of E1, then E2 is effectively unreachable. The compiler flags that situation as an error. For example:

```
import std.stdio;

void fun() {
    try {
        ...
    } catch (Exception e) {
```

```
      ...
   } catch (StdioException e) {
      ... // Error!
          // Unreachable catch handler!
   }
}
```

Although code like this is virtually always in error, dynamic masking situations across different functions may happen all the time. Some function could easily make its caller's catch handlers inoperative. Most of the time, however, that's not an error but only a normal result of call stack dynamics.

## 9.3   finally clauses

A try statement could be ended with a finally clause that basically means "Execute this code come hell or high water." Whether or not an exception was thrown, the finally clause will be executed just as the try statement concludes, be it by simply falling through, throwing, returning, breaking out of an enclosing loop—you name it. For example:

```
import std.stdio;

string fun(int x) {
   string result;
   try {
      if (x == 1) {
         throw new Exception("some exception");
      }
      result = "didn't throw";
      return result;
   } catch (Exception e) {
      if (x == 2) throw e;
      result = "thrown and caught: " ~ e.toString;
      return result;
   } finally {
      writeln("Exiting fun");
   }
}
```

Although both the normal path and the exceptional path of fun may throw or return some value, fun always prints Exiting fun to the standard output.

## 9.4  `nothrow` Functions and the Special Nature of `Throwable`

A function can be declared `nothrow`:

```
nothrow int iDontThrow(int a, int b) {
    return a / b;
}
```

§ 9.4 discussed `nothrow` functions, and now is the time to reveal a twist in the plot: `nothrow` promises that the function won't throw an `Exception`. The function is still allowed to throw the graver `Throwable` class. Essentially `Throwable` is considered unrecoverable, so the compiler is relieved of the responsibility of "thinking" of what should happen in case of an exception and consequently optimizes code under the assumption that nothing is thrown. For `nothrow` functions, the compiler simplifies entry and exit sequences to not include contingency plans in case anything gets thrown.

This clarifies and reinforces `Throwable`'s special status. The first rule of `Throwable` is you do not `catch` `Throwable`. If you do decide to `catch` it, you can't count on `struct` destructors being called and `finally` clauses being executed. That means the state of your system is undetermined and may violate any number of high-level invariants that you count on in normal operation. D does guarantee, however, that basic type safety and the integrity of its standard library are still in effect. You cannot count on the high-level integrity of your own application's state, because an arbitrary amount of code that needs to maintain said integrity has not executed. If you `catch` a `Throwable`, you may only perform a number of simple operations; most of the time, you probably want to print a message to the standard error or a log file, attempt to save whatever you can save to a separate file, stiffen that upper lip, and exit with as much dignity as possible.

## 9.5  Collateral Exceptions

There are situations in which an exception is thrown as another exception is already in flight. Consider:

```
import std.conv;

class MyException : Exception {
    this(string s) { super(s); }
}

void fun() {
    try {
        throw new Exception("thrown from fun");
    } finally {
        gun(100);
```

```
    }
}

void gun(int x) {
    try {
        throw new MyException(text("thrown from gun #", x));
    } finally {
        if (x > 1) {
            gun(x - 1);
        }
    }
}
```

What happens when fun gets called? Things are bound to go ballistic. First, fun attempts to throw, but as part of finally's aforementioned charter "come hell or high water," gun(100) gets called while an Exception is flying out of fun. In turn, gun(100) throws a MyException object carrying the string "thrown from gun #100". Let's call that second exception a *collateral exception* to distinguish it from the exception initially thrown, which we call the *primary exception*. Then gun itself uses a finally clause to spawn additional collateral exceptions—more exactly, adding to a total of 100. Machiavelli himself would be spooked by such code.

Faced with the prospect of collateral exceptions, the language may choose to

- Abort execution immediately
- Continue propagating the initial exception and ignore all others
- Have the collateral exception replace the initial exception and continue propagation
- Continue propagating the main exception and all collateral exceptions in one form or another

The last approach is the most comprehensive with regard to preserving information about what happened, but it also has the potential of being the most complicated. For example, a salvo of exceptions would be much more difficult to handle meaningfully than one.

D chose a simple and effective approach. Each Throwable object holds a reference to the next collateral Throwable object. That collateral object is accessible through the property Throwable.next. If there are no (more) collateral Throwables, Throwable.next yields null. This effectively establishes a singly linked list preserving full information about all collateral errors in the order they occurred. The list has the primary Throwable as its root. The definition of Throwable is summarized here:

```
class Throwable {
```

```
    this(string s);
    override string toString();
    @property Throwable next();
}
```

The distinction between primary and collateral exceptions makes the behavior very simple. At any `throw` point, a primary exception either is or is not in flight. If there isn't any, the exception being thrown becomes primary. Otherwise, the exception being `thrown` gets appended to the end of the singly linked list rooted in the primary exception. Continuing the example above, let's print the entire exception chain:

```
unittest {
    try {
        fun();
    } catch (Exception e) {
        writeln("Primary exception: ", typeid(e), " ", e);
        while ((e = e.next) != null) {
            writeln("Collateral exception: ", typeid(e), " ", e);
        }
    }
}
```

The code above prints

```
Primary exception: Exception thrown from fun
Collateral exception: MyException thrown from gun #100
Collateral exception: MyException thrown from gun #99
...
Collateral exception: MyException thrown from gun #1
```

The collateral exceptions come in this sequence because the append to the exceptions list is done at the `throw` point. Each `throw` fetches the primary exception (if any), registers the new exception, and initiates or continues the throwing process.

Because of collateral exceptions, D code may throw from within destructors and `scope` statements. Full information about what happened is available at the `catch` site.

## 9.6 Stack Unwinding and Exception-Safe Code

While an exception is in flight, control is transferred from the initial `throw` site all the way up to the matching `catch` handler. All of the intervening functions in the call chain are skipped. Well, almost. As part of propagating the exception, a process known as *stack unwinding* ensures orderly cleanup of functions that are being skipped. The language guarantees that the following code snippets will be executed while an exception is in flight:

- The destructors of the stack-allocated `struct` objects of all skipped functions
- The `finally` clauses of all skipped functions
- The `scope(exit)` and `scope(failure)` statements that were in effect at `throw` time

Stack unwinding is of invaluable help in ensuring program correctness in the presence of exceptions. A common liability of programs using exceptions is leaking resources. Many resources are meant to be used in acquire/release patterns, and throwing exceptions causes flows that "forget" to release resources and are difficult to detect with the naked eye. It is best to encapsulate such resources in `struct` types that release the managed resource properly in their destructor. The topic has been touched on in § 7.1.3.6 on page 252, and the standard type `File` in module `std.stdio` is an example of such encapsulation. `File` manages a system file handle and ensures that the underlying handle is properly closed when the `File` object is destroyed. The `File` object can be copied and a reference counter keeps track of all active copies; the last copy to cease existence closes the underlying file. Such idiomatic use of destructors is well known and appreciated by C++ programmers. (The idiom is known as "Resource Acquisition Is Initialization" and commonly abbreviated as RAII.) Other languages and frameworks also use manual or automated reference counting.

Resource leak is only one instance of a larger problem. Sometimes the do/undo pattern may have no palpable resource associated with it. For example, when writing an HTML file, many tags (such as `"<b>"`) must ultimately be closed with a corresponding tag (`"</b>"`). A nonlinear control flow, including throwing an exception, may cause generation of malformed HTML documents. For example:

```
void sendHTML(Connection conn) {
    conn.send("<html>");
    ... // Send the payload of the file
    conn.send("</html>");
}
```

If the code in between the two calls to `conn.send` terminates `sendHTML` early, the closing tag is not sent, resulting in an invalid stream sent down the wire. A `return` statement in the middle of `sendHTML` could cause such a problem, but at least `return` statements can be seen with the naked eye by sheer inspection of the function's body. In contrast, a `throw` may originate in any function that `sendHTML` calls (directly or indirectly), which makes it vastly more difficult and laborious for the code reviewer to assess the correctness of `sendHTML`. Furthermore, the code has major coupling problems because the correctness of `sendHTML` depends on the throwing behavior of a potentially large number of other functions.

One solution would be to mimic RAII (even if no resource is involved) and define a `struct` that sends the closing tag in its destructor. That is at best a palliative treatment.

The need is to guarantee execution of certain code, not to litter the program with types and objects.

Another possible solution is to use `finally` clauses:

```
void sendHTML(Connection conn) {
   try {
      conn.send("<html>");
      ...
   } finally {
      conn.send("</html>");
   }
}
```

This approach has a different problem: scaling, or, better said, the lack thereof. The poor scaling of `finally` becomes obvious as soon as stacking two or more call pairs is needed. For example, consider also sending a correctly paired "<body>" tag. To do so, we need to nest *two* `try/finally` blocks:

```
void sendHTML(Connection conn) {
   try {
      conn.send("<html>");
      ... // Send the head
      try {
         conn.send("<body>");
         ... // Send the body
      } finally {
         conn.send("</body>");
      }
   } finally {
      conn.send("</html>");
   }
}
```

Alternatively, the same effect could be achieved with only one `finally` block and an additional state variable that keeps track of how far along the function has gotten:

```
void sendHTML(Connection conn) {
   int step = 0;
   try {
      conn.send("<html>");
      ... // Send the head
      step = 1;
      conn.send("<body>");
      ... // Send the body
```

```
        step = 2;
    } finally {
        if (step > 1) conn.send("</body>");
        if (step > 0) conn.send("</html>");
    }
}
```

This approach works better, but now a fair chunk of code is dedicated to state management alone, which obscures the intent of the function.

Such situations are best helped with scope statements. A running function can plant scope statements as soon as execution has reached a certain point. That way whatever code snippets need to be logically paired are also physically paired.

```
void sendHTML(Connection conn) {
    conn.send("<html>");
    scope(exit) conn.send("</html>");
    ... // Send the head
    conn.send("<body>");
    scope(exit) conn.send("</body>");
    ... // Send the body
}
```

The new setup has a host of desirable properties. First, the code layout is linear—no extra nesting. This makes the approach accommodate several open/close pairs effortlessly. Second, the approach obviates the need to inspect sendHTML and all other functions it may call for hidden control flows created by possible throws. Third, related concerns are grouped together with simplified understanding and maintainability. Fourth, the code is terse because the notational overhead of scope statements is low.

## 9.7   Uncaught Exceptions

If no handler is found for an exception, a system-planted handler just prints the exception's message to the standard error console and exits with a nonzero exit code. This happens not only for exceptions that propagate out of main, but also for exceptions thrown by static this blocks.

As mentioned above, normally you should never catch Throwable objects. On very rare occasions, you might want to catch Throwable and take some contingency action, come hell or high water. You shouldn't count on a sane state throughout the system; the logic of your program has been shown to be broken so there's precious little you can assume.

# Contract Programming

Ensuring program correctness is a topic of increasing importance in a world where we trust various computing systems, large and small, with ever more bits of our existence. This chapter introduces program correctness mechanisms that kick in at runtime (as opposed to typechecking and other semantic checks, which enforce certain correctness constraints during compilation). Runtime checks for program correctness are only partially related to error handling and should not be confused with it. More specifically, there are three intertwined but distinct areas lying under the generous umbrella of "when things go wrong":

- *Error handling* (the topic of Chapter 9) deals with techniques and idioms for managing expected runtime errors.
- *Reliability engineering* is a field that studies the ability of entire systems (e.g., hardware plus software) to perform to specification. (This book does not discuss reliability engineering.)
- *Program correctness* is a field of programming language research dedicated to proving with static and dynamic means that a program is correct according to a given specification. Type systems are one of the best-known means for proving program correctness (a read of Wadler's fascinating monograph "Proofs are programs" [59] is highly recommended). This chapter discusses Contract Programming, a paradigm for enforcing program correctness.

The major aspect that distinguishes program correctness from error handling is that the latter is concerned with errors that fall *within the specification* of the program (such as dealing with a corrupt data file or invalid user input), whereas the former is concerned with programming errors that put the program's behavior *outside the specification* (such as miscalculating a percentage value that is outside the 0 through 100 range or unexpectedly obtaining a negative day of the week in a Date object). Ignoring this important distinction leads to unpardonable but, alas, still common misunderstandings such as checking file and network input with assert.

Contract Programming is an approach to defining software components introduced by Parnas [45], then further popularized by Meyer [40] along with the Eiffel programming language. Today Contract Programming has matured into a popular software development paradigm. Although most mainstream programming languages do not offer explicit support for Contract Programming, many shops have standards and conventions enforcing its underlying principles. Contracts are also an active area of research; recent work includes advanced topics such as contracts for higher-order functions [24] and static verification of contracts [61]. For the time being, D sticks with the simpler, traditional model of Contract Programming, which we'll discuss in this chapter.

## 10.1  Contracts

Contract Programming uses a real-life metaphor to improve the definition and verification of modular interfaces. The metaphor is that of *binding contract:* when entity A (person, company) commits to perform a certain service for the benefit of entity B, a contract between A and B describes what B is expected to provide to A in exchange for the service, and exactly what A commits to provide once B fulfills its part of the contract.

Similarly, the Contract Programming paradigm defines a function's specification as a contract between the function (the supplier) and its caller (the client). One part of the contract specifies what requirements the caller must fulfill in order for the function call to proceed. The other part of the contract specifies the guarantees that the function makes upon return in terms of returned value and/or side effects.

The central notions of Contract Programming are as follows:

- *Assertion:* Not tied to a particular function, an assertion is a runtime check against an if-testable condition. If the condition is nonzero, assert has no effect. Otherwise, assert throws an AssertError object. AssertError is an unrecoverable exception—it does not inherit Exception but instead inherits Error directly, which means that it shouldn't normally be caught.
- *Precondition:* The precondition of a function is the totality of conditions that a caller must fulfill in order to invoke the function. The conditions may be directly related to the call site (such as parameter values) but also related to the system state (such as availability of memory).
- *Postcondition:* The postcondition of a function is the totality of guarantees that the function makes upon normal return, assuming its precondition was satisfied.

- *Invariant:* An invariant is a condition that stays unmodified throughout a portion of a computation. In D, invariants always refer to the state of an object before and after a method invocation.

Contract Programming generalizes very nicely some time-tested notions that today we take for granted. For example, a function signature is a contract all right. Consider a function found in the standard library, module `std.math`:

```
double sqrt(double x);
```

The sheer signature imposes a contract: the caller must provide exactly one value of type `double`, and the function's return is one `double` value as well. You can't call `sqrt("hello")` or assign the result of `sqrt` to a `string`. More interestingly, you *can* call `sqrt(2)` even though 2 is an `int` and not a `double`: the signature gives the compiler enough information to help the caller fulfill the input requirement by converting 2 to a `double`. The function may have side effects, but if it doesn't, the `pure` attribute may be used to specify that:

```
// No side effects
pure double sqrt(double x);
```

This is a stronger, more binding contract for `sqrt` because it forces `sqrt` to not have any side effects. Finally, there is the `nothrow` attribute that allows us to specify an even more detailed (and restrictive) contract:

```
// No side effects, never throws
// (Actual declaration found in std.math)
pure nothrow double sqrt(double x);
```

Now we know for sure that the function either returns a `double`, terminates the program, or enters an infinite loop. There's nothing else in the world it can ever do. So we were using contracts with functions by just writing down signatures.

To appreciate the contractual power of function signatures, consider a little piece of historical evidence. The early, pre-standard version of the C language (known as "K&R C" in honor of its creators, Kernighan and Ritchie) had a quirk. If you didn't declare a function at all, K&R C would consider it a function with this signature:

```
// If you don't declare sqrt but call it, it's as if
//    you declared it as
int sqrt(...);
```

In other words, if you forgot to #include the header `math.h` (which provides the correct signature for `sqrt`), you *could* have called `sqrt("hello")` without the compiler minding it one bit. (The ellipsis introduces varargs, one of the most unsafe features of C.)

One more subtle error was that invoking sqrt(2) compiled with or without including math.h but did very different things. With the #include, the compiler converted 2 to 2.0 before calling sqrt; without it, a terrible misunderstanding between parties occurred: the caller sent the integer 2 and sqrt picked up its binary representation as if it were a floating-point number, which in 32-bit IEEE is 2.8026e-45. ANSI C recognized the gravity of this problem and fixed it by requiring prototypes for all functions.

Function attributes and types can be used to specify simple contracts. Attributes are in fixed supply, but types are easy to define whenever needed. How far can types go in describing contracts? The answer is, sadly, that (at least with the current technology) types are not an adequate vehicle for expressing even moderately complex contracts.

A designer could specify a function's contract in the documentation associated with the function, but I'm sure we all agree that setup is far from satisfactory. Users of a component don't always peruse its documentation with due care, and even when they do it's easy to make honest mistakes. Besides, documentation has a way of getting out of sync with design and implementation, particularly when specifications are nontrivial and change frequently (as often happens).

Contract Programming takes a simpler approach of specifying contractual requirements as executable predicates—snippets of code that describe the contract as pass/fail conditions. Let's take a look at each in turn.

## 10.2   Assertions

This book has defined (§ 2.3.4.1 on page 46) and already used assert in many places—an implied acknowledgment of the notion's usefulness. In addition, most languages include a sort of assertion mechanism, either as a primitive or as a library construct.

To recap, use the assert expression to ensure that an expression is supposed to be nonzero *by design, in all runs of the program regardless of input*:

```
int a, b;
...
assert(a == b);
assert(a == b, "a and b are different");
```

The asserted expression is often Boolean but may have any if-testable type: numeric, array, class reference, or pointer. If the expression is zero, assert throws an object of type AssertError; otherwise, nothing happens. An optional string parameter is made part of the error message carried by the AssertError object, if thrown. The string is evaluated only if the assertion does fail, which saves some potentially expensive computation:

```
import std.conv;

void fun() {
```

```
    int a, b;
    ...
    assert(a == b);
    assert(a == b, text(a, " and ", b, " are different"));
}
```

The `std.conv.text` function converts and concatenates all of its arguments into a `string`. That entails quite a bit of work—memory allocation, conversions, the works. It would be wasteful to do all that work if the assertion succeeds, so `assert` evaluates its second argument only if the first is zero.

What should `assert` do in case of a failure? Forcefully terminating the application is an option (and is what C's homonym macro does), but D's `assert` throws an exception. It's not an ordinary exception, however; it's an `AssertError` object, which inherits `Error`—the über-exception discussed in § 9.2 on page 302.

The `AssertError` object thrown by `assert` goes through the `catch(Exception)` handlers like a hot knife through butter. That's a good thing because `assert` failures represent logic errors in your program, and usually you want logic errors to just terminate the application as soon and as orderly as possible.

To catch an `AssertError` exception, use `Error` or `AssertError` directly in a `catch` handler instead of `Exception` or its descendants. But then again: you should seldom be in a place in life where catching `Error`s would help.

## 10.3  Preconditions

Preconditions are contractual obligations that must be satisfied upon a function's entry. For example, say we want to write a contract enforcing non-negative inputs for a function `fun`. That would be a precondition imposed by `fun` on its callers. In D, you write a precondition as follows:

```
double fun(double x)
in {
    assert(x >= 0);
}
body {
    // Implementation of fun
    ...
}
```

The `in` contract is automatically executed before the function's body. That's virtually the same as the simpler version:

```
double fun(double x) {
    assert(x >= 0);
```

```
    // Implementation of fun
    ...
}
```

but we'll see that it is important to distinguish the precondition from the function's body when objects and inheritance enter the picture.

Some languages restrict contracts to Boolean expressions and automatically throw the exception if the Boolean is false, for example:

```
// Not D
double fun(double x)
in (x >= 0)
body {
    ...
}
```

D is more flexible in that it allows you to check for preconditions that don't easily lend themselves to single Boolean expressions. Also, you have the freedom of throwing any exception you want, not only an `AssertError` exception. For example, `fun` might want to throw some exception type that records the faulty input:

```
import std.conv, std.contracts;

class CustomException : Exception {
    private string origin;
    private double val;
    this(string msg, string origin, double val) {
        super(msg);
        this.origin = origin;
        this.val = val;
    }
    override string toString() {
        return text(origin, ": ", super.toString(), val);
    }
}

double fun(double x)
in {
    if (x !>= 0) {
        throw new CustomException("fun", x);
    }
}
body {
```

```
    double y;
    // Implementation of fun
    ...
    return y;
}
```

But don't abuse that flexibility. As discussed above, `assert` throws an `AssertError` object, which is different from regular exceptions. It is best to use `AssertError` or other exceptions that inherit `Error` but not `Exception` when signaling a precondition failure. This is because precondition failure indicates a serious logic error in your program that is not supposed to get caught casually.

The compiler actually takes explicit steps to disallow contract misuse. First, inside the `in` clause you cannot execute the `return` statement, meaning that you can't use a contract to entirely skip the function's `body`. Second, D explicitly disallows changing parameters in a contract. For example, the following code is in error:

```
double fun(double x)
in {
    if (x <= 0) x = 0; // Error!
        // Cannot modify parameter 'x' inside contract!
}
body {
    double y;
    ...
    return y;
}
```

Yet, although the compiler could enforce that a contract is `pure` (which would be a logical decision), it doesn't. This means you can still alter global variables or generate output from within a contract. This freedom was granted with a purpose: impure uses are useful during debugging sessions, and it would be too restrictive to disallow them. Nevertheless, remember that generally it's not good style to alter the state of the world from within a contract. Contract code is only supposed to verify observance of the contract and throw an exception if the contract has been violated—nothing else.

## 10.4 Postconditions

With the `in` contract in tow, `fun` is asymmetric and in a certain way unfair. `fun` specifies its requirements to the caller but provides no guarantee. Why should the caller work hard to provide a non-negative number to `fun`? To check postconditions, use an `out` contract. Let's assume that `fun` guarantees a result between 0 and 1:

```
double fun(double x)
```

```
// As before
in {
   assert(x >= 0);
}
// added
out(result) {
   assert(result >= 0 && result <= 1);
}
body {
   // Implementation of fun
   double y;
   ...
   return y;
}
```

If the `in` contract or the function's body throws an exception, `out` does not execute at all. If the `in` contract passes and body `returns` normally, the `out` contract is executed. The parameter `result` passed to `out` is whatever the function is about to return. The `result` parameter is optional; `out { ... }` is also a valid `out` contract that doesn't need the result or applies to a `void`-returning function. In the example above, `result` will be a copy of y.

Just like the `in` contract, the `out` contract should only verify without modifying. The only interaction of `out` contracts with the outer world should be either doing nothing at all (pass) or throwing an exception (fail). In particular, `out` is not a good place for last-minute result adjustments. Compute the result in body, and check it with `out`. The following code does not compile for two reasons: the `out` contract attempts to rebind `result` and also attempts to (harmlessly but suspiciously) rebind an argument:

```
int fun(int x)
out(result) {
   x = 42;                        // Error!
      // Cannot modify parameter 'x' in a contract!
   if (result < 0) result = 0; // Error!
      // Cannot modify the result in a contract!
}
body {
   ...
}
```

## 10.5   Invariants

An invariant is a condition that remains satisfied at certain milestones during a computation. For example, a `pure` function ensures that the entire state of the program remains unchanged throughout the execution of the function. Such a guarantee is very strong but often too coarse to be used intensively.

A more granular invariance guarantee may be applied to an individual object, and this is the model D works with. Consider, for example, a simple `Date` class that stores the day, month, and year as individual integers:

```
class Date {
    private uint year, month, day;
    ...
}
```

It is reasonable to posit that at no point in the lifetime of a `Date` object should the year, month, and day members take nonsensical values. To express such an assumption, use an `invariant`:

```
import std.algorithm, std.range;
```

```
class Date {
private:
    uint year, month, day;
    invariant() {
        assert(1 <= month && month <= 12);
        switch (day) {
            case 29:
                assert(month != 2 || leapYear(year));
                break;
            case 30:
                assert(month != 2);
                break;
            case 31:
                assert(longMonth(month));
                break;
            default:
                assert(1 <= day && day <= 28);
                break;
        }
        // No restriction on year
    }
    // Helper functions
```

```
    static pure bool leapYear(uint y) {
        return (y % 4) == 0 && (y % 100 || (y % 400) == 0);
    }
    static pure bool longMonth(uint m) {
        return !(m & 1) == (m > 7);
    }
public:
    ...
}
```

The three tests for days 30, 31, and 29 handle the customary verifications for month February and leap year. The test in `longMonth` returns `true` if a month has 31 days and works by claiming, "A long month is an even number if and only if it is greater than July," which makes sense (months 1, 3, 5, 7, 8, 10, and 12 are long).

The `invariant` must pass for any valid `Date` object at all times. In theory the compiler could emit calls to the `invariant` whenever it wants. However, things are not that simple. Consider, for example, that the compiler makes the executive decision to insert a call to `invariant` at the end of each statement. That would be not only inefficient, but also incorrect. Consider setting a `Date` from another `Date`:

```
// Inside class Date
void copy(Date another) {
  year = another.year;
  __call_invariant();       // Inserted by the compiler
  month = another.month;
  __call_invariant();       // Inserted by the compiler
  day = another.day;
  __call_invariant();       // Inserted by the compiler
}
```

Between these statements it's quite possible that the `Date` is temporarily out of sync, so inserting an `invariant` evaluation per statement is not correct. (For example, assigning date 1 August 2015 to a date currently containing 29 February 2012 would temporarily make the date be 29 February 2015, which is an invalid date.)

How about inserting an invariant call at the beginning and end of each method? Negative again. Consider, for example, that you write a function that advances a date by one month. Such a function is useful, for example, for tracking events that happen once a month. The function must pay attention only to adjusting the day around the end of the month such that the date goes, for example, from August 31 to September 30.

```
// Inside class Date
void nextMonth() {
    __call_invariant();                // Inserted by the compiler
```

```
   scope(exit) __call_invariant(); // Inserted by the compiler
   if (month == 12) {
      ++year;
      month = 1;
   } else {
      ++month;
      adjustDay();
   }
}
// Ancillary function
private void adjustDay() {
   __call_invariant();           // Inserted by the compiler
                                 // (PROBLEMATIC)
   scope(exit) __call_invariant(); // Inserted by the compiler
                                 // (PROBLEMATIC)
   switch (day) {
      case 29:
         if (month == 2 && !leapYear(year)) day = 28;
         break;
      case 30:
         if (month == 2) day = 28 + leapYear(year);
         break;
      case 31:
         if (month == 2) day = 28 + leapYear(year);
         else if (!isLongMonth(month)) day = 30;
         break;
      default:
         // Nothing to do
         break;
   }
}
```

Function `nextMonth` takes care of year rollover and uses an ancillary `private` function `adjustDay` to ensure that the day remains inside a valid date. Here's exactly where the problem is: upon entrance in `adjustDay` the invariant may be broken. Of course it might—the sole purpose of `adjustDay` was to *fix* the `Date` object!

What makes `adjustDay` special? It's its protection level: it's a `private` function, accessible only to other functions that have the right to modify the `Date` object. Upon entrance in and exit from a `private` function, in general, it's acceptable to have a broken invariant. The places where the `invariant` must definitely be accepted are at `public` method boundaries: an object doesn't want to allow a client operation to find or leave `this` in an invalid state.

How about `protected` functions? According to the discussion in § 6.7.6 on page 201, `protected` is just one little notch better than `public`. However, it was deemed that requiring invariant satisfaction at the boundaries of `protected` functions was too restrictive.

If a class defines an invariant, the compiler automatically inserts calls to the invariant in the following places:

1. At the *end* of all constructors
2. At the *beginning* of the destructor
3. At the *beginning* and *end* of all `public` non-static methods

Say we put on X-ray vision goggles that allow us to see the code inserted by the compiler in the `Date` class. We'd then see this:

```
class Date {
   private uint day, month, year;
   invariant() { ... }
   this(uint day, uint month, uint year) {
      scope(exit) __call_invariant();
      ...
   }
   ~this() {
      __call_invariant();
      ...
   }
   void somePublicMethod() {
      __call_invariant();
      scope(exit) __call_invariant();
      ...
   }
}
```

A detail about the constructor and destructor is worth noting. Recall from the discussion of an object's lifetime (§ 6.3 on page 181) that once allocated, an object is considered valid. Therefore, even if a constructor throws, it must leave the object in an invariant-abiding state.

## 10.6   Skipping Contract Checks. Release Builds

Contracts are concerned exclusively with verifying the internal logic of an application. In keeping with that charter, most, if not all, programming systems that support contracts also allow a mode in which all contract checking is ignored. That mode is supposed to be activated only with programs that have been thoroughly reviewed, verified, and tested.

Any D compiler provides a flag (`-release` in the reference implementation) that ignores contracts altogether, that is, parses and typechecks all contract code but leaves no trace of it in the executable binary. A release build runs without contract checking (which is riskier) but also at full speed (which is, well, faster). If the application has its ducks in a row, the added risk of skipping contract checks is very low and the increase in speed is well worth that risk. The possibility of running without contracts reinforces the warning that code should *not* use contracts for routine checks that could reasonably fail. Contracts must be reserved for never-expected errors that reflect a logic bug in your program. Again, you should never use contracts to make sure that user input is correct. Also, remember the repeated warnings against doing any significant work (such as side effects) inside `assert`, `in`, and `out`? Now it's painfully obvious why: a program that does such unsavory acts would oddly behave differently in non-release and release mode.

One commonly encountered error is `assert`ing expressions with side effects, for example, `assert(++x < y)`, which is bound to cause much head scratching. It's the worst of all worlds: the bug manifests itself in release mode, when by definition you have fewer means at your disposal to find the source of the problem.

### 10.6.1   `enforce` Is Not (Quite) `assert`

It's a pity that `assert` disappears from release builds, because using it is very convenient. Instead of writing

```
if (!expr1) throw new SomeException;
...
if (!expr2) throw new SomeException;
...
if (!expr3) throw new SomeException;
```

you get to write only

```
assert(expr1);
...
assert(expr2);
...
assert(expr3);
```

Given that `assert` is so concise, many libraries provide an "always assert" feature that checks a condition and throws an exception if the condition is zero, whether you compile in release mode or not. Such checkers go in C++ by names such as VERIFY, AS-SERT_ALWAYS, or ENFORCE. D defines such a function in module `std.contracts` under the name `enforce`. Use `enforce` with the same syntax as `assert`:

```
enforce(expr1);
enforce(expr2, "That isn't quite true");
```

If the passed-in expression is zero, `enforce` throws an object of type `Exception` regardless of whether you compiled the program in release or non-release mode. If you want to throw a different type, you may specify it as follows:

```
import std.contracts;
bool something = true;
```

```
enforce(something, new Error("Something isn't right"));
```

If `something` is zero, the second argument is thrown; `enforce` evaluates it lazily such that no object creation occurs if `expr1` is nonzero.

Although `assert` and `enforce` look and feel very much alike, they serve fundamentally different purposes. Don't forget the differences between the two:

- `assert` checks your application logic, whereas `enforce` checks error conditions that don't threaten the integrity of your application.
- `assert` throws only the unrecoverable `AssertError` exception, whereas `enforce` throws by default a recoverable exception (and may throw any exception with an extra argument).
- `assert` may disappear, so don't take it into consideration when figuring the flow of your function; `enforce` never disappears, so after you call `enforce(e)` you can assume that e is nonzero.

### 10.6.2  assert(false)

An assertion against a constant that is known to be zero during compilation, such as `assert(false)`, `assert(0)`, or `assert(null)`, behaves a tad differently from a regular `assert`.

In non-release mode, `assert(false)` does not do anything special: it just throws an `AssertError` exception.

In release mode, however, `assert(false)` is *not* compiled out of existence; it will always cause a program to stop. This time, however, there would be no exception and no chance of continuing to run after an `assert(false)` was hit. The program will *crash*. This is achieved on Intel machines by executing the `HLT` ("halt") instruction, which causes the program to abort immediately.

Many of us tend to think of a crash as a highly dangerous event that indicates a program gone out of control. This disposition is prevalent most likely because many programs that do go out of control terminate, sooner or later, via a crash. But `assert(false)` is a very controlled way to terminate a program. In fact, on some operating systems, HLT automatically loads your debugger and positions it on the very `assert` that triggered the crash.

What's the purpose of this particular behavior of `assert(false)`? One obvious use has to do with system-level programs. There had to be a portable way to issue HLT, and `assert(false)` integrates well with the rest of the language. In addition, the compiler is aware of the semantics of `assert(false)`, so, for example, it disallows dead code following an `assert(false)` expression:

```
int fun(int x) {
    ++x;
    assert(false);
    return x;        // Error!
                     // Statement is not reachable!
}
```

On the contrary, in other situations you may need to add `assert(false)` to suppress a compiler error. Consider, for example, calling the standard library function `std.contracts.enforce(false)` discussed just above:

```
import std.contracts;

string fun() {
    ...
    enforce(false, "can't continue"); // Always throws
    assert(false);                    // Unreachable
}
```

The call `enforce(false)` always throws an exception, but the compiler doesn't know that. To make the compiler understand that that point cannot possibly be reached, insert an `assert(false)`. Finishing `fun` with `return "";` also works, but in that case, if someone comments out the `enforce` call later on, `fun` would start returning bogus values. The `assert(false)` is a veritable *deus ex machina* that saves your code from such situations.

## 10.7 Contracts: Not for Scrubbing Input

This section discusses a controversial matter related to contracts that is the source of continuous debate. The matter essentially boils down to this question: If a function must make some check, where should the check go—in a contract or in the function's body?

When first getting accustomed to Contract Programming, many of us are tempted to move most checks inside contracts. Consider, for example, a function called `readText` that loads a text file in its entirety as a `string`. Armed with contracts, we might define it as follows:

```
import std.file, std.utf;

string readText(in char[] filename)
out(result) {
   std.utf.validate(result);
}
body {
    return cast(string) read(filename);
}
```

(`readText` is actually a function in the standard library; you may want to look it up in module `std.file`.)

`readText` relies on two other file functions. First, it uses `read` to load an entire file into a memory buffer. The memory buffer has type `void[]`, which `readText` casts to `string`. But it would be incorrect to leave things at that: what if the file contains malformed UTF characters? To validate the `cast`, the out contract verifies the result by calling `std.utf.validate`, which throws a `UtfException` object if the buffer contains an invalid UTF character.

That would be fine, were it not for a fundamental issue: contracts must validate the *logic* of an application, not the validity of its inputs. Anything that's not considered an endemic problem of the application does not belong inside contracts. Also, contracts are not supposed to change the semantics of the application—hence D's intentional curbing of what can be modified inside a contract.

Assuming no contracts fail, an application must run with the same behavior and results with or without actually executing contracts. This is a very simple and memorable litmus test for deciding what's a contract and what isn't. Contracts are specification checks, and if the checks go away for a correct implementation, that doesn't stop the implementation from working! That's how contracts are meant to work. Expecting that a file is always valid may reveal a positive attitude but should not be part of `readText`'s specification. A correct definition of `readText` makes the check an integral part of the function:

```
import std.file, std.utf;

string readText(in char[] filename) {
   auto result = cast(string) read(filename);
   std.utf.validate(result);
   return result;
}
```

In light of the discussion so far, the answer to the question regarding check placement is: If the check concerns the application logic, it should go in a contract; otherwise, the check should go in the body of the function and never get skipped.

That sounds great, but how to define "application logic" in applications built out of separate, generic libraries written by independent entities? Consider a large general-purpose library, such as the Microsoft Windows API or the K Desktop Environment. Many applications use APIs like these, and it is inevitable that library functions receive arguments that do not conform to the spec. (In fact, an operating system API may *count* on receiving all sorts of malformed arguments.) If an application does not fulfill the precondition of a library function call, where does the blame go? It was clearly the fault of the application, but it's the library that takes the hit—in terms of instability, undefined behavior, corrupted state inside the library, crashes, all those bad things. As unfair as it may seem, such problems would reflect poorly on the library ("Library Xyz is prone to instability and surprising quirks") more than on the bug-ridden applications using it.

A general-purpose and large-distribution API should verify all inputs to all of its functions as a matter of course—not in contracts. Failure to verify an argument is unequivocally a library bug. No spokesperson would ever wave a copy of a book or paper and say, "We were using Contract Programming throughout, so we're not at fault."

Does that invalidate the argument that functions should use preconditions to specify, for example, argument ranges? Not at all. It's all a matter of defining and distinguishing "application logic" from "user input." To a function that's an integral part of an application, receiving valid arguments is part of the application logic. To a general-purpose function belonging to an independently delivered library, arguments are nothing but user input.

On the other hand, it is perfectly fine for a library to use contracts in its `private` functions. Those functions relate to the internal workings of the library and cannot be accessed by user code, so it is sensible to have them use contracts to express adherence to specification.

## 10.8 Contracts and Inheritance

The often-quoted Liskov Substitution Principle [38] states that inheritance is substitutability: an object of the derived class must be substitutable wherever an object of the base class is expected. This insight essentially determines the interaction of contracts with inheritance.

In the real world, the relationship between contracts and substitutability is as follows: once a contract is established, a substitute contractor must be *at least* as qualified to perform the job, deliver the job within *at least* the specified tolerance, and require *at most* the same compensation that was established in the contract. There is some flexibility, but never in the direction of tightening the preconditions of the contract or loosening the postconditions. If either of these happens, the contract becomes invalid and

must be rewritten.  The flexibility concerns only variations that don't negatively affect
the understanding in the contract: a substitute is allowed to require *less* and offer *more*.

### 10.8.1  Inheritance and `in` Contracts

Consider the `Date` example again.  Let's say we define a very simple, lightweight `Ba-`
`sicDate` class that offers only minimal support and leaves enhancements to derived
classes.  `BasicDate` offers a function `format` that takes a `string` representing a format
specification and returns a string with the date formatted appropriately:

```
import std.conv;

class BasicDate {
   private uint day, month, year;
   string format(string spec)
   in {
      // Require str to be equal to "%Y/%m/%d"
      assert(spec == "%Y/%m/%d");
   }
   body {
      // Simplistic implementation
      return text(year, '/', month, '/', day);
   }
   ...
}
```

The contract imposed by `Date.format` requires that the format specification be exactly `"%Y/%m/%d"`, which we assume means "year in long format followed by a slash followed by month followed by a slash followed by day." That's the only format `BasicDate`
worries about supporting.  Derived classes may add localization, internationalization,
the works.

A class `Date` that inherits `BasicDate` wants to offer a better `format` primitive—for
example, say `Date` wants to allow the specifiers `%Y`, `%m`, and `%d` in any positions and mixed
with arbitrary characters.  Also, `%%` should be allowed because it represents the actual
character `%`.  Repeated occurrences of the same specifiers should also be allowed.  To
enforce all that, `Date` writes its own contract:

```
import std.regex;

class Date : BasicDate {
   override string format(string spec)
   in {
      auto pattern = regex("(%[mdY%]|[^%])*");
```

```
        assert(!match(spec, pattern).empty);
    }
    body {
        string result;
        ...
        return result;
    }
    ...
}
```

`Date` enforces its constraints on `spec` with the help of a regular expression. Regular expressions are an invaluable aid in string manipulation; Friedl's classic *Mastering Regular Expressions* [26] is warmly recommended. This is not the place to discuss regular expressions in depth, but suffice it to say that `"(%[mdY%]|[^%])*"` means "a % followed by any of `m`, `d`, `Y`, or `%`'; or anything other than a %—repeated zero or more times." The equivalent code that would match such a pattern by hand would be considerably more verbose. The `assert` makes sure that matching the string against the pattern returns a non-empty match, that is, it worked. (For more on using regular expressions with D, you may want to peruse the online documentation of the standard module `std.regex`.)

What is the *aggregate* contract of `Date.format`? It should mind `BasicDate.format`'s contract but also relax it. It's fine if the base `in` contract fails, as long as the derived `in` contract passes. Also, `Date.format`'s contract should never strengthen `BasicDate.format`'s `in` contract. The emerging rule is as follows: In an overridden method, first execute the base class contract. If that succeeds, transfer control to the body. Otherwise, execute the derived class contract. If that succeeds, transfer control to the body. Otherwise, report contract failure.

Put another way, the `in` contracts are combined by using disjunction with short-circuit: exactly one must pass, and the base class contract is tried first. That way there is no possibility that the derived contract is more difficult to satisfy than the base class contract. On the contrary, the derived class offers a second chance for failed preconditions.

The rule above works very well for `Date` and `BasicDate`. First, the composite contract checks against the exact pattern `"%Y/%m/%d"`. If that succeeds, formatting proceeds. Failing that, conformance to the derived, more permissive, contract is checked. If that passes, again formatting may proceed.

The code generated for the combined contract looks like this:

```
void __in_contract_Date_format(string spec) {
    try {
        // Try the base contract
        this.BasicDate.__in_contract_format(spec);
    } catch (Throwable) {
        // Base contract failed, try derived contract
```

```
        this.Date.__in_contract_format(spec);
    }
    // Success, can invoke body
}
```

### 10.8.2   Inheritance and out Contracts

With out contracts the situation is exactly the opposite: when substituting a derived
object for a base object, the overridden function must offer *more* than what the contract
promised. So right off the bat, the out guarantee of the base must always be fulfilled by
the overriding method (unlike the case for the in contract).

Conversely, this means that a base class should set the contract as loose as is useful,
to avoid the risk of over-constraining derived classes. For example, if BasicDate.format
imposes that the returned string has the format year/month/day, it would effectively prevent any derived class from performing any other formatting.   Perhaps
BasicDate.format could impose a weaker contract—for example, if the formatting
string is not empty, an empty string is not allowed as output:

```
import std.range, std.string;

class BasicDate {
    private uint day, month, year;
    string format(string spec)
    out(result) {
        assert(!result.empty || spec.empty);
    }
    body {
        return std.string.format("%04s/%02s/%02s", year, month, day);
    }
    ...
}
```

Date sets its ambitions a bit higher: it computes the expected result length from the
format specification and then compares the length of the actual result to the expected
length:

```
import std.algorithm, std.regex;

class Date : BasicDate {
    override string format(string spec)
    out(result) {
        bool escaping;
```

```
            size_t expectedLength;
            foreach (c; spec) {
                switch (c) {
                    case '%':
                        if (escaping) {
                            ++expectedLength;
                            escaping = false;
                        } else {
                            escaping = true;
                        }
                        break;
                    case 'Y':
                        if (escaping) {
                            expectedLength += 4;
                            escaping = false;
                        }
                        break;
                    case 'm': case 'd':
                        if (escaping) {
                            expectedLength += 2;
                            escaping = false;
                        }
                        break;
                    default:
                        assert(!escaping);
                        ++expectedLength;
                        break;
                }
            }
            assert(walkLength(result) == expectedLength);
        }
        body {
            string result;
            ...
            return result;
        }
        ...
    }
```

(Why walkLength(result) instead of result.length? The number of characters
in a UTF-encoded string may be smaller than its length in chars.) Given these two out
contracts, what is the correct combined out contract? The answer is simple: The con-

tract of the base class must be also verified.  Then, if the derived class promises *additional* contractual obligations, those must be fulfilled as well.  It's a simple conjunction. The code below is what the compiler might generate for composing the base and derived contracts:

```
void __out_contract_Date_format(string spec) {
    this.BasicDate.__out_contract_format(spec);
    this.Date.__out_contract_format(spec);
    // Success
}
```

### 10.8.3  Inheritance and `invariant` Contracts

Just as in the case of `out` contracts, we're looking at a conjunction, an "and" relation: a class must fulfill the invariant of all of its base classes in addition to its own invariant. There is no way for a class to weaken the invariant of its base class. The current compiler calls `invariant()` clauses from the top of the hierarchy down, but that should not matter at all for the implementor of an `invariant`; as discussed, `invariant`s should have no side effects.

## 10.9  Contracts in Interfaces

Possibly the most interesting application of contracts is in conjunction with interfaces. An interface is a complex contract, so it is fitting that each of an interface's methods should describe an abstract contract—a contract without a body.  The contract is enforced in terms of the not-yet-implemented primitives defined by the interface.

Consider, for example, that we want to enhance the `Stack` interface defined in § 6.14 on page 233. Here it is for reference:

```
interface Stack(T) {
    @property bool empty();
    @property ref T top();
    void push(T value);
    void pop();
}
```

Let's attach contracts to the interface that reveal the interplay of these primitives. Interface contracts look just like regular contracts without a body.

```
interface Stack(T) {
    @property bool empty();
```

```
    @property ref T top()
    in {
        assert(!empty);
    }

    void push(T value)
    in {
        assert(!empty);
    }
    out {
        assert(value == top);
    }

    void pop()
    in {
        assert(!empty);
    }
}
```

For an interface method with a contract, the trailing semicolon is not needed anymore. With the new definition of Stack, implementations are constrained to work within the confines defined by Stack's contracts. One nice thing is that the contract-enhanced Stack is a good specification of a stack that is at the same time easy to read by a programmer and verified dynamically.

As discussed in § 10.7 on page 327, Stack's contracts may be compiled out. If you define a container library for large and general use, it may be a good idea to treat method calls as user input. In that case, the NVI idiom (§ 6.9.1 on page 213) may be better suited. A stack interface that uses NVI to always check for valid calls would look like this:

```
interface NVIStack(T) {
protected:
    ref T topImpl();
    void pushImpl(T value);
    void popImpl();

public:
    @property bool empty();

    final @property ref T top() {
        enforce(!empty);
        return topImpl();
    }
```

```
final void push(T value) {
    enforce(!empty);
    pushImpl(value);
    enforce(value == topImpl());
}

final void pop() {
    assert(!empty);
    popImpl();
}
```
}

NVIStack uses enforce throughout—a test that's impossible to compile out of existence and also makes push, pop, and top final and hence impossible to hijack by implementations. One nice effect is that all major error handling has been hoisted out of each implementation in turn into the interface—a good form of reuse and of dividing responsibilities. NVIStack implementations can assume without fear that pushImpl, popImpl, and topImpl are always called in valid states and optimize them accordingly.

# 11

# Scaling Up

An adage has it that a 100-line program can be made to work even if it breaks all rules of good programming. That adage is fractal, really—a 10,000-line program could actually be written with attention to small-scale details but without minding any larger-scale rules of proper modular development. Probably there are even quite a few million-line projects out there that break more than a few rules for large-scale design.

Many solid principles in software engineering also have a fractal feel to them. Separation of concerns and information hiding are equally at work in a small module or when connecting entire applications together. The incarnations of these principles, however, vary with the scale at which the principles apply. This chapter is concerned with assembling larger entities—entire files, directories, libraries, and programs.

D follows a few tried-and-true principles in defining its approach to large-scale modularity and also brings a couple of interesting innovations in the way it does symbol lookup.

## 11.1   Packages and Modules

The unit of compilation, protection, and encapsulation is the physical file. The unit of packaging for multiple files is the directory. And that's about as sophisticated as it gets. When viewed from a modularity standpoint, we refer to a D source file as a *module*, and to a directory containing D source files as a *package*.

There's no pretense that the program source code would really feel better in a super-duper database. D uses a "database" tuned by the best of us for a long time, integrating perfectly with security features, version control, backup, OS-grade protection, journaling, what have you, and also makes for a low entry barrier for large-scale development as the basic tools needed are an editor and a compiler.

A D module is a text file with the suffix `.d` or `.di`. The D tool chain does not handle files differently based on their suffix, but the general convention is that implementation code lies in `.d` files and interface code lies in `.di` ("D interface") files. The file must be encoded in one of UTF-8, UTF-16, or UTF-32. The endianness of the bytes in the file (in the case of UTF-16 or UTF-32) is determined by the first few bytes in a little standardized protocol known as BOM (byte order mark). Table 11.1 shows how D compilers identify the encoding of source files, which follows the Unicode standard [56, Chapter 2].

**Table 11.1:** Byte order marks (BOMs) used for distinguishing D source files. The patterns are tried in top-down order and the first successful test establishes the file's encoding. xx is any nonzero byte value.

| If the first bytes are … | Then the file's encoding is … | Throw those bytes away? |
| --- | --- | --- |
| 00 00 FE FF | UTF-32 big endian | ✔ |
| FF FE 00 00 | UTF-32 little endian | ✔ |
| FE FF | UTF-16 big endian | ✔ |
| FF FE | UTF-16 little endian | ✔ |
| 00 00 00 xx | UTF-32 big endian | |
| xx 00 00 00 | UTF-32 little endian | |
| 00 xx | UTF-16 big endian | |
| xx 00 | UTF-16 little endian | |
| Anything else | UTF-8 | |

Some files lack a BOM, but D has an unambiguous means to auto-detect the encoding. The auto-detect procedure cleverly relies on the fact that any well-formed D module must start with at least a few ASCII-based characters, that is, Unicode code points smaller than 128. This is because, owing to D's grammar, a well-formed module must start with either a D keyword (ASCII-based), ASCII whitespace, or a couple of directives starting with # that must also be ASCII characters. If the patterns in Table 11.1 are tried in top-down order, the first match deduces the encoding unambiguously. If the encoding is deduced erroneously, then no harm is done—definitely the file is in error anyway as it starts with characters that cannot be valid D code.

If the first two characters (after skipping the byte order mark, if any) of a source file are `#!`, then those characters plus all characters up to the first newline character `\n` are ignored. This is for allowing the "shebang" feature for systems that support it.

### 11.1.1  `import` Declarations

Code in previous chapters often availed itself of the `import` statement to access standard library goodies, like this:

```
import std.stdio; // Access writeln et al.
```

To import one module from another, specify the name of the module in an `import` declaration. The name must include the relative path computed from the directory where compilation takes place. For example, consider the directory hierarchy illustrated in Figure 11.1.

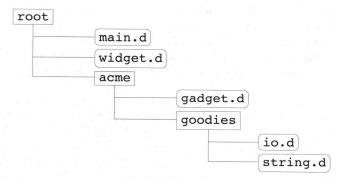

**Figure 11.1:** A sample directory structure.

Let's assume compilation proceeds in directory `root`. To access the definitions in file `widget.d`, any other file must include at the top level the declaration

```
import widget;
```

"Top level" means outside any scope (such as function, `class`, and `struct`). When encountering the `import` declaration, the compiler looks up `widget.di` (first) or `widget.d` (second), starting from the `root` directory, finds `widget.d`, and imports its symbols. To use the files deeper in the directory hierarchy, any other file in the project would have to `import` the relative path starting from `root`, using `.` as separator:

```
import acme.gadget;
import acme.goodies.io;
```

We've often used comma-separated lists in `import` declarations. The two declarations above are equivalent to

```
import acme.gadget, acme.goodies.io;
```

Note that a file situated deeper inside the directory hierarchy, such as `gadget.d`, would *still* `import` other files relative from `root`, where the compilation started, not relative from `gadget.d`'s own location. Case in point: to get access to symbols in `io.d`, `gadget.d` must use

```
import acme.goodies.io;
```

not

```
import goodies.io;
```

As another example, if io.d used string.d, it would need to import acme.goodies.string, even though the two files are in the same directory. Of course, that all assumes compilation starts in root. If you decide to go to directory acme and compile gadget.d *there*, it must import goodies.io.

importThe order of importing modules is irrelevant. The language is conceived in such a way that a module's semantics is independent of the order in which it imports other modules.

The import declaration accepts only symbols, and consequently D packages and modules must have names that are valid D symbols (§ 2.1 on page 30). For example, if you have a file called 5th_element.d, you simply cannot import it in another module because "5th_element" is not a valid D symbol. Similarly, if you put files in a directory called input-output, you cannot use that directory as a D package. Long story short—all D source files and directories must only bear names that are valid symbols. An additional convention is to make all package and module names lowercase, to avoid creating confusion on operating systems with non-strict file case handling.

### 11.1.2 Module Searching Roots

When the compiler resolves an import declaration, it searches not only from the current directory where compilation takes place. If that were the case, it would not be possible to use any of the standard library or any other libraries deployed outside the current project's directory. After all, we import modules from the package std all the time, and our projects don't have a subdirectory std in sight. How does the mechanism work?

Just like many other languages, D allows you to set up a number of *roots* where searching for modules proceeds. A command-line argument passed to the compiler allows adding any number of directories to be considered roots in the module searching process. The exact syntax of doing so is compiler-dependent; the reference compiler, dmd, uses the command-line switch −I followed immediately by a path—for example, −Ic:\Programs\dmd\src\phobos on a Windows installation, or −I/usr/local/src/phobos on a Unix installation. Any number of paths can also be added to the list of roots with additional −I switches.

To resolve import path.to.file, for example, the current directory is searched first for a subdirectory path/to.[1] If the directory exists, the file file.di is queried, and if that is not found, the file file.d is queried. If the file has been found, the search ends.

---

1. The text uses / as a generic path separator, with the understanding that the actual separator is system-dependent.

Otherwise, a similar search is performed starting with each of the directories passed with −I. The search stops at the first module found; if it goes through all directories without finding the module, a "module not found" error aborts the compilation.

If the component path.to. is missing, the module is searched directly in the roots.

It would be onerous to require the user to add a command-line switch just to access the standard library or other widely used libraries. That's why the reference compiler (and virtually any other) uses a simple configuration file containing some default command-line switches that should be appended automatically to any command line. The installation must come with the configuration file appropriately set up for finding at least the runtime support library and the standard library. So if you just type

```
% dmd main.d
```

then the artifacts of the standard library are found without requiring anything in the command line. To see exactly where each module is found, you may add the −v (verbose) flag to dmd's command line. To learn more details about how your D installation loads configuration options, you may want to consult your implementation's documentation (online [18, 19, 20, 21] in the case of dmd).

### 11.1.3   Name Lookup

Odd as it may seem, D does not have a global scope or a global namespace. In particular, there is no way to define a truly global object, function, or class name. This is because the only way to define such an entity is to put it in a module, and any module has a name. In turn, the name of the module introduces a named scope. Even the root of all class objects, Object, is not really a global name because it's actually object.Object as introduced by the installation-provided module object. For example, let's say the contents of widget.d are as follows:

```
// This is widget.d
void fun(int x) {
   ...
}
```

The definition of fun does not introduce a globally available symbol fun. Instead, whoever imports widget (e.g., main.d) gains access to the symbol widget.fun:

```
// This is main.d
import widget;

void main() {
   widget.fun(10); // Fine, look up function fun in module widget
}
```

This is all very nice and modular, but also quite verbose and unnecessarily strict. If `fun` is asked for and nobody else defines a function `fun`, couldn't the compiler just decide `widget.fun` is the winner as the sole contender?

Indeed, that's how name lookup works. Each `imported` module contributes a separate namespace, but when a symbol is looked up, the following steps take place:

1. Look up the symbol in the current scope. If found, lookup ends successfully.
2. Look up the symbol in the current module's scope. If found, lookup ends successfully.
3. Look up the symbol in *all* `imported` modules.

   - If not found, fail.
   - If found in exactly one module, lookup ends successfully.
   - If found in more than one module and if the symbol is not the name of a function, fail with "duplicated symbol" error message.
   - If found in more than one module and if the symbol is the name of a function, apply cross-module overload resolution (§ 5.5.2 on page 146).

One nice consequence of this approach is that it allows client code to be terse most of the time and verbose only when it must. In the previous example, `main.d` might simply invoke `fun` without any adornment:

```
// This is main.d
import widget;

void main() {
    fun(10); // Fine, only module widget defines fun
}
```

Let's say the file `io.d` also defines a function called `fun` with a similar signature:

```
// This is io.d in directory acme/goodies
void fun(long n) {
    ...
}
```

and then let's have `main` import both `widget.d` and `io.d`. Then an unadorned use of `fun` is in error, but qualified calls that specify the module name work properly:

```
// This is main.d
import widget, acme.goodies.io;

void main() {
```

```
fun(10); // Error!
        // Ambiguous function fun()
        //    found in widget and acme.goodies.io
  widget.fun(10);          // Fine, explicit resolution
  acme.goodies.io.fun(10); // Fine, explicit resolution
}
```

Notice how the ambiguity stays latent. If you never attempt to look up a symbol in an ambiguous manner, the compiler never complains.

### 11.1.3.1 Cross-Module Function Overloading

Chapter 5 (§ 5.5.2 on page 146 to be precise) discusses how function overloading applies across modules and gives an example in which modules defining a function with the same name do not necessarily generate any ambiguity at all. It is worth bringing closure to that discussion now that we know more about modules and modularity.

*Function hijacking* is one particularly subtle breach of modularity. Function hijacking occurs when a function in a module competes and takes over calls from a function in a different module. The typical manifestation is that a working module does different things depending on the inclusion of other modules, or on the order in which the modules are included.

Hijacking may occur as an unfortunate curdling of otherwise sound and well-intended rules. To wit, in the example above where widget defines fun(int) and acme.goodies.io defines fun(long), it seems sensible to decide that the call fun(10) made in main should go to widget.fun because that's the "better" match. However, this is one of the cases in which the better is the enemy of the good. If main imports only acme.goodies.io, then fun(10) is naturally passed to acme.goodies.io.fun as the only candidate. If, however, widget appears in the picture, fun(10) suddenly goes to widget.fun. In effect, widget both arbitrates and partakes in a contract that was initially meant to be between main and acme.goodies.io—a horrible breach of modularity.

No wonder languages are shunning hijacking. C++ allows function hijacking but most style guides advise to avoid it; Python and many other languages do not allow any hijacking at all. On the other hand, too much avoidance may lead to overly rigid rules that foster long strings of symbols in names.

D resolves hijacking in an original manner. The basic principle guiding D's approach to cross-module overloading is that adding or removing imports can't change the decision of resolving a function name. Fiddling with imports could cause compilable modules to stop compiling, and uncompilable modules to become compilable. The eliminated dangerous scenario is that in which playing with imports keeps the program compilable but with different overloading resolutions.

For any function call found in a module, if the function name is found in more than one module, *and* if the call would work in both modules, that call is in error. If, on the other hand, only one resolution could lead to a working function call, the call is legit because there is no hijacking risk.

In the given example, if widget defines fun(int) and acme.goodies.io defines fun(long), in module main the state of affairs is as follows:

```
import widget, acme.goodies.io;

void main() {
    fun(10);     // Error! Ambiguous cross-module overloading!
    fun(10L);    // Fine, unambiguously goes to acme.goodies.io.fun
    fun("10");   // Error! No match!
}
```

Adding or removing one of widget or acme.goodies.io in the import line may make a broken program work, or break a working program, or leave a working program still working—in the latter case, never with different decisions for calls to fun.

### 11.1.4  public import Declarations

By default, lookup of symbols in imported modules is not transitive; that is, in the directory hierarchy in Figure 11.1 on page 339, if module main imports module widget and module widget in turn imports module acme.gadget, then the lookup of a symbol starting from main will *not* search module acme.gadget. Whatever modules widget imports are only an implementation detail of widget, of no concern to main.

Sometimes, however, module widget is an enhancement of another module, or makes sense only in conjunction with another module. For example, widget's definitions may use and require so many of acme.goodies.io's definitions, it would be useless for any other module to use widget without also importing acme.goodies.io. In such cases, you may want to help the client by using the public import declaration:

```
// This is widget.d
// Make symbols in acme.goodies.io visible to widget's clients
public import acme.goodies.io;
```

The public import declaration shown makes all symbols defined by acme/goodies/io.d visible from modules that import widget.d (attention) *as if* widget.d *defined them itself.* Essentially public import adds an alias declaration in widget.d for each symbol in io.d. (There is no source or object code duplication, only a symbol duplication of sorts.) To wit, let's assume io.d defines a function print(string), and let's write this code in main.d:

```
import widget;

void main() {
```

```
    print("Hello");          // Fine, lookup finds print
    widget.print("Hello");   // Fine, widget effectively defines print
}
```

What if you actually imported `acme.goodies.io` from `main` as well? Let's try this:

```
import widget;
import acme.goodies.io;     // Redundant but harmless

void main() {
    print("Hello");                     // Fine ...
    widget.print("Hello");              // ... fine ...
    acme.goodies.io.print("Hello");     // ... and fine!
}
```

No harm has been done to `io.d`: the fact that `widget` defines an alias of `acme.good-ies.io.print` does not affect the original symbol in the least. The extra alias is simply an alternative means to reach the same definition.

Finally, you may see some older code using `private import`. That use is accepted and is synonymous with plain `import`.

### 11.1.5 `static import` Declarations

On occasion, the fact that any `import` declaration also adds the imported module to the implicit lookup list (per the algorithm in § 11.1.3 on page 341) may be undesirable. Sometimes it is sensible to want access to the functionality defined by a module only with explicit symbol qualification (à la `modulename.symbolname` as opposed to just `symbolname`).

The simplest case when such a decision would be sensible is using a very popular module in conjunction with a special-purpose module that overlaps several symbols in the former. For example, the standard module `std.string` defines widely used string-related routines. If you interface with a legacy system that uses a different encoding (e.g., double-byte character set aka DBCS), then you'd want to use the symbols in `std.string` most of the time, and use the symbols in your own `dbcs_string` module only occasionally and explicitly. To do so, just specify `static` with the `import` declaration for `dbcs_string`:

```
import std.string;          // Defines string toupper(string)
static import dbcs_string;  // Also defines string toupper(string)

void main() {
    auto s1 = toupper("hello");              // Fine
    auto s2 = dbcs_string.toupper("hello");  // Fine
```

```
}
```

To be more specific, if the code above didn't `import std.string`, the first call would simply fail. There is no automated lookup with `static import`, even when the symbol would be unambiguously resolved.

There are other situations when `static import` is helpful. A module `importing` a dozen others may want to rein in automated lookup and go with a more verbose but also more explicit approach. In such cases, it is useful to use `static` with comma-separated lists:

```
static import teleport, time_travel, warp;
```

or prefix a bracketed scope with `static` to the same effect:

```
static {
    import teleport;
    import time_travel, warp;
}
```

### 11.1.6 Selective imports

Another effective way of dealing with symbol clashing is to `import` only certain symbols from a module. This can be achieved with the following syntax:

```
// This is main.d
import widget : fun, gun;
```

Selective imports are laser-surgically precise: the `import` request above introduces exactly *two* symbols, namely, `fun` and `gun`. Even `widget` is not visible after the selective import! Let's assume that module `widget` defines symbols `fun`, `gun`, and `hun`. In that case, you can use `fun` and `gun` only as if `main` defined them. Any other attempts, such as `hun`, `widget.hun`, and even `widget.fun`, are invalid:

```
// This is main.d
import widget : fun, gun;

void main() {
    fun();          // Fine
    gun();          // Fine
    hun();          // Error!
    widget.fun();   // Error!
    widget.hun();   // Error!
}
```

The high precision and control of selective `import` makes it quite popular—there are programmers who swear by it, particularly if coming from languages with weaker importing and visibility mechanisms. It should be mentioned, however, that the other disambiguation mechanisms provided by D, mentioned above, are definitely no slouch. Total control of `imported` symbols would be much more of a relief if D used an error-prone default lookup mechanism.

### 11.1.7  Renaming in `imports`

Large projects tend to create quite involved package hierarchies. Overly baroque directory structures are a frequent design artifact, particularly in designs that want to establish up front a generous, comprehensive naming scheme that has stability in the face of unforeseen additions to the project. Therefore, it's not infrequent that a module finds itself in the situation of using a deeply nested module:

```
import util.container.finite.linear.list;
```

In such situations, a *renamed import* can be very useful because it allows you to assign a short name to `util.container.finite.linear.list`:

```
import list = util.container.finite.linear.list;
```

With such an `import` declaration in tow, the program can use `list.symbol` instead of the much longer `util.container.finite.linear.list.symbol`. Assuming the discussed module defines a class `List`, here's the resulting state of affairs:

```
import list = util.container.finite.linear.list;

void main() {
    auto lst1 = new list.List;                                  // Fine
    auto lst2 = new util.container.finite.linear.list.List;     // Error!
        // Undefined symbol util!
    auto lst3 = new List;                                       // Error!
        // Undefined symbol List!
}
```

The renaming `import` does not make the renamed packages (i.e., `util`, `container`, ..., `list`) visible, so attempting to use the lengthy name in the definition of `lst2` fails at the very first lookup of `util`. Also, the renamed `import` is effectively of the `static` kind (§ 11.1.5 on page 345), meaning that it does not allow automatic searching; that's why evaluating `new List` does not work. If you do want to make names visible in addition to renaming, `alias` (§ 7.4 on page 276) comes in very handy:

```
import util.container.finite.linear.list;        // Non-static
alias util.container.finite.linear.list list;    // For convenience
```

```
void main() {
    auto lst1 = new list.List;                              // Fine
    auto lst2 = new util.container.finite.linear.list.List; // Fine
    auto lst3 = new List;                                   // Fine
}
```

Renaming may also be used in conjunction with selective imports (§ 11.1.6 on page 346) like this:

```
import std.stdio : say = writeln;

void main() {
    say("Hello, world!");                   // Fine, call writeln
    std.stdio.say("Hello, world");          // Error!
    writeln("Hello, world!");               // Error!
    std.stdio.writeln("Hello, world!");     // Error!
}
```

As expected, after a selective import that also renames the symbol being imported, only the resulting name is visible, nothing else.

Finally, it's possible to rename *both* the module and the imported symbol(s):

```
import io = std.stdio : say = writeln, CFile = File;
```

The possible interactions between the two renamed imported symbols could engender a few contradictions. D's decision was to simply make the declaration above synonymous with

```
import io = std.stdio : writeln, File;
import std.stdio : say = writeln, CFile = File;
```

The doubly renaming import is equivalent to two others. One renames only the module, and the other renames only the symbols being introduced. This allows definition of semantics in terms of simpler, already known forms of import. The declaration above introduces symbols io.writeln, io.File, say, and CFile.

### 11.1.8   The module Declaration

As discussed in § 11.1 on page 337, D packages and modules that aspire to ever be importable must have names that are valid D symbols for the simple reason that import accepts only symbols.

There are a few select situations when you'd want a module to masquerade under a different module name from the file name, and a different package path from the path where the file actually resides. The simplest situation is when you have a module bearing a name that's not a valid D symbol.

Say, for example, you write a program that adheres to a larger naming convention involving dashes, for example, `gnome-cool-app.d`. Then the D compiler will refuse to compile it, even if the program is entirely correct. This is because D must generate information for each module during compilation, each module must have a name, and `gnome-cool-app` is not a valid name. A simple workaround would be to keep the source file under a different name, such as `gnome_cool_app.d`, and then rename the resulting executable as part of the build process. This definitely works, but there's a simpler and better way: just insert a `module` declaration at the beginning of the file. The `module` declaration looks like this:

```
module gnome_cool_app;
```

If such a declaration is present in `gnome-cool-app.d` (but again, only as the first declaration of the file), then the compiler is happy because it generates all module information using the name `gnome_cool_app`. For that matter, the actual name is not checked in any way; it may even be

```
module path.to.nonexistent.location.app;
```

In this case, the compiler will generate all module-level information as if the module were called `app.d` and lived in a path `path/to/nonexistent/location`. The compiler doesn't care because it does not locate that path—searching for files is associated only with `import`, and here there is no `import` in the direct compilation of `gnome-cool-app.d`.

### 11.1.9 Module Summaries

D fosters a development model that does not require separate declarations for the entities defined by a program (the "headers" and "sources" found in C and C++). You simply put code in a module and have other modules `import` that module. On occasion, however, you'd want to adopt a development model that enforces a stronger separation between the signatures that a module must implement and the code behind those signatures. In that case you need to work with the so-called *module summaries* from source code. A module summary is the minimum a module needs to know about another module in order to use it.

Practically, a module summary is a module without comments and function implementations. The implementations for functions using compile-time parameters are, however, kept as part of the module summary. This is because functions with compile-time parameters must be available during compilation for unforeseen instantiations in the client module.

Module summaries are valid D code. For example, consider the module

```
/**
This is a documentation comment for this module
*/
module acme.doitall;

/**
This is a documentation comment for class A
*/
class A {
   void fun() { ... }
   final void gun() { ... }
}

class B(T) {
   void hun() { ... }
}

void foo() {
   ...
}

void bar(int n)(float x) {
   ...
}
```

The module summary for `doitall` copies the module eliminating all comments and replacing all function bodies with ; except for the compile-time-parameterized functions, which are left intact:

```
module acme.doitall;

class A {
   void fun();
   final void gun();
}

class B(T) {
   void hun() { ... }
}

void foo();
```

```
void bar(int n)(float x) {
    ...
}
```

The summary contains the information that some module needs in order to use acme.doitall. Most of the time, the summary is managed internally by the compiler. Upon request, the compiler can generate the summary from source (using the -H flag on the reference implementation dmd). Generated summaries are useful when, for example, you want to distribute a library as headers plus a compiled library.

Notice, however, that elimination of function bodies is not guaranteed. The compiler is free to keep the bodies of very short functions for inlining purposes. For example, if acme.doitall.foo has an empty body or just calls another function, its body may be present in the generated interface file.

A development setup familiar to users of the C and C++ programming languages is to maintain manually separate header files (i.e., summaries) and implementation files. That approach entails some more work but enables certain team management techniques. For example, write access to header files could be confined to the design team, which controls all details of the APIs that modules offer to one another. The implementation team has write access to the implementation files but read-only access to the header files, which are used as active documentation guiding the implementation. The compiler verifies that the implementation conforms to the interface (well, syntactically at least).

With D you have a choice—you can (a) do away with module summaries altogether; (b) let the compiler generate them for you; or (c) manage modules and module summaries by hand. All examples in this book took option (a) of leaving the compiler to worry about figuring out everything about module summaries. To exercise the other two possibilities, you would first need to arrange modules in a hierarchy similar to that in Figure 11.2 on the next page.

Code using acme needs to add the parent directory of acme and acme_impl to the project's module searching roots (§ 11.1.2 on page 340) and then import modules in acme by using

```
// This is client.d
import acme.algebra;
import acme.io.network;
```

The acme directory includes only the summary files. To get the implementation files to cooperate, they'd have to have the module names prefixed by package acme, not acme_impl, and here's where module declarations come in handy. Even though algebra.d sits in acme_impl, it can claim it really sits in acme by including this declaration:

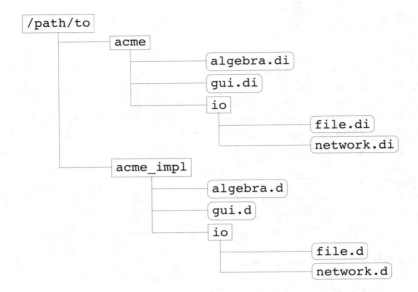

**Figure 11.2:** Directory structure for separating module summaries ("headers") from implementation files.

```
// This is acme_impl/algebra.d
module acme.algebra;
```

Correspondingly, modules in sub-package io would use

```
// This is acme_impl/io/file.d
module acme.io.file;
```

This will allow the compiler to generate the proper package and module names. To make the compiler find the function bodies during building the program, just pass the implementation files to the compiler:

```
% dmd client.d /path/to/acme_impl/algebra.d
```

The import directive in `client.d` will locate the interface file `acme.di` in directory `/path/to/acme`. Also, the compiler finds the implementation file as explicitly given in the command line, with correct package and module names.

If `client.d` uses many modules in acme, it becomes tenuous to specify all of those modules in the compiler's command line. In such cases, a better option is to package all of acme's code into a binary library and pass only that library to dmd. The syntax for building a library depends on the implementation; on the reference implementation, you'd do something like this:

```
% cd /path/to/acme_impl
% dmd -lib -ofacme algebra.d gui.d io/file.d io/network.d
```

The switch `-lib` instructs the compiler to build a library, and the switch `-of` ("output file") directs the output to a file called `acme.lib` (Windows) or `acme.a` (various Unix-derived systems). With that library in tow, all you have to do now to get client code running is something like

```
% dmd client.d acme.lib
```

If the `acme` library is used extensively, you may want to make it part of the default libraries of the project, an implementation- and system-dependent activity that requires you to read the dreaded manual.

## 11.2 Safety

Safety of programming languages has been historically a controversial notion but has gotten an increasingly focused definition in recent years.

Intuitively, a safe language is one that "protects its own abstractions" [46, Chapter 1]. As an example, consider a D class:

```
class A { int x; }
```

and a D array:

```
float[] array;
```

The D language rules (the "abstraction" provided by the language) have it that changing the x member for any object of type A cannot modify an element of `array`, and vice versa, changing `array[n]` for some n should not exact a change on member x of some object of type A. As reasonable as it seems to disallow such nonsensical operations, there are ways to make both happen in D by forging pointers with `cast` or by playing with `union`.

```
void main() {
    float[] array = new float[1024];
    auto obj = cast(A) array.ptr;
    ...
}
```

Changing one of the elements of `array` (exactly which one is platform-dependent, usually the second or the third) changes `obj.x`.

### 11.2.1   Defined and Undefined Behavior

In addition to the unsavory cast of a pointer to float to a class reference just show-cased, there are other run-time errors that could be reasonably considered failures of the language to deliver on certain promises. Good examples would be dereference of a null pointer, division by zero, or extracting the real square root of a negative number. No correct program should ever perform such operations, and the fact that they still may occur in a typechecked program may be seen as a failure of the type system.

One problem with such "nice to have" criteria for correctness is that the list could go on forever. D focuses its notion of safety around a very precise and useful definition: a safe D program is one that has no undefined behavior. The distinction of defined versus undefined behavior is as follows.

- *Defined behavior:* Execution of a program fragment in a given state has one of a number of defined outcomes. One possible outcome is to end execution abruptly. (This is exactly what happens when dereferencing the null pointer or when dividing integers by zero.)
- *Undefined behavior:* The effect of executing a program fragment in a given state is not defined. This means that anything within the realm of physical possibility could happen. The cast showcased on the previous page is a good example—a program with such a cancerous cell in it could go on for a while, until some write to array followed by a fortuitous use of obj causes execution to spiral out of control. Unchecked out-of-bounds array accesses, arbitrary pointer arithmetic, dangling pointers (§ 4.6 on page 124)—these, too, are examples of undefined behavior.

(Undefined behavior is very much akin to the notion of untrapped errors introduced by Cardelli [15]. He classifies execution errors in two broad categories: *trapped* and *untrapped*. Trapped errors cause execution to stop immediately, whereas untrapped errors cause the program to execute arbitrary instructions. A program with defined behavior may never have an untrapped error.)

There are a couple of interesting nuances regarding defined vs. untrapped behavior. For example, consider a language that defines division by zero for ints to always yield int.min. That makes division by zero defined behavior—albeit with a less than useful definition. Somewhat in the same vein, std.math actually defines sqrt(-1) to return double.nan. That's again defined behavior because double.nan is a well-defined value that is part of the specification of the language and of sqrt. Even division by zero is not an error for floating-point types: it is carefully defined to return either positive infinity, negative infinity, or Not a Number (Chapter 2). Programs would always have reproducible results as far as sqrt or floating-point division is concerned.

A program is safe if it cannot engender undefined behavior.

## 11.2.2 The `@safe`, `@trusted`, and `@system` Attributes

One simple way to make sure that no untrapped errors ever occur is to simply disallow all unsafe D constructs, such as specific uses of `cast`. However, that would mean many systems wouldn't be implementable in D. There are simply times when you must step out of the boundaries of an abstraction and, for example, make memory that seems to have a type into memory of a different type. This is exactly what happens in a memory allocator or a garbage collector. Being able to express such system-level software has always been a goal of D.

On the other hand, many applications need unsafe access to memory only in a highly encapsulated manner. A language may claim to be safe in spite of its garbage collector being implemented in an unsafe language. This is because from the safe language's perspective, there is no possible unsafe use of the collector. The collector itself is encapsulated inside the runtime support, implemented in a different language, and considered a magic primitive by the safe language. Any lack of safety in the garbage collector would be a problem of the implementation, not of the client code.

How could a large project ensure safety for most of its modules and still bend the rules in a few select places? D's approach to safety is to put the user in charge: you can state at declaration level whether code adheres to safety or needs to step outside the confines of safety. Typically you specify the features of a module right after the `module` declaration, like this:

```
module my_widget;
@safe:
...
```

At this time the properties `@safe`, `@trusted`, and `@system` are defined. These properties allow a module to advertise its level of safety. (Such an approach is not new; Modula-3 has a similar approach to distinguishing unsafe modules from safe ones.)

Code falling under the `@safe` attribute commits to using only the safe subset of D. That means

- No `cast` from a pointer type to a non-pointer type (e.g., `int`) and vice versa
- No `cast` between unrelated pointer types
- Bounds checks on all array accesses
- No unions that include pointer type, a `class` type, an array type, or a `struct` embedding such a type
- No pointer arithmetic
- Taking the address of a local is forbidden (in fact the needed restriction is to not allow such an address to escape, but that is more difficult to track)
- Function calls must invoke only other `@safe` or `@trusted` functions
- No inline assembler

- No casting away of `const`, `immutable`, or `shared`
- No use of any `@system` entities

Sometimes these rules may be overly conservative; for example, avoiding escape of pointers to local variables may rule out programs that are demonstrably legit. The power of the `@safe` subset of D (dubbed SafeD) is already considerable—entire applications may be written entirely in SafeD.

A declaration or group of declarations may specify that, on the contrary, low-level access is necessary. Such declarations should specify `@system`:

```
@system:
void * allocate(size_t size);
void deallocate(void* p);
...
```

The `@system` attribute effectively turns off all checks and can harness the unbridled power of the language—for benefit or peril.

Finally, libraries are often in the position of offering safe abstractions to clients, while they themselves use unsafe features inside. Many components of the D's standard library are in this position. Such declarations may be attributed as `@trusted`.

Modules that specify neither property are subject to the default safety choice. That choice is configurable in the compiler's configuration files and command-line options, and the exact way to do so is implementation-dependent. The reference implementation `dmd` makes `@system` the default and allows `@safe` as the default only in the presence of the command-line option `-safe`.

At the time of this writing, SafeD is of alpha quality—meaning that there may be unsafe programs that pass compilation, and safe programs that don't—but is an area of active development.

## 11.3   Module Constructors and Destructors

Sometimes, modules need to run some initialization code that primes some static data in the module. A possible way to achieve that would be to insert explicit tests ("Was this data primed?") everywhere the respective data is accessed. In cases when that may be inconvenient and/or inefficient, use module constructors.

Consider, as an example, that you write some OS-specific module that decides what to do based on a flag. Distinguishing between major operating systems (e.g., "I'm a Mac" versus "I'm a PC") is easily done during compilation. But deciding between different versions of Windows must be done at runtime.

To simplify matters a bit, let's say the code cares only to distinguish among Windows Vista, versions newer than Vista, and versions earlier than Vista. The code that does the detection at module initialization time looks like this:

```d
private enum WinVersion { preVista, vista, postVista }
private WinVersion winVersion;

static this() {
   OSVERSIONINFOEX info = { OSVERSIONINFOEX.sizeof };
   GetVersionEx(&info) || assert(false);
   if (info.dwMajorVersion < 6) {
      winVersion = WinVersion.preVista;
   } else if (info.dwMajorVersion == 6 && info.dwMinorVersion == 0) {
      winVersion = WinVersion.preVista;
   } else {
      winVersion = WinVersion.preVista;
   }
}
```

The hero of this feat is the module constructor `static this()`. Such *module constructors* are always executed before `main`. A given module may contain any number of module constructors.

Conversely, module destructors have predictable syntax:

```d
// At module level
static ~this() {
   ...
}
```

Static destructors execute after `main` finishes execution, be it by normal return or by throwing an exception. A module may define any number of module destructors and may freely interleave module constructors and module destructors.

### 11.3.1 Execution Order within a Module

The order of execution of module constructors within a given module is always top-down (lexical order). The order of execution of module destructors is bottom-up (reverse lexical order).

If one module constructor fails by throwing an exception, `main` is not executed and only the static destructors lexically situated *above* the failing module constructor are executed. If one module destructor fails by throwing an exception, no other module destructor is executed, and the application terminates by printing an error message to the standard error console.

## 11.3.2   Execution Order across Modules

Across different modules, defining an order is more complicated. The rules are identical to those defined for static class constructors (§ 6.3.6 on page 188) and are built around the notion that modules import ed by other modules must be initialized first and cleaned up last. Here are the rules deciding the order of running static constructors of modules moda and modb:

- At most one of moda and modb defines module constructors or module destructors. Then there is no ordering to worry about.
- Neither moda nor modb imports the other. Then the ordering is unspecified—any order works because the two modules don't depend on each other.
- moda imports modb. Then modb's module constructors run before moda's, and modb's module destructors run after moda's.
- modb imports moda. Then moda's module constructors run before modb's, and moda's module destructors run after modb's.
- moda imports modb and modb imports moda. Then a "cyclic dependency" error is signaled and execution is abandoned during program loading.

The check for cyclic module dependency is currently done at runtime. It is possible to detect such cycles during compilation or linking, but that would arguably not be a huge gain: the manifestation of the problem is that the program refuses to load, and it can be presumed that a program is run at least once before being shipped. Nevertheless, it is always better to detect problems earlier rather than later, so the language leaves it up to the implementation to detect and report this illegal situation.

## 11.4   Documentation Comments

Writing documentation is boring, and boredom is a programmer's ultimate anathema. As a result, typical documentation is scarce, incomplete, and out-of-date.

Automated documentation extractors do their best to infer information from the sheer code and to display interesting relationships between entities. However, today's automated extractors have a hard time documenting the high-level intent behind an implementation. Modern languages help the situation by prescribing the so-called *documentation comments*, which are stylized comments describing, for example, a user-defined entity. A language processor (either the compiler itself or a separate program) rummages through the comments in conjunction with the code and generates documentation in some popular format (such as XML, HTML, or PDF).

D defines a documentation comments specification that describes both the format of the stylized comments and the process of transforming them into the target format. The process is not dependent on the target format; a simple and flexible translation template (also defined by the user) directs the translator to generate virtually any needed format.

A full treatment of the documentation comments translation system is beyond the scope of this book. Suffice it to say that you'd be well advised to give it a close look; many D projects and the entire Web site of the reference implementation and its standard library are generated using D's documentation comments.

## 11.5 Interfacing with C and C++

D modules can interface directly with C and C++ functions. The restriction is that template C++ functions are not allowed because that would require the D compiler to include a full-fledged C++ compiler. Also, D's `class` layout is not compatible with C++ classes that use `virtual` inheritance.

To call functions defined in C and C++, simply specify the language in the function declaration and make sure to link your module with the appropriate libraries:

```
extern(C) int foo(char*);
extern(C++) double bar(double);
```

The declarations cue the D compiler to generate calls with the appropriate stack layout, calling convention, and name encoding (aka name mangling), even though D functions themselves are different in some or all of these aspects.

To call D functions from within C and C++, simply provide an implementation with a declaration like the one above:

```
extern(C) int foo(char*) {
    ... // Implementation
}
extern(C++) double bar(double) {
    ... // Implementation
}
```

The compiler, again, generates the proper name mangling and calling convention that fits the client language. The function can therefore be called from foreign and D modules alike.

## 11.6 `deprecated`

Any declaration (type, function, or data) can be prefixed with `deprecated`. The keyword acts like a storage class but does not influence actual code generation in the least. Instead, it only informs the compiler that the marked entity is not supposed to be used. The compiler emits a warning if that entity does get used and may actually refuse compilation if passed the right flag (`-w` for `dmd`).

Using `deprecated` allows you to establish a slow and organized migration path from old versions of APIs to newer versions. After deprecating the appropriate declarations, you can set the compiler to either accept or reject `deprecated` declarations. When you're ready for the step, the errors will pinpoint the work areas and allow incremental code updates.

## 11.7  `version` Declarations

In an ideal world, you write once and run anywhere. Here on Earth, however, you occasionally need to deal with sources of variability in your program—be they library versions, special-purpose builds, or platform dependencies. To help with that, D defines a `version` declaration that you can use to conditionally compile code.

Using `version` is deliberately simple and straightforward. You either set a version or you test for it. The version itself can be an integer constant or a symbol:

```
version = 20100501;
version = FinalRelease;
```

To test for a version, write this:

```
version(20100501) {
    ... // Declarations
}
version (PreFinalRelease) {
    ... // Declarations
} else {
    ... // More declarations
}
```

If a `version` has been previously assigned, the declarations guarded by the test are compiled; otherwise, they are ignored. A `version` may have an `else` clause with the obvious meaning.

You can set a version only before any read of that version. Attempting to set a `version` after it has been tested is a compile-time error:

```
version (ProEdition) {
    ... // Declarations
}
version = ProEdition; // Error!
```

This is because version assignments are not supposed to be mutable—a `version` must be the same regardless of the portion of the program you're looking at.

In addition to specifying `version` inside source files, you may do so in the compiler's command line (`-version=123` or `-version=xyz` for the reference implementation dmd). Attempting to set a `version` in both the command line and a source file is, again, in error.

The simplicity of `version` is not incidental. It would have been easy to make `version` more powerful in many ways, but that would soon have started to work against its purpose. For example, C's version handling by using `#if/#elif/#else` offers arguably more possible tactics in defining versioning—which is exactly why versioning in the typical C project has some tangled hairballs of conditional compiles. D's `version` is intentionally underpowered in order to support only simple, uniform versioning.

Compilers routinely feature a number of predefined `versions`, such as the platform (e.g., `Win32`, `Posix`, or `Mac`), endianness (`LittleEndian`, `BigEndian`), and more. `version(unittest)` is already defined when the program has unit testing enabled. The special running symbols `__FILE__` and `__LINE__` denote the current file name and line in the file, respectively. Consult your compiler's documentation for a complete list of `version` definitions.

## 11.8  debug Declarations

A `debug` declaration is a specialized `version` with identical assignment and test syntaxes. The debug was defined especially to standardize the manner in which programs define their debugging mode and facilities.

A typical use of `debug` is as follows:

```
module mymodule;
...
void fun() {
   int x;
   ...
   debug(mymodule) writeln("x=", x);
   ...
}
```

If you want to debug `mymodule`, define `-debug=mymodule` in the command line when you compile that module, and `debug(mymodule)` will evaluate to `true`, compiling all guarded code. Just as with `version`, you cannot assign a `debug` symbol after you have tested for it.

## 11.9  D's Standard Library

D's standard library, code-named Phobos, has evolved organically together with the language. As such, it includes older-style APIs and also newfangled library artifacts using the language's newer features.

The library consists of two main packages, `core` and `std`. The first contains the fundamental runtime support, including the implementations of built-in types, the garbage collector, the startup and shutdown code, the support for concurrency, the definitions needed for accessing the C runtime library, and other related components. The `std` package contains higher-level functionality. The advantage of this setup is that other libraries may plug in on top of `core` and coexist with `std` without requiring it.

The `std` package has a flat structure—most modules lie straight in that package. Modules are dedicated to functional areas. Table 11.2 highlights and discusses a few of the more important Phobos modules.

**Table 11.2:** Standard Modules Summary

| Module name | Description |
| --- | --- |
| std.algorithm | This module is arguably the flagship of the powerful generic programming capabilities of the language and is inspired by C++'s Standard Template Library (STL) [51]. It contains over 70 important algorithms, implemented in very general terms. Most algorithms concern structured sequences of identical elements. In the STL the basic sequence abstraction is the iterator, whereas in D the corresponding primitive is the *range*. A brief overview wouldn't do the subject justice; comprehensive introductions to D's ranges are available online [3]. |
| std.array | Convenience functions for array manipulation |
| std.bigint | Variable-length integer with a heavily optimized implementation |
| std.bitmanip | Low-level bit manipulation types and routines |
| std.concurrency | Concurrency-related facilities, discussed in detail in Chapter 13 |
| std.container | Implementations of various containers |
| std.complex | Complex numbers. Historically, complex numbers have been a built-in feature. Advances in the language and in compiler technology permitted a switch to a library implementation without significant loss of efficiency. |
| std.contracts | The home of a few contract-related and error handling facilities, notably `enforce`, which is used fairly often throughout this book |
| std.conv | A one-stop shop for all conversion-related needs. Many useful functions such as `to` and `text` are defined here. |
| std.date | Date and time amenities |
| std.file | File utilities. This module generally manipulates files as a unit; for example, there is a function `std.file.read` that reads an entire file, but `std.file` has no notion of opening a file and reading from it in small chunks. (See also `std.stdio` below.) |
| std.functional | Functional definition and composition primitives |

**Table 11.2:** Standard Modules Summary *(continued)*

| Module name | Description |
| --- | --- |
| std.getopt | Command-line parsing |
| std.json | Handling of the JSON data format |
| std.math | Highly optimized math routines |
| std.numeric | General numeric algorithms and kernels |
| std.path | File path manipulation utilities |
| std.random | A variety of random number generators |
| std.range | Range-related definitions and classification primitives |
| std.regex | Regular expression engine |
| std.stdio | The standard I/O library facilities, built on top of C's stdio library. Input and output files offer range-style interfaces, which means that many of the algorithms defined in std.algorithm can operate directly on files. |
| std.string | String-specific functions. Strings are highly integrated with std.algorithm, so this module is relatively small and mostly emphasizes (by defining aliases) the bits of std.algorithm applicable to strings. |
| std.traits | Type traits and introspection |
| std.typecons | Facilities for defining new types such as Tuple |
| std.utf | Functions for manipulating UTF encodings |
| std.variant | Discriminated union types |

# Operator Overloading

We programmers tend to dislike excessive separation between built-in types and user-defined types. Endowing built-in types with magic properties works against the openness and extensibility of any language because user-defined types are forever condemned to second-class status. Yet language designers have legitimate reasons to give built-in types the red carpet treatment. One such reason is that a language that's too configurable becomes difficult to teach and also difficult to parse both by the human and by the machine. Each language tries to strike a good balance between the built-in and the configurable, some making it a point to get close to one of the two extremes.

D's take on the matter is pragmatic: it recognizes the importance of configurability, but also the practicality of built-in types. More specifically, D takes advantage of built-in types in exactly three ways:

1. *Type name syntax:* Arrays and associative arrays are used all over the place, and let's face it, `int[]` and `int[string]` look better than `Array!int` and `AssociativeArray!(string, int)`. User code does not have the ability to define new ways of expressing type names such as, for example, `int[[]]`.
2. *Literals:* Numeric, string, array, and associative array literals are "special"—their set cannot be extended. Constructed `struct` objects such as `Point(5, 3)` are literals, too, but a type cannot define new literal syntax such as `(3, 5)pt`.
3. *Semantics:* The compiler uses knowledge of the semantics of certain types and their operations to optimize code. For example, `"Hello" ~ ", " ~ "world"` does not execute any concatenation at runtime because the compiler knows what concatenation does on strings and fuses the strings during compilation. Similarly, the compiler uses knowledge of arithmetic to simplify and optimize arithmetic expressions.

Some languages add operators to this list. They make operators special; in order to do any operation against user-defined types you must use the standard language facilities, such as invoking functions or macros. Though that's a perfectly legitimate decision, it does create problems for a host of numeric code. Many numeric programs define their own types with algebras (infinite-precision numbers, custom floats, complex numbers, quaternions, octonions, vectors, matrices of various layouts, tensors ... the language can't reasonably make them all built-in). For such types, code expressiveness suffers a steep decay. Operators typically require less space and fewer parentheses than the equivalent functional syntax and often yield code that's instantly recognizable. Consider, for example, computing the harmonic mean of three nonzero numbers x, y, and z. The operator-based expression is very close to the mathematical definition:

```
m = 3 / (1/x + 1/y + 1/z);
```

In a language that requires function calls instead of operators, things don't look that good at all:

```
m = divide(3, add(add(divide(1, x), divide(1, y)), divide(1, z)));
```

Code containing many such arithmetic operations quickly becomes much more difficult to read and modify than code using infix operators.

D is a very appealing language for numeric programming. It has solid floating-point arithmetic and an excellent library of transcendental functions that sometimes yield better precision than system-native libraries, and it offers elaborate modeling abilities. That appeal is enhanced by a powerful operator overloading facility. With operator overloading you can define your own numeric types (such as fixed-point or decimal for financial and accounting programs, unbound integers, or infinite-precision reals) that closely mimic built-in numeric types. Operator overloading also offers the ability to define types that have numeric-like algebras, such as vectors and matrices. Let's see how to define types that make use of this feature.

## 12.1    Overloading Operators

D's approach to operator overloading is simple: whenever at least one participant in an operator expression is of user-defined type, the compiler *rewrites* the expression into a regular method call with a specific name. Then the regular language rules apply. As such, overloaded operators are nothing but syntactic sugar for method calls, so there is no need to learn the vagaries of a full-blown language feature. For example, if a has some user-defined type, the expression a + 5 is rewritten as a.opBinary!"+"(5). The usual checks and rules apply to the method opBinary, which a's type must define if it wants to support operator overloading.

Rewriting (or more precisely *lowering* because the process transforms higher-level constructs to lower-level code) is a very effective tool for implementing new features on top of existing ones, and D uses it a fair amount. We've seen lowering at work for the `scope` statement (§ 3.13 on page 84). Essentially `scope` is just sugar over specially crafted `try` statements, but you certainly wouldn't want to write the lowered code directly—`scope` raises the level of discourse considerably. Operator overloading continues in the same tradition by defining all operator invocations in terms of rewrites to function calls, thereby leveraging regular function definitions. Without further ado, let's see how the compiler lowers different categories of operators.

## 12.2 Overloading Unary Operators

For the unary operators + (plus), - (negate), ~ (bitwise "not"), * (pointer dereference), ++ (increment), and -- (decrement), the compiler rewrites the expression

```
‹op› a
```

to

```
a.opUnary!"‹op›"()
```

for all values of user-defined types. The rewrite is an invocation of method `opUnary` against a with one compile-time argument "`‹op›`" and no runtime arguments. For example, ++a is rewritten as `a.opUnary!"++"()`.

To overload one or more unary operators for a type `T`, define a method called `T.opUnary` with the following signature:

```
struct T {
    SomeType opUnary(string op)();
}
```

The method as defined above would be called for all unary operators. If you want to define separate methods for certain operators, signature constraints (§ 5.4 on page 140) can help. Consider, for example, defining a `CheckedInt` type that wraps the primitive numeric types and makes sure their operations never go out of bounds. `CheckedInt` should be parameterized on the wrapped type (e.g., `CheckedInt!int`, `CheckedInt!long`, etc.). A partial definition of `CheckedInt` along with its preincrement and predecrement operators is shown here:

```
struct CheckedInt(N) if (isIntegral!N) {
    private N value;
    ref CheckedInt opUnary(string op)() if (op == "++") {
        enforce(value != value.max);
        ++value;
        return this;
    }
}
```

```
   ref CheckedInt opUnary(string op)() if (op == "--") {
      enforce(value != value.min);
      --value;
      return this;
   }
   ...
}
```

### 12.2.1   Using `mixin` to Consolidate Operator Definitions

A very powerful technique allows defining not one, but a bunch of operators in one shot.
For example, `CheckedInt`'s unary operators +, -, and ~ all do the same thing—they just
forward the respective operation to the `value` member. Although they are not identical,
they certainly follow the same pattern. We could just define one specialized method
for each, but that results in duplication of uninteresting boilerplate code. A better way
is to use string `mixins` (§ 2.3.4.2 on page 47) to directly assemble the operations from
the operand names and the operator symbol. The code below implements all relevant
unary operators for `CheckedInt`.

```
struct CheckedInt(N) if (isIntegral!N) {
   private N value;
   this(N value) {
      this.value = value;
   }
   CheckedInt opUnary(string op)()
         if (op == "+" || op == "-" || op == "~") {
      return CheckedInt(mixin(op ~ "value"));
   }
   bool opUnary(string op)() if (op == "!") {
      return !value;
   }
   ref CheckedInt opUnary(string op)() if (op == "++" || op == "--") {
      enum limit = op == "++" ? N.max : N.min;
      enforce(value != limit);
      mixin(op ~ "value");
      return this;
   }
   ...
}
```

The savings in code size are already obvious and only get better once we get to binary operators and indexing expressions. The star of the approach is the `mixin` expres-

sion, which allows you to take a string and ask the compiler to compile it. The string is obtained by literally putting together by hand the operand and the operator. The serendipitous availability of string op virtually enables the idiom; in fact, the whole feature was designed with mixin in mind. Historically, D used a separate name for each operator (opAdd, opSub, opMul ...), an approach that required rote memorization of the correspondence of names to operators and writing a bunch of functions with near-identical bodies.

### 12.2.2 Postincrement and Postdecrement

The postincrement (a++) and postdecrement (a--) operators are odd—they use the same symbols as their "pre" counterparts, so distinguishing by symbol does not help. An additional challenge is that the caller fetching the result of the operator must see the old value of the incremented entity. Finally, increment and decrement must be consistent over their pre- and post- versions.

Postincrement and postdecrement can be generated entirely from preincrement and predecrement respectively by means of a little boilerplate code. Instead of requiring you to write that boilerplate code, D writes it for you. The rewrite of a++ is performed as follows (postdecrement handling is similar):

- If the result of a++ is not needed, the rewrite is ++a, which is subsequently rewritten to a.opUnary!"++"().
- If the result of a++ is taken (for example, arr[a++]), the rewrite is (let's take a deep breath here) ((ref x) {auto t=x; ++x; return t;})(a).

The first case simply acknowledges that postincrement without using the result is the same as preincrement. The second case defines a lambda function (§ 5.6 on page 148) that handles the needed boilerplate: create a fresh copy of the input, increment the input, and return the copy. The lambda function is immediately applied to the value being incremented.

### 12.2.3 Overloading the cast Operator

The explicit cast is a unary operator spelled cast(T) a. It is a bit different from all others in that it specifies a type, and therefore it has a dedicated lowering. For a value val of some user-defined type and some other type T,

```
cast(T) val
```

is rewritten as

```
val.opCast!T()
```

The `opCast` implementation should of course return a value of type `T`, a detail enforced by the compiler. Although overloading of functions by return value is not allowed, constrained templates do allow multiple `opCast` definitions. For example, to define `cast` to `string` and `cast` to `int` for some type `T`, you'd write

```
struct T {
    string opCast(T)() if (is(T == string)) {
        ...
    }
    int opCast(T)() if (is(T == int)) {
        ...
    }
}
```

You can define `casting` to an entire category of types. Let's build on the `CheckedInt` example by defining `casting` to all built-in integral types. The trick is that some of those types may have a more restrictive range, and we want to `enforce` that there is no loss in the conversion. An additional challenge is that we want to avoid `enforceing` unless necessary (for example, there's no need to check bounds on a conversion from `CheckedInt!int` to `long`). Since the bounds information is present during compilation, we can avail ourselves of `static if` (§ 3.4 on page 68) to insert only the necessary `enforcements`.

```
struct CheckedInt(N) if (isIntegral!N) {
    private N value;
    // Conversions to all integrals
    N1 opCast(N1)() if (isIntegral!N1) {
        static if (N.min < N1.min) {
            enforce(N1.min <= value);
        }
        static if (N.max > N1.max) {
            enforce(N1.max >= value);
        }
        // It is now safe to do a raw cast
        return cast(N1) value;
    }
    ...
}
```

### 12.2.4  Overloading Ternary Operator Tests and `if` Tests

Given a value a of user-defined type, the compiler rewrites code of the shape

```
a ? ‹expr₁› : ‹expr₂›
```

into

```
cast(bool) a ? ‹expr₁› : ‹expr₂›
```

Similarly, the compiler rewrites a test inside of an `if` statement from

```
if (a) ‹stmt› // With or without an else clause
```

to

```
if (cast(bool) a) ‹stmt›
```

The negation operator `!` is also rewritten as the negation of the `cast`.
To enable such tests, define the `cast` to `bool`, like this:

```
struct MyArray(T) {
    private T[] data;
    bool opCast(T)() if (is(T == bool)) {
        return !data.empty;
    }
    ...
}
```

## 12.3  Overloading Binary Operators

For binary operators + (addition), - (subtraction), * (multiplication), / (division), %
(modulus), & (bitwise "and"), | (bitwise "or"), ^ (bitwise "xor"), << (left shift), >> (right
shift), >>> (unsigned right shift), ~ (concatenation), and `in` (set membership test), the
expression

```
a ‹op› b
```

where at least one of a and b has a user-defined type, is rewritten as

```
a.opBinary!"‹op›"(b)
```

and also

```
b.opBinaryRight!"‹op›"(a)
```

If exactly one of these invocations passes lookup and overloading checks, that
rewrite is chosen. If both invocations are valid, that's an ambiguity error. If no invocation is valid, obviously that's a "symbol not found" error.

Continuing our `CheckedInt` example in § 12.2 on page 367, let's define all binary operators:

```d
struct CheckedInt(N) if (isIntegral!N) {
   private N value;
   // Addition
   CheckedInt opBinary(string op)(CheckedInt rhs) if (op == "+") {
      auto result = value + rhs.value;
      enforce(rhs.value >= 0 ? result >= value : result < value);
      return result;
   }
   // Subtraction
   CheckedInt opBinary(string op)(CheckedInt rhs) if (op == "-") {
      auto result = value - rhs.value;
      enforce(rhs.value >= 0 ? result <= value : result > value);
      return result;
   }
   // Multiplication
   CheckedInt opBinary(string op)(CheckedInt rhs) if (op == "*") {
      auto result = value * rhs.value;
      enforce(value && result / value == rhs.value ||
          rhs.value && result / rhs.value == value ||
          result == 0);
      return result;
   }
   // Division and remainder
   CheckedInt opBinary(string op)(CheckedInt rhs)
          if (op == "/" || op == "%") {
      enforce(rhs.value != 0);
      return CheckedInt(mixin("value" ~ op ~ "rhs.value"));
   }
   // Shift
   CheckedInt opBinary(string op)(CheckedInt rhs)
          if (op == "<<" || op == ">>" || op == ">>>") {
      enforce(rhs.value >= 0 && rhs.value <= N.sizeof * 8);
      return CheckedInt(mixin("value" ~ op ~ "rhs.value"));
   }
   // Bitwise (unchecked, can't overflow)
   CheckedInt opBinary(string op)(CheckedInt rhs)
          if (op == "&" || op == "|" || op == "^") {
      return CheckedInt(mixin("value" ~ op ~ "rhs.value"));
   }
```

```
    ...
}
```

(Many of the checks could be made cheaper but more machine-dependent by using Intel processors' overflow bit, which is set or cleared by all arithmetic operations.) The code above defines one distinct operator for each operator-specific test. Whenever two or more operators have the same code shape, they are fused together. This is the case for / and % because they both do the same test, for all shift operators, and also for the three bitwise operators, which require no testing. Again, the approach is to assemble the operation as a string and then use `mixin` to compile the string into an expression.

### 12.3.1 Operator Overloading[2]

If operator overloading is allowing types to define their own implementation of operators, then operator overloading overloading, or operator overloading[2], is allowing types to define several overloaded versions of the overloaded operators.

Consider, for example, the expression a * 5, where a has `CheckedInt!int` type. That won't compile because so far `CheckedInt` defines `opBinary` to require a `CheckedInt` on the right-hand side. So the client code would have to write a * `CheckedInt!int(5)` to get the job done, which is quite unpleasant.

The right way to solve this problem is to define one or more additional `opBinary` implementations for `CheckedInt!N`, this time taking type N on the right-hand side. It would appear that defining the new `opBinary` is a fair amount of repetitive work, but in fact it's a one-liner:

```
struct CheckedInt(N) if (isIntegral!N) {
    ... // As before
    // Operations with raw numbers
    CheckedInt opBinary(string op)(N rhs) {
        return opBinary!op(CheckedInt(rhs));
    }
}
```

The simple beauty of the approach is owed to the transformation of the operator into a regular symbol that can then be forwarded to another operator implementation.

### 12.3.2 Commutativity

The presence of `opBinaryRight` is necessary for cases in which the type defining the operator occurs on the right-hand side of an operation, as in 5 * a. In this case, a's type has a chance of hooking the operator by defining `opBinaryRight!"*"(int)`. There is a redundancy involved—if you want to support, for example, operations with an integer on either side (e.g., 5 * a and also a * 5), you need to define `opBinary!"*"(int)` and `opBinaryRight!"*"(int)`, which is wasteful because multiplication is commutative. However, having the language make a decision on operator commutativity may be unnecessarily limiting: the property of commutativity depends on the algebra; for example, * is not commutative for matrices. Therefore the compiler leaves the user to define operators on the left- and right-hand sides separately and declines taking any responsibility for the commutativity of operators.

To support a ‹*op*› b and b ‹*op*› a when one operand converts cheaply to the other's type, the following one-liner suffices.

```
struct CheckedInt(N) if (isIntegral!N) {
   ... // As before
   // Implement right-hand operators
   CheckedInt opBinaryRight(string op)(N lhs) {
      return CheckedInt(lhs).opBinary!op(this);
   }
}
```

All we need to do is obtain the corresponding expression with a `CheckedInt` on the left-hand side. Then the already defined operators kick in.

There are situations in which going through a conversion would require additional superfluous steps. For example, consider 5 * c, where c has type `Complex!double`. The solution above would forward the multiplication to `Complex!double(5) * c`, which would convert 5 to a complex number with the imaginary part equal to zero, and then would unnecessarily get busy with the multiplication of complex numbers, when in fact only two real multiplications would suffice. The result would still be correct, just obtained with more sweat than necessary. For such cases, it's best to decompose the right-hand side operations differently, in commutative and non-commutative operations. The commutative operations can be handled simply by swapping the arguments around. The non-commutative operations can be implemented on a per-case basis either from scratch or by leveraging other already implemented primitives.

```
struct Complex(N) if (isFloatingPoint!N) {
   N re, im;
   // Implement commutative operators
   Complex opBinaryRight(string op)(N lhs)
      if (op == "+" || op == "*")
   {
      // Assumes the left-hand-side operator is implemented
      return opBinary!op(lhs);
   }
   // Implement non-commutative operators by hand
   Complex opBinaryRight(string op)(N lhs) if (op == "-") {
      return Complex(lhs - re, -im);
```

```
    }
    Complex opBinaryRight(string op)(N lhs) if (op == "/") {
        auto norm2 = re * re + im * im;
        enforce(norm2 != 0);
        auto t = lhs / norm2;
        return Complex(re * t, -im * t);
    }
}
```

Other types may choose to group certain operation groups differently, in which case the already described techniques for constraining op can be of help.

## 12.4 Overloading Comparison Operators

For comparison operators (equality and ordering), D follows the design we have encountered for classes (§ 6.8.3 on page 205, § 6.8.4 on page 209). This seems mainly a historically motivated decision, but there are other good reasons to pursue a different design for comparisons from the general opBinary. For one thing, there are very strong relationships between == and != and also between all four of <, <=, >, and >=. Such relationships suggest that the use of two named functions is better than allowing symbol-based code that defines each operator individually. Plus, many more types are likely to define equality and ordering than the full-blown set of operators. In view of that fact, the language provides a small and simple facility for defining comparisons instead of forcing the use of the power tool opBinary.

The rewrite of a == b, where at least one of a and b has user-defined type, proceeds by the following algorithm:

- If a and b are both class types, the rewrite is object.opEquals(a, b). As described in § 6.8.3 on page 205, comparisons between classes obey a little protocol that is implemented by module object in the core library.
- Otherwise, if a.opEquals(b) and b.opEquals(a) resolve to the same function, the rewrite is a.opEquals(b). This could happen when a and b have the same type with the same or with different qualifiers.
- Otherwise, exactly one of a.opEquals(b) and b.opEquals(a) must be compilable and becomes the rewrite.

Expressions using the four ordering comparison operators <, <=, >, and >= are rewritten as follows:

- If a.opCmp(b) and b.opCmp(a) resolve to the same function, the rewrite is a.opCmp(b) ‹*op*› 0.

- Otherwise, exactly one of a.opCmp(b) and b.opCmp(a) must be compilable. If the first is compilable, the rewrite is a.opCmp(b) ‹*op*› 0. Otherwise, the rewrite is 0 ‹*op*› b.opCmp(a).

It is worth mentioning again the reason for the existence of both opEquals and opCmp. At first glance, it would appear that opCmp is sufficient (equality would be a.opCmp(b) == 0). However, whereas most types can define equality, many cannot easily define an inequality relation. For example, matrices or complex numbers do have equality but lack a canonical ordering relation.

## 12.5   Overloading Assignment Operators

Assignment operators include a = b but also in-place binary operators such as a += b and a *= b. We already saw in § 7.1.5.1 on page 256 that

```
a = b
```

is rewritten as

```
a.opAssign(b)
```

For in-place binary operators, the rewrite of

```
a ‹op›= b
```

is

```
a.opOpAssign!"‹op›"(b)
```

The rewrite gives a's type an opportunity to implement in-place operations following the techniques described above. For example, consider implementing += for CheckedInt:

```
struct CheckedInt(N) if (isIntegral!N) {
    private N value;
    ref CheckedInt opOpAssign(string op)(CheckedInt rhs)
            if (op == "+") {
        auto result = value + rhs.value;
        enforce(rhs.value >= 0 ? result >= value : result <= value);
        value = result;
        return this;
    }
    ...
}
```

Three details are worth noting in the definition above. First, `opOpAssign` returns a reference to the current object, which makes it compatible with the way built-in types work. Second, the actual computation is not done in place but instead on the side. The actual state of the object is changed only after the verification has passed. Otherwise, we risk corrupting the current object in case `enforce` throws. Third, the body of the operator is virtually a duplicate of `opBinary!"+"` on page 372. Let's use this last observation to leverage the existing implementations of all binary operators in defining the in-place assignment operators. The definition would look like this:

```
struct CheckedInt(N) if (isIntegral!N) {
    ... // As before
    // Define all assignment operators
    ref CheckedInt opOpAssign(string op)(CheckedInt rhs) {
        value = opBinary!op(rhs).value;
        return this;
    }
}
```

Alternatively, a type might choose to define the binary operators in terms of the assignment operators, which are defined from scratch. Efficiency considerations may drive such a decision; for many types, modifying an object in place uses less space and is faster than creating a new object.

## 12.6 Overloading Indexing Operators

D allows efficient definition of completely abstract arrays: arrays that support all of the operations normally expected from an array but that never expose the address of their elements to client code. Overloading of indexing operators is an essential contributor to that capability. To effect proper indexed access, the compiler distinguishes between element reads and element writes. The latter have an array element as the left-hand side of an assignment operator, be it plain = or an in-place binary operator such as +=.

When no assignment is in effect, the compiler rewrites the expression

```
a[b1, b2,..., bk]
```

into

```
a.opIndex(b1, b2,..., bk)
```

for any number of arguments $k$. It is up to the implementation of the `opIndex` method to decide how many arguments are accepted, what their types should be, and what the return type is.

If the result of an indexing operator is assigned to, the lowering transforms

```
a[b₁, b₂,..., bₖ] = c
```

into

```
a.opIndexAssign(c, b₁, b₂,..., bₖ)
```

If an increment or decrement operator is used against an index expression, the expression

```
‹op› a[b₁, b₂,..., bₖ]
```

where ‹*op*› is either ++ or - -, is rewritten as

```
a.opIndexUnary!"‹op›"(b₁, b₂,..., bₖ)
```

Postincrement and postdecrement are generated automatically from preincrement and predecrement, as described in § 12.2.2 on page 369.

Finally, if an indexed element is modified in place, the lowering transforms

```
a[b₁, b₂,..., bₖ] ‹op›= c
```

into

```
a.opIndexOpAssign!"‹op›"(c, b₁, b₂,..., bₖ)
```

These rewrites give a's type the ability to fully define how indexed elements are accessed and operated upon. Why does the indexed type take responsibility for the assignment operators? An apparently better design would be to just have `opIndex` return a reference to the stored element, for example:

```
struct MyArray(T) {
    ref T opIndex(uint i) { ... }
}
```

Then, whatever assignment and modify-assignment operations T supports will work properly. For example, given a `MyArray!int` named a, the expression a[7] *= 2 would first fetch a `ref int` off `opIndex` and then use that reference to effect multiplication in place by 2. That is, in fact, how built-in arrays work.

Alas, this simple design is flawed. One issue is that many array-like collections wouldn't want to give `ref` access to their members. They would, if at all possible, encapsulate and abstract away the location of their members. The benefits are the usual advantages of information hiding—the container has more freedom to choose the best storage strategy for its elements. A simple example is defining a container holding `bool` objects. If the container were forced to give access to `ref bool`, it would have to store each value at a separate address. If the container can hide away addresses, it can store eight `bool` values in 1 byte.

Another example is that for some containers, data access is indistinguishable from data manipulation. For example, consider a sparse array. Sparse arrays may ostensibly have many millions of elements, but only a handful of them are nonzero, which allows sparse arrays to use space-efficient storage strategies. Now consider the following code:

```
SparseArray!double a;
...
a[8] += 2;
```

What the array should do depends at the same time on the current contents of the array, as well as the new data: if the slot a[8] was previously unfilled, create the slot with value 2; if the slot was filled with value -2, remove the slot because its new value would be zero, which is not stored explicitly; and if the slot contained anything but -2, make the addition and store it back into the slot. There is no way to effect that or even a good part of that if opIndex is required to return a reference.

## 12.7 Overloading Slicing Operators

D arrays offer the slicing operators a[] and a[$b_1$ .. $b_2$] (§ 4.1.3 on page 97). Both of these can be overloaded by user-defined types. The compiler performs lowerings similar to those for the index operator.

When there is no assignment involved, the compiler rewrites a[] into a.opSlice() and a[$b_1$ .. $b_2$] into a.opSlice($b_1$, $b_2$).

Lowerings for slice operations follow the same mold as those defined for arrays. The method names substitute "slice" for "array" throughout: ‹op› a[] is lowered into a.opSliceUnary!"‹op›"(), ‹op› a[$b_1$ .. $b_2$] becomes a.opSliceUnary!"‹op›"($b_1$, $b_2$), a[] = c becomes a.opSliceAssign(c), a[$b_1$ .. $b_2$] = c becomes a.opSliceAssign(c, $b_1$, $b_2$), a[] ‹op›= c becomes a.opSliceOpAssign!"‹op›"(c), and finally a[$b_1$ .. $b_2$] ‹op›= c becomes a.opSliceOpAssign!"‹op›"(c, $b_1$, $b_2$).

## 12.8 The $ Operator

Inside index and slice expressions for built-in arrays, D allows the symbol $ to stand in for the length of the array. For example, a[0 .. $ - 1] selects all but the last element of built-in array a.

Although it seems like quite a minor feature, $ has consistently been an important contributor to people's enjoyment of using D arrays. Conversely, the fact that $ was "magic" and couldn't be overloaded has been a perennial source of irritation—evidence supporting the view that built-in types should seldom have powers inaccessible to user-defined ones.

Operator $ can be overloaded for user-defined types as follows:

- In the expression a[‹*expr*›], where a is a value of user-defined type, if $ occurs in ‹*expr*›, it is rewritten as a.opDollar(). The rewrite is the same whether or not the expression is assigned to.
- In the expression a[‹*expr*$_1$›,..., ‹*expr*$_k$›], if $ occurs in ‹*expr*$_i$›, it is rewritten as a.opDollar!(i)().
- In the expression a[‹*expr*$_1$› .. ‹*expr*$_2$›], if $ occurs in ‹*expr*$_1$› or ‹*expr*$_2$›, it is rewritten as a.opDollar().

If a is the result of an expression, that expression is evaluated only once.

## 12.9  Overloading `foreach`

User-defined types have the ability to essentially define how `foreach` works with them. This is a huge boon for types modeling collections, ranges, streams, and other entities that can be iterated. Better yet, there are two distinct ways in which you can go about it, choosing different trade-offs.

### 12.9.1  `foreach` with Iteration Primitives

One way to define how `foreach` works with your type (`struct` or `class`) is to define three iteration primitives: property `empty` of type `bool` telling whether there are any elements left; property `front` returning the current element being iterated; and method `popFront()` that moves to the next element. A typical implementation of the three primitives is shown here:

```
struct SimpleList(T) {
private:
   struct Node {
      T _payload;
      Node * _next;
   }
   Node * _root;
public:
   @property bool empty() { return !_root; }
   @property ref T front() { return _root._payload; }
   void popFront() { _root = _root._next; }
   ...
}
```

With this definition in hand, iterating a list is as simple as

```
void process(SimpleList!int lst) {
   foreach (value; lst) {
```

```
    ... // Use value of type int
  }
}
```

The compiler rewrites the `foreach` control code into its clumsier but fine-grained `for` loop that uses the three primitives:

```
void process(SimpleList!int lst) {
  for (auto __c = lst; !__c.empty; __c.popFront()) {
    auto value = __c.front;
    ... // Use value of type int
  }
}
```

If you specify `ref` with `value`, the compiler replaces all uses of `value` with calls to `__c.front` throughout the body of the loop. That way, you get to directly replace elements in the list. Of course, your `front` property must return a `ref` itself; otherwise, attempts to use it as an lvalue will be in error.

Last but not least, if the iterated object offers the slice operator with no arguments `lst[]`, `__c` is initialized with `lst[]` instead of `lst`. This is in order to allow "extracting" the iteration means out of a container without requiring the container to define the three iteration primitives.

### 12.9.2  foreach with Internal Iteration

The primitives above expose an iteration interface that client code may use any way it wants. Sometimes it is better to use *internal iteration,* meaning that the iterated entity takes complete control of the iteration process and executes the loop body on its own. Such inversion of control can be useful in a number of instances, particularly when spanning the collection is best done recursively (as is the case for trees).

To effect `foreach` with internal iteration, you need to define a method `opApply` for your `struct` or `class`. For example:

```
import std.stdio;

class SimpleTree(T) {
private:
  T _payload;
  SimpleTree _left, _right;

public:
  this(T payload) {
    _payload = payload;
```

```
    }

    // inorder traversal of the tree
    int opApply(int delegate(ref T) dg) {
        auto result = dg(_payload);
        if (result) return result;
        if (_left) {
            result = _left.opApply(dg);
            if (result) return result;
        }
        if (_right) {
            result = _right.opApply(dg);
            if (result) return result;
        }
        return 0;
    }
}

void main() {
    auto obj = new SimpleTree!int(1);
    obj._left = new SimpleTree!int(5);
    obj._right = new SimpleTree!int(42);
    obj._right._left = new SimpleTree!int(50);
    obj._right._right = new SimpleTree!int(100);
    foreach (i; obj) {
        writeln(i);
    }
}
```

The program effects an inorder traversal of the tree and prints

```
1
5
42
50
100
```

The compiler packages the loop body (in this case { writeln(i); }) as a delegate
and passes it to opApply. The compiler arranges things such that code that breaks out of
the loop prematurely returns 1 out of the delegate, hence the manipulation of result
inside opApply.

With that information in hand, reading opApply is really easy: first apply the body of
the loop to the root node, and then recurse to the left and right nodes.  The simplicity

of implementation is the point, really. If you try to implement tree iteration in terms of empty, front, and popFront, things become significantly more complicated. This is because in opApply the iteration state is maintained implicitly on the call stack. With the three iteration primitives you'll need to maintain that state explicitly.

There is one more detail worth noting in the interaction between foreach and opApply. The variable i used in foreach is made part of the delegate type. Fortunately, the type of that variable and even the number of bound variables used in foreach are completely configurable. If you define opApply to take a delegate of two arguments, you can use foreach like this:

```
foreach (k, v; object) { // Calls object.opApply(k, v)
   ...
}
```

In fact, iteration of keys and values for built-in associative arrays is implemented using opApply. For an associative array of type V[K], the delegate accepted by opApply takes K and ref V as parameters.

## 12.10 Defining Overloaded Operators in Classes

Most of the rewrites above use methods with compile-time parameters such as opBinary(string)(T). Such methods work very well inside classes as well as structs. The only issue is that methods with compile-time parameters are implicitly final and cannot be overridden, so defining a class or an interface with overridable members must take additional steps. The simplest solution is to have opBinary, for example, forward to a regular method that can be overridden:

```
class A {
   // Non-overridable method
   A opBinary(string op)(A rhs) {
      // Forward to an overridable function
      return opBinary(op, rhs);
   }
   // Overridable method, dispatch string at runtime
   A opBinary(string op, A rhs) {
      switch (op) {
         case "+":
            ... // Implement addition
            break;
         case "-":
            ... // Implement subtraction
            break;
         ...
```

```
        }
    }
}
```

This approach is effective but suboptimal because it tests the operator during runtime, an activity that could be carried out during compilation. The following solution eliminates that inefficiency by moving the test inside the generic `opBinary`:

```
class A {
    // Non-overridable method
    A opBinary(string op)(A rhs) {
        // Forward to an overridable function
        static if (op == "+") {
            return opAdd(rhs);
        } else static if (op == "+") {
            return opSubtract(rhs);
        } ...
    }
    // Overridable methods
    A opAdd(A rhs) {
        ... // Implement addition
    }
    A opSubtract(A rhs) {
        ... // Implement subtraction
    }
    ...
}
```

This time there is one overridable method per operator. You may, of course, choose the operators to overload and the ways to group them as needed.

## 12.11 And Now for Something Completely Different: `opDispatch`

Perhaps the most interesting and idiom-enabling rewrite is `opDispatch`, which takes D to places usually reserved for much more dynamic languages.

If a type `T` defines the method `opDispatch`, the compiler will rewrite

```
a.fun(‹arg₁›, ..., ‹argₖ›)
```

into

```
a.opDispatch!"fun"(‹arg₁›, ..., ‹argₖ›)
```

for all would-be methods `fun` that a's type does *not* define, that is, calls that would otherwise result in a "method not defined" error.

The definition of `opDispatch` may implement a number of very interesting designs featuring varying amounts of dynamism. For example, consider an `opDispatch` implementation that implements an alternate naming convention for a `class`' methods. For starters, let's implement a simple function that converts a symbol `written_like_this` to its camel-case counterpart `writtenLikeThis`:

```
import std.ctype;

string underscoresToCamelCase(string sym) {
   string result;
   bool makeUpper;
   foreach (c; sym) {
      if (c == '_') {
         makeUpper = true;
      } else {
         if (makeUpper) {
            result ~= toupper(c);
            makeUpper = false;
         } else {
            result ~= c;
         }
      }
   }
   return result;
}

unittest {
   assert(underscoresToCamelCase("hello_world") == "helloWorld");
   assert(underscoresToCamelCase("_a") == "A");
   assert(underscoresToCamelCase("abc") == "abc");
   assert(underscoresToCamelCase("a_bc_d_") == "aBcD");
}
```

Armed with `underscoresToCamelCase`, we can easily define `opDispatch` for a `class` to convince it to accept calls of the form `a.method_like_this()` and automatically forward them to `a.methodLikeThis()`—all during compilation.

```
class A {
   auto opDispatch(string m, Args...)(Args args) {
      return mixin("this."~underscoresToCamelCase(m)~"(args)");
   }
```

```
    int doSomethingCool(int x, int y) {
        ...
        return 0;
    }
}

unittest {
    auto a = new A;
    a.doSomethingCool(5, 6);    // Straight call
    a.do_something_cool(5, 6);  // Same call going via opDispatch
}
```

The second call does not refer to any of A's methods, so it gets routed through opDispatch via the call `a.opDispatch!"do_something_cool"(5, 6)"`. In turn, opDispatch generates the string `"this.doSomethingCool(args)"` and then compiles it by using mixin. Given that args is bound to the argument pair 5, 6, the mixin is ultimately forwarded to `a.doSomethingCool(5, 6)`—good old forwarding at its best. Mission accomplished.

### 12.11.1  Dynamic Dispatch with `opDispatch`

Although it is certainly interesting to use opDispatch for various compile-time shenanigans, the really interesting applications involve dynamism. Dynamic languages such as JavaScript or Smalltalk allow adding methods to objects at runtime. Let's try to do something similar in D by defining a class Dynamic that allows adding, removing, and calling methods dynamically.

First, we need to define a runtime signature for such dynamic methods, which is where the jack-of-all-trades type Variant found in std.variant may be of help. A Variant object can hold just about any value, which makes it the ideal candidate for the parameter and the return type of a dynamic method. So let's define the signature of such a dynamic method as a delegate that takes a Dynamic as its first parameter (filling the role of this) and an array of Variant for parameters and returns a Variant.

```
import std.variant;

alias Variant delegate(Dynamic self, Variant[] args...) DynMethod;
```

Because of the . . . , we can call a DynMethod with any number of arguments and have the compiler package them into an array. Let's now define Dynamic, which, as promised, allows manipulating methods at runtime. To do so, Dynamic defines an associative array that maps strings to DynMethods:

```
class Dynamic {
```

```
    private DynMethod[string] methods;
    void addMethod(string name, DynMethod m) {
        methods[name] = m;
    }
    void removeMethod(string name) {
        methods.remove(name);
    }
    // Dispatch dynamically on method
    Variant call(string methodName, Variant[] args...) {
        return methods[methodName](this, args);
    }
    // Provide syntactic sugar with opDispatch
    Variant opDispatch(string m, Args)(Args args...) {
        Variant[] packedArgs = new Variant[args.length];
        foreach (i, arg; args) {
            packedArgs[i] = Variant(arg);
        }
        return call(m, args);
    }
}
```

Let's take `Dynamic` for a test drive:

```
unittest {
    auto obj = new Dynamic;
    obj.addMethod("sayHello",
        Variant(Dynamic, Variant[]) {
            writeln("Hello, world!");
            return Variant();
        });
    obj.sayHello();   // Prints "Hello, world!"
}
```

Adding a method entails some amount of syntactic chaff because all methods must conform to the same signature. In the example above, there's quite a bit of unused stuff because the added `delegate` does not use any of its parameters and does not return an interesting value. The call syntax, however, is very clean, which is important because typically methods are added rarely and called often. `Dynamic` can be improved in many ways, for example, by defining a `getMethodInfo(string)` inspection function that returns the parameter count and types for a given method.

It is worth noting that the usual trade-offs between doing things statically versus dynamically are in effect. The more you do at runtime, the more you need to conform to common data formats (i.e., `Variant`) and compromise on efficiency (for example, by looking up method names during runtime). The payoff is increased flexibility—you can manipulate `class` definitions during runtime as needed, define dynamic inheritance relationships, interface with scripting languages, define scripting for your own objects, and much more.

## 12.12   Summary and Quick Reference

User-defined types can overload most operators. There are a few exceptions, such as the comma operator `,`, the logical conjunction operator `&&`, the logical disjunction operator `||`, the identity test `is`, the ternary operator `?:`, the unary operators address-of `&`, and `typeid`. These operators were considered to create more confusion than flexibility if ever overloaded.

Speaking of confusion, operator overloading is a powerful tool that comes with a correspondingly strong warning. In D you'd be best advised to avoid uses of operators for exotic purposes such as defining entire domain-specific embedded languages (DSELs); if you want to define DSELs, you should at best use strings, string `mixins` (§ 2.3.4.2 on page 47), and compile-time function evaluation (§ 5.12 on page 169) to parse the DSEL input from a compile-time string and then generate the corresponding D code. That entails more work, but your library's clients will appreciate it.

Defining `opDispatch` opens new vistas but should also be used responsibly. Too much dynamism might introduce unnecessary inefficiencies and weaken typechecking—for example, don't forget that if you wrote `a.heloWorld()` instead of `a.helloWorld()` in the example above, the code would still compile only to fail during runtime.

Table 12.1 summarizes the information provided in this chapter. Use it as a cheat sheet when overloading operators for your own types.

**Table 12.1:** Overloaded operators

| Expression ... | Is rewritten as ... |
|---|---|
| ‹op›a for ‹op› ∈ {+, -, ~, *, ++, --} | `a.opUnary!"‹op›"()` |
| a++ | `((ref x) {auto t=x; ++x; return t;})(a)` |
| a-- | `((ref x) {auto t=x; --x; return t;})(a)` |
| cast(T) a | `a.opCast!(T)()` |
| a ? ‹expr₁› : ‹expr₂› | `cast(bool) a ? ‹expr₁› : ‹expr₂›` |
| if (a) ‹stmt› | `if (cast(bool) a) ‹stmt›` |
| a ‹op› b for ‹op› ∈ { +, -, *, /, %, &, \|, ^, <<, >>, >>>, ~, in} | `a.opBinary!"‹op›"(b)` or `b.opBinaryRight!"‹op›"(a)` |

**Table 12.1:** Overloaded operators *(continued)*

| Expression ... | Is rewritten as ... |
|---|---|
| a == b | If a, b classes: `object.opEquals(a, b)` (see § 6.8.3 on page 205). Otherwise, if a and b have the same type: `a.opEquals(b)`. Otherwise, the only compilable of `a.opEquals(b)` and `b.opEquals(a)`. |
| a != b | `!(a == b)`, then refer to the rewrite above |
| a < b | `a.opCmp(b) < 0` or `b.opCmp(a) > 0` |
| a <= b | `a.opCmp(b) <= 0` or `b.opCmp(a) >= 0` |
| a > b | `a.opCmp(b) > 0` or `b.opCmp(a) < 0` |
| a >= b | `a.opCmp(b) >= 0` or `b.opCmp(a) <= 0` |
| a = b | `a.opAssign(b)` |
| a ‹*op*›= b for ‹*op*› ∈ {+, -, *, /, %, &, \|, ^, <<, >>, >>>, ~} | `a.opOpAssign!"‹`*op*`›"(b)` |
| a[$b_1$, $b_2$,..., $b_k$] | `a.opIndex(`$b_1$`, `$b_2$`,..., `$b_k$`)` |
| a[$b_1$, $b_2$,..., $b_k$] = c | `a.opIndexAssign(c, `$b_1$`, `$b_2$`,..., `$b_k$`)` |
| ‹*op*›a[$b_1$, $b_2$,..., $b_k$] if ‹*op*› ∈ {++,--} | `a.opIndexUnary(`$b_1$`, `$b_2$`, ..., `$b_k$`)` |
| a[$b_1$, $b_2$,..., $b_k$] ‹*op*›= c for ‹*op*› ∈ {+, -, *, /, %, &, \|, ^, <<, >>, >>>, ~} | `a.opIndexOpAssign!"‹`*op*`›"(c, `$b_1$`, `$b_2$`,..., `$b_k$`)` |
| a[$b_1$ .. $b_2$] | `a.opSlice(`$b_1$` .. `$b_2$`)` |
| ‹*op*›a[$b_1$ .. $b_2$] | `a.opSliceUnary!"‹`*op*`›"(`$b_1$`, `$b_2$`)` |
| a[] = c | `a.opSliceAssign(c)` |
| a[$b_1$ .. $b_2$] = c | `a.opSliceAssign(c, `$b_1$`, `$b_2$`)` |
| a[] ‹*op*›= c | `a.opSliceOpAssign!"‹`*op*`›"(c)` |
| a[$b_1$ .. $b_2$] ‹*op*›= c | `a.opSliceOpAssign!"‹`*op*`›"(c, `$b_1$`, `$b_2$`)` |

# 13

# Concurrency

Convergence of various factors in the hardware industry has led to qualitative changes in the way we are able to access computing resources, which in turn prompts profound changes in the ways we approach computing and in the language abstractions we use. Concurrency is now virtually everywhere, and it is software's responsibility to tap into it.

Although the software industry as a whole does not yet have ultimate responses to the challenges brought about by the concurrency revolution, D's youth allowed its creators to make informed decisions regarding concurrency without being tied down by obsoleted past choices or large legacy code bases. A major break with the mold of concurrent imperative languages is that D does not foster sharing of data between threads; by default, concurrent threads are virtually isolated by language mechanisms. Data sharing is allowed but only in limited, controlled ways that offer the compiler the ability to provide strong global guarantees.

At the same time, D remains at heart a systems programming language, so it does allow you to use a variety of low-level, maverick approaches to concurrency. (Some of these mechanisms are not, however, allowed in safe programs.)

In brief, here's how D's concurrency offering is layered:

- The flagship approach to concurrency is to use isolated threads or processes that communicate via messages. This paradigm, known as *message passing*, leads to safe and modular programs that are easy to understand and maintain. A variety of languages and libraries have used message passing successfully. Historically message passing has been slower than approaches based on memory sharing—which explains why it was not unanimously adopted—but that trend has recently undergone a definite and lasting reversal. Concurrent D programs are encouraged

391

to use message passing, a paradigm that benefits from extensive infrastructure support.

- D also provides support for old-style synchronization based on critical sections protected by mutexes and event variables. This approach to concurrency has recently come under heavy criticism because of its failure to scale well to today's and tomorrow's highly parallel architectures. D imposes strict control over data sharing, which in turn curbs lock-based programming styles. Such restrictions may seem quite harsh at first, but they cure lock-based code of its worst enemy: low-level data races. Data sharing remains, however, the most efficient means to pass large quantities of data across threads, so it should not be neglected.

- In the tradition of system-level languages, D programs not marked as `@safe` may use casts to obtain hot, bubbly, unchecked data sharing. The correctness of such programs becomes largely your responsibility.

- If that level of control is insufficient for you, you can use `asm` statements for ultimate control of your machine's resources. To go any lower-level than that, you'd need a miniature soldering iron and a very, very steady hand.

Before getting into the thick of these topics, let's take a brief detour in order to gain a better understanding of the hardware developments that have shaken our world.

## 13.1   Concurrentgate

When it comes to concurrency, we are living in the proverbial interesting times more than ever before. Interesting times come in the form of a mix of good and bad news that contributes to a complex landscape of trade-offs, forces, and trends.

The good news is that density of integration is still increasing by Moore's law; with what we know and what we can reasonably project right now, that trend will continue for at least one more decade after the time of this writing. Increased miniaturization begets increased computing power density because more transistors can be put to work together per area unit. Since components are closer together, connections are also shorter, which means faster local interconnectivity. It's an efficiency bonanza.

Unfortunately, there are a number of sentences starting with "unfortunately" that curb the enthusiasm around increased computational density. For one, connectivity is not only local—it forms a hierarchy [16]: closely connected components form units that must connect to other units, forming larger units. In turn, the larger units also connect to other larger units, forming even larger functional blocks, and so on. Connectivity-wise, such larger blocks remain "far away" from each other. Worse, increased complexity of each block increases the complexity of connectivity between blocks, which is achieved by reducing the thickness of wires and the distance between them. That means an increase of resistance, capacity, and crosstalk. Resistance and capacity worsen propagation speed in the wire. Crosstalk is the propensity of the signal in one wire to propagate to a nearby wire by (in this case) electromagnetic field. At high frequencies, a wire is just an antenna and crosstalk becomes so unbearable that serial communication increasingly replaces parallel communication (a somewhat counterintuitive phenomenon visible at all scales—USB replaced the parallel port, SATA replaced PATA as the disk data connector, and serial buses are replacing parallel buses in memory subsystems, all because of crosstalk. Where are the days when parallel was fast and serial was slow?).

Also, the speed gap between processing elements and memory is also increasing. Whereas memory density has been increasing at predictably the same rate as general integration density, its access speed is increasingly lagging behind computation speed for a variety of physical, technological, and market-related reasons [22]. It is unclear at this time how the speed gap could be significantly reduced, and it is only growing. Hundreds of cycles may separate the processor from a word in memory; only a few years ago, you could buy "zero wait states" memory chips accessible in one clock cycle.

The existence of a spectrum of memory architectures that navigate different trade-offs among density, price, and speed, has caused an increased sophistication of memory hierarchies; accessing one memory word has become a detective investigation that involves questioning several cache levels, starting with precious on-chip static RAM and going possibly all the way to mass storage. Conversely, a given datum could be found replicated in a number of places throughout the cache hierarchy, which in turn influences programming models. We can't afford anymore to think of memory as a big, monolithic chunk comfortably shared by all processors in a system: caches foster local memory traffic and make shared data an illusion that is increasingly difficult to maintain [37].

In related, late-breaking news, the speed of light has obstinately decided to stay constant (`immutable` if you wish) at about 300,000,000 meters per second. The speed of light in silicon oxide (relevant to signal propagation inside today's chips) is about half that, and the speed we can achieve today for transmitting actual data is significantly below that theoretical limit. That spells more trouble for global interconnectivity at high frequencies. If we wanted to build a 10GHz chip, under ideal conditions it would take three cycles just to transport a bit across a 4.5-centimeter-wide chip while essentially performing no computation.

In brief, we are converging toward processors of very high density and huge computational power that are, however, becoming increasingly isolated and difficult to reach and use because of limits dictated by interconnectivity, signal propagation speed, and memory access speed.

The computing industry is naturally flowing around these barriers. One phenomenon has been the implosion of the size and energy required for a given computational power; today's addictive portable digital assistants could not have been fabricated at the same size and capabilities with technology only five years old. Today's trends, however, don't help traditional computers that want to achieve increased computational power at about the same size. For those, chip makers decided to give up the battle for faster clock rates and instead decided to offer computing power packaged in already known ways: several identical central processing unit (CPUs) connected to each other and to memory via buses. Thus, in a matter of a few short years, the responsibility for making computers faster has largely shifted from the hardware crowd to the software crowd. More CPUs may seem like an advantageous proposition, but for regular desktop computer workloads it becomes tenuous to gainfully employ more than around eight processors. Future trends project an exponential expansion of the number of available CPUs well into the dozens, hundreds, and thousands. To speed up one given program, a lot of hard programming work is needed to put those CPUs to good use.

The computing industry has always had moves and shakes caused by various technological and human factors, but this time around we seem to be at the end of the rope. Since only a short time ago, taking a vacation is not an option for increasing the speed of your program. It's a scandal. It's an outrage. It's Concurrentgate.

## 13.2   A Brief History of Data Sharing

One aspect of the shift happening in computing is the suddenness with which processing and concurrency models are changing today, particularly in comparison and contrast to the pace of development of programming languages and paradigms. It takes years and decades for programming languages and their associated styles to become imprinted into a community's lore, whereas changes in concurrency matters turned a definite exponential elbow starting around the beginning of the 2000s.

For example, our yesteryear understanding of general concurrency[1] was centered around time sharing, which in turn originated with the mainframes of the 1960s. Back then, CPU time was so expensive, it made sense to share the CPU across multiple programs controlled from multiple consoles so as to increase overall utilization. A *process* was and is defined as the state and the resources of a running program. To implement time sharing, the CPU uses a timer interrupt in conjunction with a software scheduler. Upon each timer interrupt, the scheduler decides which process gets CPU time for the next time quantum, thus giving the illusion that several processes are running simultaneously, when in fact they all use the same CPU.

To prevent buggy processes from stomping over one another and over operating system code, *hardware memory protection* has been introduced. In today's systems, memory protection is combined with *memory virtualization* to ensure robust process isolation: each process thinks it "owns" the machine's memory, whereas in fact a translation layer from logical addresses (as the process sees memory) to physical addresses (as the machine accesses memory) intermediates all interaction of processes with memory and isolates processes from one another. The good news is that runaway processes can harm only themselves, but not other processes or the operating system kernel. The less

---

1. The following discussion focuses on general concurrency and does not discuss vector operation parallelization and other specialized parallel kernels.

good news is that upon each task switching, a potentially expensive swapping of address translation paraphernalia also has to occur, not to mention that every just-switched-to process wakes up with cache amnesia as the global shared cache was most likely used by other processes. And that's how *threads* were born.

A thread is a process without associated address translation information—a bare execution context: processor state plus stack. Several threads share the address space of a process, which means that threads are relatively cheap to start and switch among, and also that they can easily and cheaply share data with each other. Sharing memory across threads running against one CPU is as straightforward as possible—one thread writes, another reads. With time sharing, the order in which data is written by one thread is naturally the same as the order in which those writes are seen by others. Maintaining higher-level data invariants is ensured by using interlocking mechanisms such as critical sections protected by synchronization primitives (such as semaphores and mutexes). Through the late twentieth century, a large body of knowledge, folklore, and anecdotes has grown around what could be called "classic" multithreaded programming, characterized by shared address space, simple rules for memory effect visibility, and mutex-driven synchronization. Other models of concurrency existed, but classic multithreading was the most used on mainstream hardware.

Today's mainstream imperative languages such as C, C++, Java, or C# have been developed during the classic multithreading age—the good old days of simple memory architectures, straightforward data sharing, and well-understood interlocking primitives. Naturally, languages modeled the realities of that hardware by accommodating threads that all share the same memory. After all, the very definition of multithreading entails that all threads share the same address space, unlike operating system processes. In addition, message-passing APIs (such as the MPI specification [29]) have been available in library form, initially for high-end hardware such as (super)computer clusters.

During the same historical period, the then-nascent functional languages adopted a principled position based on mathematical purity: we're not interested in modeling hardware, they said, but we'd like to model math. And math for the most part does not have mutation and is time-invariant, which makes it an ideal candidate for parallelization. (Imagine the moment when those first mathematicians-turned-programmers heard about concurrency—they must have slapped their foreheads: "Wait a *minute!...*") It was well noted in functional programming circles that such a computational model does inherently favor out-of-order, concurrent execution, but that potential was more of a latent energy than a realized goal until recent times.

Finally, Erlang was developed starting in the late 1980s as a domain-specific embedded language for telephony applications. The domain required tens of thousands of simultaneous programs running on the same machine and strongly favored a message-passing, "fire-and-forget" communication style. Although mainstream hardware and operating systems were not optimized for such workloads, Erlang initially ran on specialized hardware. The result was a language that originally combined an impure functional style with heavy concurrency abilities and a staunch message-passing, no-sharing approach to communication.

Fast-forward to the 2010s. Today, even run-of-the-mill machines have more than one processor, and the decade's main challenge is to stick ever more CPUs on a chip. This has had a number of consequences, the most important being the demise of seamless shared memory.

One time-shared CPU has one memory subsystem attached to it—with buffers, several levels of caches, the works. No matter how the CPU is time-shared, reads and writes go through the same pipeline; as such, a coherent view of memory is maintained across all threads. In contrast, multiple interconnected CPUs cannot afford to share the cache subsystem: such a cache would need multiport access (expensive and poorly scalable) and would be difficult to place in the proximity of all CPUs simultaneously. Therefore, today's CPUs, almost without exception, come with their own dedicated cache memory. The hardware and protocols connecting the CPU + cache combos together are a crucial factor influencing multiprocessor system performance.

The existence of multiple caches makes data sharing across threads devilishly difficult. Now reads and writes in different threads may hit different caches, so sharing data from one thread to another is not straightforward anymore and, in fact, becomes a message passing of sorts:[2] for any such sharing, a sort of handshake must occur among cache subsystems to ensure that shared data makes it from the latest writer to the reader and also to the main memory.

As if things weren't interesting enough already, cache synchronization protocols add one more twist to the plot: they manipulate data in blocks, not individual word reads and word writes. This means that communicating processors "forget" the exact order in which data was written, leading to paradoxical behavior that apparently defies causality and common sense: one thread writes x and then y and for a while another thread sees the new y but only the old x. Such causality violations are extremely difficult to integrate within the general model of classic multithreading, which is imbued with the intuition of time slicing and with a simple memory model. Even the most expert programmers in classic multithreading find it unbelievably difficult to adapt their programming styles and patterns to the new memory architectures.

To illustrate the rapid changes in today's concurrency world and also the heavy influence of data sharing on languages' approach to concurrency, consider the following piece of advice given in the 2001 edition of the excellent book *Effective Java* [8, Item 51, page 204]:

> When multiple threads are runnable, the thread scheduler determines which threads get to run and for how long. ... The best way to write a robust, responsive, portable multithreaded application is to ensure that there are few runnable threads at any given time.

---

2. This is ironic because shared memory has been faster than message passing in the classic multithreading days.

One startling detail for today's observer is that single-processor, time-sliced thread-ing is not only addressed by the quote above, but actually assumed without being stated. Naturally, the book's 2008 edition[3] [9] changes the advice to "ensure that the average number of runnable threads is not significantly greater than the number of processors." Interestingly, even that advice, although it looks reasonable, makes a couple of unstated assumptions: one, that there will be high data contention between threads, which in turn causes degradation of performance due to interlocking overheads; and two, that the number of processors does not vary dramatically across machines that may exe-cute the program. As such, the advice is contrary to that given, repeatedly and in the strongest terms, in the *Programming Erlang* book [5, Chapter 20, page 363]:

> **Use Lots of Processes** This is important—we have to keep the CPUs busy. All the CPUs must be busy all the time. The easiest way to achieve this is to have lots of processes.[4] When I say lots of processes, I mean lots in relation to the number of CPUs. If we have lots of processes, then we won't need to worry about keeping the CPUs busy.

Which recommendation is correct? As usual, it all depends. The first recommenda-tion works well on 2001-vintage hardware; the second works well in scenarios of inten-sive data sharing and consequently high contention; and the third works best in low-contention, high-CPU-count scenarios.

Because of the increasing difficulty of sharing memory, today's trends make data sharing tenuous and favor functional and message-passing approaches. Not inciden-tally, recent years have witnessed an increased interest in Erlang and other functional languages for concurrent applications.

## 13.3 Look, Ma, No (Default) Sharing

In the wake of the recent hardware and software developments, D chose to make a rad-ical departure from other imperative languages: yes, D does support threads, but they do not share any mutable data by default—they are isolated from each other. Isolation is not achieved via hardware as in the case of processes, and it is not achieved through runtime checks; it is a natural consequence of the way D's type system is designed.

Such a decision is inspired by functional languages, which also strive to disallow all mutation and consequently mutable sharing. There are two differences. First, D pro-grams can still use mutation freely—it's just that mutable data is not unwittingly acces-sible to other threads. Second, no sharing is a *default* choice, not the *only* one. To define data as being shared across threads, you must qualify its type with `shared`. Consider, for example, two simple module-scope definitions:

---

3. Even the topic title was changed from "Threads" to "Concurrency" to reflect the fact that threads are but one concurrency model.

4. Erlang processes are distinct from OS processes.

```
int perThread;
shared int perProcess;
```

In most languages, the first definition (or its syntactic equivalent) would introduce a global variable used by all threads; however, in D, perThread has a separate copy for each thread. The second declaration allocates only one int that is shared across all threads, so in a way it is closer (but not identical) to a traditional global variable.

The variable perThread is stored using an operating system facility known as thread-local storage (TLS). The access speed of TLS-allocated data is dependent upon the compiler implementation and the underlying operating system. Generally it is negligibly slower than accessing a regular global variable in a C program, for example. In the rare cases when that may be a concern, you may want to load the global into a stack variable in access-intensive loops.

This setup has two important advantages. First, default-share languages must carefully synchronize access around global data; that is not necessary for perThread because it is private to each thread. Second, the shared qualifier means that the type system and the human user are both in the know that perProcess is accessed by multiple threads simultaneously. In particular, the type system will actively guard the use of shared data and disallow uses that are obviously mistaken. This turns the traditional setup on its head: under a default-share regime, the programmer must keep track manually of which data is shared and which isn't, and indeed most concurrency-related bugs are caused by undue or unprotected sharing. Under the explicit shared regime, the programmer knows for sure that data *not* marked as shared is never indeed visible to more than one thread. (To ensure that guarantee, shared values undergo additional checks that we'll get to soon.)

Using shared data remains an advanced topic because although low-level coherence is automatically ensured by the type system, high-level invariants may not be. To provide safe, simple, and efficient communication between threads, the preferred method is to use a paradigm known as *message passing*. Memory-isolated threads communicate by sending each other asynchronous messages, which consist simply of D values packaged together.

Isolated workers communicating via simple channels are a very robust, time-proven approach to concurrency. Erlang has done that for years, as have applications based on the Message Passing Interface (MPI) specification [29].

To add acclaim to remedy,[5] good programming practice even in default-share multi-threaded languages actually enshrines that threads ought to be isolated. Herb Sutter, a world-class expert in concurrency, writes in an article eloquently entitled "Use threads correctly = isolation + asynchronous messages" [54]:

---

5. That must be an antonym for the phrase "to add insult to injury."

Threads are a low-level tool for expressing asynchronous work. "Uplevel" them by applying discipline: strive to make their data private, and have them communicate and synchronize using asynchronous messages. Each thread that needs to get information from other threads or from people should have a message queue, whether a simple FIFO queue or a priority queue, and organize its work around an event-driven message pump mainline; replacing spaghetti with event-driven logic is a great way to improve the clarity and determinism of your code.

If there is one thing that decades of computing have taught us, it must be that discipline-oriented programming does not scale. It is reassuring, then, to reckon that the quote above pretty much summarizes quite accurately the following few sections, save for the discipline part.

## 13.4  Starting a Thread

To start a thread, use the spawn function like this:

```
import std.concurrency, std.stdio;

void main() {
   auto low = 0, high = 100;
   spawn(&fun, low, high);
   foreach (i; low .. high) {
      writeln("Main thread: ", i);
   }
}

void fun(int low, int high) {
   foreach (i; low .. high) {
      writeln("Secondary thread: ", i);
   }
}
```

The spawn function takes the address of a function &fun and a number of arguments ‹$a_1$›, ‹$a_2$›, ..., ‹$a_n$›. The number of arguments $n$ and their types must match fun's signature, that is, the call fun(‹$a_1$›, ‹$a_2$›, ..., ‹$a_n$›) must be correct. This check is done at compile time. spawn creates a new execution thread, which will issue the call fun(‹$a_1$›, ‹$a_2$›, ..., ‹$a_n$›) and then terminate. Of course, spawn does not wait for the thread to terminate—it returns as soon as the thread is created and the arguments are passed to it (in this case, two integers).

The program above outputs a total of 200 lines to the standard output. The interleaving of lines depends on a variety of factors; it's possible that you would see 100 lines from the main thread followed by 100 lines from the secondary thread, the exact opposite, or some seemingly random interleaving. There will never be, however, a mix of two messages on the same line. This is because `writeln` is defined to make each call atomic with regard to its output stream. Also, the order of lines emitted by each thread will be respected.

Even if the execution of `main` may end before the execution of `fun` in the secondary thread, the program patiently waits for all threads to finish before exiting. This is because the runtime support library follows a little protocol for program termination, which we'll discuss later; for now, let's just note that other threads don't suddenly die just because `main` returns.

As promised by the isolation guarantee, the newly created thread shares nothing with the caller thread. Well, almost nothing: the global file handle `stdout` is *de facto* shared across the two threads. But there is no cheating: if you look at the `std.stdio` module's implementation, you will see that `stdout` is defined as a global `shared` variable. Everything is properly accounted for in the type system.

### 13.4.1 `immutable` Sharing

What kind of functions can you call via `spawn`? The no-sharing stance imposes certain restrictions—you may use only by-value parameters for the thread starter function (`fun` in the example above). Any pass by reference, either explicit (by use of a `ref` parameter) or implicit (e.g., by use of an array) should be verboten. With that in mind, let's take a look at the following rewrite of the example:

```d
import std.concurrency, std.stdio;

void main() {
   auto low = 0, high = 100;
   auto message = "Yeah, hi #";
   spawn(&fun, message, low, high);
   foreach (i; low .. high) {
      writeln("Main thread: ", message, i);
   }
}

void fun(string text, int low, int high) {
   foreach (i; low .. high) {
      writeln("Secondary thread: ", text, i);
   }
}
```

The rewritten example is similar to the original, but it prints an additional string. That string is created in the main thread and passed without copying into the secondary thread. Effectively, the contents of `message` are shared between the two threads. This violates the aforementioned principle that all data sharing must be explicitly marked through the use of the `shared` keyword. Yet the example compiles and runs. What is happening?

Chapter 8 explains that `immutable` provides a strong guarantee: an `immutable` value is guaranteed never to change throughout its lifetime. The same chapter explains (§ 8.2 on page 291) that the type `string` is actually an alias for `immutable(char)[]`. Finally, we know that all contention is caused by sharing of *writable* data—as long as nobody changes it, you can share data freely as everybody will see the exact same thing. The type system and the entire threading infrastructure acknowledge that fact by allowing all `immutable` data to be freely sharable across threads. In particular, `string` values can be shared because their characters can't be changed. In fact, a large part of the motivation behind introducing `immutable` into the language was the help it brings with sharing structured data across threads.

## 13.5 Exchanging Messages between Threads

Threads that print messages with arbitrary interleavings are hardly interesting. Let's modify the example to ensure that threads work in tandem to print messages as follows:

```
Main thread: 0
Secondary thread: 0
Main thread: 1
Secondary thread: 1
...
Main thread: 999
Secondary thread: 999
```

To achieve that, we need to define a little protocol between the two threads: the main thread should send the message "Print this number" to the secondary thread, and the secondary thread must answer back, "Done printing." There is hardly any concurrency going on, but the example serves well the purpose of explaining pure communication. In real applications, threads should spend most of their time doing useful work and spend relatively little time communicating with each other.

First off, in order for two threads to communicate, they need to know how to address each other. A program may have many threads chattering away, so an identification means is necessary. To address a thread, you must get a grip on its *thread id*, nicknamed henceforth as "tid," which is returned by `spawn`. (The name of a tid's type is actually `Tid`.) In turn, the secondary thread also needs a tid to send the response back. That's easy to do by having the sender specify its own `Tid` the same way you'd write the sender's address on a snail mail envelope. Here's what the code looks like:

```
import std.concurrency, std.stdio;
```

```
void main() {
   auto low = 0, high = 100;
   auto tid = spawn(&writer);
   foreach (i; low .. high) {
      writeln("Main thread: ", i);
      tid.send(thisTid, i);
      enforce(receiveOnly!Tid() == tid);
   }
}

void writer() {
   for (;;) {
      auto msg = receiveOnly!(Tid, int)();
      writeln("Secondary thread: ", msg[1]);
      msg[0].send(thisTid);
   }
}
```

This time around `writer` takes no more arguments because it receives the information it needs in the form of messages. The main thread saves the `Tid` returned by `spawn` and then uses it in the call to the `send` method. The call sends two pieces of data to the other thread: the current thread's `Tid`, accessed via the global property `thisTid`, and the integer to be printed. After throwing that data over the fence to the other thread, the main thread waits for acknowledgment in the form of a call to `receiveOnly`. The `send` and `receiveOnly` functions work in tandem: one call to `send` in one thread is met by a call to `receiveOnly` in the other. The "only" in `receiveOnly` is present because `receiveOnly` accepts only specific types—for example, in the call `receiveOnly!bool()`, the caller accepts only a message consisting of a `bool` value; if another thread sends anything else, `receiveOnly` throws a `MessageMismatch` exception.

Let's leave `main` rummaging around the `foreach` loop and focus on `writer`'s implementation, which implements the other side of the mini-protocol. `writer` spends time in a loop starting with the receipt of a message that must consist of a `Tid` and an `int`. That's what the call `receiveOnly!(Tid, int)()` ensures; again, if the main thread sent a message with some different number or types of arguments, `receiveOnly` would fail by throwing an exception. As written, the `receiveOnly` call in `writer` matches perfectly the call `tid.send(thisTid, i)` made from `main`.

The type of `msg` is `Tuple!(Tid, int)`. Generally, messages with multiple arguments are packed in `Tuple` objects with one member per argument. If, however, the message consists only of one value, there's no redundant packing in a `Tuple`. For example, `receiveOnly!int()` returns an `int`, not a `Tuple!int`.

Continuing with `writer`, the next line performs the actual printing. Recall that for the tuple `msg`, `msg[0]` accesses the first member (i.e., the `Tid`) and `msg[1]` accesses the second member (the `int`). Finally, `writer` acknowledges that it finished writing to the console by simply sending its own `Tid` back to the sender—a sort of a blank letter that only confirms the originating address. "Yes, I got your message," the empty letter implies, "and acted upon it. Your turn." The main thread waits for that confirmation before continuing its work, and the loop goes on.

Sending back the `Tid` of the secondary thread is superfluous in this case; any dummy value, such as an `int` or a `bool`, would have sufficed. But in the general case there are many threads sending messages to one another, so self-identification becomes important.

## 13.6  Pattern Matching with `receive`

Most useful communication protocols are more complex than the one we defined above, and `receiveOnly` is quite limited. For example, it is quite difficult to implement with `receiveOnly` an action such as "receive an `int` or a `string`."

A more powerful primitive is `receive`, which matches and dispatches messages based on their type. A typical call to `receive` looks like this:

```
receive(
    (string s) { writeln("Got a string with value ", s); },
    (int x) { writeln("Got an int with value ", x); }
);
```

The call above matches any of the following `send` calls:

```
send(tid, "hello");
send(tid, 5);
send(tid, 'a');
send(tid, 42u);
```

The first `send` call matches a `string` and is therefore dispatched to the first function literal in `receive`, and the other three match an `int` and are passed to the second function literal. By the way, the handler functions don't need to be literals—some or all of them may be addresses of named functions:

```
void handleString(string s) { ... }
receive(
    &handleString,
    (int x) { writeln("Got an int with value ", x); }
);
```

Matching is not exact; instead, it follows normal overloading rules, by which `char`
and `uint` are implicitly convertible to `int`. Conversely, the following calls will *not* be
matched:

```
send(tid, "hello"w); // UTF-16 string (§ 4.5 on page 118)
send(tid, 5L);       // long
send(tid, 42.0);     // double
```

When `receive` sees a message of an unexpected type, it doesn't throw an exception (as `receiveOnly` does). The message-passing subsystem simply saves the non-
matching messages in a queue, colloquially known as the thread's *mailbox*. `receive`
waits patiently for the arrival of a message of a matching type in the mailbox. This makes
`receive` and the protocols implemented on top of it more flexible, but also more sus-
ceptible to blocking and mailbox crowding. One communication misunderstanding is
enough for a thread's mailbox to accumulate messages of the wrong type while `receive`
is waiting for a message type that never arrives.

The `send`/`receive` combo handles multiple arguments easily by using `Tuple` as an
intermediary. For example:

```
receive(
    (long x, double y) { ... },
    (int x) { ... }
);
```

matches the same messages as

```
receive(
    (Tuple!(long, double) tp) { ... },
    (int x) { ... }
);
```

A call like `send(tid, 5, 6.3)` matches the first function literal in both examples
above.

To allow a thread to take contingency action in case messages are delayed, `receive`
has a variant `receiveTimeout` that expires after a specified time. The expiration is signaled by `receiveTimeout` returning `false`:

```
auto gotMessage = receiveTimeout(
    1000, // Time in milliseconds
    (string s) { writeln("Got a string with value ", s); },
    (int x) { writeln("Got an int with value ", x); }
);
if (!gotMessage) {
    stderr.writeln("Timed out after one second.");
}
```

### 13.6.1 First Match

Consider the following example:

```
receive(
    (long x) { ... },
    (string x) { ... },
    (int x) { ... }
);
```

This call will not compile: `receive` rejects the call because the third handler could never be reached. Any `int` sent down the pipe stops at the first handler.

In `receive`, the order of arguments dictates how matches are attempted. This is similar, for example, to how `catch` clauses are evaluated in a `try` statement but is unlike object-oriented function dispatch. Reasonable people may disagree on the relative qualities of first match and best match; suffice it to say that first match seems to serve this particular form of `receive` quite well.

The compile-time enforcement performed by `receive` is simple: for any message types ‹$Msg_1$› and ‹$Msg_2$› with ‹$Msg_2$›'s handler coming after ‹$Msg_1$›'s in the `receive` call, `receive` makes sure that ‹$Msg_2$› is *not* convertible to ‹$Msg_1$›. If it is, that means ‹$Msg_1$› will match messages of type ‹$Msg_2$› so compilation of the call is refused. In the example above, the check fails when ‹$Msg_1$› is `long` and ‹$Msg_2$› is `int`.

### 13.6.2 Matching Any Message

What if you wanted to make sure you're looking at any and all messages in a mailbox—for example, to make sure it doesn't get filled with junk mail?

The answer is simple—just accept the type `Variant` in the last position of `receive`, like this:

```
receive(
    (long x) { ... },
    (string x) { ... },
    (double x, double y) { ... },
    ...
    (Variant any) { ... }
);
```

The `Variant` type defined in module `std.variant` is a dynamic type able to hold exactly one value of any other type. `receive` recognizes `Variant` as a generic holder for any message type, and as such a call to `receive` that has a handler for `Variant` will always return as soon as at least one message is in the queue.

Planting a `Variant` handler at the bottom of the message handling food chain is a good method to make sure that stray messages aren't left in your mailbox.

## 13.7    File Copying—with a Twist

Let's write a short program that copies files—a popular way to get acquainted with a language's file system interface. Ah, the joy of K&R's classic `getchar`/`putchar` example [34, Chapter 1, page 15]. Of course, the system-provided programs that copy files use buffered reads and writes and many other optimizations to accelerate transfer speed, so it would be difficult to write a competitive program, but concurrency may give an edge.

The usual approach to file copying goes like this:

1.  Read data from the source file into a buffer.
2.  If nothing was read, done.
3.  Write the buffer into the target file.
4.  Repeat from step 1.

Adding appropriate error handling completes a useful (if unoriginal) program. If you select a large enough buffer and both the source and destination files reside on the same disk, the performance of the algorithm is near optimal.

Nowadays a variety of physical devices count as file repositories, such as hard drives, thumb drives, optical disks, connected smart phones, and remotely connected network services. These devices have various latency and speed profiles and connect to the computer via different hardware and software interfaces. Such interfaces could and should be put to work in parallel, not one at a time as the "read buffer/write buffer" algorithm above prescribes. Ideally, both the source and the target device should be kept as busy as possible, something we could effect with two threads following the producer-consumer protocol:

1.  Spawn one secondary thread that listens to messages containing memory buffers and writes them to the target file in a loop.
2.  Read data from the source file in a newly allocated buffer.
3.  If nothing was read, done.
4.  Send a message containing the read buffer to the secondary thread.
5.  Repeat from step 2.

In the new setup, one thread keeps the source busy and the other keeps the target busy. Depending on the nature of the source and target, significant acceleration could be obtained. If the device speeds are comparable and relatively slow compared to the bandwidth of the memory bus, the speed of copying could theoretically be doubled. Let's write a simple producer-consumer program that copies `stdin` to `stdout`:

```
import std.algorithm, std.concurrency, std.stdio;

void main() {
```

```
    enum bufferSize = 1024 * 100;
    auto tid = spawn(&fileWriter);
    // Read loop
    foreach (immutable(ubyte)[] buffer; stdin.byChunk(bufferSize)) {
        send(tid, buffer);
    }
}

void fileWriter() {
    // Write loop
    for (;;) {
        auto buffer = receiveOnly!(immutable(ubyte)[])();
        tgt.write(buffer);
    }
}
```

The program above transfers data from the main thread to the secondary thread through `immutable` sharing: the messages passed have the type `immutable(ubyte)[]`, that is, arrays of `immutable` unsigned bytes. Those buffers are acquired in the `foreach` loop by reading input in chunks of type `immutable(ubyte)[]`, each of size `bufferSize`. At each pass through the loop, one new buffer is allocated, read into, and bound to `buffer`. The `foreach` control part does most of the hard work; all the body has to do is send off the buffer to the secondary thread. As discussed, passing data around is possible because of `immutable`; if you replaced `immutable(ubyte)[]` with `ubyte[]`, the call to `send` would not compile.

## 13.8 Thread Termination

There's something unusual about the examples given so far, in particular `writer` defined on page 402 and `fileWriter` defined on the facing page: both functions contain an infinite loop. In fact, a closer look at the file copy example reveals that `main` and `fileWriter` understand each other well regarding copying things around but never discuss application termination; in other words, `main` does not ever tell `fileWriter`, "We're done; let's finish and go home."

Termination of multithreaded applications has always been tricky. Threads are easy to start, but once started they are difficult to finish; the application shutdown event is asynchronous and may catch a thread in the middle of an arbitrary operation. Low-level threading APIs do offer a means to forcefully terminate threads, but invariably with the cautionary note that such a function is a blunt tool that should be replaced with a higher-level shutdown protocol.

D offers a simple and robust thread termination protocol. Each thread has an *owner* thread; by default the owner is the thread that initiated the `spawn`. You can change the current thread's owner dynamically by calling `setOwner(tid)`. Each thread has exactly one owner but a given thread may own multiple threads.

The most important manifestation of the owner/owned relationship is that when the owner thread terminates, the calls to `receive` in the owned thread will throw the `OwnerTerminated` exception. The exception is thrown only if `receive` has no more matching messages and must wait for a new message; as long as `receive` has something to fetch from the mailbox, it will not throw. In other words, when the owner thread terminates, the owned threads' calls to `receive` (or `receiveOnly` for that matter) will throw `OwnerTerminated` if and only if they would otherwise block waiting for a new message. The ownership relation is not necessarily unidirectional. In fact, two threads may even own each other; in that case, whichever thread finishes will notify the other.

With thread ownership in mind, let's take a fresh look at the file copy program on page 406. At any given moment, there are a number of messages in flight between the main thread and the secondary thread. The faster the reads are relative to writes, the more buffers will wait in the writer thread's mailbox waiting to be processed. When `main` returns, it will cause the call to `receive` to throw an exception, but not before all of the pending messages are handled. Right after the mailbox of the writer is cleared (and the last drop of data is written to the target file), the next call to `receive` throws. The writer thread exits with the `OwnerTerminated` exception, which is recognized by the runtime system, which simply ignores it. The operating system closes `stdin` and `stdout` as it always does, and the copy operation succeeds.

It may appear there is a race between the moment the last message is sent from `main` and the moment `main` returns (causing `receive` to throw). What if the exception "makes it" before the last message—or worse, before the last few messages? In fact there is no race because causality is always respected in the posting thread: the last message is posted onto the secondary thread's queue *before* the `OwnerTerminated` exception makes its way (in fact, propagating the exception is done via the same queue as regular messages). However, a race *would* exist if `main` exits while a different, third thread is posting messages onto `fileWriter`'s queue.

A similar reasoning shows that our previous simple example that writes 200 messages in lockstep is also correct: `main` exits after mailing (in the nick of time) the last message to the secondary thread. The secondary thread first exhausts the queue and then ends with the `OwnerTerminated` exception.

If you find throwing an exception too harsh a mechanism for handling a thread's exit, you can always handle `OwnerTerminated` explicitly:

```
// Ends without an exception
void fileWriter() {
   // Write loop
   for (bool running = true; running; ) {
      receive(
         (immutable(ubyte)[] buffer) { tgt.write(buffer); },
```

```
        (OwnerTerminated) { running = false; }
    );
  }
  stderr.writeln("Normally terminated.");
}
```

In this case, `fileWriter` returns peacefully when `main` exits and everyone's happy. But what happens in the case when the secondary thread—the writer—throws an exception? The call to the `write` function may fail if there's a problem writing data to `tgt`. In that case, the call to `send` from the primary thread will fail by throwing an `OwnedFailed` exception, which is exactly what should happen. By the way, if an owned thread exits normally (as opposed to throwing an exception), subsequent calls to `send` to that thread also fail, just with a different exception type: `OwnedTerminated`.

The file copy program is more robust than its simplicity may suggest. However, it should be said that relying on the default termination protocol works smoothly when the relationships between threads are simple and well understood. When there are many participating threads and the ownership graph is complex, it is best to establish explicit "end-of-communication" protocols throughout. In the file copy example, a simple idea would be to send by convention a buffer of size zero to signal the writer that the reading thread has finished successfully. Then the writer acknowledges termination to the reader, which finally can exit. Such an explicit protocol scales well to cases when there are multiple threads processing the data stream between the reader and the writer.

## 13.9   Out-of-Band Communication

Consider that you're using the presumably smart file-copying program we just defined to copy a large file from a fast local store to a slow network drive. Midway through the copy, there's a read error—the file is corrupt. That causes `read` and subsequently `main` to throw an exception while there are many buffers in flight that haven't yet been written. More generally, we saw that if the owner terminates *normally*, any blocking call to `receive` from its owned threads will throw. What happens if the owner exits with an exception?

If a thread terminates by means of an exception, that indicates a serious issue that must be signaled with relative urgency to the owned threads. Indeed this is carried out via an *out-of-band* message.

Recall that `receive` cares only about matching messages and lets all others accumulate in the queue. There is one amendment to that behavior. A thread may initiate an out-of-band message by calling `prioritySend` instead of `send`. The two functions accept the same parameters but exhibit different behaviors that actually manifest themselves on the receiving side. Passing a message of type `T` with `prioritySend` causes `receive` in the receiving thread to act as follows:

- If the call to `receive` handles type `T`, then the priority message will be the next message handled, even though it arrived later than other regular (non-priority) messages. Priority messages are always pushed to the beginning of the queue, so the latest priority message sent is always the first fetched by `receive` (even if other priority messages are already waiting).
- If the call to `receive` does not handle type `T` (i.e., would leave the message waiting in the mailbox) and if `T` inherits `Exception`, `receive` throws the message directly.
- If the call to `receive` does not handle type `T` and `T` does not inherit `Exception`, `receive` throws an exception of type `PriorityMessageException!T`. That exception holds a copy of the message sent in the form of a member called `message`.

If a thread exits via an exception, the exception `OwnerFailed` propagates to all of its owned threads by means of `prioritySend`. In the file copy program, `main` throwing also causes `fileWriter` to throw as soon as it calls `receive`, and the entire process terminates by printing an error message and returning a nonzero exit code. Unlike the normal termination case, there may be buffers in flight that have been read but not yet written.

## 13.10   Mailbox Crowding

The producer-consumer file copy program works quite well but has an important shortcoming.  Consider copying a large file between two devices of different speeds, for example, copying a legally acquired movie file from an internal drive (fast) to a network drive (possibly considerably slower). In that case, the producer (the `main` thread) issues buffers at considerable speed, much faster than the speed with which the consumer is able to unload them in the target file. The difference in the two speeds causes a net accumulation of buffers, which may cause the program to consume a lot of memory without achieving a boost in efficiency.

To avoid mailbox crowding, the concurrency API allows setting the maximum size of a thread's message queue, and also setting the action to take in case the maximum size has been reached. The signatures of relevance here are

```
// Inside std.concurrency
void setMaxMailboxSize(Tid tid, size_t messages,
   bool(Tid) onCrowdingDoThis);
```

The call `setMaxMailboxSize(tid, messages, onCrowdingDoThis)` directs the concurrency API to call `onCrowdingDoThis(tid)` whenever a new message is to be passed but the queue already contains `messages` entries. If `onCrowdingDoThis(tid)` returns `false` or throws an exception, the new message is ignored. Otherwise, the size of the thread's queue is checked again, and if it is less than `messages`, the new message is posted to thread `tid`. Otherwise, the entire loop is resumed.

The call occurs in the caller thread, not the callee. In other words, the thread that initiates sending a message is also responsible for taking contingency action in case the maximum mailbox size of the recipient has been reached. It seems reasonable to ask why the call should not occur in the callee; that would, however, scale the wrong way in heavily threaded programs because threads with full mailboxes may become crippled by many calls from other threads attempting to send messages.

There are a few prepackaged actions to perform when the mailbox is full: block the caller until the queue becomes smaller, throw an exception, or ignore the new message. Such predefined actions are conveniently packaged as follows:

```
// Inside std.concurrency
enum OnCrowding { block, throwException, ignore }
void setMaxMailboxSize(Tid tid, size_t messages, OnCrowding doThis);
```

In our case, it's best to simply block the reader thread once the mailbox becomes too large, which we can effect by inserting the call

```
setMaxMailboxSize(tid, 1024, OnCrowding.block);
```

right after the call to spawn.

The following sections describe approaches to inter-thread communication that are alternative or complementary to message passing. Message passing is the recommended method of inter-thread communication; it is easy to understand, fast, well behaved, reliable, and scalable. You should descend to lower-level communication mechanisms only in special circumstances—and don't forget, "special" is not always as special as it seems.

## 13.11   The shared Type Qualifier

We already got acquainted with shared in § 13.3 on page 397. To the type system, shared indicates that several threads have access to a piece of data. The compiler acknowledges that reality by restricting operations on shared data and by generating special code for the accepted operations.

The global definition

```
shared uint threadsCount;
```

introduces a value of type shared(uint), which corresponds to a global unsigned int in a C program. Such a variable is visible to all threads in the system. The annotation helps the compiler a great deal: the language "knows" that threadsCount is freely accessible from multiple threads and forbids naïve access to it. For example:

```
void bumpThreadsCount() {
   ++threadsCount; // Error!
```

```
                     // Cannot increment a shared int!
}
```

What's happening? Down at machine level, `++threadsCount` is not an atomic operation; it's a read-modify-write operation: `threadsCount` is loaded into a register, the register value is incremented, and then `threadsCount` is written back to memory. For the whole operation to be correct, these three steps need to be performed as an indivisible unit. The correct way to increment a `shared` integer is to use whatever specialized atomic increment primitives the processor offers, which are portably packaged in the `std.concurrency` module:

```
import std.concurrency;
shared uint threadsCount;

void bumpThreadsCount() {
    // std.concurrency defines
    //    atomicOp(string op)(ref shared uint, int)
    atomicOp!"+="(threadsCount, 1); // Fine
}
```

Because all shared data is accounted for and protected under the aegis of the language, passing `shared` data via `send` and `receive` is allowed.

### 13.11.1   The Plot Thickens: shared Is Transitive

Chapter 8 explains why `const` and `immutable` must be *transitive* (aka deep or recursive): following any indirections starting from an `immutable` object must keep data `immutable`. Otherwise, the `immutable` guarantee has the power of a comment in the code. You can't say something is immutable "up to a point" after which it changes its mind. You can, however, say that data is *mutable* up to a point, where it becomes immutable through and through. Stepping into immutability is veering down a one-way street. We've seen that `immutable` facilitates a number of correct and pain-free idioms, including functional style and sharing of data across threads. If immutability applied "up to a point," then so would program correctness.

The same exact reasoning goes for `shared`. In fact, with `shared` the necessity of transitivity becomes painfully obvious. Consider:

```
shared int* pInt;
```

which according to the qualifier syntax (§ 8.2 on page 291) is equivalent to

```
shared(int*) pInt;
```

The correct meaning of `pInt` is "The pointer is shared and the data pointed to by the pointer is also shared." A shallow, non-transitive approach to sharing would make `pInt` "a shared pointer to non-shared memory," which would be great if it weren't untenable. It's like saying, "I'll share this wallet with everyone; just please remember that the money in it ain't shared."[6] Claiming the pointer is shared across threads but the pointed-to data is not takes us back to the wonderful programming-by-honor-system paradigm that has failed so successfully throughout history. It's not the voluntary malicious uses, it's the honest mistakes that form the bulk of problems. Software is large, complex, and ever-changing, traits that never go well with maintaining guarantees through convention.

There is, however, a notion of "unshared pointer to shared data" that does hold water. Some thread holds a private pointer, and the pointer "looks" at shared data. That is easily expressible syntactically as

```
shared(int)* pInt;
```

As an aside, if there exists a "Best Form-Follows-Function" award, then the notation `qualifier(type)` should snatch it. It's perfect. You can't even syntactically create the wrong pointer type, because it would look like this:

```
int shared(*) pInt;
```

which does not make sense even syntactically because (`*`) is not a type (granted, it *is* a nice emoticon for a cyclops).

Transitivity of `shared` applies not only to pointers, but also to fields of `struct` and `class` objects: fields of a `shared` object are automatically qualified as `shared` as well. We'll discuss in detail the ways in which `shared` interacts with `classes` and `structs` later in this chapter.

## 13.12 Operations with `shared` Data and Their Effects

Working with `shared` data is peculiar because multiple threads may read and write it at any moment. Therefore, the compiler makes sure that all operations preserve integrity of data and also causality of operations.

Reads and writes of `shared` values are allowed and guaranteed to be atomic: numeric types (save for `real`), pointers, arrays, function pointers, delegates, and class references. `struct` types containing exactly one of the mentioned types are also readable and writable atomically. Notably absent is `real`, which is the only platform-dependent type with which the implementation has discretion regarding atomic sharing. On Intel machines, `real` has 80 bits, which makes it difficult to assign atomically in 32-bit programs. Anyway, `real` is meant mostly for high-precision temporary results and not for data interchange, so it makes little sense to want to share it anyway.

---

6. Incidentally, you can share a wallet with theft-protected money with the help of `const` by using the type `shared(const(Money)*)`.

For all numeric types and function pointers, shared-qualified values are convertible implicitly to and from unqualified values. Pointer conversions between shared(T*) and shared(T)* are allowed in both directions. Primitives in std.concurrency allow you to do arithmetic on shared numeric types.

### 13.12.1  Sequential Consistency of shared Data

With regard to the visibility of shared data operations across threads, D makes two guarantees:

- The order of reads and writes of shared data issued by one thread is the same as the order specified by the source code.
- The global order of reads and writes of shared data is some interleaving of reads and writes from multiple threads.

That seems to be a very reasonable set of assumptions—self-evident even. In fact, the two guarantees fit time-sliced threads implemented on a uniprocessor system quite well.

On multiprocessors, however, these guarantees are very restrictive. The problem is that in order to ensure the guarantees, all writes must be instantly visible throughout all threads. To effect that, shared accesses must be surrounded by special machine code instructions called *memory barriers*, ensuring that the order of reads and writes of shared data is the same as seen by all running threads. Such serialization is considerably more expensive in the presence of elaborate cache hierarchies. Also, staunch adherence to sequential consistency prevents reordering of operations, an important source of compiler-level optimizations. Combined, the two restrictions lead to dramatic slowdown—as much as one order of magnitude.

The good news is that such a speed loss occurs only with shared data, which tends to be rare. In real programs, most data is not shared and therefore need not meet sequential consistency requirements. The compiler optimizes code using non-shared data to the maximum, in full confidence that no other thread can ever access it, and only tiptoes around shared data. A common and recommended programming style with shared data is to copy shared values into thread-local working copies, work on the copies, and then write the copies back into the shared values.

## 13.13  Lock-Based Synchronization with synchronized classes

A historically popular method of writing multithreaded programs is *lock-based synchronization*. Under that discipline, access to shared data is protected by *mutexes*—synchronization objects that serialize execution of portions of the code that temporarily break data coherence, or that might see such a temporary breakage. Such portions of code are called *critical sections.*[7]

A lock-based program's correctness is ensured by introducing ordered, serial access to shared data. A thread that needs access to a piece of shared data must acquire (lock) a mutex, operate on the data, and then release (unlock) that mutex. Only one thread at a time may acquire a given mutex, which is how serialization is effected: when several threads want to acquire the same mutex, one "wins" and the others wait nicely in line. (The way the line is served—that is, thread priority—is important and may affect applications and the operating system quite visibly.)

Arguably the "Hello, world!" of multithreaded programs is the bank account example—an object accessible from multiple threads that must expose a safe interface for depositing and withdrawing funds. The single-threaded baseline version looks like this:

```
import std.contracts;

// Single-threaded bank account
class BankAccount {
   private double _balance;
   void deposit(double amount) {
      _balance += amount;
   }
   void withdraw(double amount) {
      enforce(_balance >= amount);
      _balance -= amount;
   }
   @property double balance() {
      return _balance;
   }
}
```

In a free-threaded world, += and -= are a tad misleading because they "look" atomic but are not—both are read-modify-write operations. Really `_balance += amount` is encoded as `_balance = _balance + amount`, which means the processor loads `_balance` and `_amount` into its own operating memory (registers or an internal stack), adds them, and deposits the result back into `_balance`.

Unprotected concurrent read-modify-write operations lead to incorrect behavior. Say your account has `_balance == 100.0` and one thread triggered by a check deposit calls `deposit(50)`. The call gets interrupted, right after having loaded `100.0` from mem-

---

7. A potential source of confusion is that Windows uses the term *critical section* for lightweight mutex objects that protect a critical section and *mutex* for heavier-weight mutexes that help inter-process communication.

ory, by another thread calling `withdraw(2.5)`. (That's you at the corner coffee shop getting a latte with your debit card.) Let's say the coffee shop thread finishes the entire call uninterrupted and updates `_balance` to `97.5`, but that event happens unbeknownst to the `deposit` thread, which has loaded `100` into a CPU register already and still thinks that's the right amount. The call `deposit(50)` computes a new balance of `150` and writes that number back into `_balance`. That is a typical *race condition*. Congratulations—free coffee for you (be warned, though; buggy book examples may be rigged in your favor, but buggy production code isn't). To introduce proper synchronization, many languages offer a `Mutex` type that lock-based threaded programs use to protect access to `balance`:

```
// This is not D code
// Multithreaded bank account in a language with explicit mutexes
class BankAccount {
   private double _balance;
   private Mutex _guard;
   void deposit(double amount) {
      _guard.lock();
      _balance += amount;
      _guard.unlock();
   }
   void withdraw(double amount) {
      _guard.lock();
      try {
         enforce(_balance >= amount);
         _balance -= amount;
      } finally {
         _guard.unlock();
      }
   }
   @property double balance() {
      _guard.lock();
      double result = _balance;
      _guard.unlock();
      return result;
   }
}
```

All operations on `_balance` are now protected by acquiring `_guard`. It may seem there is no need to protect `balance` with `_guard` because a `double` can be read atomically, but protection must be there for reasons hiding themselves under multiple layers of Maya veils. In brief, because of today's aggressive optimizing compilers and relaxed memory models, *all* access to shared data must entail some odd secret handshake that has the writing thread, the reading thread, and the optimizing compiler as participants; absolutely any bald read of shared data throws you into a world of pain (so it's great that D disallows such baldness by design). First and most obvious, the optimizing compiler, seeing no attempt at synchronization on your part, feels entitled to optimize access to `_balance` by holding it in a processor register. Second, in all but the most trivial examples, the compiler *and* the CPU feel entitled to freely reorder bald, unqualified access to shared data because they consider themselves to be dealing with thread-local data. (Why? Because that's most often the case and yields the fastest code, and besides, why hurt the plebes instead of the few and the virtuous?) This is one of the ways in which modern multithreading defies intuition and confuses programmers versed in classic multithreading. In brief, the `balance` property must be synchronized to make sure the secret handshake takes place.

To guarantee proper unlocking of `Mutex` in the presence of exceptions and early returns, languages with scoped object lifetime and destructors define an ancillary `Lock` type to acquire the lock in its constructor and release it in the destructor. The ensuing idiom is known as *scoped locking* [50] and its application to `BankAccount` looks like this:

```cpp
// C++ version of an interlocked bank account using scoped locking
class BankAccount {
private:
   double _balance;
   Mutex _guard;
public:
   void deposit(double amount) {
      auto lock = Lock(_guard);
      _balance += amount;
   }
   void withdraw(double amount) {
      auto lock = Lock(_guard);
      enforce(_balance >= amount);
      _balance -= amount;
   }
   double balance() {
      auto lock = Lock(_guard);
      return _balance;
   }
}
```

`Lock` simplifies code and improves its correctness by automating the pairing of locking and unlocking. Java, C#, and other languages simplify matters further by embedding `_guard` as a hidden member and hoisting locking logic up to the signature of the method. In Java, the example would look like this:

```
// Java version of an interlocked bank account using
//    automated scoped locking with the synchronized statement
class BankAccount {
   private double _balance;
   public synchronized void deposit(double amount) {
      _balance += amount;
   }
   public synchronized void withdraw(double amount) {
      enforce(_balance >= amount);
      _balance -= amount;
   }
   public synchronized double balance() {
      return _balance;
   }
}
```

The corresponding C# code looks similar, though synchronized should be replaced with [MethodImpl(MethodImplOptions.Synchronized)].

Well, you've just seen the good news: in the small, lock-based programming is easy to understand and seems to work well. The bad news is that in the large, it is very difficult to pair locks with data appropriately, choose locking scope and granularity, and use locks consistently across several objects (not paying attention to the latter issue leads to threads waiting for each other in a *deadlock*). Such issues made lock-based coding difficult enough in the good ole days of classic multithreading; modern multithreading (with massive concurrency, relaxed memory models, and expensive data sharing) has put lock-based programming under increasing attack [53]. Nevertheless, lock-based synchronization is still useful in a variety of designs.

D offers limited mechanisms for lock-based synchronization. The limits are deliberate and have the advantage of ensuring strong guarantees. In the particular case of BankAccount, the D version is very simple:

```
// D interlocked bank account using a synchronized class
synchronized class BankAccount {
   private double _balance;
   void deposit(double amount) {
      _balance += amount;
   }
   void withdraw(double amount) {
      enforce(_balance >= amount);
      _balance -= amount;
   }
   double balance() {
```

```
        return _balance;
    }
}
```

D hoists `synchronized` one level up to the entire `class`. This allows D's `BankAc-count` to provides stronger guarantees: even if you wanted to make a mistake, there is no way to offer back-door unsynchronized access to `_balance`. If D allowed mixing `synchronized` and unsynchronized methods in the same class, all bets would be off. In fact, experience with method-level `synchronized` has shown that it's best to either define all or none as `synchronized`; dual-purpose `classes` are more trouble than they're worth.

The `synchronized` class-level attribute affects objects of type `shared(BankAccount)` and automatically serializes calls to any method of the class. Also, protection checks get stricter for `synchronized` classes. Recall that according to § 11.1 on page 337, normal protection checks ordinarily do allow access to non-`public` members for all code within a module. Not so for `synchronized` classes, which obey the following rules:

- No `public` data is allowed at all.
- Access to `protected` members is restricted to methods of the `class` and its descendants.
- Access to `private` members is restricted to methods of the `class`.

## 13.14 Field Typing in synchronized classes

The transitivity rule for `shared` objects dictates that a `shared` class object propagates the `shared` qualifier down to its fields. Clearly `synchronized` brings some additional law and order to the table, which is reflected in relaxed typechecking of fields inside the methods of `synchronized` classes. In order to provide strong guarantees, `synchronized` affects semantic checking of fields in a slightly peculiar manner, which tracks the correspondingly peculiar semantics of `synchronized`.

Synchronized methods' protection against races is *temporary* and *local*. The temporary aspect is caused by the fact that as soon as the method returns, fields are not protected against races anymore. The local aspect concerns the fact that `synchronized` ensures protection of data directly embedded inside the object, but not data indirectly referred by the object (i.e., through class references, pointers, or arrays). Let's look at each in turn.

### 13.14.1 Temporary Protection == No Escape

Maybe not very intuitively, the temporary nature of `synchronized` entails the rule that no address of a field can escape a `synchronized` address. If that happened, some other portion of the code could access some data beyond the temporary protection conferred by method-level synchronization.

The compiler will reject any attempt to return a `ref` or a pointer to a field out of a method, or to pass a field by `ref` or by pointer to some function. To illustrate why that rule is sensible, consider the following example:

```
double * nyukNyuk; // N.B.: not shared

void sneaky(ref double r) { nyukNyuk = &r; }

synchronized class BankAccount {
   private double _balance;
   void fun() {
      nyukNyuk = &_balance; // Error!  (as there should be)
      sneaky(_balance);     // Error!  (as there should be)
   }
}
```

The first line of `fun` attempts to take the address of `_balance` and assign it to a global. If that operation were to succeed, the type system's guarantee would have failed—henceforth, the program would have shared access to data through a non-`shared` value. The assignment fails to typecheck. The second operation is a tad more subtle in that it attempts to do the aliasing via a function call that takes a `ref` parameter. That also fails; practically, passing a value by means of `ref` entails taking the address prior to the call. Taking the address is forbidden, so the call fails.

### 13.14.2  Local Protection == Tail Sharing

The protection offered by `synchronized` is also local in the sense that it doesn't necessarily protect data beyond the direct fields of the object. As soon as indirection enters into play, the guarantee that only one thread has access to data is lost. If you think of data as consisting of a "head" (the part sitting in the physical memory occupied by the `BankAccount` object) and possibly a "tail" (memory accessed indirectly), then a `synchronized` class is able to protect the "head" of the data, whereas the "tail" remains `shared`. In light of that reality, typing of fields of a `synchronized` class inside a method goes as follows:

- All numeric types are not `shared` (they have no tail) so they can be manipulated normally.
- Array fields declared with type `T[]` receive type `shared(T)[]`; that is, the head (the slice limits) is not `shared` and the tail (the contents of the array) remains `shared`.
- Pointer fields declared with type `T*` receive type `shared(T)*`; that is, the head (the pointer itself) is not `shared` and the tail (the pointed-to data) remains `shared`.

- Class fields declared with type T receive type shared(T). Classes are automatically by-reference, so they're "all tail."

These rules apply on top of the no-escape rule described in the previous section. One direct consequence is that operations affecting direct fields of the object can be freely reordered and optimized inside the method, as if sharing has been temporarily suspended for them—which is exactly what synchronized does.

There are cases in which an object completely owns another. Consider, for example, that the BankAccount stores all of its past transactions in a list of double:

```
// Not synchronized and generally thread-agnostic
class List(T) {
   ...
   void append(T value) {
      ...
   }
}

// Keeps a List of transactions
synchronized class BankAccount {
   private double _balance;
   private List!double _transactions;
   void deposit(double amount) {
      _balance += amount;
      _transactions.append(amount);
   }
   void withdraw(double amount) {
      enforce(_balance >= amount);
      _balance -= amount;
      _transactions.append(-amount);
   }
   double balance() {
      return _balance;
   }
}
```

The List class was not designed to be shared across threads so it does not use any synchronization mechanism, but it is in fact never shared! All of its uses are entirely private to the BankAccount object and completely protected inside synchronized methods. Assuming List does not do senseless shenanigans such as saving some internal pointer into a global variable, the code should be good to go.

Unfortunately, it isn't. Code like the above would not work in D because append is not callable against a shared(List!double) object. One obvious reason for the compiler's refusal is that the honor system doesn't go well with compilers. `List` may be a well-behaved class and all, but the compiler would have to have somewhat harder evidence to know that there is no sneaky aliasing of shared data afoot. The compiler could, in theory, go ahead and inspect `List`'s class definition, but in turn, `List` may be using some other components found in other modules, and before you can say "interprocedural analysis," things are getting out of hand.

*Interprocedural analysis* is a technique used by compilers and program analyzers to prove facts about a program by looking at more functions at once. Such analyses are typically slow, scale poorly with program size, and are sworn enemies of separate compilation. Although there exist systems that use interprocedural analysis, most of today's languages (including D) do all of their typechecking without requiring it.

An alternative solution to the owned subobject problem is to add new qualifiers that describe ownership relationships such as "BankAccount owns its `_transactions` member and therefore its mutex also serializes operations on `_transactions`." With the proper annotations in place, the compiler could verify that `_transactions` is entirely encapsulated inside `BankAccount` and therefore can be safely used without worrying about undue sharing. Systems and languages that do that have been proposed [25, 2, 11, 6] but for the time being they are not mainstream. Such ownership systems introduce significant complications in the language and its compiler. With lock-based synchronization as a whole coming under attack, D shunned beefing up support for an ailing programming technique. It is not impossible that the issue might be revisited later (ownership systems have been proposed for D [42]), but for the time being certain lock-based designs must step outside the confines of the type system, as discussed next.

### 13.14.3   Forcing Identical Mutexes

D allows dynamically what the type system is unable to guarantee statically: an owner-owned relationship in terms of locking. The following global primitive function is accessible:

```
// Inside object.d
setSameMutex(shared Object ownee, shared Object owner);
```

A `class` object `obj` may call `obj.setMutex(owner)` to effectively throw away its associated synchronization object and start using the same synchronization object as `owner`. That way you can be sure that locking `owner` really locks `obj`, too. Let's see how that would work with the `BankAccount` and the `List`.

```
// Thread-aware
synchronized class List(T) {
   ...
   void append(T value) {
```

```
      ...
   }
}


// Keeps a List of transactions
synchronized class BankAccount {
   private double _balance;
   private List!double _transactions;

   this() {
      // The account owns the list
      setSameMutex(_transactions, this);
   }
   ...
}
```

The way the scheme works requires that List (the owned object) be synchronized. Subsequent operations on _transactions would lock the _transactions field per the normal rules, but in fact they go ahead and acquire BankAccount object's mutex directly. That way the compiler is happy because it thinks every object is locked in separation. Also, the program is happy because in fact only one mutex controls the BankAccount and also the List subobject. Acquiring the mutex of _transactions is in reality acquiring the already locked mutex of this. Fortunately, such a recursive acquisition of an already owned, uncontested lock is relatively cheap, so the code is correct and not too locking-intensive.

### 13.14.4   The Unthinkable: casting Away shared

Continuing the preceding example, if you are absolutely positive that the _transactions list is completely private to the BankAccount object, you can cast away shared and use it without any regard to threads like this:

```
// Not synchronized and generally thread-agnostic
class List(T) {
   ...
   void append(T value) {
      ...
   }
}


synchronized class BankAccount {
   private double _balance;
   private List!double _transactions;
```

```
   void deposit(double amount) {
      _balance += amount;
      (cast(List!double) _transactions).append(amount);
   }
   void withdraw(double amount) {
      enforce(_balance >= amount);
      _balance -= amount;
      (cast(List!double) _transactions).append(-amount);
   }
   double balance() {
      return _balance;
   }
}
```

Now the code does compile and run. The only caveat is that now correctness of the lock-based discipline in the program is ensured by you, not by the language's type system, so you're not much better off than with languages that use default sharing. The advantage you are still enjoying is that casts are localized and can be searched for and carefully reviewed.

## 13.15  Deadlocks and the synchronized Statement

If the bank account example is the "Hello, world!" of threaded programs, the bank account transfer example must be the corresponding (if grimmer) introduction to threads that deadlock. The example goes like this: Assume you have two BankAccount objects, say, checking and savings. The challenge is to define an atomic transfer of some money from one account to another.

The naïve approach goes like this:

```
// Transfer version 1: non-atomic
void transfer(shared BankAccount source, shared BankAccount target,
      double amount) {
   source.withdraw(amount);
   target.deposit(amount);
}
```

This version is not atomic, however; between the two calls there is a quantum of time when money is missing from both accounts. If just at that time a thread executes the inspectForAuditing function, things may get a little tense.

To make the transfer atomic, you need to acquire the hidden mutexes of the two objects outside their methods, at the beginning of transfer. You can effect that with the help of synchronized statements:

```
// Transfer version 2: PROBLEMATIC
void transfer(shared BankAccount source, shared BankAccount target,
     double amount) {
   synchronized (source) {
     synchronized (target) {
        source.withdraw(amount);
        target.deposit(amount);
     }
   }
}
```

The synchronized statement acquires an object's hidden mutex through the exe-cution of the statement's body. Any method call against that object benefits from an already acquired lock.

The problem with the second version of transfer is that it's prone to deadlock: if two threads attempt to execute a transfer between the same accounts but *in opposite directions*, the threads may block forever. A thread attempting to transfer money from checking to savings locks checking exactly as another thread attempting to transfer money from savings to checking manages to lock savings. At that point, each thread holds a lock, and each thread needs the other thread's lock. They will never work out an understanding.

To really fix the problem, you need to use synchronized with *two* arguments:

```
// Transfer version 3: correct
void transfer(shared BankAccount source, shared BankAccount target,
     double amount) {
   synchronized (source, target) {
     source.withdraw(amount);
     target.deposit(amount);
   }
}
```

Synchronizing on several objects in the same synchronized statement is different from successively synchronizing on each. The generated code always acquires mutexes in the same order in all threads, regardless of the syntactic order in which you specify the objects. That way, deadlock is averted.

The actual order in the reference implementation is the increasing order of object addresses. Any global ordering would work just as well.

Multi-argument synchronized is helpful but, unfortunately, not a panacea. General deadlock may occur non-locally—one mutex is acquired in one function, then another in a different function, and so on, until a deadlock cycle closes. But synchronized with multiple arguments raises awareness of the issue and fosters correct code with modular mutex acquisition.

## 13.16   Lock-Free Coding with `shared classes`

The theory of lock-based synchronization was established in the 1960s. As early as 1972 [23], researchers started making inroads toward avoiding the slow, ham-fisted mutexes as much as possible in multithreaded programs. For example, some types were assignable atomically so people reckoned there was no ostensible need to guard such assignments with mutex acquisition. Also, some processors offered more advanced lightweight interlocked instructions such as atomic increment or test-and-set. About three decades later, in 1990, there was a definite beam of hope that some clever combination of atomic read-write registers could help avoid the tyranny of locks. At that point, a seminal piece of work had the last word in a line of work and the first word in another.

Herlihy's 1991 paper "Wait-free synchronization" [31] marked an absolutely powerful development in concurrent programming. Prior to that, it was unclear to hardware and software developers alike what kind of synchronization primitives would be best to work with. For example, a processor with atomic reads and writes for `int`s could intuitively be considered less powerful than one that also offers atomic +=. It may appear that one that offers atomic *= is even better; generally, the more atomic primitives one has at one's disposal, the merrier.

Herlihy blew that theory out of the water and in particular has shown that certain seemingly powerful synchronization primitives, such as test-and-set, fetch-and-add, and even one global shared FIFO queue, are virtually useless. These *impossibility results* were proven clearly enough to instantly disabuse anyone of the illusion that such mechanisms could provide the magic concurrency potion. Fortunately, Herlihy has also proved *universality results*—certain synchronization primitives may theoretically synchronize an infinite number of concurrent threads. Remarkably, the "good" primitives are not more difficult to implement than the "bad" ones and don't look particularly powerful to the naked eye. Of the useful synchronization primitives, one known as *compare-and-swap* has caught on and is implemented today by virtually all processors. Compare-and-swap has the following semantics:

```
// This function executes atomically
bool cas(T)(shared(T) * here, shared(T) ifThis, shared(T) writeThis) {
    if (*here == ifThis) {
        *here = writeThis;
        return true;
    }
    return false;
}
```

In plain language, `cas` atomically compares a memory location with a given value, and if the location is equal to that value, it stores a new value; otherwise, it does nothing. The result of the operation tells whether the store took place. The entire `cas` operation is atomic and must be provided as a primitive. The set of possible Ts is limited to integers of the native word size of the host machine (i.e., 32 or 64 bits). An increasing number of machines offer *double-word compare-and-swap*, sometimes dubbed `cas2`. That operation atomically manipulates 64-bit data on a 32-bit machine and 128-bit data on a 64-bit machine. In view of the increasing support for `cas2` on contemporary machines, D offers double-word compare-and-swap under the same name (`cas`) as an overloaded intrinsic function. So in D you can `cas` values of types `int`, `long`, `float`, `double`, all arrays, all pointers, and all `class` references.

### 13.16.1 `shared classes`

Following Herlihy's universality proofs, many data structures and algorithms took off around the nascent "cas-based programming." Now, if a `cas`-based implementation is possible for theoretically any synchronization problem, nobody has said it's easy. Defining `cas`-based data structures and algorithms, and particularly proving that they work correctly, is a difficult feat. Fortunately, once such an entity is defined and encapsulated, it can be reused to the benefit of many [57].

To tap into `cas`-based lock-free goodness, use the `shared` attribute with a `class` or `struct` definition:

```
shared struct LockFreeStruct {
    ...
}

shared class LockFreeClass {
    ...
}
```

The usual transitivity rules apply: `shared` propagates to the fields of the `struct` or `class`, and methods offer no special protection. All you can count on are atomic assignments, `cas` calls, the guarantee that the compiler and machine won't do any reordering of operations, and your unbridled confidence. But be warned—if coding were walking and message passing were jogging, lock-free programming would be no less than the Olympics.

### 13.16.2 A Couple of Lock-Free Structures

As a warmup exercise, let's implement a lock-free stack type. The basic idea is simple: the stack is maintained as a singly linked list, and insertions as well as removals proceed at the front of the list:

```
shared struct Stack(T) {
  private shared struct Node {
    T _payload;
    Node * _next;
  }
  private Node * _root;

  void push(T value) {
    auto n = new Node(value);
    shared(Node)* oldRoot;
    do {
      oldRoot = _root;
      n._next = oldRoot;
    } while (!cas(&_root, oldRoot, n));
  }

  shared(T)* pop() {
    typeof(return) result;
    shared(Node)* oldRoot;
    do {
      oldRoot = _root;
      if (!oldRoot) return null;
      result = & oldRoot._payload;
    } while (!cas(&_root, oldRoot, oldRoot._next));
    return result;
  }
}
```

Stack is a shared struct, and as a direct consequence pretty much everything inside of it is also shared. The internal type Node has the classic payload-and-pointer structure, and the Stack itself stores the root of the list.

The do/while loops in the two primitives may look a bit odd, but they are very common; slowly but surely, they dig a deep groove in the cortex of every cas-based programming expert-to-be. The way push works is to first create a new Node that will store the new value. Then, in a loop, _root is assigned the pointer to the new node, but *only* if in the meantime no other thread has changed it! It's quite possible that another thread has also performed a stack operation, so push needs to make sure that the root assumed in oldRoot has not changed while the new node was being primed.

The pop method does not return by value, but instead by pointer. This is because pop may find the queue empty, which is not an exceptional condition (as it would be in a single-threaded stack). For a shared stack, checking for an element, removing it, and returning it are one organic operation. Aside from the return aspect, pop is similar in the implementation to push: _root is replaced with care such that no other thread changes it while the payload is being fetched. At the end of the loop, the extracted value is off the stack and can be safely returned to its caller.

If Stack didn't seem that complicated, let's look at actually exposing a richer singly linked interface; after all, most of the infrastructure is built inside Stack already.

Unfortunately, for a list things are bound to become more difficult. How much more difficult? Brutally more difficult. One fundamental problem is insertion and deletion of nodes at arbitrary positions in the list. Say we have a list of int containing a node with payload 5 followed by a node with payload 10, and we want to remove the 5 node. No problem here—just do the cas magic to swing _root to point to the 10 node. The problem is, if at the same time another thread inserts a new node right after the 5 node, that node will be irretrievably lost: _root knows nothing about it.

Several solutions exist in the literature; none of them is trivially simple. The implementation described below, first proposed by Harris [30] in the suggestively entitled paper "A pragmatic implementation of non-blocking linked-lists," has a hackish flavor to it because it relies on setting the unused least significant bit of the _next pointer. The idea is first to mark that pointer as "logically deleted" by setting its bit to zero, and then to excise the node entirely in a second step:

```
shared struct SharedList(T) {
   shared struct Node {
      private T _payload;
      private Node * _next;

      @property shared(Node)* next() {
         return clearlsb(_next);
      }

      bool removeAfter() {
         shared(Node)* thisNext, afterNext;
         // Step 1: set the lsb of _next for the node to delete
         do {
            thisNext = next;
            if (!thisNext) return false;
            afterNext = thisNext.next;
         } while (!cas(&thisNext._next, afterNext, setlsb(afterNext)));
         // Step 2: excise the node to delete
         if (!cas(&_next, thisNext, afterNext)) {
            afterNext = thisNext._next;
            while (!haslsb(afterNext)) {
               thisNext._next = thisNext._next.next;
```

```
        }
        _next = afterNext;
    }
}

void insertAfter(T value) {
    auto newNode = new Node(value);
    for (;;) {
        // Attempt to find an insertion point
        auto n = _next;
        while (n && haslsb(n)) {
            n = n._next;
        }
        // Found a possible insertion point, attempt insert
        auto afterN = n._next;
        newNode._next = afterN;
        if (cas(&n._next, afterN, newNode)) {
            break;
        }
    }
}

private Node * _root;

void pushFront(T value) {
    ... // Same as for Stack.push
}

shared(T)* popFront() {
    ... // Same as for Stack.pop
}
}
```

The implementation is tricky but can be understood if you keep in mind a couple of invariants. First, it's OK for logically deleted nodes (i.e., Node objects with the field _next having its least significant bit set) to hang around for a little bit. Second, a node is never inserted after a logically deleted node. That way, the list stays coherent even though nodes may appear and disappear at any time.

The implementation of clearlsb, setlsb and haslsb is as barbaric as it gets; for example:

```
T* setlsb(T)(T* p) {
   return cast(T*) (cast(size_t) p | 1);
}
```

## 13.17  Summary

The implementation of setlsb, dirty and leaking some grease at the seams, is a fitting finale for a chapter that has started with the simple beauty of message passing and has gradually descended into the underworld of sharing.

D has an ample offering of threading amenities. For most applications on modern machines, the preferred mechanism is defining protocols built around message passing. Immutable sharing should be of great help there. You'd be well advised to use message passing for defining robust, scalable concurrent applications.

If you need to do synchronization based on mutual exclusion, you can do so with the help of synchronized classes. Be warned that support for lock-based programming is limited compared to other languages, and for good reasons.

If you need simple sharing of data, you may want to use shared values. D guarantees that operations on shared values are performed in the order specified in your code and do not cause visibility paradoxes and low-level races.

Finally, if activities such as bungee jumping, crocodile taming, or walking on coals seem sheer boredom to you, you'll be glad that lock-free programming exists, and that you can do it in D by using shared structs and classes.

# Bibliography

[1]   ALAGIĆ, S., AND ROYER, M. Genericity in Java: Persistent and database systems implications. *The VLDB Journal 17*, 4 (2008), 847–878. (Cited on page 236.)

[2]   ALDRICH, J., KOSTADINOV, V., AND CHAMBERS, C. Alias annotations for program understanding. In *OOPSLA: Object-Oriented Programming, Systems, Languages, and Applications* (New York, NY, 2002), ACM Press, pp. 311–330. (Cited on page 422.)

[3]   ALEXANDRESCU, A. On Iteration. *InformIT* (November 2009). http://erdani.com/publications/on-iteration.html. (Cited on page 362.)

[4]   AMSTERDAM, J. Java's new considered harmful. *Dr. Dobb's Journal* (April 2002). http://www.ddj.com/java/184405016. (Cited on page 211.)

[5]   ARMSTRONG, J. *Programming Erlang: Software for a Concurrent World.* The Pragmatic Programmers, LLC, Raleigh, NC, and Dallas, TX, 2007. (Cited on page 397.)

[6]   BACON, D. F., STROM, R. E., AND TARAFDAR, A. Guava: A dialect of Java without data races. In *OOPSLA: Object-Oriented Programming, Systems, Languages, and Applications* (New York, NY, 2000), ACM Press, pp. 382–400. (Cited on page 422.)

[7]   BENOIT, F., REIMER, J., AND CARLBORG, J. The D Widget Toolkit (DWT). http://www.dsource.org/projects/dwt. (Cited on page 226.)

[8]   BLOCH, J. *Effective Java Programming Language Guide.* Sun Microsystems, Inc., Mountain View, CA, 2001. (Cited on pages 272, 396.)

[9]   BLOCH, J. *Effective Java, Second Edition.* Prentice Hall PTR, Upper Saddle River, NJ, 2008. (Cited on pages 207, 397.)

[10]  BÖHM, C., AND JACOPINI, G. Flow diagrams, Turing machines and languages with only two formation rules. *Commun. ACM 9*, 5 (1966), 366–371. (Cited on page 6.)

[11]  BOYAPATI, C., LEE, R., AND RINARD, M. Ownership types for safe programming: Preventing data races and deadlocks. In *OOPSLA: Object-Oriented Programming, Systems, Languages, and Applications* (New York, NY, 2002), ACM Press, pp. 211–230. (Cited on page 422.)

[12] BRIGHT, W. The D assembler. `http://digitalmars.com/d/1.0/iasm.html`. (Cited on page 89.)

[13] BROOKS, JR., F. P. *The Mythical Man-Month: Essays on Software Engineering, 20th Anniversary Edition.* Addison-Wesley, Reading, MA, August 1995. (Cited on page 199.)

[14] CABANA, B., ALAGIĆ, S., AND FAULKNER, J. Parametric polymorphism for Java: Is there any hope in sight? *SIGPLAN Notices 39*, 12 (2004), 22–31. (Cited on page 236.)

[15] CARDELLI, L. Type Systems. In *The Computer Science and Engineering Handbook*, A. B. Tucker, Ed. CRC Press, Boca Raton, FL, 1997, ch. 103, pp. 2208–2236. (Cited on page 354.)

[16] CHANG, R. "Near Speed-of-Light On-Chip Electrical Interconnects". PhD thesis, Stanford University, 2003. (Cited on page 392.)

[17] COHEN, T. Java Q&A: How do I correctly implement the `equals()` method? *Dr. Dobb's Journal* (May 2002). `http://www.ddj.com/java/184405053`. (Cited on page 207.)

[18] DIGITAL MARS. dmd—FreeBSD D Compiler. `http://digitalmars.com/d/2.0/dmd-freebsd.html`, 2009. (Cited on page 341.)

[19] DIGITAL MARS. dmd—Linux D Compiler. `http://digitalmars.com/d/2.0/dmd-linux.html`, 2009. (Cited on page 341.)

[20] DIGITAL MARS. dmd—OSX D Compiler. `http://digitalmars.com/d/2.0/dmd-osx.html`, 2009. (Cited on page 341.)

[21] DIGITAL MARS. dmd—Windows D Compiler. `http://digitalmars.com/d/2.0/dmd-windows.html`, 2009. (Cited on page 341.)

[22] DREPPER, U. What every programmer should know about memory. *Eklektix, Inc.* (October 2007). (Cited on page 393.)

[23] EASTON, W. B. Process synchronization without long-term interlock. *ACM SIGOPS Operating Systems Review 6*, 1/2 (1972), 95–100. (Cited on page 426.)

[24] FINDLER, R. B., AND FELLEISEN, M. Contracts for higher-order functions. *ACM SIGPLAN Notices 37*, 9 (2002), 48–59. (Cited on page 314.)

[25] FLANAGAN, C., AND ABADI, M. Object types against races. In *CONCUR '99: Proceedings of the 10th International Conference on Concurrency Theory* (London, UK, 1999), Springer-Verlag, pp. 288–303. (Cited on page 422.)

[26] FRIEDL, J. *Mastering Regular Expressions*. O'Reilly Media, Inc., Sebastopol, CA, 2006. (Cited on page 331.)

[27] GAMMA, E., HELM, R., JOHNSON, R., AND VLISSIDES, J. *Design Patterns: Elements of Reusable Object-Oriented Software*. Addison-Wesley, Reading, MA, 1995. (Cited on pages 157, 197, 211, 282.)

[28] GOVE, D. *Solaris Application Programming*. Prentice Hall PTR, Upper Saddle River, NJ, 2008. (Cited on page 267.)

[29] GROPP, W., LUSK, E., AND SKJELLUM, A. *Using MPI: Portable Parallel Programming with the Message-Passing Interface*. MIT Press, Cambdridge, MA, 1999. (Cited on pages 395, 398.)

[30] HARRIS, T. L. A pragmatic implementation of non-blocking linked-lists. *Lecture Notes in Computer Science 2180* (2001), 300–314. (Cited on page 429.)

[31] HERLIHY, M. Wait-free synchronization. *TOPLAS: ACM Transactions on Programming Languages and Systems 13*, 1 (1991), 124–149. (Cited on page 426.)

[32] HOFFMAN, D. M., AND WEISS, D. M., Eds. *Software Fundamentals: Collected Papers by David L. Parnas*. Addison-Wesley, Reading, MA, 2001. (Cited on page 200.)

[33] ISO. The ANSI C standard (C99). Tech. Rep. WG14 N1124, ISO/IEC, 1999. (Cited on page 30.)

[34] KERNIGHAN, B. W., AND RITCHIE, D. M. *The C Programming Language*. Prentice Hall, Englewood Cliffs, NJ, 1978. (Cited on pages 83, 406.)

[35] KNUTH, D. E. *The Art of Computer Programming, Vol. 2: Seminumerical Algorithms*. Addison-Wesley, Reading, MA, 1997. (Cited on page 169.)

[36] KORPELA, J. K. *Unicode Explained*. O'Reilly Media, Inc., Sebastopol, CA, 2006. (Cited on page 118.)

[37] LEE, E. A. The problem with threads. *Computer 39*, 5 (2006), 33–42. (Cited on page 393.)

[38] LISKOV, B. Keynote address—Data Abstraction and Hierarchy. In *OOPSLA: Object-Oriented Programming, Systems, Languages, and Applications* (New York, NY, 1987), pp. 17–34. (Cited on page 329.)

[39] MARTIN, R. C. *Agile Software Development, Principles, Patterns, and Practices*. Prentice Hall, October 2002. (Cited on page 21.)

[40] MEYER, B. *Object-Oriented Software Construction*. Prentice Hall, Inc., Upper Saddle River, NJ, 1988. (Cited on pages 175, 211, 314.)

[41] MEYERS, S. How non-member functions improve encapsulation. *C++ Users Journal 18*, 2 (2000), 44–52. (Cited on page 202.)

[42] MILEWSKI, B. Race-free multithreading: Ownership. Blog post at `http://bartoszmilewski.wordpress.com/2009/06/02/race-free-multithreading-ownership/`. (Cited on page 422.)

[43] ODERSKY, M., AND WADLER, P. Pizza into Java: Translating theory into practice. In *Proceedings of the 24th ACM SIGPLAN-SIGACT symposium on Principles of programming languages* (Paris, France, 1997), ACM, pp. 146–159. (Cited on page 139.)

[44] PARNAS, D. L. On the criteria to be used in decomposing systems into modules. *Commun. ACM 15*, 12 (1972), 1053–1058. (Cited on page 200.)

[45] PARNAS, D. L. A technique for software module specification with examples. *Commun. ACM 15*, 5 (1972), 330–336. (Cited on page 314.)

[46] PIERCE, B. C. *Types and Programming Languages*. MIT Press, Cambridge, MA, 2002. (Cited on pages 175, 353.)

[47] PIKE, R. UTF-8 history. `http://www.cl.cam.ac.uk/~mgk25/ucs/utf-8-history.txt`, 2003. (Cited on page 119.)

[48] PRESS, W. H., TEUKOLSKY, S. A., VETTERLING, W. T., AND FLANNERY, B. P. *Numerical Recipes: The art of scientific computing*. Cambridge University Press, New York, NY, 2007. (Cited on page 173.)

[49] RADENSKI, A., FURLONG, J., AND ZANEV, V. The Java 5 generics compromise orthogonality to keep compatibility. *J. Syst. Softw. 81*, 11 (2008), 2069–2078. (Cited on page 236.)

[50] SCHMIDT, D. C. Strategized locking, thread-safe interface, and scoped locking. *C++ Report 11*, 9 (1999). (Cited on page 417.)

[51] STEPANOV, A., AND LEE, M. The Standard Template Library. Tech. rep., WG21 X3J16/94-0095, 1994. (Cited on pages 157, 362.)

[52] SUTTER, H. Virtuality. *C/C++ Users Journal* (September 2001). `http://www.gotw.ca/publications/mill18.htm`. (Cited on page 213.)

[53] SUTTER, H. The free lunch is over: A fundamental turn toward concurrency in software. *Dr. Dobb's Journal 30*, 3 (2005), 202–210. (Cited on page 418.)

[54] SUTTER, H. Use threads correctly = isolation + asynchronous messages. *Sutter's Mill* (March 2009). `http://herbsutter.com/2009/03/16/`. (Cited on page 398.)

[55] SUTTER, H., AND ALEXANDRESCU, A. *C++ Coding Standards: 101 Rules, Guidelines, and Best Practices*. Addison-Wesley, Reading, MA, 2004. (Cited on page 213.)

[56] THE UNICODE CONSORTIUM. *The Unicode Standard, Version 5.0*. Addison-Wesley, Reading, MA, 2006. (Cited on pages 118, 338.)

[57] VALOIS, J. D. Lock-free linked lists using compare-and-swap. In *Proceedings of the fourteenth annual ACM symposium on Principles of distributed computing* (1995), ACM New York, NY, pp. 214–222. (Cited on page 427.)

[58] VON RONNE, J., GAMPE, A., NIEDZIELSKI, D., AND PSARRIS, K. Safe bounds check annotations. *Concurrency and Computation: Practice and Experience 21*, 1 (2009). (Cited on page 96.)

[59] WADLER, P. Proofs are programs: 19th century logic and 21st century computing. *Dr. Dobb's Journal* (December 2000). (Cited on page 313.)

[60] WEGNER, P. A technique for counting ones in a binary computer. *Communications of the ACM 3*, 5 (1960), 322. (Cited on page 83.)

[61] XU, D. N., PEYTON JONES, S., AND CLAESSEN, K. Static contract checking for Haskell. *SIGPLAN Not. 44*, 1 (2009), 41–52. (Cited on page 314.)

# Index

random number generator, 169
range, 132, 157, 380
        input, 157
range violation, 115
RangeError, 50, 51
raw data definition, 36
rdmd, 2, 133
read-modify-write, 106, 412
read-modify-write operations, 415
read-only, 37
read, 328
readf, 23
readText, 328
real, 29, 413
rebinding, 178
receive. Tuple, 404
receive, 403–405, 408
receiveOnly, 402, 404
receiveTimeout, 404
recursive definition, 191
recursive function, 11
red-black tree, 131
reduce, 157, 158
*reductio ad absurdum*, 210
redundant inheritance paths, 227
ref, 6, 7, 9, 76, 94, 108, 110, 113, 135,
        136, 156, 243, 381
        and conversions, 76
        giving access, 378
refactoring, 67
reference implementation, 351, 353,
        356
reference semantics, 15, 26, 177, 180,
        239, 242, 246
reference versus object, 177
referential structure, 180
reflexive, 144
reflexivity, 206, 209
regex, 15, 17
regular expression, 15, 331
relational algebra, 131
relative primality, 170

relaxed memory model, 416, 418
release mode, 326
reliability engineering, 313
relocatable objects, 249
remainder, 54
removing method at runtime, 386
renaming in import, *see* import, re-
        naming
reordering, 414, 416
reordering of field access, 421
require less, 329
resistance, 392
Resource Acquisition Is Initialization,
        310
resource disposal, 188
resource leak, 310
return, 81, 319
reusability, 139
reverse video, 124
reversed turtles, 190
rewriting
        for overloaded operators, 366
rigidity, 139
Ripolles, Pablo, xxvii
Ritchie, Dennis, 82, 315
Roberts, Brad, xxvii
root, 204
run-of-the-mill machine, 396
runaway process, 394
runnable thread, 396
runtime check, 313
rvalue, 42, 101, 102, 135, 182, 249, 251,
        257, 265, 266
rvalue versus lvalue, *see* lvalue versus
        rvalue
Rynn, Michael, xxvii

# S

safe interface, 96
safe module
        versus system module, 96

# FREE Online Edition

Your purchase of **The D Programming Language** includes access to a free online edition for 45 days through the Safari Books Online subscription service. Nearly every Addison-Wesley Professional book is available online through Safari Books Online, along with more than 5,000 other technical books and videos from publishers such as Cisco Press, Exam Cram, IBM Press, O'Reilly, Prentice Hall, Que, and Sams.

**SAFARI BOOKS ONLINE** allows you to search for a specific answer, cut and paste code, download chapters, and stay current with emerging technologies.

## Activate your FREE Online Edition at www.informit.com/safarifree

> **STEP 1:** Enter the coupon code: LRKPFDB.

> **STEP 2:** New Safari users, complete the brief registration form.
> Safari subscribers, just log in.

If you have difficulty registering on Safari or accessing the online edition, please e-mail customer-service@safaribooksonline.com